LABOR IN THE SOVIET UNION

SOLOMON M. SCHWARZ

LABOR
IN THE
SOVIET UNION

PRAEGER - NEW YORK

Copyright, 1951, by Solomon M. Schwarz.

Library of Congress Catalog Card Number: 52-7491

FOREWORD

The reader of a book on Russian labor policy may expect more than the author will, and can, promise him. The Soviet Union claims—or at least claimed for many years—to be a workers' state and to have created a socialist planned economy. The labor policy of the Soviet state is one of the most important guides to knowledge and understanding of present-day Russia. The reader may expect that a work on Russian labor policy in the period of universal planning will answer the fundamental question which has stirred controversy for years: What is the essence, the social content of the Russian economic and social order? Is it socialism? Is it "state capitalism?" Is it a "transitional form" from capitalism to socialism? Or is it something else?

At the risk of disappointing the reader, I have refrained from even touching the question in this book. No analysis of labor policy alone can fully answer it. Important as knowledge of Russian labor policy must be to any answer, understanding of Russia's economics and, last but not least, the particularly difficult precise sociological analysis of modern Russia are of no lesser importance. On a smaller scale I have tried elsewhere[1] to illuminate certain sides of this last complex of questions. Yet that was hardly more than a modest beginning, while nothing short of an intensive sociological analysis of present-day Russia and especially of the Soviet Communist Party and its development since the first years of the Revolution can scientifically clarify a great many basic questions which today can mostly be answered only with reservations.

---

[1] See my brief study, "Heads of Russian Factories," *Social Research*, New School for Social Research, New York, September, 1942, and Chapter IX of *Management in Russian Industry and Agriculture* by Gregory Bienstock, Solomon M. Schwarz, and Aaron A. Yugov, Oxford University Press, New York. 1944.

v

In the present book I have in the main confined myself to showing and analyzing the complicated actual evolution of Russian labor policy—not only in the form it has taken in laws and ordinances and legal textbooks but in its practical results, i.e. in its impact on the every-day lives of workers and employees. In other words, I have sought to describe not merely the formal labor policy of the Soviet Union—so to speak, its "paper" policy—but also the real policy as it evolved in constant adjustment to the goals of official economic policy.

The field of Russian labor policy is very extensive. It was not possible for me to take up all of its problems in the desired detail. To keep the size of the book from jeopardizing publication, I have chiefly confined myself to showing Russian labor policy since the Soviet Union's adoption of universal planning (Five-Year-Plan policy). Previous developments were sketched in only insofar as it seemed necessary to a better presentation of developments since the second half of the 1920's. Otherwise, too, I was often obliged to condense extensively, giving to some chapters (Chapter Seven, for example) almost the character of a reference and probably detracting from the reader's pleasure. For the same reason I had to forego treating many of the peripheral problems of labor policy which call for special research and discussion. Thus the problems of vocational training were almost completely ignored and the measures to increase the productivity of labor mentioned only now and then; similarly, in Chapter Four, I have shown only the beginnings of the so-called socialist competition and refrained from analyzing its further development. Finally, I have withdrawn and discarded the already written major chapter about the trade unions. Some day I hope to have an apportunity to relate the story of unionism in the USSR in a separate book.

I have to make one further qualification. This book deals only with what I should call normal, regular labor relations and does not consider the conditions of forced labor which apply to millions of Soviet citizens (in the so-called labor camps and elsewhere). The labor of these millions of slaves plays a tremendous role in the economy of the Soviet Union, but the labor laws do not cover them.

This book is based almost exclusively on Soviet sources. Other sources were used in a few cases. But Soviet literature of the past decade is extraordinarily deficient in the systematic presentation of labor problems. Virtually no regular comprehensive labor statistics have been published since the mid-Thirties. To show the actual development of labor policy and labor conditions, therefore, I had to rely largely on innumerable individual press dispatches, newspaper and magazine articles, and frequently incidental remarks in official documents and speeches, collecting and systematizing the scattered statistical data I was able to find. I have indicated these sources and explained, wherever necessary, the manner in which I made use of this material. In part, therefore, the book may seem overloaded with detail. But I hope to win the inquisitive reader's consent to this manner of presentation, and to make his own study of Russian developments easier for him.

The writing of this book was facilitated by the generosity of the Rockefeller Foundation and the New York School for Social Research. I wish to acknowledge my gratitude to both institutions.

The Slavonic Division of the New York Public Library offered assistance and co-operation. The opportunity to use the Division's comprehensive collection of Soviet materials was a great advantage, and I take pleasure in thanking the staff for its active and expert help.

Many critical suggestions and valuable advice were offered by the members of the Graduate Faculty, New School for Social Research. In particular I wish to express my thanks to Dr. Frieda Wunderlich for her encouragement and criticism.

The manuscript was written partly in German, partly in English. I am indebted to E. B. Ashton and A. R. L. Gurland for the preparation of the final English text and to Louis J. Herman for editorial and technical assistance in the publication of the book.

This study was first written in 1941-1943 and analyzed the development of Soviet labor policy up to 1941. In 1946, I brought it up to date and prepared it for publication, but could not find a publisher who would accept a book with such limited commercial prospects. In its present form, the book has again been expanded and brought up to date (1951).

I am very grateful to my daring publisher, Frederick A. Praeger, who took the risk of letting it see the light of day.

New York City,   SOLOMON M. SCHWARZ
February 1952

NOTE ON SOURCE MATERIAL

With a few instances the material used in this book is from Soviet sources: books, magazines, bulletins, newspapers published in the Soviet Union either by government agencies or by officially recognized public bodies, such as the Soviet trade unions, or by government-owned and strictly supervised publishing houses.

Quotations from statutory texts are from different official sources as they are not always available in the official Soviet collection, *Sobraniye Zakonov i Rasporyazhenii Pravitel'stva SSSR* (after 1938, *Sobraniye Postanovlenni i Rasporyazhenii Pravitel'stva SSR*). The latter is referred to here as *Laws and Ordinances*, with reference to the year and current number of legal document; for example, *Laws and Ordinances*, 1939:1.

Titles of Russian books are given in English translation, titles of magazines, bulletins, newspapers in the Russian version; transliteration is, with slight deviation, in accordance with the usage adopted by the New York Public Library. The list of Soviet periodicals below, quoted or referred to, supplies the English translation of the titles, indicating the nature of the publication, by whom issued, etc.

Bol'shevik (Bolshevik): magazine published fortnightly by the Central Committee of the Communist Party of the Soviet Union.

Ekonomicheskoye Obozreniye (Economic Review): monthly, absorbed in May 1930 by *Planovoye Khozyaistvo* (see below); originally issued by the staff of the now also defunct *Ekonomicheskaya Zhizn'*, daily newspaper of the former Council for Labor and Defense, an interdepartmental committee within the Council of the People's Commissars of the USSR.

Industriya (Industry): see *Torgovo-Promyshlennaya Gazeta.*

Izvestiya (News): daily newspaper, published since the early days of the Revolution by the Central Executive Committee of the Soviets, later—since January 1938—by the Presidium of the Supreme Soviet of the USSR.

Izvestiya Akademii Nauk, Otdeleniye Ekonomiki i Prava (News of the Academy of Sciences, Economics and Law Department): journal issued 6 times a year by the Academy of Sciences of the USSR.

Izvestiya Narkomtruda (News of the People's Commissariat for Labor): official bulletin of the People's Commissariat for Labor, containing legislative and administrative material in the field of labor.

Na Agrarnom Fronte (On the Agrarian Front): bi-monthly, later monthly journal of the Agrarian Institute of the Communist Academy; ceased publication in 1935.

Na Planovom Fronte (On the Planning Front): fortnightly published by the State Planning Commission; discontinued in 1937.

Planovoye Khozyaistvo (Planned Economy): monthly journal of the State Planning Commission; discontinued in the second half of 1941; resumed publication as a bi-monthly in the second half of 1944.

Pravda (Truth): daily newspaper of the Central Committee of the Communist Party of the Soviet Union.

Problemy Ekonomiki (Problems of Economics): monthly, since 1935 bi-monthly publication of the Economic Institute of the Academy of Sciences of the USSR; discontinued in 1941.

Snabzheniye, Kooperatsiya i Torgovlya (Supply, Cooperatives, and Trade): see *Sovetskaya Torgovlya*.

Sotsialisticheskoye Zemedeliye (Socialist Agriculture): newspaper of the People's Commissariat for Agriculture of the USSR.

Sovetskaya Torgovlya (Soviet Trade): daily newspaper of the People's Commissariat for Domestic Trade of the USSR (prior to 1935 under the title *Snabzheniye, Kooperatsiya i Torgovlya*).

Sovetskaya Yustitsiya (Soviet Justice): periodical issued by the People's Commissariat for Justice of the USSR, weekly prior to 1930; three times a month 1930 through 1936; semi-monthly 1937 through 1940; weekly again in 1941.

Sovetskaya Zakonnost' (Soviet Legality): monthly publication of the Office of the Public Prosecutor of the USSR.

Sovetskoye Gosudarstvo (Soviet State): published in 1930 and 1931 under the title *Sovetskoye Gosudarstvo i Revolyutv* under the title *Sovetskoye Gosudarstvo i Revolyutsiya Prava,* and since 1939 under the title *Sovetskoye* monthly, later bi-monthly; issued prior to 1935 by the Institute for Soviet Construction and Law of the Communist Academy, in 1935 by the same Institute of the Academy of Sciences of the USSR, and since 1936 by the latter's Law Institute; discontinued in the second half of 1941, resumed in 1946.

Sputnik Agitatora (Agitator's Handbook): semi-monthly publication for Party officials, agitators, speakers, etc., issued by the CC of the CPSU.

Statistika Truda (Labor Statistics): monthly statistical publication of the All-Union Central Trade Union Council, ceased publication in 1929.

Statisticheskoye Obozreniye (Statistical Review): monthly issued by the Central Statistical Office (TsUNKhU), ceased publication in 1930.

Torgovo-Promyshlennaya Gazeta (Newspaper of Commerce and Industry): daily newspaper of the economic administration and industrial management; title changed to *Za Industrializatsiyu* in 1930 and again to *Industriya* in September 1937; originally issued by the Supreme Economic Council of the USSR, became the official organ of the People's Commissariat for Heavy Industry in January 1932 and later also of other People's Commissariats in charge of individual industries; discontinued in the fall of 1940 to be replaced by newspapers for various industries, such as *Chernaya Metallurgiya* (Iron and Steel), *Ugol'* (Coal), *Neft'* (Oil). etc.

Trud (Labor): daily newspaper of the All-Union Central Trade Union Council.

Vedomostii Verkhovnogo Soveta (News of Supreme Soviet): official journal published by the Presidium of the Supreme Soviet of the USSR, carrying legislative acts, edicts, etc. emanating from the Persidium, and the laws passed by the Supreme Soviet *in pleno.*

Vestnik Truda (Labor Herald): monthly issued by the All-Union Central Trade Union Council; ceased publication in 1929.

Voprosy Ekonomiki (Problems of Economics): monthly issued since 1948 by the Economic Institute of the Academy of Sciences of the USSR.

Voprosy Strakhovaniya (Insurance Problems): originally weekly, since 1924 monthly issued by the Central Social Insurance Administration of the People's Commissariat for Labor, taken over by the AUCTUC in 1933.

Voprosy Truda (Labor Problems): monthly issued by the People's Commissariat for Labor of the USSR; ceased publication in 1933.

Za Industrializatsiyu (For Industrialization): see *Torgovo-Promyshlennaya Gazeta.*

ABBREVIATIONS

USSR   Union of Soviet Socialist Republics.

RSFSR   Russian Soviet Federative Socialist Republic, major constituent part of the USSR.

CEC   Central Executive Committee of the Soviets of Workers', Peasants' and Red Army Soldiers' Deputies' between sessions of the All- Union Soviet Congress the legislative branch of the Soviet Government; more often than not its legislative functions were exercised by its Presidium or by the CPC (see below); under the 1936 Constitution the CEC and the Soviet Congress have been supplanted by the Supreme Soviet of the USSR.

CPC   Council of the People's Commissars, executive branch of the Soviet Government; abolished in March 1946 to give way to the Council of Ministers of the USSR.

CPSU   Communist Party of the Soviet Union (Bolsheviks).

CC   Central Committee, national governing body of the CPSU; barely functions *in pleno*, most of its powers having passed to its executive agency, the Politbureau (Political Bureau of the Central Committee).

AUCTUC   All-Union Central Trade Union Council, national governing body of the trade union movement, elected by and accountable to the All-Union Trade Union Convention; assembling irregularly in plenary session, operates mainly through its Presidium and/or Secretariat.

TABLE OF CONTENTS

Chapter One:
GROWTH AND TRANSFORMATION OF
THE WORKING CLASS

Chapter Two:
TRANSFORMATION OF THE LABOR MARKET

Chapter Three:

TRANSFORMATION OF THE LABOR RELATIONSHIP

Chapter Four:

WAGES AND LIVING STANDARDS, I (Up to 1941)

Chapter Five:
WAGES AND LIVING STANDARDS, II (Since 1941)

Chapter Six:
HOURS AND WORKING CONDITIONS

xvii

Chapter Seven:
SOCIAL INSURANCE

LABOR IN THE SOVIET UNION

Chapter One

GROWTH AND TRANSFORMATION OF THE WORKING CLASS

Distinctive Traits of Russian Labor

In most continental European countries it was the city people, mainly artisans and other urban groups, whose proletarianization produced the industrial working class. By origin and by tradition, the latter was a predominantly urban social stratum. New-comers from the countryside kept swelling the ranks of industrial labor all over Europe, but in most cases this influx was quickly assimilated by the city. The rural ties of the migrants loosened rapidly. The children of the country-bred new industrial workers retained hardlly a trace of their peasant background.

This is the vital difference between the evolution of labor in Russia and the rest of Europe. In Russia the city as such, and urban handicraft in particular, had never risen to levels comparable to the flowering of urban civilization in Western and Central Europe. Russian industry originated in the country, and until 1861, when serfdom was abolished, much of its labor was done by peasant serfs. Even after it invaded the cities it drew the bulk of the needed manpower from the ranks of the rural populace.

Until quite recently a vast majority of Russian industrial

1

workers was not only of peasant stock but closely linked with the countryside. The continuing bond was not only psychological, resting on family ties as elsewhere in Europe; there also were economic ties, and precisely these were of profound importance. The industrial worker in the city often kept a farm in his native village, and had it run by the women, children, and old men of his family. Very often, too, he would go back to the village himself, tilling his soil for weeks and even months, and then return to the factory after the harvest.

This close connection of urban workers with the farm led many Russian economists and sociologists for a long time simply to deny the existence of a Russian industrial working class.

As late as the 1890's this skepticism was widespread. An outstanding pioneer in the study of labor conditions, E. M. Dement'yev, wrote in 1893: "From olden times the opinion has crystallized in our literature that our factory workers are simply peasants who eke out the scanty income they derive from agriculture by supplementary work in factories; and all statistical and economic investigations for the province of Moscow have hitherto regarded factory work of peasants as a sideline." [1] Dr. Dement'yev opposed this obsolete view on the basis of a survey he had conducted in the 1880's in three counties of Moscow province, on behalf of the Moscow Zemstvo (provincial self-government).

But the ties which bound industrial workers to village and homestead remained close. Dr. Dement'yev himself pointed out that 91.5 per cent of the factory workers covered by his survey were legally members of the peasantry,[2] and that 14.1 per cent of all workers over eighteen years of age would return regularly to do farm work in their native village.[3]

---

[1] E. M. Dement'yev, *The Factory. What It Gives the Population and What It Takes Away*, 2d ed., Moscow, 1897, p. 1.

[2] In Tsarist Russia, individual citizens were legally bound to "estates," which implied privileges for the upper classes and restrictions for the lower ones, particularly the peasantry. Until 1917, when the institution was fully abolished, urban workers who came from the country had remained legally peasants for a long time.

[3] *Op. cit.*, pp. 4 and 18. A recent Russian work on the origin of the Russian industrial working class rightly emphasizes that Dement'yev's figures fail to make the rural connection of industrial labor fully apparent:

"In analyzing these figures, it must be taken into accout that the survey was made during a crisis, as a result of which only groups of workers most closely tied

In other provinces the workers' connection with the rural economy was even closer. Official figures issued for 1893 on the nine factory inspection districts placed the proportion of factory workers periodically returning to the villages for farm work at 28.2 per cent.[4] There were wide fluctuations from industry to industry; according to the same statistics, the seasonal migration quota ranged from 11.1 per cent in the metal trades to 65.4 per cent in the processing of food and beverages.[5]

How much the rural economy meant to industrial workers is not fully expressed by the numbers returning seasonally to work in the fields. It can be seen better from a survey made in a large Moscow textile factory in 1898.[6] Of 2,553 workers employed there, 1,417 (all male) were thoroughly interviewed. 94.2 per cent turned out to be of peasant stock. The following figures reveal their specific rural interests:

---

to production remained in the factories." (A. G. Rashin, *The Formation of the Industrial Proletariat in Russia,* Moscow, 1940, p. 405.)

[4] Data of factory inspectors supplied by A. V. Pogozhev, *Establishing the Magnitude and Distribution of Russia's Workers' Population,* published by the Academy of Sciences, St. Petersburg, 1906, p. 101. The following table indicates the regional distribution, St. Petersburg and the more highly developed Polish districts showing the least "agricultural residues" among industrial workers:

District	Percent returning to the villages for agricultural labor
Voronezh	76.3%
Kiev	57.5
Kharkov	51.2
Vladimir	19.8
Moscow	19.5
Warsaw	17.1
Piotrkow	14.7
Vilna	12.4
St. Petersburg	10.8

Average 9 factory inspection districts 28.2%

[5] Data from Pogozhev, as quoted *supra,* n. 4, p. 100. Percentage oscillations by industries were as follows:

Industry	Percentage returning
Metal trades	11.1%
Textiles	16.5
Lumber	30.3
Processing of minerals	35.4
Processing of animal produce	46.1
Food and beverages	65.4

[6] V. Shestakov, *The Workers of the Emil Zindel Factory,* Moscow, 1900, quoted from M. Tugan-Baranovsky, *The Russian Factory, Past and Present,* vol. 1, 3d ed., St. Petersburg, 1907, p. 448.

Return to village for seasonal work in their own fields	11.9%
Do not return, having relatives till fields	61.4
Do not farm for themselves, leasing fields	12.3
Own no fields but keep a village homestead	3.6
Without village connections	10.8
Total	100.0%

Here the proportion of workers who still had ties with the rural economy was as high as 89.2 per cent, many times the number of those returning to the village to lend a hand in the fields.

With the growth of industry, especially since that last decade of the nineteenth century, these ties were gradually severed in spite of the laws that held factory workers bound to the "peasant estate." The break was especially open among workers in the metal trades, and even more so in printing. Yet even the printers often remained linked with the farm.

According to a survey made by the Moscow printers union in 1907, 46.0 per cent of all workers employed in Moscow print shops had fields which they tilled themselves or through family labor (mostly the latter); an additional 16.4 per cent leased the fields or kept at least a homestead in their native village. Only 37.6 per cent had cut all property ties with the rural economy. Of all the workers covered by the survey, 65 per cent had been born on farms.[7]

Hardly any comparable figures are available for the years following World War I.[8] Industrial labor moved farther from its

[7] A. Svavitsky and V. Sher, *The Condition of Workers in the Moscow Printing Industry*, St. Petersburg, 1909, pp. 5 f.

[8] In this context mention ought to be made of the industrial labor census of 1918, when the workers among other things were asked about their pre-revolutionary connection with agriculture. The results have to be used with caution, however —not only because the questions concerned the past and the answers were accordingly less reliable. A fact of much more profound influence on the survey was that the workers' flight from the factories to the land (due to the disruption of the urban economy and to the agragrian revolution in the country) had set in many months before the census. The rural ties of the remaining part were scarcely representative of industrial labor on the threshold of the revolution. Altogether, out of nearly a million workers whose replies were statistically evaluated, 31.3 per cent said they had owned rural property before the revolution, and two-thirds of these (20.9 per cent) had operated farms, tilling the soil in person or through family labor.

These figures are far too low to correspond with reality just before the revolu-

farm background, yet strong country connections remained even after 1917. They accounted for the mass exodus of urban workers between 1918 and 1921 and exerted a decisive influence on the trend of unemployment during the first revolutionary years as well as in the later period, between 1922 and 1928.

The trend of industrial manpower in the first revolutionary decade cannot be understood unless it is seen in terms of the rural background of a large proportion of industrial workers. Though industrial employment decreased sharply between 1918 and 1921, there was no visible unemployment. On the contrary, there was a noticeable tightening of the labor market. Conversely, the beginning of industrial recovery and reconstruction in 1922 brought a steady increase in the number of employed along with a considerable increase in the number of unemployed.[9]

Employment Figures until 1928

The first years of the revolution saw a disastrous contraction of the entire economy, particularly of industry. There was an abrupt decrease in the number of employed. Though the nadir of economic decline was reached in the first half of 1921, the shrinkage of employment continued even after the economic policy was reversed with the introduction of the NEP (New Economic Policy). Employers who hitherto, for one reason or another, had hesitated to discharge superfluous workers, did so now, in keeping with the reestablished principles of commercial accounting.

The low point of industrial employment was not reached

---

tion. Yet the survey retains a certain significance as an illustration of the relative rural ties of the workers in different branches of industry. If we assume that farms were operated by 20.9 per cent of industrial labor as a whole, we find that the corresponding figure was 38.7 per cent among the miners, 29.2 per cent among the food workers, 26 per cent in the linen industry, 21 per cent among the metal workers, 20.4 per cent in the cotton industry, 19.6 per cent in the lumber industry, and 9.6 per cent in the graphic arts.

The results of this census were published in Russian in *Industry 1913-18— Part Two, Occupational Census* by the Central Statistical Administration, Moscow, 1926. For a comprehensive summary of the results, see A. G. Rashin (cf. note 3), pp. 412-415.

[9] Cf. my articles "Bevölkerungsbewegung und Arbeitslosigkeit in Russland," *Die Gesellschaft*, Berlin, February 1927; "Unemployment in Russia, 1917 to 1925," *International Labour Review*, November 1926; and "The Five-Year Plan and the Regulation of the Labour Market in the U.S.S.R.," *International Labour Review*, March 1933.

until the summer of 1922. It was only after this time that employment in industry and other economic fields rose steadily.

Some figures may illuminate this trend. The last census of Tsarist Russia, held on February 2, 1897, revealed that, out of a total population of approximately 126,400,000, some 10,500,-000 were wage and salary earners (including civil servants but excluding the military). This figure must be corrected to make allowances for the territorial reduction of Russia after World War I; within the borders of the Soviet Union prior to World War II, the number of wage and salary earners in 1897 would have been about 7,900,000 out of a total population of about 104,000,-000. For 1913 the corresponding figure (after territorial allowances) has been estimated at 11,200,000, out of a total population of some 140,000,000. But in 1921/22,[10] the number of wage and salary earners[11] had fallen far below the level of 1913, indeed below that of 1897, to about 6,500,000 in a population of approximately 133,000,000.[12]

Conditions in industry proper were worse. Industry (not including handicraft and home workers) employed the following numbers:[13]

1897	1,515,000
1913	2,552,000
1921/22 [14]	1,243,000

From the summer of 1922 on, the number of wage and salary earners in the national economy in general and in industry in

---

[10] Soviet statistics during the first revolutionary decade were not based on calendar years. Data usually refer to the "economic year" ending September 30.

[11] Data from B. Gukhman, *The Size of the Proletariat and Wages in the USSR*, Moscow, 1926, p. 29.

[12] The number of wage and salary earners in all fields of economic activity for the economic year 1921-22 was never officially released. Such figures are available only since 1922-23, at which time there were 6,800,000. However, the number of wage earners in industry for both years is ascertainable. It was 1,243,400 in 1921-22; 1,445,900 in 1922-23, an increase of 202,500 (data from Gukhman, as quoted *supra*, n. 11, p. 73). The total number of wage and salary earners in all fields of economic activity in 1921-22 may thus be estimated as somewhat less than 6,500,000.

[13] Gukhman, as quoted *supra*, n. 11, pp. 13, 74.

[14] The lowest monthly employment figures were recorded in July, August and September, 1922. The employment trend can be seen from a comparison with the corresponding months of 1921 and 1923 (data from Gukhman, as quoted *supra*, n. 11, pp. 74 ff.):

	1921	1922	1923
		(in thousands)	
July	1,395	1,191	1,563
August	1,306	1,161	1,539
September	1,253	1,209	1,498

particular increased continuously. In 1928 the total in all occupational divisions was 11,600,000,[15] for the first time surpassing the 1913 figures. However, the population as a whole had grown rapidly. In 1928 it approximated 151,000,000[16] as against 140,000,-000 in 1913. Out of each 1,000 inhabitants, 76.8 were employed as wage or salary earners in 1928. This compares with a ratio of 80.0 in 1913, and of 76.0 in 1897.

The trend was slightly more favorable with respect to manual labor in industry proper (excluding handicraft, home workers, and salaried employees):

Wage Earners in Industry[17]

1897	1,515,000
1913	2,552,000
1928	2,822,000

On the other hand, the number of farm workers dropped considerably over the same period of years, as a result of the agrarian revolution.[18]

It took six years (1922-1928) to restore the working class (statistically speaking, wage and salary earners in all occupational divisions) to the size it had attained prior to World War I. When the Five-Year-Plan policy of speedy industrialization was put into effect, the pace increased rapidly.

The First Five-Year Plan: Project and Achievement

The First Five-Year Plan, as adopted by the Sixteenth Communist Party Conference in April, 1929, was to run from October 1, 1928, to September 30, 1933. Actually it ran its course in less than five years, and was proclaimed to have been completed by December 31, 1932. It was designed to bring about a vast expansion of national production, especially of industrial output. Accordingly, it envisioned a large increase in the number of workers and employees.

However, the authors of the Plan displayed some caution in

---

[15] *Socialist Construction of the USSR. Statistical Yearbook,* Moscow, 1936, p. 508.

[16] *Five-Year Plan of Economic Construction of the USSR,* Moscow, 1929, vol. II, 2, p. 163.

[17] Data for 1897 and 1913 from Gukhman, as quoted *supra,* n. 11, p. 29; for 1928, from *Socialist Construction . . .* as quoted *supra,* n. 15, p. 508.

[18] Agricultural laborers numbered approximately 2,775,000 in 1897, 3,000,000 in 1913, and 2,007,000 in 1928, according to sources indicated in n. 17 *supra.*

mapping out the growth of the working class. The projected increase was to be slower than the actual one in the five years preceding the Five-Year Plan, as can be seen from the following table:[19]

Year	Number of Employed (in millions)	Increase over Preceding year
	Past Development	
1922/23	6.8	...
1923/24	7.6	11.1%
1924/25	8.5	13.0
1925/26	10.2	19.8
1926/27	11.0	7.8
1927/28	11.3	3.7
	Five-Year Plan Schedule	
1928/29	11.9	4.9
1929/30	12.8	7.5
1930/31	13.8	7.7
1931/32	14.7	7.0
1932/33	15.8	6.9

The relatively moderate pace indicated in these figures for the projected increase in employment was clearly underscored by the authors of the Plan themselves. They wrote: [20]

"The increase in the number of wage and salary earners, as provided for in the Plan, is relatively moderate as compared with the preceding five years, during which the yearly increases in the number of workers and salaried employees averaged 11 to 12 per cent and the total increase for the period equaled 70 per cent. It is necessary to take into consideration, however, that the growth of the working class during the reconstruction years profited chiefly from the opportunity to use existing plant, while new investment was relatively small; that is to say, this growth took place on the old basis of production. Conversely, employment in the coming five-year period will increase through addition of new, more efficient plant.

"The numerical change in the employment of wage and salary earners, as it is to take place from one year to the other, shows an increase in pace in 1929/30 and a somewhat slowed-up development during the following years. The increase in the

---

[19] *Five-Year Plan* . . ., as quoted *supra*, n. 16, vol. I, p. 129.
[20] *Op. cit.*, vol. II, 2, pp. 165 f.

number of wage and salary earners during the five-year period will average about 6 per cent annually."

Altogether, the number of employed was to rise from approximately 11,300,000 in 1927/28 to 15,800,000 in 1932/33,—a total increase of some 4,500,000 or 38.9 per cent.

However, the number of wage and salary earners in the national economy as a whole approximated 22,800,000 in the calendar year 1932, as against the 15,800,000 envisioned for the economic year 1932/33. In less than five years labor more than doubled its size. In industry proper, the figure attained in 1932 was approximately 6,300,000. This compares with 3,106,000 in 1928 and an estimated 4,100,000 for the economic year 1932/33 according to the Five-Year Plan.[21]

The official report on the execution of the First Five-Year Plan summarized the facts as follows: [22]

"From 1928 to 1932 a total of about 12,500,000 new wage and salary earners were drawn into all occupational divisions (including 1,300,000 who replaced those eliminated by death, disability, or assignment to study). According to preliminary estimates this increase was derived from the following sources: About 4,000,000 were city dwellers working for wages for the first time (viz., 1,700,000 adolescents, some 500,000 college graduates, 1,400,000 adult women not previously engaged in production, and about 400,000 former artisans and home workers). The remaining 8,500,000 were peasants."

The number of newly-employed workers manifestly exceeded the manpower reserves available at the beginning of the Five-Year Plan.[23] This would have been impossible but for the tremendous influx of new workers from the villages. In the second half of the five-year period, however, this tide began visibly to recede. The rural manpower reserves were not exhausted, rather the contrary. But in the meantime something new and decisive had happened to the agrarian economy. The collectivization of

---

[21] *Fulfilling the First Five-Year Plan for the Economic Development of the USSR*, Moscow, 1933, pp. 253 f., 267. Later the figures for 1932 were slightly revised upward. According to *Socialist Construction . . .*, as quoted *supra*, n. 15, p. 508, the total number of wage and salary earners was estimated at 22,900,000 and the corresponding figure for industry proper at 6,500,000.

[22] *Fulfilling . . .*, as quoted *supra*, n. 21, p. 174.

[23] For the development of unemployment, cf. Chapter Two below.

agriculture, which put a new complexion on the labor market, had begun.

Rural Overpopulation and Collectivization of Agriculture

The effects of the collectivization of agriculture on the labor market are closely interwoven with the age-old crux of Russia's rural economy: rural overpopulation. For many decades it was one of the central issues of the country's social evolution. Due to the limited absorptive capacity of an underdeveloped industry, the population surplus on the farms had become quasi-permanent.

The agrarian revolution did not basically change matters. The big landowners were expropriated, and their lands largely distributed among the peasants, but as the bulk of the land had been in peasant hands even before the revolution, this did not solve the real agrarian problem, the question of "land hunger." The results of the redistribution of land, the People's Commissariat for Agriculture reported in 1920, were "much less than many had anticipated." [24]

Reviewing achievements during the first three years of the Revolution (1917-1920), the People's Commissariat explained: [25] "Small indeed were the results of distributing a giant acreage among the millions of peasants. A special survey by the Central Agricultural Board has found that the *per capita* increase of peasant acreage is very small, amounting to a few tenths or hundredths of a desyatine.[26] In a vast majority of provinces the additional acreage did not exceed half a desyatine; and only in a few did it reach one desyatine."

According to official figures, the average size of peasant holdings in 29 provinces of European Russia rose from 1.67 to 2.26 desyatines *per capita* of the peasant population.[27] The actual increase was even less impressive, for a portion of the newly acquired land had already been tenanted by the peasants prior to the revolution.

---

[24] B. N. Knipovich, *Summary of Three Years' Activity (1917-1920) of the People's Commissariat for Agriculture,* issued by the People's Commissariat for Agriculture, Moscow, 1920, p. 9.

[25] *Ibid.*

[26] One desyatine is equivalent to 1.093 hectares=2.6997 acres.

[27] From data cited in the Russian-language publication by S. N. Prokopovicz, *Studies in Soviet Economy,* Berlin, 1923, p. 70.

Thus the redistribution of land could do little to ease the pressure of rual overpopulation. Whatever slight improvement there was, was largely offset by a new migration from the cities to the country that began in the first year of the Revolution, and by the damage that war and civil war had inflicted on agriculture. The density of the rural population remained menacing. It had actually grown in comparison with prewar days, as shown by the following table:[28]

Male Adult Farm Workers
Per 100 Desyatines of Arable Land

Region	1913	1923	Ratio 1923:1913
Western	10.5	13.9	1.32
Northwestern	14.4	13.8	.96
Central Industrial	11.0	18.7	1.70
Northeastern	11.1	15.6	1.41
Wyatka-Vetluga	10.1	11.7	1.16
Ural	7.2	8.7	1.21
Central Agrarian	13.5	15.4	1.14
Middle Volga	10.8	12.3	1.14
Lower Volga	6.9	7.5	1.09
Crimea	3.4	3.9	1.15

The change in ownership did nothing to change the fact that the numbers of employables working on farms exceeded that required for cultivation. On the basis of rural tax returns for 1924/25, N. Organovsky, an authority on farm statistics, showed that the per capita amount of work accomplished increases with the size of the farm. The acreage planted per person was as follows:

Size of Farm	Desyatines Planted per Person
Small (up to 4 desyatines)	0.58
Lower medium (4 to 8 desyatines)	1.38
Upper medium (8 to 15 desyatines)	2.13
Large (more than 15 desyatines)	3.56
All brackets	1.42

Oganovsky commented: [29]

---

[28] Data from N. Kondrat'yev and N. Oganovsky, *The Outlook for the Development of Agriculture in the Soviet Union,* issued by the People's Commissariat for Agriculture, Moscow, 1924, p. 122.

[29] N. Oganovsky, "Results of the Agrarian Revolution and Recent Differentiation Trends within the Peasantry," *Planovoye Khozyaistvo,* May, 1925, pp. 55 f.

"If the small farmers could utilize their working capacity as efficiently as the lower medium farmers, the labor of 57 per cent of the former would be superfluous; if working efficiency in the lowest bracket could be increased to the level of the upper medium group, the proportion of unusable manpower among the small farmers would amount to 73 per cent. Now, the total available manpower in the small-farmer category throughout the Soviet Union amounts to 13,100,000. Consequently, in the small-farmer category, on the basis of the productivity of labor in the lower medium bracket, the number of persons employed in excess of requirements totals 7,500,000; computed on the basis of the degree of productivity characteristic of the upper medium bracket, it would come to 9,600,000. In addition, using this latter ratio, the number of persons employed in excess of requirements in the lower-medium category may be calculated at 10,300,000. This would bring the total unusable manpower up to 19,900-000, or 43 per cent of the manpower in the villages of the Soviet Union."

Though the data on which these computations were based may not have been wholly accurate, the general picture was true. The extent of rural overpopulation in the Soviet Union was enormous.

For the moment, migrations to the city could hardly be expected to bring relief. Not only did the rural population overbalance the urban one; there also was its high rate of natural increase. It was not until the middle 1930's that the cities had grown enough to absorb at least the natural rural population increase in the course of their further expansion, lessening the overcrowding on the farms.

This was still far off when the Five-Year Plan era began. In percentage, the First Five-Year Plan foresaw a relatively slight increase in the size of the rural population: 9.0 per cent in five years, as against a 24.4 per cent increase in the cities. In absolute figures, however, the rural increase thus envisioned considerably exceeded that planned for the cities. The rural population was to grow by 11,100,000, as against 6,800,000 for the urban one.[30] The actual development was different. It was deeply influenced

---

[30] The rural population was seen increasing from 123,400,000 in 1927-28 to 134,500,000 in 1932-33, while the urban population was expected to advance during the same time from 27,900,000 to 34,700,000. (Data from *Five-Year Plan* . . ., as quoted *supra*, n. 16, vol. I, p. 129.)

by the sudden turn in official farm policy toward the wholesale collectivization of agriculture.

The year 1929, the first of the First Five-Year Plan, also saw the Soviet Government begin to collectivize peasant holdings by massive official pressure, disrupting all traditional socio-economic relationships in the villages. Some elements of collective farming had been introduced as early as 1918, but until 1929 the process was generally limited to government-fostered merger of farms into farm coöperatives, and in no sense affected a major part of the peasantry. Only 3.9 per cent of all peasant farms (comprising 3.6 per cent of available arable land) had been collectivized by the spring of 1929 [31] when the First Five-Year Plan was approved by the CPSU Conference. The Plan itself confined collectivization to a relatively moderate scope: by 1933, 13.6 per cent of the farming population was to be organized in collective farms (*kolkhozes*) operating on 14.1 per cent of the entire arable land.[32]

But before the end of the summer these moderate plans were abondoned, and by 1930 collectivization had advanced beyond the scope planned for 1933. Thereafter it proceeded by leaps and bounds: [33]

July 1 of . . .	Farms Collectivized as Percentage of All Peasant Farms	Per Cent Peasant-held Planted Acreage Collectivized
1929	3.9	4.9
1930	23.6	33.6
1931	52.7	67.8
1932	61.5	77.6
1933	64.4	83.1
1934	71.1	87.4
1935	83.2	94.1
1938	93.5	99.3

The march of collectivization revolutionized the urban labor market and left an indelible imprint on the social physiognomy of the Russian working class.

From a purely statistical point of view collectivization was bound to enlarge the surplus of labor in the villages. All other

[31] *Socialist Construction* . . ., as quoted *supra*, n. 15, p. 159.

[32] *Five-Year Plan* . . ., as quoted *supra*, n. 16, vol. II, 1, p. 337.

[33] Data for 1929-1935 from *Socialist Construction* . . ., as quoted *supra*, n. 15, p. 278; for 1938, from *Socialist Construction of the USSR*, 1933-1938, Moscow, 1939, p. 85.

conditions being equal, the expenditure of labor per unit of acreage is less on collective farms than in independent peasant holdings; large-scale farming favors labor-saving division of work.

This was clearly shown by an investigation which the *Kolkhoz* Center (an agency operating under the People's Commissariat for Agriculture) conducted in 1930 in four districts of the Ukraine, North Caucasus, the Central Black-Soil Area, and Siberia. Collective farms using larger-sized equipment unknown to the small peasant farmer were excluded, to eliminate differences in the level of mechanization. In terms of man-days of male adults per hectare of planted acreage, expenditure of labor was as follows: [34]

	Fall Planting		Spring Planting	
	Collective Farms	Independent Peasant Farms	Collective Farms	Independent Peasant Farms
Ukraine	5.31	7.89	...	...
North Caucasus	5.61	11.16	5.48	7.80
Central Black-Soil Area	7.22	11.41	7.46	12.23
Siberia	...	...	5.54	16.99

The difference in size alone makes for a considerable saving of labor in collective farming. Introduction of heavy machinery, spurred by collectivization, is another labor-saving device. To determine the expenditure of labor before and after mechanization of the principal phases of agricultural work (cultivation and harvesting), another study was carried out by the *Kolkhoz* Institute (People's Commissariat for Agriculture) in October, 1930. This survey of 68 collective farms scattered all over the country disclosed a labor saving of 48.2 per cent for spring seeds, and of 50.2 per cent for autumn seeds, by means of mechanization.[35]

Numerous surveys have shown that collective agriculture can use only a fraction of the total available manpower. In 1930 a study of 102 *kolkhozes* revealed that days worked per able-bodied person averaged not more than one hundred a year. Even in August, the busiest month in agricultural work, the number of days worked per able-bodied *kolkhoz* member averaged eighteen in

[34] I. Reznikov, "Release of Manpower by Collective Farms, and the Tasks of Organizing *Otkhod*," *Na Agrarnom Fronte*, June, 1931, p. 38.
[35] *Op. cit.*, p. 42.

Bashkiria, fourteen in the North Caucasus and the Leningrad and Western areas, and only eight in the Ivanovo area.[36]

Still less satisfactory was the situation uncovered by other surveys: "A survey by the Research Institute for Large-scale Farming disclosed that in the Volga area only 18.9 per cent of the available manpower was utilized by the *arteli* and 28.7 per cent by the *kommuny;*[37] in the North Caucasus, 18.3 per cent by the former and 38.1 per cent by the latter. According to a comprehensive study undertaken by the *Kolkhoz* Institute in 1930 and based on production plans, less than half the available manpower was used on 31.0 per cent of all collective farms in the Central Black-Soil Region, on 31.6 per cent in the Ukraine, on 25 per cent in the Middle-Volga Area, etc."[38]

As efficiency of work improved with the development of collectivized agriculture, the manpower surplus became more pronounced. Labor expenditures per unit of acreage in a large number of *kolkhozes* under survey in 1933 and 1937 compared as follows:[39]

Days Worked per Hectare of Grain Acreage

Area	1933	1937	Ratio 1937:1933
Azov-Black-Sea	8.67	6.96	.803
Voronezh	14.68	10.63	.724
Western Siberia	9.91	8.27	.835
Kalinin	28.43	26.63	.937
White Russia	23.55	19.42	.825
Ukraine	11.32	10.45	.923
Average	12.30	10.55	.856

The figures may not always be reliable in every detail, as the surveys from which they were drawn had the primary purpose of proving the presence of large manpower reserves in the *kolkhoz* organization. Still, they may be assumed to give a correct picture of the basic trend.

There is no doubt that at first the *kolkhozes* could make efficient use of only part of the manpower available in a peasant

[36] *Op. cit.,* p. 35.
[37] *Arteli* and *kommuny* are different organizational types of collective farms.
[38] A. Libkind, *Agrarian Overpopulation and Collectivization of the Villages,* issued by the Agrarian Institute of the Communist Academy, Moscow, 1931, p. 182.
[39] I. Merinov, "Productivity of Labor in the *Kolkhozes,*" *Planovoye Khozyaistvo,* December, 1939, pp. 142 f.

economy. With farming collectivized and mechanized, the total rural labor force capable of economically efficient agricultural employment diminished considerably. Did this not justify the expectation that collectivization would rapidly aggravate the pressure of rural overpopulation and spur migration to the cities?

In fact, developments were much more complicated and led to various contradictory trends.

Collectivization of Agriculture and Urban Labor Market

In the early years of forcible collectivization, many millions of peasants left for the city. Eight and a half million workers from the country were absorbed by the urban labor market between 1928 and 1932. Most of them, however, did not come from collective farms. They were cast-offs of the collectivization process: either formerly well-to-do peasants who had been "dekulakized"—expropriated and expelled—or pauperized independents who balked at joining the *kolkhozes*.

Within the "collectivized sector," on the other hand, it soon turned out that collectivization, despite its labor-saving effect, kept farmers from migrating to the city and often made it imperative for industrial workers to return to the villages whence they had come long ago.

The first year of forcible collectivization, 1929/30, already showed the extent to which the urban labor market was upset by the agrarian upheaval. Early in 1930, the newspapers were full of items about the new phenomenon of "flight from the cities." Workers who had remained economically linked with the farm rushed back there, lest they miss out in the agrarian reshuffle.

The greatest number of such reports came from mining districts, where the semi-peasant was a common type. The following dispatches were typical:

> "The mines are being deserted. Miner, construction worker, mechanic, each and every one is off to the country to the *kolkhoz*. What else can you expect? That's where their families are. And whoever stays away from the *kolkhoz* is in danger of being branded a *kulak* by the blundering local officials." [40]
>
> "In their administrative zeal the collectivization reformers

---

[40] *Za Industrializatsiyu*, March 22, 1930.

failed to remember that 30 per cent of the miners have farms of their own, and have subjected the families of these miners to so much pressure that their husbands, brothers and fathers are now deluged with letters urging them to come home as soon as possible, to 'save the farm.' In many cases, miners' farms were simply expropriated as *kulak* property and their families refused membership in the *kolkhozes*. It is not surprising that hordes of excited miners have been running for home." [41]

As a rule, Soviet newspapers confined themselves to attributing the miners' flight from the mines to "blundering" enforcement of collectivization by overzealous officials. But the real cause was a phenomenon far more serious than individual excesses.

Under normal conditions, work in the mines was a customary objective of the so-called "temporary migration"*(otkhod, othkodnichestvo)* of farm labor. Without giving up their farms, peasant families who were not fully employed in agriculture would move temporarily to take industrial or semi-industrial seasonal jobs. The collectivization of agriculture upset the urban labor market peculiarly through its effect on *otkhod*. While increasing the manpower surplus on the farms, it reduced the industrial labor supply which temporary migration had normally provided.

Those peasants who had not yet been forced into *kolkhozes* feared to leave for the city or for temporary work lest absence furnish a pretext for expropriating their farms. Those who had already joined collective farms were even more averse to leaving their villages, because they risked discrimination within the *kolkhoz:* with too many people working on collective farms, there was a tendency to withhold work assignments from families whose sons, brothers or fathers were absent and drew pay from non-farm jobs.

The Soviet press during that period constantly discussed the decrease of *otkhod*. "The ratio of collectivization" was said to be "in inverse proportion to the ratio of *otkhod*." In other words, the farther collectivization progressed, the more the number of those willing to accept permanent or temporary employment in the city dwindled. Figures from several areas may illustrate this "inverse proportion": [42]

---

[41] *Trud,* April 15, 1930.
[42] Ye. Bronshtein, "The Manpower Issue in the Third Year of the Five-Year Plan," *Planovoye Khozyaistvo,* December, 1930, p. 201.

Area	Per cent Farms Collectivized	Number of Otkhodniki Per 1,000 Rural Inhabitants
Mordva	8.9 '	47.4
Penza	11.0	20.8
Kuznetsk	11.9	28.6
Syzran'	18.1	36.3
Ul'yanovsk	18.7	30.2
Buguruslan	31.1	26.4
Samara	35.6	17.4
Orenburg	40.2	12.7

This decrease in "temporary migration" noticeably reduced the labor supply in the cities. The difficulties of filling industry's requirements multiplied apace. Repeated attempts at legislative or administrative remedial action (cf. Chapter Two below) were only partially successful.

Urbanization Trends

Today there can no longer be any doubt that the half-rustic nature of the Russian working class was due to the prevalence of the small peasant farm, an economic unit that could neither sustain nor adequately occupy the peasant family. If he could not make a livelihood on the farm, the peasant went to the city to look for work and often stayed for the major part of the year. For the head of the family to take industrial or semi-industrial jobs was not only economically feasible but often imperative. Frequently it was more profitable to hire a farm hand for a while than to have the head of the family forego remunerative non-farm employment. Collectivization changed all that.

Of course, rural overpopulation did not disappear and did not even lessen appreciably. In fact, collectivization initially served to increase the manpower surplus on the farms.[43] And yet, *otkhod* declined. Besides, there appeared a new phenomenon, a pronounced "flight from the city." Even old industrial workers, loyal to industry during the stormy years of collectivization (1929-

---

[43] The opposite trend did not become apparent until several years later. Then, in the late 1930's, new projects were launched on the collective farms and new employment possibilities materialized, provided by soil improvement and conservation, cultivation of commercial plants, construction work, etc. This "industrialization" of agriculture tended to ease the pressure of overpopulation.

1931), seemed to gravitate back to the farm now that the *kolhozes* were growing strong.

Thus the official newspaper for industry wrote in 1934: [44]

> "Considerable changes in the composition of the labor force in the Donets mines are more clearly visible from year to year. Whereas the Donets Basin used to have a surplus of manpower in the winter months, today whole trusts, not just single mines, complain of manpower shortages . . . Nearly 50 per cent of the workers of the OGPU Mine (250 people) have announced their intention to quit, and more than a hundred add that they want to go 'home,' to the village. Things are no better in the largest mines of the Kadiyev coal trust, such as 'Il'yitch,' 'Krivorozh'ye,' etc. Unfortunately, the case of the Kadiyev coal trust is by no means exceptional."

The industry newspaper sounded a warning: "'There are not a few jobs being quit by miners who have been at work in the mines for eight or ten years." The same trend, though less conspicuously, showed up in other industries. It was surely no accident that in 1933, despite a 600,000 drop in industrial employment, there were no visible signs of unemployment in the urban labor market.

Yet although *otkhod* in the usual sense decreased and in additon there were people leaving the cities, a cross-current set in eventually.

In the most turbulent years in the countryside (principally 1930 and 1931) a stream of people moved from the villages into the cities. Certainly it is no accident that Soviet novels, dealing with the workers' life in factories and above all on the vast industrial construction jobs of the early thirties, keep bringing up "de-kulakized" and "*kulak* children." But this movement did not stop with the *kulaks*. It was soon clear that the families of *kolkhoz* members also furnished multitudes of "country fugitives," although the influx of migrants from the *kolkhozes* was not large enough to meet the manpower demands of urban industry.

Taking place in already collectivized agriculture, this new exodus differed essentially from earlier peasant migrations. The bulk of the migrants no longer were heads of families, departing for a time. They were no longer interested in keeping their eco-

---

[44] *Za Industrializatsiyu,* March 16, 1934.

nomic connections with the farm. Increasing numbers resembled the majority of rural migrants in Western and Central Europe, young people who did not care to farm any more, who were ready to become city folks. They came to represent what was to Russia a rather new type: the urbanized industrial worker.

In 1934 a correspondent of the official industry newspaper drew a vivid picture of the change: [45]

> "The social composition of the workers who apply for work in the mines has changed; so has their attitude toward the mine. There was a time when the most common sight in the Donets coal mines was the temporary migrant who would spend part of the year working in the mine and would return to his village in summer, year in, year out. In recent years, quite a few of these workers have definitely settled down in the mining towns, while others have gone back to the country for good . . . But a completely new type of worker has been coming from the country. These are people who have not yet made up their minds where they will ultimately settle, near the mine or back in the village."

The same correspondent quoted figures taken from surveys among Donets miners in 1929 and 1932. The proportion of country-bred miners had not changed in those years; they numbered 61.5 per cent of the total in 1929, and 61.9 per cent in 1932. And yet an essential transformation had taken place. While 27.8 per cent of the miners interviewed in 1929 maintained close economic connections with the country, the corresponding figure in 1932 was only 17.9 per cent. In 1929, 10.1 per cent of the miners questioned had taken leave of absence to do farm labor during the busy season, in 1932 only 0.5 per cent.[46]

The disengagement of industrial labor from its rural background was in full swing.

Working Class Growth from 1932 to 1941

Under the First Five-Year Plan (1928-1932), the grand total of wage and salary earners rose from 11,600,000 to 22,900,000. This was far in excess of the goal set by the Plan, and caused misgivings among government and industrial leaders. In the fall

---

[45] *Za Industrializatsiyu*, February 14, 1934.
[46] *Ibid.*

of 1931 the Supreme Economic Council issued a circular letter (published October 30, 1931) which directed the management of all industrial plants "instantly" to bring the number employed in line with the level of industrial production, and henceforth to refrain from hiring new personnel unless specifically authorized. And when the trade union daily, *Trud*, ventured, in December, 1931, to announced a further increase in employment for 1932, the responsible editor was fired for vi 'ation of government directives.[47]

However, the increase in the number of wage and salary earners in the whole economy envisioned for 1932 was still considerable. It was to rise from 18,700,000 to 21,000,000, i.e., 12.3 per cent.[48] Details of the projected expansion were not released, but official comment indicated that the new personnel would be recruited mainly by employing more apprentices and apparently also more construction workers. On the whole, the government for the time being showed reluctance to increase industrial employment any further.[49]

Again, actual developments surpassed Plan estimates. In 1932 employment reached a new high. It rose 20.8 instead of 12.3 per cent, tantamount to an additional employment of 4,000,000.[50]

---

[47] The incident was mentioned in *Trud* when it occurred. This once, I am unable to furnish an exact reference to the source. In Paris, during the war, I lost my file of *Trud*, and this newspaper has not been completely preserved in this country. Shortly after the incident occurred I related it at length in an article "Unemployment Again?" in the Russian-language *Sotsialisticheskii Vestnik (Social-i.. ...urier)*, Berlin, 1932, No. 3.

[48] *Izvestiya*, December 26, 1931.

[49] Official reluctance toward further expansion in industrial employment found its expression in an editorial of the official trade union newspaper (*Trud*, January 21, 1932), which said: "This year the increase in the productivity of labor will be based chiefly on the most rigidly planned restriction of the number of wage and salary earners. The basic attitude of the Plan for 1932 is decisive reversal of the attitude toward hiring new employees . . . The increase in the number of wage and salary earners during the year will be very moderate as compared with the figure for the end of last year. Industrial establishments controlled by the Supreme Economic Council will hardly employ more workers on the yearly average than they did during the last quarter of 1931. Average railroad employment for the year will be 30,000 less than during the last quarter of the preceding year. Employees on the pay roll of the administration and public institutions will be reduced in number in 1932, in accordance with the directive for cutbacks in administrative expenses. The only group which, according to the Plan, is to undergo a further rapid increase is the apprentices; the number of apprentices is to increase 52 per cent in industrial establishments controlled by the Supreme Economic Council, 70 per cent in rail transport, 53 per cent in waterway transport, etc."

[50] Railroads as well as the administration and public institutions had been instructed to carry out cutbacks in 1932. Instead, there was increase in employment in both occupational divisions by 200,000 each. Cf. *Socialist Construction . . .*, as quoted *supra*, n. 15, p. 508

For the first time since the start of large-scale economic planning, a substantial cut in employment was foreseen in the annual plan for 1933—from 22,900,000 to 21,300,000 [51]—but the actual decrease was only 600,000 instead of 1,600,000.[52]

From 1934 on, employment climbed anew. The Second Five-Year Plan (1933-1937), passed in the beginning of 1934, envisioned a 6,000,000 increase in the number of wage and salary earners in all occupational divisions, from 22,900,000 to 28,900,000, a gain of 26.0 per cent.[53]

But while the First Five-Year Plan had seen its estimates far exceeded, the Second Five-Year Plan failed to see them fulfilled. Though the projected rate of increase was modest in comparison with that of the previous Plan, it was not attained. By 1937 the number of employed had risen 4,000,000 instead of 6,000,000, i.e., 17.6 instead of 26.0 per cent.[54]

Supplying industry with labor was more difficult than foreseen. Accordingly, a lower rate of increase was projected for the Third Five-Year Plan (1938-1942): total employment was to rise from 27,000,000 to 32,700,000 or 21.0 per cent.[55] On the eve of the war it seemed likely that this Plan would succeed; according to data published in 1941, the number employed in 1940 totaled 30,400,000, with 31,600,000 planned for 1941.[56]

How did this affect labor's share within the total population? The census of January 19, 1939 showed the population of the Soviet Union as 170,500,000. By 1940, it presumably approximated 174,000,000. This would account for a ratio of 175 wage and salary earners per thousand inhabitants, as compared with 77 per thousand in 1928, and 80 in 1913.

The numerical increase in wage workers and salaried employees under the three Five-Year Plans can be summarized in the following figures:

---

[51] *Izvestiya*, January 31, 1933.

[52] The number employed was reduced by 250,000 in industry and by as much as 750,000 in building (approximately). This was compensated for by additional employment in a number of other occupational divisions. Cf. *Socialist Construction . . .*, as quoted *supra*, n. 15, p. 508

[53] *Second Five-Year Plan for the National Economy of the USSR*, Moscow, 1934, vol I, pp. 504 f.

[54] *Results of Fulfilling the Second Five-Year Plan*, Moscow, 1939, p. 104.

[55] *Resolutions of the Eighteenth Convention of the CPSU*, Moscow, 1939, p. 36.

[56] Nikolai A. Voznesensky, "The Economic Results of the Year 1940 and the Plan for the Economic Development of the USSR for 1941. Report to the Eighteenth Conference of the CPSU," *Bol'shevik*, 1941, Nos. 3-4, p. 53.

Working Class Growth from 1928 to 1942

Employment (in millions)

	Last Year Before Plan	Last Year Under Plan proposed	achieved
1st Five-Year Plan[57]			
(1928/29-32)	11.3	15.8	22.9
2nd Five-Year Plan			
(1933-37)	22.9	28.9	27.0
3rd Five-Year Plan			
(1938-42)	27.0	32.7	...

Per Cent Increase

	Plan Estimate	Actual
1st Five-Year Plan (1928/29-1932)	38.9	102.0
2nd Five-Year Plan (1933-1937)	26.0	17.6
3rd Five-Year Plan (1938-1942)	21.0	....

The enormous growth of the working class in less than one and a half decades of overall planning is a fact of great sociological importance, especially as the stratification of labor also underwent substantial changes. There was a marked increase in the proportion of manual workers, in particular in industry proper. Both processes involved transformations which reshaped the social pattern of the country.

At this point we shall add a few additional remarks on the growth of the working class, in so far as it reveals the metamorphosis of Russian labor—the formation of a new working class without rural ties.

Out of 12,500,000 new wage and salary earners who swelled the ranks of labor under the First Five-Year Plan, roughly 8,500,-000 had come from the peasantry. Under the Second Five-Year Plan the industrial manpower supply was to depend much less on the rural influx. The number of employed was to rise by 6,000,-000 from 1932 to 1937; in addition, 3,400,000 were needed to replace those eliminated by death, disability, etc. Of this total of 9,400,000 new wage and salary earners, only 3,200,000 were to be recruited on the farms; nearly two-thirds had to come from the cities.[58]

---

[57] Under the First Five-Year Plan, figures proposed for the fifth year refer to the economic year of 1932-33, figures of actual results to the calendar year 1932.
[58] *Second Five-Year Plan* . . ., as quoted *supra*, n. 53, vol. I, pp. 338 f.

Not even this modest influx from the countryside was certain; the authors of the Second Plan did not expect it to flow automatically, but proposed to assure it by rigorous labor control measures. With the scope of rural migration not safely predictable, the problem of mobilizing the urban manpower reserves—particularly that of inducing housewives to work for wages— assumed paramount importance. (See below, Chapter Two.)

The scarcity of statistical material prevents an exact analysis of these trends between 1932 and 1937. The increase in the total number of wage and salary earners lagged considerably behind the Plan estimate. But there was a very substantial rise in the industrial employment of women. As a recruitment source of industrial labor, the city obviously played an even larger part than it had been assigned in the Plan. It is safe to assume that this trend has gained in significance during the subsequent years.

The Working Class in the War and Postwar Years

The war added considerable momentum to the trend here described. Above all, it brought on an acute labor shortage. Industry had to give up a great many workers for service in the armed forces. No data were ever published on the number of military draftees nor on that of occupational exemptions and deferments;[59] neither were there any indications as to the rules which governed releases from draft on occupational grounds. As far as can be judged from reports on conditions in industry, only limited numbers of workers subject to military service were retained in the plants (especially in the first one to one-and-a-half years of the war), and only among skilled workers in war industry proper was there a considerable percentage of exemptions.

Even more affected by the draft was rural labor, an import-

---

[59] The information available on the numbers of persons drafted into the armed forces, or classes called up, is neither exact nor comprehensive. According to unverified data circulating outside of the Soviet Union, the wartime draft covered men between 18 and 54 or 55 and comprised 37 or 38 classes (probably taking into account the age shifts in wartime). To a certain extent this assumption is borne out by official data on discharges. The first three demobilization orders (*Pravda*, June 24, and September 26, 1945; March 21, 1946) referred to 13, 10 or 6 classes respectively, a total of 29. After these 29 classes had been discharged, the Soviet Union retained armed forces far in excess of peacetime effectives. The fourth demobilization act (*Pravda*, October 23, 1946) merely ordered the discharge of "the seriatim oldest age group."

ant source of manpower for industry, and notably for "mass projects" which did not require special skills. Suffice it to say that the proportion of women in the able-bodied rural population had risen from 52 per cent at the beginning of 1939 to 71 per cent at the beginning of 1943.[60] The farm population diminished so rapidly in the early stages of the war that organized recruitment of manpower on the farms (see Chapter Two) had to be discontinued in the first war year. The conscription of city dwellers for farm work was finally introduced in 1942 (see Chapter Three).

Under these circumstances the greatest possible utilization of urban labor reserves became a necessity. Above all, it manifested itself in a vast increase in female industrial labor (see Chapter Two). In addition, the employment of youth in industry was greatly expanded, and older workers, already eliminated from the labor process, were "re-activated." The result was a shift in the age structure of the industrial working class. Beween 1939 and 1942 the quota of boys and girls under eighteen rose from 6 to 15 per cent of the total industrial labor force, the quota of workers from eighteen to forty-nine years of age dropped from 85 to 73 per cent, and the quota of older workers, aged fifty or more, rose from 9 to 12 per cent.[61] A definite compilation of the figures for male and female industrial workers would have made the shift in the male age groups even more evident. Nor was the process completed by 1942. There were simply no later statistics published.

However significant, the influx of these new workers could not insure the replenishment of the war-depleted plant labor pools. Between 1940 and 1943, there was a 38 per cent drop in the number of workers and employees in the whole economy and administration.[62] In industry proper, while less marked, it still amounted to 31 per cent.[63] Of course, this drop was partly due to the fact that important areas of the Soviet Union were still German-occupied in 1943, and economic reconstruction in the parts already liberated had only just begun. But even in 1945, when the war was over and the work of reconstruction far advanced, the number of employed workers remained considerably below pre-war levels.

---

[60] N. A. Vosnesensky, *The War Economy of the USSR in the Period of the War for the Fatherland,* Moscow, 1947, p. 113.
[61] *Ibid.,* pp. 112 f.
[62] *Ibid.,* p. 109.
[63] Calculated on the basis of Voznesensky's figures, *ibid.,* p. 109.

It has been mentioned before that the over-all total of wage workers and salaried employees in all branches of the Soviet economy and administration had reached 30,400,000 by 1940. This figure referred to the Soviet Union within its old borders. Expansion has since increased the Soviet population by some 14 per cent, and the 1940 employment totals in present Soviet territory must have substantially surpassed the figure of 30,400,000. Yet by 1945 the total number of manual and white-collar workers employed within the Soviet boundaries amounted to no more than 27,250,000.[64]

Toward the end of the war, and in the first postwar year, frequent complaints of an extraordinary labor shortage appeared in the Soviet press. The first news referred to peat. Only 76,200 workers worked on peat banks operated by the People's Commissariat for Power Generation, the main consumer of peat, by April 1, 1945, as against 97,800 a year earlier.[65] This, of course, may have been influenced by specific conditions.

But things were no better in textiles, although the textile industry as a whole suffered least from the war, as relatively few textile plants were located in occupied territory. Nevertheless, the press recorded in October, 1945, that plant and equipment in textile factories were largely idle for lack of manpower.[66] In March, 1946, it was announced on the floor of the Supreme Soviet that because of the labor shortage "about one-third of all spindles and looms in textile factories of Moscow city and Moscow province [were] kept in reserve, out of operation." [67] Machinery was also idle in the textile plants of Ivanovo province,[68] next to Moscow the largest textile district of the USSR. According to Aleksei N. Kosygin, vice-chairman of the Council of Ministers of the USSR, the total number employed in the textile industry dropped from 808,000 in 1940 to 400,000 in 1946.[69]

Similar conditions prevailed in hosiery, clothing, leather, shoe factories and other light-industry establishments. In Octo-

---

[64] Calculated on the basis of figures announced by Voznesensky, in reporting to the Supreme Soviet on the Fourth Five-Year Plan. S. *Proceedings in the 1st Session of the Supreme Soviet of the USSR*, March, 1946, p. 66.
[65] *Pravda*, April 8, 1945.
[66] *Pravda*, October 28, 1945.
[67] Georgi M. Popov, deputy from Moscow, speaking during debates on the Fourth Five-Year Plan, *Proceedings . . .*, as quoted *supra*, n. 64, p. 256.
[68] *Pravda*, April 20, 1946.
[69] *Proceedings . . .*, as quoted *supra*, n. 64, p. 156.

ber, 1945, an official announcement referring to these industries said: [70] "In many factories . . . equipment is not being utilized, remaining idle because of lack of workers." In March, 1946, Vice-Premier Kosygin said [71] that "the number of workers in these industries contracted considerably" in comparison with prewar standards.

Naturally, coal mining, too, was seriously affected. Even metallurgy and metal manufactures which enjoyed manpower priorities during the war reported instances of acute manpower shortage. "Not enough workers" was indicated in October, 1945, as the chief reason why industrial plants in Yaroslavl failed to comply with plan assignments, and it was stressed that metal plants there were the worst hit.[72] At a session of the Supreme Soviet in March, 1946, Piotr F. Lomako, Minister for Non-Ferrous Industry, complained about the shortage of workers in plants under his Ministry.[73] Of course, the complaints of metallurgical and metal-manufacturing plants seemed almost reassuring, compared with the manpower tragedy that befell the textile industry and kindred consumer goods manufactures.

The Soviet leaders knew well that no large-scale influx of manpower from rural areas could be counted on to overcome these difficulties. In March, 1946, when the Fourth Five-Year Plan was confirmed, it was decided to resume the so-called organized enlistment of workers in the *kolkhozes;* but no great results seem to have been expected from this measure, and the main stress was laid on the mass production of skilled and semi-skilled labor by the occupational training of youth (see Chapter Two).

A few data may illustrate this. When the Fourth Five-Year Plan (1946-50) was drawn up, the total number of workers and employees in all economic and administrative branches was set at 33,500,000 for 1950 as against 27,250,000 in 1945.[74] The number of manual workers projected for industry proper in 1950 was not announced, and neither was the actual one in 1945. But as the latest available Soviet figures place the number of manual workers in industry (including apprentices and the so-called "lower

[70] A. Shchegolev [the People's Commissar for Light Industry of the RSFSR], "Light-Industry Potentialities," *Pravda,* October 20, 1945.

[71] See n. 69 above.

[72] *Izvestiya,* October 26, 1945.

[73] *Proceedings* . . ., as quoted *supra,* n. 64, p. 300.

[74] *Ibid.,* p. 66.

service personnel") at somewhat less than one-third of the total employed labor force,[75] we may estimate that they numbered about 9,000,000 in 1945, and about 11,000,000 (according to plan) in 1950.

In planning to add about two million more industrial workers, the number of juveniles to be enlisted and trained for skilled or semi-skilled labor in the course of the Five-Year Plan had been set at 4,500,000. While part of these were not to be trained for industry proper but for transportation and the building trades, which in the Soviet Union do not count as industrial branches, the bulk was—and still is—destined for industry. Even if we take regular replacement requirements into consideration, we find that an overwhelming majority of the new industrial workers was to consist of these juvenile trainees.

A great many of them are, of course, drafted from rural areas. (For more on that subject, and on this form of occupational training in general, see Chapter Two). Once trained, however, they do not go back to the country. Their assimilation into industrial labor is final. They no longer resemble the traditional half-rustic type of Russian worker.

Actual developments under the Fourth Five-Year Plan differed in detail from the projected ones. In particular, the total of workers and employees rose faster than had been envisioned, while the occupational training program could not quite produce the planned number of new, young workers. But in principle there was no change.

The plan envisioned a five-year increase of 6,250,000 in the total of workers and employees. In fact, the number of those employed in all economic and administrative branches rose as follows: [76]

---

[75] According to the figures for 1937, workers and employees in all economic and administrative branches numbered 26,989,500, and manual workers in industry proper 8,827,500, or 32.7 per cent. For the year 1942 the draft of the Third Five-Year Plan estimated the total of workers and employees at 32,000,000 and the total of workers in industry proper at 10,314,000, or 32.2 per cent. Calculated according to figures quoted in *The Third Five-Year Plan of National Economic Development in the USSR* (Draft), Moscow, 1939, pp. 228-29.

[76] Taken from the yearly economic progress reports on the years 1946-50, published by the Central Statistical Administration in *Izvestiya* of January 21, 1947, January 18, 1948, January 20, 1949, January 18, 1950, and January 27, 1951. In the 1950 report, unlike those on the years from 1946 to 1949, the increase in employ-

in 1946 by 3,000,000
" 1947 " 1,200,000
" 1948 " 2,000,000
" 1949 " 1,800,000
" 1950 " 2,200,000

Thus the five-year increase was not 6,250,000, as it should have been according to plan, but approximately 10,200,000, and by 1950 the total number of workers and employees had not reached 33,500,000 but nearly 37,500,000. Correspondingly the number of manual industrial workers reached between 12,000,- 000 and 12,500,000 in 1950—an increase over 1945 of from 3,000,- 000 to 3,500,000. The number of juveniles drafted for occupational training and trained amounted to some 3,400,000 in the five years (see Chapter Two). The influx into industry of the specially trained juveniles remained decisive.

Another interesting point shown by these statistics is the unusually sharp rise in employment figures during 1946, although in that particular year the number of juveniles delivered to industry by the occupational training program was a modest 382,- 000. The bulk of the new manpower in 1946 came from another source, and the assumption suggests itself that an unexpectedly large number of men discharged from the army sought and found employment as manual and white-collar workers. Hundreds of thousands, possibly millions who went to war from the villages and had as yet no families of their own did not return to their villages after the war years. Instead, they were absorbed into the

---

ment is not given as an anual average. Instead, the total of workers and employees at the end of 1950 is given as 39,200,000, and at the same time this figure is said to exceed that of the end of 1949 by 2,000,000. As we know from the quarterly reports on the first nine months of 1950 (*Izvestiya* of April 27, July 28, and October 24, 1950) that the average employment totals in these quarters exceeded the corresponding figures for 1949 by 2,000,000, 2,400,000, and 2,400,000, respectively, we may assume that the annual average of workers and employees increased by 2,200,- 000 from 1949 to 1950, and that the average for 1950 was close to 37,500,000.

As the number of workers and employees rose approximately evenly, the difference between the annual average and the figure at the year's end should amount to about half the annual increase. For 1950 that would mean about 1,100,000—some 600,000 less than the difference between the nearly 37,500,000 just calculated as the 1950 average and the 39,200,000 announced as the end-of-the-year figure. Presumably this discrepancy is due to the fact that some social group not previously classified as "workers and employees" was now counted in that category—perhaps the students of the occupational training schools of the so-called "State Labor Reserve" (cf. Chapter Two).

great mass of urban workers and employees, partly by the lower administrative machine. They, too, turned into workers who ceased to resemble the half-rustic worker type.

Today the process of developing a modern working class without rural ties is all but completed in the Soviet Union.

APPENDIX

Statistical Material on the Working Class

Available statistical data on the development of industrial labor in Russia during the last half-century are not easily compared and summarized. Statistical methods and sociological classifications differed so widely during the period under review that the coördination of individual data meets with great obstacles.

Data on the number of wage and salary earners vary considerably according to different sources. But if their juxtaposition in a single table would hardly make sense, the statistical evidence on hand can be presented in several individual surveys.

A study published in 1926 by a Soviet author [77] offers processed census data which may be used for the purposes of the present survey. The following table draws on this particular source, presenting material for the period from 1897 to 1924. All data refer to the pre-1939 territory of the Soviet Union, for both the Soviet period and the pre-revolutionary period:

Wage and Salary Earners in Russia
(in thousands)

	1897	1913	1922/23	1923/24
Grand Total	7,905	11,200	6,636	7,397
Thereof:				
Industry, all classes	2,202	3,636	1,958	2,150
(a) large-scale	1,622	2,776	1,659	1,815
(b) small-scale	580	860	300	335
Railroads	347	705	862	875
Communications	37	72	92	87
Commerce	367	451	306	380
Agriculture	2,775	3,000	1,100	1,300

[77] B. Gukhman, *The Size of the Proletariat and Wages in the USSR*, Moscow, 1926, p. 29.

Official publications under the Five-Year Plans followed a different, more detailed pattern, but even within the framework of this new pattern the figures for the individual years are not always comparable. In consequence, the following table does not go beyond 1935; data are based on the official statistical abstract issued in 1934, and completed or revised in accordance with the 1936 edition of the same source.[78]

Wage and Salary Earners in the USSR, 1924-1935
(in thousands)

	1923/24	1924/25	1925/26	1926/27	1928	1929
Grand Total	...	8,532	10,173	10,944	11,599	12,168
Thereof:						
Large-scale industry	1,795	2,107	2,678	2,839	3,096	3,366
Building	194	287	426	547	723	918
Transportation:						
Total	1,038	1,058	1,240	1,302	1,270	1,302
(a) Railroads	802	806	962	1,006	971	984
(b) Waterways	82	86	99	111	104	111
(c) Other	154	166	179	185	195	207
Communications	81	82	94	95	95	120
Commerce	248	374	471	515	532	627
Public eating places	21	33	45	49	55	79
Education	493	551	603	715	789	819
Public health	252	271	324	365	399	438
Finance	48	66	82	86	95	108
Other government services	887	965	1,082	1,120	1,174	1,255
Agriculture	...	...	...	...	1,676	1,576
Lumber	...	...	...	...	337	415
Domestic service	133	193	253	317	377	396

[78] *Socialist Construction of the USSR. Statistical Year-Book*, Moscow, 1934, pp. 306 f.; 1936, pp. 508 f.

	1930	1931	1932	1933	1934	1935
Grand Total	14,531	18,990	22,943	22,325	23,681	24,770
Thereof:						
Large-scale						
industry	4,264	5,483	6,481	6,229	6,531	7,066
Building	1,623	2,549	3,126	2,361	2,618	2,204
Transportation:						
Total	1,499	1,927	2,222	2,305	2,556	2,922
(a) Railroads	1,084	1,320	1,527	1,474	1,603	1,789
(b) Waterways	132	177	196	189	222	246
(c) Other	283	430	500	642	730	887
Communications	153	197	224	258	295	334
Commerce	815	1,078	1,411	1,375	1,465	1,650
Public eating						
places	181	365	515	532	546	485
Education	921	1,153	1,347	1,463	1,569	1,725
Public Health	477	562	647	681	739	809
Finance	101	116	128	132	134	152
Other govern-						
ment services	1,470	1,712	1,918	1,753	1,680	1,745
Agriculture	1,552	2,060	2,858	2,819	3,094	2,974
Lumber	611	857	1,140	1,193	1,209	1,300
Domestic service	253	228	216	...	...	...

More recently, data referring to the last years covered by the table above were partly revised and regrouped so as to offer a basis for comparison with subsequent years. The statistical abstract issued in 1939 [79] compared the number of wage and salary earners in 1932, the last year of the First Five-Year Plan, with that in 1937, the last year of the Second Five-Year Plan. These data, complemented by projected figures for 1942, the last year of the Third Five-Year Plan,[80] follow:

[79] *Socialist Construction in the USSR, 1933-1938,* Moscow, 1939, p. 138.

[80] See the draft of the Third Five-Year Plan, as quoted *supra,* n. 75, pp. 228 f.—When the Third Five-Year Plan was approved, the projected figure for wage and salary earners in 1942 was raised by 700,000 (to 32,700,000). The approved figures for the different branches of economy were not made public.

*Wage and Salary Earners in the USSR at the end of the
First and Second Five-Year Plans, and Projected Figures
of the Third Five-Year Plan* (in thousands)

	1932	1937	1942 (planned)
Grand Total	22,942.8	26,989.5	32,000
Thereof:			
Industry	7,999.8	10,111.7	11,899
thereof:			
manual workers		8,048.0	9,184
technical employees		697.7	910
other white-collar workers		586.5	675
lower service personnel		475.2	630
apprentices		303.4	500
Building	2,835.1	2,023.2	1,829
thereof:			
manual workers		1,672.6	1,497
technical employees		119.9	129
other white-collar workers		122.5	98
lower service personnel		97.5	91
apprentices		10.7	14
Railway transportation	1,296.6	1,512.2	1,700
Water transportation	145.5	179.5	230
Other transportation	598.5	1,092.1	1,735
Communications	224.3	375.0	500
Commerce	1,410.8	1,993.9	2,500
Public eating places	515.1	395.5	560
Finance	128.4	192.8	230
Education	1,351.1	2,303.0	2,900
Arts	84.5	122.0	165
Health service	647.2	1,117.6	1,600
Other government services	1,833.5	1,743.3	2,000
Housing and municipal services		753.7	920
Agriculture	2,857.5	2,482.6	2,650
Lumber	196.1	247.9	325
Others		246.0	195

The proportion of wage and salary earners within the total population is even more difficult to establish. All figures above refer to persons gainfully employed as wage or salary earners and do not include dependents. As for social groups other than wage or salary earners, Soviet statistics do not supply data on persons gainfully employed but list gainfully employed and dependents together. The only figures available for these groups indicate merely the proportion of different "social groups" within the total population. The following grouping of social strata within the Soviet Union's population is of some interest:[81]

Percent Distribution of USSR Population, by Social Groups

	1913	1928	1934	1937
Wage and salary earners	16.7	17.3	28.1	34.7
Peasants on collectivized farms and artisans [82] organized in producers' cooperatives	—	2.9	45.9	55.5
Peasants on independent individual farms and artisans [82] not organized in cooperatives	65.1	72.9	22.5	5.6
Bourgeoisie (landowners; urban upper and lower class bourgeoisie; tradesmen and *kulaki*)	15.9	4.5	.1	—
Others (students, military, beneficiaries of pensions, etc.)	2.3	2.4	3.4	4.2
Total	100.0	100.0	100.0	100.0

These percentages show clearly that the social weight of labor increased tremendously between 1928 and 1937. For subsequent years reliable comparable data are lacking. Results of the population census taken in January 1939 were only partly disclosed. Percentage data published would, if true, indicate a rather fantastic social regrouping within a period of two years—from 1937 to 1939. According to these figures,[83] the social distribution of the population in January 1939 was as follows:

---

[81] *Socialist Construction* . . . , as quoted *supra*, n. 79, p. 16.

[82] Russian statistics as well as legislation use a special term, *kustari*, for small producers in more or less primitive handicraft establishments. Prior to the 1920's the term applied only to small industrial producers within the framework of rural economy. Later it usually also referred to small-scale handicraft in the cities.

[83] *Izvestiya*, April 29, 1940

Social Group	Per Cent of Total Population	
Wage earners	32.19	} 49.73
Salary earners	17.54	
Peasants on collevtivized farms	44.61	} 46.90
Artisans organized in producers' cooperatives	2.29	
Peasants on independent individual farms	1.78	} 2.60
Artisans not organized in cooperatives	.82	
Others	.77	
Total	100.00	

These figures should be treated with caution. The precentage of workers and employees was put at 34.7 for 1937 in the statistical reference work cited above, which appeared in 1939. It is true that certain shifts took place between 1937 and January, 1939, and the percentage of workers and employees might—in view of the shifts in the immediately preceding years—be estimated at perhaps 37, but under no circumstances at 49.7. Whence this sudden rise of a full third in the percentage total?

It is apparent that the data for workers and employees in the two tables given above do not refer to the same group of persons. In the compilation of the first table (through 1937), only persons occupying a regular work status were considered to be workers and employees, in accordance with the data in the current statistics for the labor force; in the compilation of the second table (for 1939), however, several million additional persons were counted as workers and employees. It is known from the statements of former Soviet slaves that the slaves (in concentration camps, etc.) were included in the national census of 1939 and that they were registered, not according to their former professions, but according to their work in the camps, i.e., in all cases as workers and employees. This was confirmed recently in a work by a former Soviet statistician, who took part in the census of 1939.[84] The number of workers and employees according to the census of 1939 therefore had to be considerably higher than the number of workers and employees according to the current statistics for the labor force.

If this were the only cause of the great discrepancy between the two figures given (37.0 and 49.7 per cent), the number of slaves in 1939 would have to equal about a third of the number of workers and employees holding a regular work status, that is, it would have to reach a total of some 10,000,000. In reality, however, the number of

---

[84] N. Galin, *How Censuses Were Carried Out in the USSR.* (Russian), Munich, 1951, p. 20.

slaves at the beginning of 1939 was probably somewhat smaller, since part of the group "workers and employees (with families)" in the 1939 census should perhaps be attributed to certain tricks on the part of the official statisticians, who were set the task of computing the highest possible percentage figure for the "workers and employees" group. For this reason, a farm family perhaps, whose head had been employed however briefly as a worker in industry, building, etc., was counted in its entirety as a workers' family (note the great difference between the 1937 and 1939 data for collective farmers and, even more, for individual farmers). Some other statistical tricks were perhaps also employed. All this, however, can explain only a relatively limited part of the 10,000,000 discrepancy. These 10,000,000 were undoubtedly, for the most part, slaves.[85]

---

[85] See my article, "Statistics on Slave Labor," in *Sotsialisticheskii Vestnik*, December, 1951.

Chapter Two

TRANSFORMATION OF
THE LABOR MARKET

Labor Market and Labor Market Policy Until 1930.—The Turning Point: Tightening of the Labor Supply.—Main Problem after 1930: Industrial Labor Supply.—The End of Unemployment Insurance and of the Labor Market.—Manpower Recruitment on the Farms.—"Activation" of Urban Labor Reserves: Female Labor.—"Activation" of Juvenile Reserves.— Preparations for a Planned Distribution of Manpower.

Labor Market and Labor Market Policy Until 1930

From the very outset, the Soviet labor market was influenced by the distinctive features of Russian industrial labor and its close ties with the rural economy. Between 1918 and 1921, in the years of economic disintegration, millions fled from the cities to the country. The urban labor market was deserted to the point where even the shrunken urban economy could only be kept functioning by the introduction of compulsory labor.[1] Economic recovery, which began in 1921, and the reemployment of millions started an influx of migrants from the countryside. Unemployment, hitherto latent, became manifest. Russia presented a peculiar phenomenon: the number of unemployed rose right along with the number of employed.

As the rise in employment was dealt with in the preceding chapter, it remains to point out the unemployment trend. According to employment exchange statistics, unemployment increased

---

[1] Cf. my article "Die Arbeitspflicht in Russland," *Archiv für Rechts- und Wirtschaftsphilosophie*, October, 1925.

37

rapidly from early in 1922, as will be seen from the following figures: [2]

		Registered Unemployed (in thousands)
1922	January	175
	July	436
1923	January	625
	July	1,000
1924	January	1,240
	July	1,340

In the second half of 1924 a reorganization of the employment exchanges was initiated. With the reorganization of the service, compulsory hiring through these exchanges was relaxed and the sifting of the waiting lists of job applicants ordered. As an immediate consequence, the number of registered unemployed dropped from July 1924 on, if only for a short time. For 1924/25 and the following years the yearly average figures were as follows: [3]

	Registered Unemployed (in thousands)
1924/25	848
1925/26	1,017
1926/27	1,242
1927/28	1,290

Corresponding yearly averages for 1928/29 and 1929/30 are not known. The following figures reveal a further increase in unemployment until it began to recede in the second half of 1929: [4]

Years	Registered Unemployed (in thousands)	
	April 1	October 1
1927	1,478	1,041
1928	1,576	1,365
1929	1,741	1,242
1930	1,081	. . .

---

[2] A. Mints, "The Labor Market in 1924," *Voprosy Truda*, March, 1925, p. 24.
[3] *Control Figures for the National Economy of the USSR for 1927/28*, Moscow, 1928, p. 213; *Control Figures . . . for 1928/29*, Moscow, 1929, p. 156.
[4] M. Romanov, "Labor Market Prospects in the USSR," *Voprosy Truda*, July-August, 1930, p. 46.

A labor shortage, which we shall later take up in detail, began to develop and soon led to basic changes in manpower policy—changes which affected all subsequent trends. Before discussing these trends, however, let us look briefly at the organization of the labor market in the second half of the 1920's.

The reorganization of the government-operated employment exchanges, begun in the second half of 1924, was completed early in 1925. Sec. 7 of the Labor Code, which required that hiring be done only through employment exchanges, was repealed.[5] Employers were now free to hire whomever they wanted, and employees were free to take any job they wished.

Did the government mean to relax its rigid hold on the labor market—so to speak, to leave the balancing supply and demand to the "free play of forces"? Certainly not. It was soon clear that this was neither intended nor did it actually take place.

The formal repeal of compulsory hiring through the employment exchanges did not inaugurate any "liberal" policy. The governmental employment exchanges, as organized prior to 1925, were simply not up to the tasks facing them in the framework of a labor policy based on their hiring monopoly. There was no end to the complaint of their red tape and inefficiency. The abrogation of Sec. 7 of the Labor Code was merely the first step toward a reorganization that had become inevitable.

The sequel to this first step was a unionist labor market policy that revived the idea of compulsory hiring through the employment exchanges and put it into practice in a new form: by incorporating it in union contracts. There could be no question, under Soviet conditions, of a conflict between governmental and union measures in the field of labor market policy. The repeal of Sec. 7 of the Labor Code and the use of collective bargaining to reintroduce compulsory hiring through the employment exchanges were two links in a single chain of events.

The new method of letting the unions enforce compulsory hiring through employment exchanges was first applied in 1925. By 1926 its use was widespread. The Seventh Trade Union Convention, meeting in December 1926, resolved: [6] "In negotiating

---

[5] Decision of the CEC and CPC of the USSR, January 2, 1925, *Izvestiya*, January 14, 1925.
[6] Ya. Gindin, "The Seventh Trade Union Convention of the USSR and Unemployment," *Vestnik Truda*, February, 1927, p. 2.

collective agreements, trade unions shall insist that the necessary personnel be hired through the employment exchanges, with exceptions permitted only for specially skilled workers in special jobs, and with the consent of the unions." This practice was soon the rule.

Under different conditions, exclusive hiring through employment exchanges means different things. There is no space here to discuss its varying effects; I should like only to repeat some general observations I made more than fifteen years ago: [7]

> "Labor organizations in Western Europe fight for the acceptance of compulsory hiring through employment offices as a guiding principle of labor market policy. Wherever a strong labor union movement enjoys true freedom and independence, and labor unions actively participate in the administration of employment offices and in the supervision of hiring, the compulsion to hire through these offices protects employees from discriminatory selection of job applicants by employers and acts as a safeguard to prevent employers from using the plight of backward groups of workers to cut wages and worsen working condition. . .

> "In Soviet Russia exclusive hiring through employment offices never had this particular significance. There, trade unions do not, and never did, enjoy enough freedom and independence to ensure the protective function of compulsory hiring through employment offices. Nor do, or did, the employers there (i.e., primarily the government-owned enterprises) have enough freedom to fix wages and to use a free labor market to depress the workers' living standards.

> "What is more, exclusive hiring through employment offices, patterned after the most progressive social ideas of the West, though officially announced as early as 1917, was not actually introduced until later, when a manpower shortage, due to the mass exodus from the city to the country, came to be acutely felt.

> "At that time compulsory hiring through employment offices could not possibly protect the workers' interests; it became a device to rob job seekers of the last vestiges of the freedom to dispose of their labor. It was a step on the road to the intro-

---

[7] Cf. my article "Crisis of Labor Market Policy," *Sotsialisticheskii Vestnik*, Paris, 1935, no. 16.

duction of compulsory labor. It is not surprising that it should have been regarded by the masses of wage and salary earners in the period of War Communism as a measure to oppress them not to improve their condition.

"During the years of the NEP, with unemployment rising visibly, exclusive hiring through employment offices lost this adverse meaning. Workers became used to it, the hardships involved lessened as time went by, and though it did not perform the protective function which makes labor organizations in Western countries advocate it, it became at least a guarantee of the more or less satisfactory functioning of the labor market setup."

With the unions enforcing hiring through the employment exchanges, another feature of unionist policy became evident. Restrictions were placed on admission to unions, and a tendency appeared to reserve the jobs for members.

To be eligible for membership, applicants had to be employed for a certain time (varying in different unions) and no one who was not a union member could be referred to a job which unemployed members were seeking. The result was a vicious circle: non-union men had hardly a chance to get jobs, and the jobless could not join unions. Under these circumstances, the unions' reintroduction of compulsory hiring through employment exchanges acquired special significance.

Leading union circles were aware of this. An article published by the trade union newspaper, *Trud,* in the summer of 1925 and significantly headed, "The Unions and the Right to Work," set forth the principles on which the monopolistic and restrictive union policies were based. It said: [8]

"The unions have never made it their task to defend the interests of people who do not do salaried work. The mere intention to get a job and join the union is not enough. The unions fight for organized work, for organized securing of jobs and as a matter of course [sic] for the employment of those who are already organized. By doing otherwise the unions would lose their class character [sic] and deny their essence—the protection of their members' interests . . .

"Unemployed who are not union members will not agree with us on this issue, because they want to get jobs. There are

[8] *Trud,* July 1, 1925.

many of them, not only at the employment exchanges but also in every worker, employee and peasant family. Yet it must be stressed again that the unions will not and cannot undertake to protect all those who are not working for wages."

In the pursuit of this monopolistic policy, emphasis was laid on the conflict of interests between the employed and the unemployed.[9] Quite often unions took a determined stand against newcomers from the country and opposed "artificial inflation of unemployment among union members through inclusion of peasant and semi-peasant elements and of the urban petty bourgeoisie."[10]

Analogous trends prevailed in the government regulation of the labor market. In March 1927 an order was issued to the effect that "only real unemployed" were to be registered as job applicants by employment exchanges.[11] Only those applicants were admitted to registration who had held jobs before and could prove "previous employment" of a certain length of time. The only exemption was for children of wage and salary earners, and for graduates of technical schools (secondary and higher education).

On this basis, the People's Commissariat for Labor of the USSR issued further regulations on the registration of unemployed.[12] "Previous employment" now established eligibility for registration only if shown for the last year prior to the application. Skilled workers had only to show that they had held any job in the course of that year, regardless of the length of employment; but unskilled unemployed were required to submit proof of "uninterrupted employment for six consecutive months" in the year preceding registration.

These restrictions were mainly aimed against the influx of job seekers from the country. Children of wage and salary earners were admitted to registration until their twenty-first year, without proof of previous employment. So were union members

9 V. Kuz'menko, "Rejection of Liberalism in the Admission to Trade Union Membership," *Vestnik Truda*, December, 1927, pp. 53 f.

10 For further details regarding this peculiar Russian version of "closed shop" policies, cf. my article on "Monopolistic Tendencies in the Russian Trade Unions," *Gewerkschafts-Zeitung*, weekly issued by the German Federation of Trade Unions (ADGB), Berlin, 1928, no. 31.

11 Decision of the CEC and the CPC of the USSR on "measures for the regulation of the labor market," March 4, 1927, *Izvestiya*, March 12, 1927.

12 *Izvestiya Narkomtruda*, 1927, No. 13.

generally; union affiliation was taken as proof of having worked for wages.[13]

Unemployed who failed to meet the requirements could be listed in special records and had a chance to get a job if there were not enough "registered unemployed." It was left to the employment agencies to decide, depending on the condition of the labor market, whether or not they would grant such additional listings.

As it did not seem feasible to set up a countryside network of exchanges, auxiliary employment agencies, so-called "correspondence points," were created, especially in rural regions. Their first task was not to further employment but mainly to bar "migration of seasonal workers from the countryside." [14]

Govermental and unionist labor market policies were complementary. Their close coordination produced a homogeneous system of measures designed to curb the invasion of the urban labor market by rural migrants.

The Turning Point: Tightening of the Labor Supply

By mid-1929 the labor market showed the first signs of shortages. Some observers pointed to a "deterioration" in distribution of unemployed. Out of 1,335,000 unemployed registered with the employment exchanges on April 1, 1929, only 349,000, lcss than one-quarter, were industrial workers.[15] Bottlenecks in the supply of labor for industrial employment were already foreseeable, though no one dared yet to think that unemployment might vanish.

The First Five-Year Plan, approved in April 1929, envisioned a reduction of the unemployed from 1,135,000 in April, 1928, to 511,000 by April, 1933.[16] The annual plan for the year 1929/30 reckoned with a more modest decline: to an annual average of

---

[13] Further exemptions were provided for some categories of female applicants for employment by an ordinance of the People's Commissariat for Labor of the USSR of February 23, 1928. Admission to registration without proof of previous employment record was granted to widows of union members for a period of two years following the husband's death, also to women belonging to national minority groups in eastern regions. Cf. *Izvestiya Narkomtruda*, 1928, p. 190.

[14] I. Voitinsky, ed., *ABC of Soviet Labor Law*, 5th ed., Moscow, 1929, p. 36.

[15] S. Tarasov, "Tasks of Supplying Industry with Manpower," *Voprosy Truda*, August, 1929, p. 31.

[16] *Five-Year Plan of Economic Construction of the USSR*, Moscow, 1929, Vol. II, 2, p. 179.

1,106,000, against 1,224,000 in the preceding year.[17] It was not until early 1930 that the basic changes taking place in the labor market began to be understood.

The first definite drop in unemployment appeared in the winter of 1929-30. Details were given in the official periodical of the People's Commissariat for Labor: [18]

> "Sharp declines in unemployment were observed in Moscow and Leningrad where it had been rampant up to the preceding year. In Moscow the total number of unemployed receded from 302,000 on April 1, 1929, to 169,000 on April 1, 1930, a decrease of 44 per cent. The decline was still greater in industry proper where the number of unemployed fell from 51,500 to 20,500, i.e., more than 60 per cent. . . A heavy decline in unemployment also was recorded in Leningrad, where it was most clearly visible in industrial categories: 42.1 per cent among metal workers, 39.0 per cent among textile workers, 36.4 per cent among clothing workers; at a slower pace among unskilled workers, where the decrease was 22.5 per cent, and among non-manual workers, where it was 28.7 per cent."

In seasonal occupations an acute country-wide shortage manifested itself as early as the summer of 1930. In particular, the inadequate manpower supply created bottlenecks in industrial construction and other important construction projects. Data supplied by the People's Commissariat for Labor of the USSR for July 1930, the busiest month of the building season, gave an indication of the stringency. Figures referring to the most important construction projects in different regions are as follows: [19]

Region	Workers Needed	Workers Employed	Shortage
Leningrad	15,795	10,897	31.0%
Moscow	6,208	5,375	13.3
Siberia	47,873	31,094	35.1
Ural	153,453	95,206	37.9

The building industry was not the only one hit by lack of labor. During the summer and fall of 1930, other industries too

---

[17] *Control Figures for the National Economy of the USSR for* 1929/30, Moscow, 1930, p. 486.
[18] M. Romanov, as quoted *supra,* n. 4, pp. 47 f.
[19] Ye. Bronshtein, "The Manpower Problem in the Third Year of the Five-Year-Plan Period," *Planovoye Khozyaistvo,* December, 1930, pp. 209 f.

experienced substantial difficulties: [20]

> "Labor supply in coal mining in July 1930 was only 89.3 per cent of requirements. In the Donets Basin the number of miners in the pits declined considerably (by 12,000) in September, preventing fulfilment of the coal production plan.

> "Labor scarcity was no less acutely felt in waterways and railroad freight handling. 2,000 workers were required in the Mid-Volga region, while only 600 were at hand; in all waterway districts of the RSFSR, 27,500 workers were employed in mid-August, while 15,000 more were needed. In October, only 46,947 freight cars were loaded instead of 63,777 as planned, that is, only 75 per cent. By September 1, railroads were in need of 155,000 freight loaders, but only 68,300 were available.

> "Of 427,800 workers needed for lumber rafting by August 1, only 197,000, i.e., 46 per cent, were available; of the 315,900 needed by September 1, 155,400 were at hand, i.e., 43 per cent."

The scarcity of labor was due to different causes. The rise in employment was not the whole story, for in spots there was even a drop in the number employed. What made the shortage so acute was mainly the collectivization of agriculture, which reduced the manpower supply from the farms (cf. Chapter One). Another reason was the deterioration of living standards in the cities under the First Five-Year Plan (cf. Chapter Four).

The transformation of the labor market led only gradually to the formation of new labor policies. As late as December 5, 1929, in a resolution dealing with the "growth of the ranks of the working class, the size of unemployment and measures to combat it," [21] the CC of the CPSU still insisted on restricting access to the labor market. Employment exchanges still were directed to "reduce the scope of those to be registered as unemployed, so that only real unemployed remain registered who can prove previous employment over a fixed period of time and show a genuine interest in finding work." Local committees of the CP were expressly "forbidden" to order or tolerate any relaxation of the rigid registration requirements.

The CC also rebuked the unions for "inadequate regulation of the increase in union membership," which was said to have

---

[20] *Op. cit.*, p. 210.
[21] *Pravda*, December 9, 1929.

caused "a number of non-industrial unions to become a channel for the invasion of industry by non-union workers, partly even by socially alien and hostile elements." The AUCTUC was instructed to tighten its regulations regarding proof of previous employment as an eligibility requirement for union membership; it also was to "take steps to make it harder for class-hostile urban and rural elements to invade industry by way of the unions."

Shortly afterwards, the tenor of this resolution was made the law of the land. It was incorporated into a decree issued by the CPC of the USSR on February 14, 1930, on "measures for a planned manpower supply of the plants, for the training of the labor cadres, the organization of the labor market, and the battle against unemployment." [22] Government circles were still concerned with holding back migration to the cities.

Yet certain new overtones were discernible in both the resolution of the CC and the decision of CPC. They foreshadowed a policy of "actively" directing the labor market. Actual reversal of policy got under way in the fall of 1930.

Early in September, 1930, the CC of the CPSU published a manifesto addressed to "all Party, economic, trade union, and Communist Youth organizations" and explaining the urgent tasks of the third year under the Five-Year Plan.[23] It stressed in particular that legislation on employment exchanges was no longer in line with "present conditions," that reorganization of the labor supply was "urgent," and that it would have to enable new masses of workers to be "increasingly drawn into production."

Along with the manpower shortage, a new trouble added to the headaches of industry. Workers had started "floating," wandering from one factory to another. This was now to be stopped.

On October 20, 1930, six weeks after the manifesto quoted above, another comprehensive resolution was adopted by the CC of the CPSU, again dealing with the labor shortage and discussing "measures for a planned supply of the national economy with manpower and for combating labor turnover." [24] This resolution ordered: "Employment exchanges shall be reorganized within twenty days with a view to a planned distribution of manpower."

---

[22] *Laws and Ordinances*, 1930:147. Only those sections of the CC's resolution which referred to local Party committees and to trade unions were omitted in the decree. The omission probably was due to purely formal considerations.

[23] *Pravda*, September 3, 1930.

[24] *Pravda*, October 22, 1930.

Steps to counteract "floating" were decreed, and at the same time eligibility requirements for the registration of the unemployed were to be eased.

This was the beginning of a shift from a controlled labor market to a directed labor supply, to the manipulation of manpower, i.e., the planned allocation of the manpower to individual industries and individual plants. No longer market automatism, even not a limited one, but compulsory action on the basis of a "plan"—this though apparently not yet clearly recognized, was the idea in the minds of the authors of the CC resolution, soon to be expressed in a series of legal provisions, administrative orders, and statements by the makers of labor and economic policy.

Main Problem after 1930: Industrial Labor Supply

The shift in labor policy led to the dropping of the very term "employment exchanges." The designation disappeared, and curiously no new one found acceptance. In discussing the new labor policy, the Board of the People's Commissariat for Labor of the USSR favored the replacement of employment exchanges with a "labor force administration."[25] Analogous suggestions emanated from a conference of employment exchange officials, called in November 1930.[26] However, when the new labor policy was finally embodied in a decree of the CEC and CPC of the USSR on December 15, 1930,[27] there was no mention either of employment exchanges or of a labor force administration. The new statute merely referred to "labor organs" (i.e., labor agencies) and "agencies charged with the utilization of manpower."

The vague nomenclature was well suited to the fundamentally empirical, trial-and-error method of working out the future labor policy. But it was also the first sign of decline of the agencies under the Commissariat for Labor as executive organs of this policy. Circumscribing the functions of the labor administration in a decree of December 28, 1930, the People's Commissariat for Labor of the USSR once more fell back on the term "labor force administration." [28] Even so, it did not catch.

---

[25] Izvestiya, November 5, 1930.
[26] Voprosy Truda, October-November, 1930, p. 143.
[27] Izvestiya, December 17, 1930.
[28] Izvestiya Narkomtruda, 1931, No. 1-2

Vague terminology did not prevent the new policy from taking shape. There was no point any more in restricting registration of the unemployed with the employment agencies. Though the restrictions were not canceled at once, they were largely relaxed. Whatever remained in force was not so much designed to regulate the labor market as to police both the employed and the unemployed.

At that very time—as previously pointed out in another context—a singular rural influx made itself felt. Peasants resisting collectivization, as well as the *dekulakized,* appeared in growing numbers on the urban labor market. Government circles feared that the attitudes of these rural migrants might impair the morale of urban labor, already undermined by its visibly deteriorating material conditions. It was this contagion by rural migrants which the continuing restrictions on the registration of job seekers were intended to check. They were openly described as measures to protect the "class character" of urban labor.

The above-mentioned resolution of the CC of the CPSU of October 20, 1930, sounded a warning against the invasion of industry by "socially alien elements." A joint manifesto, issued on the same day by the People's Commissariat for Labor of the USSR, the AUCTUC, and the CC of the Young Communist League,[29] put it more bluntly. It called on the labor agencies, the unions, and the youth organizations to "examine the social complexion of people who are given jobs, and to prevent the infiltration of alien elements into the ranks of labor."

To what extent such considerations dominated the scene in the early 1930's may be seen from one characteristic example. In 1930 the leading Soviet law journal carried an *ex post facto* indictment of the labor administration for having failed to enforce the "class point of view" in the legislation of the 1920's. The following charges were preferred: [30]

"The regulations issued by the People's Commissariat for Labor on March 28, 1927,[31] establishing the guiding principles for the registration of the unemployed, failed to introduce clear-

---

[29] *Izvestiya,* October 22, 1930.
[30] Z. Grishin, "On Deficiencies and Opportunistic Deviations in Labor Legislation," *Sovetskoye Gosudarstvo i Revolyutsiya Prava,* November-December, 1930, p. 169.
[31] Cf. above in the present chapter, esp. to n. 12.

cut class requirements. Under prevailing conditions the eligibility requirements provided for in the regulations, such as union membership, particularly with respect to non-industrial unions, and the required proof of previous employment, did not provide industrial production and employment exchanges with sufficient guarantees against the infiltration of class-alien elements. The decisions of the conference of labor agency officials, which the People's Commissariat for Labor convened late in 1928, also completely overlooked the issue of selecting manpower according to class principles. In the same manner, numerous directives issued by the People's Commissariat for Labor with respect to the seasonal labor market were not imbued with the necessary political sensitivity. . ."

These efforts to preserve "class purity" characterize the political climate in which the new labor policy crystallized in the 1930's especially at the beginning of the decade. But they do not tell us enough about the form and contents of the policy, manifested in some significant novel features.

To begin with, hiring through governmental employment agencies was again made mandatory on December 15, 1930,[32] but for another purpose than in the 1920's. Then, the compulsion had primarily served to halt the influx of new labor. Now that labor was scarce, it was to aid above all in the better utilization and distribution of available manpower. The agencies in charge of manpower control had to be in a position to see that plants did not employ or hire unnecessary workers, and compulsory hiring through government agencies was but one of many means to that end.

Its revival was short-lived, however. Putting special agencies in charge of manpower supply conflicted with a newly prevailing tendency to leave hiring like other tasks of labor policy to the "economic organs": the agencies of the economic administration and their subordinates, the managers of the plants.

In the field of labor supply, this tendency found its earliest expression in a decree of September 13, 1931.[33] Plant management was empowered to hire men "directly, without recourse to agencies of the labor administration." Under this plain lan-

---

[32] Cf. n. 27 above.
[33] Decision of the CEC and the CPC of the USSR, *Laws and Ordinances,* 1931:385.

guage there could be no revival of compulsory hiring through labor exchanges by the collective bargaining route, either.

The shift in labor policy brought several more complex problems to the fore. How to secure an adequate labor supply, how to improve utilization of the available manpower—all this called for new solutions.

The End of Unemployment Insurance and of the Labor Market

The first solution was purely disciplinary. Maximum utilization of manpower reserves conflicted with the jobless worker's right to reject employment offered to him. Previous, highly complicated provisions, while not exactly favoring the unemployed, were by and large tolerable. Now, under the decree of February 14, 1930, the labor exchanges were empowered to deal severely with the jobless worker who refused an offer of a job or of vocational retraining.[34]

A whole series of subsequent measures narrowed the freedom of the unemployed to accept or reject work. They need not be discussed in detail as they were soon suspended by a decree of October 9, 1930,[35] whose very title aimed at the "immediate employment of the unemployed" and the "suspension of unemployment benefit payments."

It was an epochal step. Benefit payments to the unemployed were stopped—by wire! The labor exchanges were enjoined to "take all steps necessary to put the unemployed to work at once." Some clauses merit special attention: "The unemployed are to be given jobs not only within their vocational qualifications but also other work requiring no special skills." And: "With the sole exception of sickness attested by a medical certificate, no reasons for refusing work shall be accepted." Finally: "Applicants refusing work will be stricken from the rolls of the labor exchanges"—i.e., in many cases deprived of any chance of work.

This was the end of unemployment insurance in the Soviet Union.

To justify the move, the press announced that there was no

---

[34] For details regarding previous legislation, see Voitinsky, as quoted *supra*, n. 14, pp. 41 f.; the provisions of February 14, 1930, were discussed above, cf. n. 22.
[35] Issued by the People's Commissariat for Labor of the USSR, cf. *Izvestiya*, October 11, 1930.

more unemployment. But if there was none, why the ban on benefit payments—by wire? Without unemployment, presumably, such payments would have stopped by themselves. In fact, there were many hundreds of thousands of unemployed listed with the labor exchanges when relief was canceled. The suspension of unemployment benefits was a means of pressure to force the unemployed worker to accept any job offered, even if it was outside his trade, beneath his skill, and far from his place of residence.

Officially there has been no unemployment since. The absence of unemployment in the Soviet Union has become so unimpeachable a tenet that even the employment service idea gave way. The employment agencies began to wither about 1931. Some of their functions were taken over by the economic administration and by plant management. But the employment service organization was not subordinated to the "economic organs." It simply withered away.

In 1933, when the People's Commissariat for Labor of the USSR was dissolved and an important part of its jurisdiction was handed over to the trade unions, there was neither a word about transferring its power and duties in the field of manpower distribution, nor any mention of the labor exchanges—as if all this had simply been forgotten.

Thus the market automatism of labor supply and demand vanished without being replaced by an overall organization for the planned allocation of manpower. Strange as is may seem, methodical control and allocation of labor was put into practice neither methodically nor consistently but piecemeal, by trial and error. Two special labor supply organizations were established—one to recruit manpower on the farms, the other, created much later, to give vocational training to juveniles and supervise their employment afterward—but general machinery for the regulation of the labor market ceased to exist in 1933. After the war—in 1946—the two mentioned special employment organizations were joined under a single command in the newly created Ministry of State Labor Reserves. To date, however, this ministry has also remained without general jurisdiction over manpower policy.

As there was no general organization, the idea of one inevitably kept cropping up—always empirically, dictated by everyday requirements. In the mid-Thirties it even looked for a while as if the idea of labor exchanges were regaining ground: in the spring of 1935, 105 " information bureaus" were opened in Moscow providing job seekers with "information on vacancies in plants and government departments." [36] Plant and department heads in turn would "advise the Board of the Moscow Central Information Bureau of manpower requirements." For the time being there was no thought of making recourse to the information bureaus compulsory.

The activity of these agencies was initially modest in scope. The press paid hardly any attention to them. Still, it was announced on occasion that in their first three months of operation (April through June, 1935) the Moscow information bureaus had referred 39,739 job seekers to positions, and that 31,655 of these had actually been hired.[37]

There were attempts to broach the problem on a general scale. In June, 1935, the official organ of Soviet Industry published an article cautiously headed "Job Information," written with great caution and dressed up as a local report from Kharkov.[38] Obviously intended as a trial balloon, it told of "a new phenomenon in Kharkov." More and more people were knocking at the doors of union offices in search of work. "Productivity of labor is increasing, and many a plant is forced to discharge surplus personnel. The Kharkov Tractor Works released some 1,500 persons in the course of the past year. The Kharkov Electro-Mechanical Works also reduced the number of its workers."

It was not too hard to find work for skilled workers, the correspondent went on, but the unskilled and semi-skilled remained "unoccupied" (the term "unemployed" was carefully avoided) and had to turn to their unions. Would not organized "job information" be helpful? "Right now, in Kharkov, people wonder whether some kind of information center should not be set up to give information on the local labor demand." But that would be only a makeshift. "A sensible job information service must be set up beyond the confines of Kharkov. The demand for manual and white-collar workers and specialists must be organized in every major industrial center—not only for the particular city itself but for other districts . . ."

Similar views and organizational beginnings appeared else-

---

[36] *Pravda,* April 1, 1935.
[37] *Pravda,* July 20, 1935.
[38] *Za Industrializatsiyu,* June 10, 1935.

where at that time, always rather timidly. But the concept that a revival of employment agencies was incompatible with the new manpower utilization policy evidently prevailed. After 1935, "information bureaus" or "job information" were no longer heard of. The concept of the labor market had finally been laid to rest.

Manpower Recruitment on the Farms

The central problem of Russian labor policy until close to the end of the Second Five-Year Plan was to assure a steady flow of workers from the countryside. The need for planning and direction of this flow was already recognized in NEP days. At that time, of course, the question was not so much how to promote the influx as how to channel, how to dam, and how—if need be—to stop it. The problem changed fundamentally about 1930, when labor became scarce. Now the Soviet Government was chiefly concerned with the influx of rural labor.

A sufficient supply of labor for industrial production depended largely on the attitude the *kolkhozes* displayed towards the exodus of their members. Consequently, in the following years, the cardinal problems of government intervention concerned the relations between *kolkhozes* and *kolkhoz* members, on the one hand, and plant and economic authorities interested in an adequate manpower supply on the other hand.

Rules were laid down by the interested government departments—the People's Commissariats for Labor and for Agriculture and the Supreme Economic Council—in a circular letter of March 3, 1930, concerning "measures to channel manpower from the *kolkhozes* into the seasonal branches of the national econmy." [39] Collective farms were obliged to release men to industry in numbers to be jointly fixed in each instance by governmental planning agencies, and with the selection of the individuals who were to report for industrial work left to the *kolkhoz* managing boards. "Failure to carry out orders issued by the *kolkhoz* managing boards," the circular letter continued, "shall be regarded as noncompliance with *kolkhoz* decisions and as a violation of work rules."

It was not as easy as that, though. Not only did *kolkhoz* mem-

---

[39] *Za Industrializatsiyu*, March 4, 1930.

bers refuse to be summarily ordered into factories; the managing boards themselves resisted an automatic transfer of their labor to industry. After all, it was to their own direct interest to keep their members on the farms, or, if they approved of the transfer, to try to profit by it—which, in turn, as a rule, happened at the expense of the migrants themselves, provoking further resistance.

Frequently, managing boards of collective farms refused to provide migrating members with identification papers[40] as a means of preventing their departure—without such papers, the migrants could not get jobs. In other cases they were required to give up part of the wages they would earn in the factories: "The *kolkhozes* prevent their members from leaving for seasonal employment by insisting that they turn over 35 to 50 per cent of their wages to the *kolkhoz*." [41] Or: "*Kolkhozes* sometimes show an enormous appetite. In the Mozyr' district, migratory *kolkhoz* members were forced to yield 40 to 50 per cent of their wages to the *kolkhoz*, in some instances as much as 75 per cent." [42]

There were dramatic incidents: "Recruiting agents for 'Ugol' ['Coal' Trust] have terrible trouble recruiting a few dozen workers . . . In the Volkhovatsk district an agent had to flee after local authorities threatened to jail him unless he 'stopped bothering.'" [43] "The chairmen of the village Soviets in Khvorostyansk and Samarino bluntly told the agents to get out or be thrown out." [44] During the early 1930's the press was full of similar complaints.

A decree issued in March 1930 expressly prohibited "any kind of interference with the departure of peasants, particularly peasants on collective farms." [45] Violations were made punishable. This did not help much. More than two years later the monthly publication of the People's Commissariat for Labor of the USSR reported: [46]

"We observe various forms of resistance to organized recruitment of workers from the country. To cite some characteristic facts:

[40] *Za Industrializatsiyu,* June 8, 9 and 12, 1931.
[41] *Trud,* March 24, 1930.
[42] *Pravda,* April 6, 1930.
[43] *Za Industrializatsiyu,* June 8, 1931.
[44] *Za Industrializatsiyu,* June 9, 1931.
[45] Issued by th CPC of the USSR, March 16, 1930, in *Izvestiya,* March 17, 1930.
[46] L. Ginzburg, "Weak Points of Organized Manpower Recruitment," *Voprosy Truda,* July, 1932, p. 16.

"The managing board of the Dem'yan Bednyi *kolkhoz* (Tula district) informed members employed on construction at the Shterovka Electro-Works that unless they returned immediately to the *kolkhoz* they would be fined 10 rubles for every day of absence.

"*Kolkhoz* managing boards in the villages of Dyakovo, Kuchki, and Teremovo, Konstantinovka district, decided to demand 80 per cent of the earnings of their members employed in industry. As a result, many *kolkhoz* members have quit their jobs and returned to the collective farms.

"There have been instances of *kolkhoz* peasants being fined and their belongings attached or even confiscated (Rakitino and Arkhityansk districts, Central Black-Soil Province); of *kolkhozes* permitting their members to leave only on condition that they took their families along (Buzuluk district, Mid-Volga Province). There was even a case of *kolkhoz* members who had been going to work in Moscow for six years and more and were now directed in writing to 'stop moving off and go to work in the *kolkhoz*.' In case of non-compliance the managing board threatened to expel not only the 'refractory' migrants from the collective farm but their families as well (Vyshneye village, Ugarovo district, Moscow province).

"One *kolkhoz* in the Sudzha district expelled a whole group of peasants for taking jobs in the Kharkov Tractor Works.

"In the Krasnoyarsk district there were cases of migrants being disfranchised."

The resistance put up, tacitly or vocally, by the *kolkhozes* greatly hampered the recruitment of labor among collectivized farmers. In order to break it, legal means were sought to permit the *kolkhozes* to derive certain benefits from the industrial employment of their members.

First, in the spring of 1930, they were permitted to claim ten per cent of their members' earnings on industrial jobs. A year later, a different means was evolved: in March 1931, recruitment of workers on collective farms was removed from the jurisdiction of the labor authorities, on the ground that it was to be "integrated with the work of the economic organs." In other words, agencies of the economic administration and plant managers would henceforth negotiate directly with the *kolkhozes* about the release of *kolkhoz* peasants. That the *kolkhozes* would be able to get something in return out of the "economic organs" was tacitly understood. The labor authorities kept only the job of "assigning recruitment districts to the economic organs, supervising recruitment operations, and, if necessary, assisting the economic agencies in the recruitment of manpower." [47]

The details of the new recruitment setup were laid down in a decree of June 30, 1931.[48] Agreements between industrial management and *kolkhoz* boards were to be reciprocal, not just in form but in essence. In particular, industry was obliged in any future recruitment deals to provide the collective farms with "special means of raising production, corresponding to the number of *kolkhoz* members released."

Kolkhozes supplying labor for industrial use were promised different kinds of compensation to help them increase their production. Aside from industry, as the direct beneficiary, other government agencies also had to support the "release" of rural labor. Agricultural and other authorities were instructed to give preference in the allocation of farm equipment, in school construction, social services, etc., to *kolkhozes* willing to release workers in bulk. The collective farms, on the other hand, were forbidden to share in the industrial earnings of their members. Families of the migratory *kolkhoz* members were guaranteed a grain supply from *kolkhoz* stocks (at the official, artificially low price) and assured of work assignments on the collective farm with the resulting claims to share in *kolkhoz* returns.

The rights of individual *kolkhoz* members were somewhat further protected when it was decreed in August 1931 [49] that the agreement between the recruiting agency and the "releasing" *kolkhoz* had to be supplemented by labor contracts to be agreed upon with every peasant hired for industrial work. The signing of a contract with the collective farm was now merely the starting point of a recruiting campaign among the members. It was only if this campaign failed to bring enough volunteers that the management of the *kolkhoz* was to use coercion to supply the needed manpower.

To be sure, as adopted in 1931, this entire system of recruit-

[47] Z. Mokhov, "From Laissez-Faire to Organized Manpower Recruitment," *Voprosy Truda*, August-September, 1932, p. 51.
[48] Decree of the CEC and the CPC of the USSR "on *otkhod*," June 30, 1931, *Izvestiya*, July 1, 1931.
[49] *Izvestiya*, September 10, 1931.

ing future industrial workers from the collectivized peasantry rested upon scarcely disguised compulsion. The *kolkhozes* were compelled to provide a fixed number of workers. The *kolkhoz* peasants in turn were compelled to hire out for industrial labor. But this coercion did not yet amount to a fullfledged system of compulsory labor, although the *kolkhozes'* bargaining freedom was severely limited. Their manpower deals with industry were free transactions only to the extent that they could negotiate about what the economic agencies would give them in return. The recruitment quotas imposed on them had to be met in any case.

Individual *kolkhoz* members had somewhat more freedom of movement, on paper as well as in fact. As the number of workers to be recruited by industry was invariably limited in comparison with total *kolkhoz* membership, the quotas could often be met without resorting to compulsion—provided the recruits received protection of their interests toward their own *kolkhoz*.

The leading circles of industry did not want *kolkhoz* members to retain even this freedom of movement. They called for intensified pressure in recruiting, but at first they did not succeed. Their coercive notions were authoritatively rejected as "leftist deviationism," as expressed by *Bol'shevik*, the official semi-monthly of the CC of the CPSU:[50]

> "The desire of some industrial executives for 'delivery' of manpower from the kolhozes is wrong on principle. On issues of agricultural migration, a 'leftist deviationism' is as possible as the rightist opportunistic reliance on spontaneity . . . Trying to create a system of perfectly planned manpower distribution in town and country by the automatic ejection of surplus labor from the *kolkhozes*, in accord with migration quotas set from above, would be to anticipate developments. . . The task of the *kolkhozes* in the field of migration is to distribute and use their own manpower so as to release workers for migration; to enlighten their members about the political importance and the practical benefits of transferring to industrial work; finally to give the recruiting agents all possible assistance in the recruitment of individual workers."

---

[50] V. Revzina, "New Organization of *Otkhod*," Bol'shevik, 1931, No. 13, pp. 34 f.

This complicated combination of friendly advice, promises of "practical benefits," and veiled threats of punishment met with numerous obstacles. In spite of the legislation of 1931, *kolkhoz* boards went on claiming a share in their members' industrial earnings, and they continued to exert pressure to keep them on the farms. It took time to change this attitude; complaints about it were heard until the mid-Thirties.

Still more persistent were complaints about recruiting practice. Local authorities, both political and agricultural, were accused of pressuring *kolkhoz* members to take industrial jobs. Recruiting agents were charged with making all sorts of promises that were not kept later. Industrial managers finally were blamed for efforts to hold the migrant workers in the plants by every possible unlawful means and to prevent their return to the villages.

To push recruitment, industrial management generally did not resort to outright coercion as much as to misleading and fraudulent promises. "Some particularly characteristic cases" were cited by the daily newspaper of the industrial administration in the spring of 1931: [51]

"The industrial combine in Lipetsk recruits 5,000 workers. A week later they are back, angry and exhausted. It turns out that crowds of people came and found housing facilities provided for only 300.

"Recruiting is going on for a construction project of the Siberian Farm Combine Works. The conditions offered are acceptible. The men go to Novosibirsk to 'look around'; if they like it, they will 'send for the others.' They arrive, and lo and behold: no canteen, no housing, no bath—nothing but a tent with a Central Workers Cooperative store. Naturally, no one 'sent for the others,' and anyone who had any money left pulled out to look for something better.

"Sandhogs wanted for the Dnieper power dam—Dnieprostroi! Resolutions of the district labor office, six-foot posters, stirring appeals. All set! With song and flying streamers the men ride to Dnieprostroi. On arrival they learn that excavations are 'nearly completed' and sandhogs are 'not needed.' Needless to say, the return trip was not so festive, with men riding on foot·

---

[51] *Za Industrializatsiyu,* April 15, 1931.

boards, running boards, or on the roof, frantically clinging to the exhaust pipe. . .

"Almost everywhere you find cases of management failing to employ seasonal workers on jobs corresponding to their skills. Bricklayers report for work, but as the bricks have not been delivered they are put to nailing boards, making 2.50 or 3 rubles instead of 6 or 7. Even in the Donets Basin, where craft lines are so sharply drawn, someone managed not only to put recruited miners to work on other jobs but to keep them waiting weeks and weeks for assignment."

Some plants recruiting workers in rural areas resorted to means reminiscent of the worst colonial practices. A recruiting agent in the Morshansk district failing to find volunteers, "arranged drinking bouts where *kolkhoz* peasants were plied with liquor until they signed contracts." In the Bogucharovo district, agents secretly passed out shawls among the peasant women to dissuade them "from keeping the men at home." [52]

Such methods were hardly apt to improve morale. Their main effect was to spread unrest in the plants and to increase labor turnover. Workers who had fared badly in one plant tried out another and still another, and quickly turned into "floaters." As the turnover of personnel assumed appalling proportions, creating major bottlenecks under the First Five-Year Plan, the obnoxious recruitment practices came in for sharp criticism in the official economic press. But redress was slow in coming; the same conditions, only slightly improved, were commonplace until the mid-Thirties.

A reportedly typical case was related in the Moscow trade union paper. [53] In its labor contracts, the management of the Verkhne-Isetsk Works in the Urals had undertaken to provide single men with "living space in a house, including bunk, mattress, and all facilities" and married men with "a separate room within a month's time." This obligation turned out to be "not worth the paper it was written on." When the men arrived they wer crowded into a barn, married and single alike, and had to sleep on the floor. "The barn is unlightened except for two or three small kerosene burners without lamp chimneys; the cold

---

[52] *Za Industrializatsiyu,* May 12, 1931.
[53] *Trud,* March 3, 1934.

and filth are terrible. . ." For these accommodations the newly arrived workers were charged as much rent as would have been appropriate for proper quarters.

Under such conditions it was not surprising that the new industrial recruits would try to quit their jobs and look for better work. To curb this "floating," the oddest means were devised. For example, the mine administration of Stalino in the Donets Basin permitted workers to give notice only on a certain day of the month. The men replied by trying to get fired for violations of work discipline. As a result, in the course of twenty-five days, 85 workers gave proper notice to quit and 1,102 had to be discharged for absenteeism. In the Gor'ki Automobile Works, a number of *kolkhoz* peasants who had served out their contracts and wished to return to their farms had to go to court to obtain their discharges.[54]

On August 14, 1933, the Public Prosecutor of the USSR directed his subordinates to act under Sec. 131 of the Criminal Code against *kolkhoz* members who would quit their industrial jobs without being authorized or otherwise "break their contracts with economic agencies." Such cases were to be dealt with in speeded-up proceedings.[55] Sec. 131 of the Soviet Criminal Code concerns "economic crimes" committed by "felonious non-compliance with the provisions of a contract entered into with a public enterprise." It provides for punishment of not less than six months in jail and confiscation of all or part of the delinquent's property. At the time of its enactment Sect. 131 was certainly not intended to make felons out of workers who quit their jobs without authority. Even the Public Prosecutor refrained from applying it to all violations of labor contracts by workers. The penalties of Sec. 131 were reserved exclusively for breach of contract by *kolkhoz* migrants.

The flaws in recruitment practice aroused misgivings even within the economic administration. In fact, recruitment not only failed to assure an adequate labor supply, it also cost huge sums of money. In 1934, industrial establishments in Leningrad province alone spent 19,500,000 rubles on recruitment (mainly on staff salaries)—a cost of from 80 to 120 rubles per worker

---

[54] *Za Industrializatsiyu,* August 2, 1933.
[55] *Sovetskaya Yustitsiya,* 1933, No. 17, p. 21.

hired.[56] In the Kama Electro Works, recruitment expenses per construction worker hired amounted to 150 rubles. But the average construction worker did not stay on the job for more than fifty days.[57] Thus recruitment came as high as three rubles per manday.

High costs were not the only trouble. The actual manpower yield also left much to be desired. As far as is known, complete statistical data on the results of recruitment on collective farms have never been published; the latest available figures refer to 1938 and cover 36 provinces and autonomous republics of the RSFSR.[58] According to these, 2,800,000 workers were to be recruited on collective farms in 1938. In fact, not quite 1,700,000 were recruited, and only 1,500,000 of these were "dispatched" to places of work.[59] How many of those dispatched got there and stayed on the job is not known. We may safely assume that they numbered less than 50 per cent of the Plan figure.

In the second half of the 1930's, rural recruitment gradually lost its importance. On the one hand, the hidden urban manpower reserves were progressively mobilized to meet labor requirements; on the other hand, as mentioned before, migration to the cities changed its complexion. In the framework of collective agriculture the departure of manpower for industry could not be maintained in its old forms. Increasingly, the place of the migrating heads of farm families was taken by young people ready to settle in the city for good. These new migrants were less difficult to win for industrial labor, so no cumbersome recruiting setup was needed.

The decline of organized labor recruiting in the *kolkhozes* was apparent in the economic plan for 1941, the details of which were made public only a short time ago.[60] It shows that in 1941

56 *Za Industrializatsiyu*, May 29, 1935.
57 *Za Industrializatsiyu*, June 15, 1935.
58 At the beginning of 1938, the RSFSR, the largest constituent part of the Soviet Union, was administratively divided into 49 provinces and autonomous republics. The above data cover the most important ones.
59 *Pravda*, April 5, 1939.
60 Until recently, nothing was known of the 1941 plan except for the few data to be gleaned from Voznesensky's report to the Eighteenth CPSU Conference in February 1941. The detailed figures were contained in the statistical "appendix" —a fat volume of nearly 750 printed pages—to the plan which the CPC and CC of the CPSU approved on January 17, 1941. The appendix, like the plan itself, was "not for publication," but during the war the Germans somehow got hold of it,

organized recruiting in the *kolkhozes* was to be carried out in a total of 25 regions and autonomous republics of the Russian Socialist Soviet Republic, and the total number of recruits was to be 628,500—i.e., less than one-fourth the Plan figure for 1938 (see above). Besides, 76,500 were to be recruited in the Ukraine, 34,-800 in Byelo-Russia, 20,000 in the Moldavian republic, and 4,400 in the Kazakh republic—a total of 764,200 in the Soviet Union. The plan also reveals the distribution of the recruits among the several people's commissariat: 114,000 were earmarked for power plants, 67,000 for construction, 60,000 for transportation, 50,000 for coal mining, 39,000 for the oil industry, 38,500 for fishing, 35,000 for non-ferrous metals, 30,000 each for steel and lumber, 28,000 each for the textile and food industries, 10,000 for the paper industry, and so forth.

On the whole, recruitment kept functioning for quite some time under rules laid down in 1931. The number of laws, decrees, executive orders, etc. supplementing these rules in subsequent years was enormous, but no substantial changes were introduced. When the People's Commissariat for Labor of the USSR was disbanded in 1933, most of its functions were transferred to the trade unions, but neither then nor later were the latter entrusted with the supervision of recruitment operations by industrial management.

The organizational scheme in which recruitment has been operating in recent yetars was worked out in 1938.[61] It provided for general supervision by national and local "commissions for the organized recruitment of manpower." On the top level (for the USSR as a whole and its component republics) the commissioners were the Vice-Chairman of the Council of People's Commissars, the People's Commissar for Agriculture, and the Chairman of the State Planning Commission *(Gosplan);* on the provincial and regional level the commissions were made up of officials of the corresponding provincial and regional authorities.

Geographically, recruitment was so organized as to give every People's Commissariat in charge of specific industries a well-de-

---

and after the war it came into American hands but was kept secret until 1950. In 1951, it was published (in Russian) by the American Council of Learned Societies. For the figures quoted in the following text see p. 563.

[61] Decree of the CPC of the USSR, July 21, 1938, *Laws and Ordinances,* 1938: 208.

fined area in which only those industries were allowed to recruit. The People's Commissariats sent to the provinces or parts of provinces assigned to them special administrators, each operating with a small staff of two or three inspectors for every district and entitled to call on the services of all local Soviet and *kolkhoz* agencies.

Recruitment quotas—nation-wide, for the individual republics, and mostly also for smaller administrative units—were fixed annually and had to be approved by the CPC of the USSR.

During the war—with rural manpower becoming scarcer than ever—the organized recruiting of labor in the *kolkhozes* was suspended at an early stage. In March 1946 its resumption was decided upon,[62] and in the same year it was placed under the Ministry of State Labor Reserves. A special Central Administration for the Organized Enlistment of Manpower in the *Kolkhozes* was set up in the framework of the ministry, with its local agencies taking the place of the above-mentioned commissions for the organized recruitment of manpower. For several important industries the Central Administration itself through its local agencies has to recruit manpower in the *Kolkhozes*.[63]

Special provisions apply to recruitment for industries in which seasonal work is of particular importance, such as lumber, rafting, peat, etc. Here we can mention only the special regime instituted for lumber work with its peculiar conditions. Workers hiring out for the lumber season often furnish their own horses; yet the horses do not belong to them but to the *kolkhozes*. The usual procedure until 1937 was to pay the wages of *kolkhoz* members employed in lumbering to the collective farm, which in turn paid the lumbermen under the rules governing the income of members working in the *kolkhoz* itself. That is to say, their seasonal work was credited in "man-days," and remunerated when the entire *kolkhoz* income was divided according to "man-days" worked.[64]

In 1937 this arrangement was suspended. Since then a sea-

---

62 *Proceedings of the Supreme Soviet of the USSR*, March, 1946, p, 396.

63 N. G. Aleksandrov, ed., *Soviet Labor Law*, published by the People's Commissariat for Justice of the USSR, Moscow, 1949, p. 130.

64 For further details on the distribution of *kolkhoz* returns in proportion to "man-days" credited to individual members, cf. Gregory Bienstock, Solomon M. Schwartz and Aaron Yugow, *Management in Russian Industry and Agriculture*, New York, 1944, pp. 164 ff.

sonal worker without a horse is paid his full lumber wages directly, and one furnishing a horse gets half his wages, with the
other half going to the collective farm.[65] Besides being subject
to the work rules of the lumber industry, the seasonal workers
are answerable to the *kolkhoz* for their conduct outside the collective farm and liable to substantial penalties for infraction of
rules. The official textbook on *kolkhoz* law comments: [66]

> "The operation of the law on the departure of *kolkhoz*
> peasants for participation in lumber work has posed the con-
> troversial question of whether the collective farms may punish
> the transferees for violating labor contracts in the lumber in-
> dustry (leaving the job ahead of time, etc.). Inasmuch as agree-
> ments between the *kolkhozes* and the management of the lumber
> industry render the *kolkhozes* responsible for the fulfillment of
> the plan for lumbering operations [!], the management of the
> *kolkhozes* must be granted the authority to act, under Sec. 17 of
> the By-laws of the Agricultural *Artel'*, against *kolkhoz* members
> who neglect their duties under the labor contract and leave their
> jobs before its expiration. The same rule applies to those who
> violate work discipline and obstruct the government plan for
> the supply of lumber."

Sec. 17 of the Model By-laws for Agricultural *Arteli* (the
basic organizational type of collective farms), as enacted in 1935,[67]
empowers the managing board of a collective farm to impose
penalties ranging up to exclusion on *kolkhoz* members for negligence at work, violation of the by-laws, non-compliance with decisions taken by the board or the general meeting, etc. Thus,
according to the official textbook interpretation, if a farmer was
forced to take a seasonal job in the lumber industry and later
quit to go back to the farm, he was liable to be expelled from the
kolkhoz, i.e. to lose his home and livelihood.

"Activation" of Urban Labor Reserves: Female Labor

Along with labor recruitment on the farms, the problem of
the fullest utilization or—to use the official term—"activation" of
urban manpower resources was soon tackled in the Soviet Union.

---

[65] *Kolkhoz Law. Textbook for Law Schools,* issued by the People's Commissariat for Justice, Moscow, 1939, p. 291.
[66] *Op. cit.,* p. 292.
[67] *Laws and Ordinances,* 1935:82.

The main objective[68] was to win for industrial employment women who had not heretofore worked for wages.

Lively public discussions of increasing the proportion of paid jobs held by women had been going on for years prior to the reversal of Soviet labor policy in 1930-31. In those days, of course, the issue was not mobilization of hidden manpower reserves as much as work for women as a means to raise their status. The controlling point of view was women's emancipation rather than labor market policy.

The authors of the First Five-Year Plan, too, looked at women's labor only from the point of view of their economic and social position. As the Plan contemplated a considerable expansion of basic industries which employed only relatively few women, the ratio of women in industry as a whole was bound to decline. To counteract this, the planners recommended " intensified enrollment of women in various occupational divisions." They said: [69]

> "If the proportion of women employed in various occupational divisions remained unchanged, the different pace of developing the several sections of the national economy would result in a decline of the percentage of women among the total of wage earners ... This would be quite unsound; we must make it our task to widen the scope of women's work everywhere."

In particular, it was deemed necessary to raise the number of women in skilled occupation, notably by a general and vocational training program for girls and by expanding welfare institutions which would reduce household work. "Socialization of the living standard" and "socialization of everyday life" were the official slogans on the threshold of the 1930's.

As envisioned in the First Five-Year Plan, vigorous promotion of female labor was not just to maintain the ratio of women wage earners in all economic divisions but to raise it from 27.0 per cent in 1927/28 to 32.5 per cent in 1932/33.[70]

The decree of February 14, 1930, on "measures for a planned manpower supply of the plants" [71] also regarded the desired in-

---

68 Another major project within the scope of the "activation" program was to expand employment of juvenile workers. This will be discussed below.

69 *Five-Year Plan* . . ., as quoted *supra*, n. 16, vol. II, 2, p. 180.

70 *Op. cit.*, pp. 180 f.

71 *Laws and Ordinances*, 1930:147. Cf. above to n. 22.

crease in the number of employed women (and juveniles) from the point of view of "reducing unemployment among juveniles and women."

It was not until September, 1930, that a new attitude began to appear in official documents. The previously quoted manifesto of the CC of the CPSU on the tasks to be accomplished during the third Plan year[72] said that "to insure the fulfillment of the production program for the third year of the five-year period" it was necessary to "draw more juvenile workers as well as wives of workers and other toilers into production."

Intensified utilization of urban manpower reserves was an alluring prospect, the more so as it permitted increases in the labor supply without aggravating the housing and food shortages in the cities—both particularly knotty problems in the early 1930's. By employing more workers' wives, it was also hoped to lessen personnel turnover in the plants. Experience has shown that women are less inclined to change their jobs, and if a married couple works in the same plant the husband is more likely to stay put. Finally, if jobs were held by several members of a family, it might alleviate the drop in living standards, also most acutely felt in those years.

In addition to these considerations, the view was soon expressed that more extensive employment of women could be important from the preparedness angle. One of the leading economic periodicals wrote as early as the spring of 1931: [73]

> "Economic, Soviet, and Party organs will have to consider that even in peacetime the problem of women workers is of the greatest importance to national defense, for the training of manpower takes time and vocational skill is determined not only by an apprenticeship but by practical experience on the job."

On September 6, 1930, following the lead of the Party manifesto of September 3, the CPC of the RSFSR authorized the People's Commissariat for Labor of the RSFSR to take the following steps: [74]

---

[72] Cf. n. 23 above.

[73] S. Gimmelfarb, "Elimination of Unemployment and the Problem of the Labor Force," *Problemy Ekonomiki*, April-May 1931, p. 31.

[74] Decree "concerning regulations for supplying manpower to the national economy and promoting the training of skilled labor," *Izvestiya*, September 8, 1930.

(1) within a month to draw up a list of trades and professions to be reserved predominantly for women;

(2) in accord with other competent government agencies to raise the quota of girls in all vocational schools and training classes;

(3) also in accord with other agencies, to draw up plans for improving such social services as day nurseries, kindergartens, communal kitchens, etc. which notably ease the burdens of working women.

This program of measures to spur the gainful employment of women was carried out during the years that followed. It was quite successful, although the establishment of social services failed to keep pace with the spread of women's employment. To implement the directive just mentioned the People's Commissariat for Labor of the RSFSR issued on January 16, 1931, two catalogues, one of occupations to be reserved exclusively, and the other to be reserved predominantly, for women,[75]—an interesting idea which so far, outside of the Soviet Union, seems to have become law only in Cuba.[76]

The legislation of the USSR accepted the idea in a less decisive form. A decree of the CPC of the USSR of May 19, 1931, contained a list of occupations "in which the use of female labor shall be greatly expanded."[77] This practically superseded the catalogues of occupations "exclusively" or "predominantly" reserved for women which had been worked out for the RSFSR; in time they were tacitly abolished. On the other hand, the official designation of many occupations as suitable for a "great expansion" of female labor actually had a strong practical influence for several years. Planning agencies annually set quotas for the various industries, obliging plant managers to employ a fixed percentage of women.[78] This percentage rose from year to year.

In the mid-Thirties, compulsory regulation of female labor

---

[75] *Izvestiya Narkomtruda,* 1931, No. 5-6.

[76] Legislation enacted in 1917 and in the course of the following years; cf. *The Law and Women's Work,* International Labour Office, Studies and Reports, Series I, No. 4, Geneva, 1939, p. 353.

[77] *Izvestiya Narkomtruda,* 1931, pp. 268 ff.; an additional list was issued on April 10, 1932, *op. cit.,* 1931, pp. 295 f.

[78] See e.g., the decree of the CEC of the RSFSR, issued on December 3, 1931, "on the implementation of Party directives and government decisions relative to the recruitment of women into industry," *Laws and Ordinances of the RSFSR,* 1931:515.

quotas seemed to have lost its importance: the wide spread of female labor became an established fact. The directives of May
19, 1931, were gradually forgotten. After 1936 they were no
longer mentioned in textbooks on labor law or in collections of
laws and statutes compiled for everyday use.

Clauses stipulating "exclusive," "predominant," or "greatly
expanded" employment of women could only take effect if there
were adequate training facilities. The urgency of "systematic improvement of vocational skills and retraining of women" was
stressed as early as July 1929 by the People's Commissariat for
Labor of the USSR and the AUCTUC in a circular letter concerning "more extensive use of women in production."[79] In December, 1929, the People's Commissariat for Labor of the USSR
ordered a minimum quota of places in factory training schools
reserved for girls; the quota was to exceed the proportion of
women actually employed in each particular industry, and to average 35 per cent in industry as a whole.[80]

A year later the CEC of the USSR went a step farther, in a
decree of January 10, 1931, concerning "measures to train skilled
labor for the national economy of the USSR."[81] The minimum
quota for girls in the trade schools for industrial, building and
agricultural enterprises was raised to "about 50 per cent" of the
student body. Detailed regulations were issued by the People's
Commissariat for Labor of the USSR on February 8, 1931.[82]

None of these regulations was fully carried out; there often
were just not enough girls to fill the minimum quota, especially
as the student bodies of these factory institutions rose enormously
in the early 1930's.[83] Still, the quota provisions had a great effect.

---

[79] *Izvestiya Narkomtruda*, 1929, pp. 627 ff.
[80] B. Marsheva, "Female Labor in 1931," *Voprosy Truda*, January, 1931, p. 34.
[81] *Izvestiya*, January 14, 1931.
[82] *Izvestiya Narkomtruda*, 1931, No. 5-6
[83] The number of factory trade schools and the number of students attending
them rose rapidly from the inception of the Five-Year-Plan policy until 1932; then
it declined, slowly at first, later swiftly. Official figures (for the beginning of years)
are as follows:

	Number of Schools	Number of Students
1928	1,814	178,300
1931	3,265	584,700
1932	3,970	975,000
1933	3,900	958,900
1934	1,974	355,800
1935	1,712	246,300

Data are from *Socialist Construction of the USSR. Statistical Year-Book*, Moscow, 1935, p. 616; 1936, p. 578.

The proportion of girls in the factory trade schools rose considerably:[84]

January 1	Female Students
1929	24.9%
1930	31.1
1931	36.6
1932	38.4

1932 was the peak year. Thereafter, factory trade schools in general grew less important, and in time the rules about girl student quotas were forgotten. They were no longer mentioned when vocational training in the plants was reorganized on September 15, 1933. According to the latest available data, 32.2 per cent of the factory trade school graduates were girls in 1937, and 31.1 per cent in 1938.[85] In 1937, girls made up 33.9 per cent of the student bodies.[86]

The measures taken to encourage the industrial employment of women had largely served their purpose by the mid-Thirties; their disappearance could not reverse the trend. Female labor has risen tremendously. Multitudes of women are employed in all economic divisions, especially in industry, and increasing numbers in skilled occupations. Details on the history and the problems of female labor in different industries would exceed the scope of this book.[87] The following is merely a brief summary.

Although envisioning a considerable rise in the proportion of female wage and salary earners, the First Five-Year Plan offered no detailed plan to increase the employment of women. Such a plan was not worked out until the spring of 1930, after the CEC of the USSR had urged it on two occasions.[88] Never published in full, it was revealed in outline by one of its co-authors.[89]

The objectives proposed in this plan went beyond the orig-

[84] G. Serebrennikov, *Female Labor in the USSR,* Moscow, 1934, p. 115.

[85] Computed from data for individual industries as indicated in *Cultural Construction of the USSR. Statistical Year-Book,* 1940, p. 136.

[86] S. Trubnikov, "Sources of Manpower Recruitment in the USSR," *Problemy Ekonomiki,* November-December, 1939, p. 155.

[87] For more details, see Judith Grunfeld, "Women's Work in Russia's Planned Economy," *Social Research,* February, 1942.

[88] Statements of January 30, 1929, and February 16, 1930, reported in *Izvestiya,* February 28, 1930.

[89] Ye. Bronshtein, "Immediate Prospects of Female Labor. Female Labor in the Five-Year Plan Period," *Na Planovom Fronte,* 1950, No. 11, pp. 48-54.

inal goals of the First Five-Year Plan. The latter had contemplated an increase in the proportion of women in all occupational divisions of from 27.0 to 32.5 per cent between 1927/28 and 1932/33; the new plan aimed at a 34 to 35 percentage by 1932/33.[90]

The increase was to be largest in the production of capital goods: the proportion of women employed in these industries was to reach 20.2 per cent by 1932/33, as compared with 10.3 per cent in 1928/29. In consumer goods industries, where female labor previously had been widespread, it was to rise from 51.6 to 58.8 per cent. Over the same period the number of women employed in the building trades was to increase tenfold, from 51,000 to between 500,000 and 550,000. In commerce (hitherto a near-monopoly of men) the number of women was to rise from 105,500 to 321,000; in education, from 390,000 to 942,000; in communications, from 27,000 to 98,000, etc.

The bulk of the new women workers was to be recruited from the ranks of housewives. Accordingly, the proportion of housewives who were not gainfully employed—and thus, according to the prevailing concept, economically "inactive"—had to drop from 57 to 44 per cent of the total employable female population of the cities.

The First Five-Year Plan had contemplated an increase of from 3,060,000 to 5,120,000 in the total of female wage and salary earners.[91] The goal of the special plan was set somewhat higher, providing for 5,600,000 or even more in 1932/33.[92]

In absolute figures, the Plan was not only fulfilled but surpassed. As regards the proportion of women among the total of wage and salary earners, however, achievements fell strikingly short of expectations. As mentioned before, the total employment recorded in 1932 far exceeded all Plan estimates, and by the same year some 6,000,000 women were gainfully employed. Yet the ratio

---

[90] If there had been no special provisions for expanding the employment of women in industry, the percentage of women among wage and salary earners would have dropped from 27.0 to 24.5 per cent, according to Bronshtein (cf. preceding note), as industries employing few women were scheduled to expand much more rapidly than those which usually employed them in large number, mainly consumer goods industries.

[91] Computed from the total number of wage and salary earners given in *Five-Year Plan* . . ., as quoted *supra*, n. 16, Vol. 11, 2, pp. 206 f., and the percentage of female labor as cited in the text.

[92] Computed from the total number of wage and salary earners given in *Control Figures* . . ., as quoted *supra*, n. 17, p. 487, and the percentage of female labor indicated by Bronshtein, as quoted *supra*, n. 89.

of women remained at 27.4 per cent, almost unchanged since 1927/28.[93]

The increase varied greatly in the different occupational divisions. Some figures may illustrate this:[94]

Women Employed (in thousands)

	Plan for 1932/33	Actual Figures for 1932
Industry	...	2,043
Construction	500 to 550	380
Commerce	321	374
Health Services	641	426
Education	942	692

Percentage of Women Employed

	Plan for 1932/33	Actual Figures for 1932
Industry	34.8	32.2
Construction	18.2	12.8
Commerce	36.0	29.3
Health Services	70.0	70.2
Education	60.0	53.6

The most significant gains were made in industry proper, especially in industries where women workers had been virtually unknown. This trend continued under the Second Five-Year Plan (1933-1937) which proposed to increase the number of female wage and salary earners from 6,820,000 by the end of 1932 to 9,850,000 by the end of 1937,[95] or from 29.9 to 33.9 per cent of total employment.[96]

The employment goals set by this Plan for wage and salary earners of both sexes were not achieved, but the average number of women employed in 1937 came close to the Plan figure for the end of the year. The proportion of employed women increased considerably, in excess of Plan estimates. In 1937 there were 9,357,000 women employed in all economic divisions, or 35.4 per cent. Their proportion in industry proper was 39.8 per cent; in

[93] Trubnikov, as quoted *supra*, n. 86, p. 156.
[94] Plan estimates, according to Bronshtein, as quoted *supra*, n. 89, pp. 51 f.; figures for 1932 from Trubnikov, as quoted *supra*, n. 86, p. 156.
[95] Figures previously cited indicate the yearly average; employment figures taken from the Second Five-Year Plan refer to the end of the year.
[96] *Second Five-Year Plan for the Nation Economy of the USSR*, Moscow, 1934, Vol. I, p. 507.

construction, 20.6 per cent; in commerce, 34.0 per cent; in the
health services, 72.4 per cent; in education, 56.6 per cent.[97]

Women were in the overwhelming majority among newly
employed workers. Between 1932 and 1937 total employment increased by 4,047,000, of which 3,350,000, or 82 per cent, comprised women.[98]

Under the Third Five-Year Plan (1938-1942), total employment was to increase by 5,700,000; the number of employed
women was to rise by 3,500,000 to 12,900,000, or 39.3 per cent
of the total.[99] [100]

The following table will summarize the trend under the first
three Five-Year Plans:

	Millions Employed	Millions of Women Employed	Percentage of Women Employed
1927/28	11.3	3.1	27.0
1932	22.9	6.0	27.4
1937	27.0	9.4	34.7
1942 (Plan estimate)	32.7	12.9	39.3

By November 1, 1939, the proportion of women among all
wage and salary earners in industry proper had risen to 41.6 per
cent; among manual workers, to 43.4 per cent.[101] It is interesting
to note the high percentage of women among manual workers
in some industries where female labor was new. The following
figures were given for November 1, 1939:[102]

Industry	Percentage of Women Employed
Coal mining	24.8
Iron ore mining	23.6
Iron and steel	24.9
Metal trades	31.7
Woodworking	43.9
Bakeries	55.5

[97] V. Orlikova, "Soviet Woman in Society's Production," *Problemy Ekonomiki*,
July, 1940, p. 112.

[98] Trubnikov, as quoted *supra,* n. 86, p. 157.

[99] *Ibid.*

[100] In the meantime there was a report in a Party publication for CP organizers and speakers (*Sputnik Agitatora*, 1941, No. 3, p. 22) to the effect that the
number of female wage and salary earners had surpassed 11,000,000 in 1940, two
years prior to the expiration of the planning period, attaining 38.4 per cent of
the total number of wage and salary earners.

[101] Orlikova, as quoted *supra*, n. 97, p. 114.

[102] *Ibid.*

The trend shown in these figures prepared the ground for the near-universal resort to female labor in the war years.

In the very first years of the war, women soon made up a majority of wage and salary earners in general, and of those in industry proper in particular. Voznesensky, in his well-known book on the Soviet economy in wartime, stated that the proportion of women among wage and salary earners as a whole had risen from 38 per cent in 1940 to 53 per cent in 1942, and in industry from 41 to 52 per cent.[103] Female labor was now extensively utilized even in places where it had made small inroads, if any, in the past. For instance, 6 per cent of all steam engine operators were women early in 1941, and 33 per cent late in 1942. Corresponding figures were 6 and 27 per cent for boiler stokers, 12 and 32 per cent for hand-molders, 29 and 39 per cent for machine-molders, 16 and 33 per cent for lathe operators, 17 and 31 per cent for welders, etc.[104] The picture in mechanized agriculture was no different: 4 per cent of the tractor operators on Machine and Tractor Stations (MTS) were women in 1940, 45 per cent in 1942; among combine operators their proportion rose from 6 to 43 per cent, and among MTS drivers from 5 to 36 per cent.[105] The vast increase in the proportion of women between 1940 and 1942 marked all fields of employment.[106]

railroads	from 25 to 36 per cent
communications	" 48 " 67 " "
communal economy	" 42 " 64 " "
trade	" 37 " 55 " "
education	" 58 " 73 " "
health services	" 76 " 83 " "
government administration	" 35 " 55 " "

Voznesensky's figures do not go beyond 1942, but in that year the trend had certainly not reached its peak. Scattered through the daily press we can find many items indicating that the utilization of female labor continued to expand in the later years of the war.

By the spring of 1944 the number of women in steel and iron had reached—incredibly enough—40 per cent of the total number

---

103 Voznesensky (cf. Chapter One, n. 6o), p. 111.
104 *Ibid.*
105 *Op. cit.,* pp. 92-93.
106 *Op. cit.,* p. 111.

employed,[107] as against 24.9 per cent on November 1, 1939.[108] Female labor spread in occupations where no women or almost none had been employed. In December 1943 a dispatch from Baku said:[109] "In the [oil] fields, where there had been but scattered women before the war, women workers now account for 30 to 40 per cent of total personnel employed." In the Urals women in large numbers were employed in charcoal-burning for high-grade metal furnaces, a man's trade from olden times.[110]

The range of female labor in mining was astounding. Yet, in the 1930's numerous women had worked in mines, and notwithstanding statutory prohibition, even on below-surface jobs, to which they were then admitted *post factum* by law in October 1940. But while the general prohibition of female labor underground was abrogated, women still were prevented from working in particularly strenuous jobs, such as coal cutting, digging, shovel work, etc.[111] These restrictions were frequently ignored from the outset, and no one bothered about them any more during the war. In the Chelyabinsk mines (Urals), special women's teams were set up for all coal-digging; they proved so successful that a special mine district was set aside for women in Kopeisk (near Chelyabinsk), and this women's mine earned wide renown for its high rate of output.[112]

After the liberation of the badly devastated Donets coal basin, women assumed a high share of responsibility for reconstruction work. Summing up the results of one year's reconstruction achievements, the secretary of the Stalino Provincial Committee of the Communist Party specifically mentioned the role of women miners in Stalino Coal, one of the three largest Donest coal combines, which prior to the war accounted for half the coal mined in the region. He said:[113] "In the pits of the Stalino Coal Combine women today represent more than one-third of all workers employed." And a few months later, in December, 1944:[114] "In many pits women have become the basic, decisive power. In various

107 *Pravda*, March 8, 1944.
108 V. Orlikova, as quoted *supra*, n. 97, p. 114.
109 *Trud*, December 11, 1943.
110 *Izvestiya*, September 7, 1944.
111 Decree of the CPC of the USSR "on employing the labor of women in the mining industry" of October 25, 1940, *Laws and Ordinances*, 1940:730.
112 *Trud*, December 24, 1944.
113 L. Mel'nikov, "The Renascent Donets Basin," *Pravda*, September 7, 1944.
114 L. Mel'nikov, "Donets Women Coal-diggers," *op. cit.*, December 6, 1944.

coal trusts, such as Kuibyshevugol', Artemugol', Sovetskugol', the proportion of women among the total number of miners is 50 to 60 per cent."

Widespread employment of women miners and their record performance were stressed in reports dealing with the two other Donets combines, Voroshilovgrad Coal[115] and Rostov Coal.[116] Praise was also lavished on women in Krivorosh'ye iron ore mines.[117]

With a view to the expanding employment of women in coal mines, the Central Board of the Donets Basin Union of Coal Industry Workers suggested that mine management establish special (presumably reduced) job quotas for women.[118] I was unable to find any references in the press as to whether the suggestion was followed up.

On the postwar trend of female labor the Soviet press maintains a silence unusual even under Soviet conditions. Even on March 8—"Women's Day"—when the Soviet papers print articles praising the social rise of women in the USSR and reporting on women-engineers, physicians, teachers, kolkhoz chairmen, deputies of Soviets, etc.—no comprehensive data on women wage and salary earners are published. Only once—on March 8, 1948—Pravda mentioned in passing that in 1947 the proportion of women in the total number of wage and salary earners in all branches of economy and administration amounted to 47 per cent. No corresponding figures for the following years were ever published, either for the entire economy, or for the industry. It is true that, on March 8, 1951, Pravda reported that in the industry of the Kazah SSR 41 per cent of all workers and employees were women, and in the industry of the Tadzhik SSR as much as 47 per cent. For republics with a strong Moslem tradition these figures appear almost incredibly high.

The exact scope of female labor in the USSR cannot be determined. There can be no doubt, however, that it remains very large, and though the percentage is lower now than at the peak of the war-time trend, it surely remains considerably above that of 1940.

---

[115] Trud, November 22, 1944.
[116] Trud, September 7, 1944.
[117] Izvestiya, October 7, 1944.
[118] Trud, December 26, 1944.

"Activation" of Juvenile Labor Reserves

Besides expanding the use of female labor, "activation" of the urban manpower reserves implied an increased utilization of juvenile labor. The difficulties of recruiting urban youth for productive labor were due not so much to problems of labor market policy as to vocational training problems which are outside the scope of this book. Here the question of juvenile labor can be considered only in its connection with the steps that were taken to facilitate the absorption of youth in the labor process. In large measure, the point was to put adolescents to work—whether by means of training or in other ways—and to keep them at work.

In the 1920's it had been rather difficult to find jobs for youngsters. Widespread unemployment and strict child labor laws made industrial managers reluctant to employ them. As a result there were no jobs to be had, and as no special schools had yet been set up, teenagers often had little chance to get vocational training. Thus the jobless youngsters were at a twofold disadvantage: their chance of getting work was slight, and if they remained out of work they were barred from vocational training and consequently from entry into skilled trades.

To remove this disadvantage, a minimum quota of workers under eighteen was prescribed for all industries in 1922. Termed "armor" (in Russian *"bronya"*), this minimum quota ranged from 5 to 6 per cent of the total number of employed. In the late 1920's, additional "super-armor" quotas were set for individual industries or single plants, to be agreed upon between the economic administration and plant management on the one hand, and the trade unions and labor authorities on the other, with part of the extra payroll expenses defrayed by the social insurance system (from funds earmarked for unemployment insurance).

The transformation of the labor market in the early 1930's made such special devices to assure employment of a minimum number of juveniles unnecessary. They were abrogated in somewhat unusual fashion. On April 20, 1932, the People's Commissariat for Labor of the USSR released a long list of its own decrees and orders issued between 1923 and 1931, which, it said, had been "invalidated although not formally repealed."[119] Among those listed were eleven concerning the "armor."

---

[119] *Izvestiya Narkomtruda*, 1932, pp. 273-285.

Nor did youth need special protection from the threat of unemployment now that labor was no longer in over-supply. The problem now was how to induce sufficient numbers of young people to learn a trade and work for wages. Up to the late 1930's, they were largely trusted to take the desired trade by themselves, spurred by the propaganda of trade unions and the Young Communist League. No real coercion was applied, although the Supreme Economic Council by decree of November 27, 1929,[120] obliged all graduates of factory trade schools to go to work for three years after graduation, under orders of the economic agencies which had paid for their training.

Similar provisions were made when vocational training was reorganized in September, 1933, but management and economic agencies had no means to enforce or supervise compliance. In practice, the idea that juveniles should "work out" the costs of their training was generally ineffective.

Compulsory vocational training and a kind of compulsory labor system for the trainees are of much more recent date. On October 2, 1940, a decree of the Presidium of the Supreme Soviet of the USSR[121] ordered "mobilization" (sic!) of teenagers for vocational training to meet the manpower requirements of industry and transportation. And "mobilization," in this case, was no metaphor but a precise, technical description of the process.

Between 800,000 and 1,000,000 boys were to be drafted annually from cities and collective farms. Fourteen- and fifteen-year olds were to attend vocational schools and complete two-year training courses for skilled jobs; sixteen- and seventeen-year olds were to prepare in six-month courses for jobs classified as "mass trades." On completion of their training, both age groups had to work in government-owned enterprises for four years, under orders and supervision of the Central Administration for State Labor Reserves[122] whose establishment was announced on the same day as the "mobilization."

In practice, this was compulsory labor for youth, similar to compulsory military service—a similarity underscored by the fact

---

[120] *Izvestiya Narkomtruda,* 1929, p. 787.
[121] *Izvestiya,* October 3, 1940.
[122] Since October, 1940, the term "State Labor Reserve" has been used for the student bodies of the vocational training schools set up on the basis of the decree of October 2, 1940, and for graduates of these schools for the four years they remain under the control of the Central Administration.

that the "mobilization" applied to boys only. The quotas set were to be filled primarily by volunteers; only if there were not enough of these were compulsory inductions to make up the difference. Incidentally, when the Soviet Union entered the war, compulsory training was extended to girls as well.

But this compulsory labor still fell short of general labor service for youths,—first of all, because the draft quotas for training were always set far below the total number of juveniles in the corresponding age groups. Another important provision restricted universal application of the labor service while giving it a strangely distinctive social—or, perhaps better, anti-social—cast. Students of secondary schools and institutions of higher learning were exempted from compulsory training and subsequent compulsory four-year employment; and on the same day when the "mobilization" was ordered, a decree of the CPC of the USSR[123] reintroduced tuition fees in public schools above the seventh grade (practically abolishing free secondary education) and in all higher institutions of learning. Thus, in a way, higher education became the privilege of children of higher-income families. And with secondary school and college students exempt from compulsory vocational training and the subsequent four years of labor service, the "mobilization" was practically confined to children of families in the lower income brackets.[124]

In wartime, conscription for training was applied on a large scale, but the results were below the original estimates. According to peacetime plans, some 800,000 to 1,000,000 boys were to graduate annually from "manpower-reserve" schools. Actually, from 1941 through 1945, a total of 2,460,000 boys and girls completed training school courses, a yearly average of somewhat less than 500,000.[125] Incomplete data, which account for 1,840,000 juvenile

---

123 *Izvestiya,* October 3, 1940.

124 Cf. my article, "Heads of Russian Factories, A Sociological Study," *Social Research,* New York, September, 1942. My analysis was sharply attacked by A A. Yugov who took the view that the purpose of abolishing free higher education was to achieve a better selection of the students. Cf. A. A. Yugov, "On Ruling Groups in the USSR," *Novyi Put,* New York, December 1942, and February, 1943, and my replies, "On Social Processes in the Soviet Union," *Sotsialisticheskii Vestnik,* New York, January and April, 1943.

125 Piotr G. Moskatov, chief, Central Administration for Labor Reserves, speaking in the Supreme Soviet during deliberations of the Fourth Five-Year Plan, cf. *Izvestiya,* March 23, 1946.

workers, show the following distribution, by industries, of graduates of both sexes: [126]

Industry	Number of Juveniles (in thousands)
Metallurgy (ferrous and other)	250
Machine building	150
Armament industry	600
Coal mining	180
Oil (extraction and refining)	70
Electric Power	80
Building materials, industrial construction	200
Transportation (rail, water)	310

Only fragmentary data are available for other industries. The chemical industry was supplied with some 40,000 juvenile workers, the industry attached to the People's Commassariat for Communications with 30,000.[127] Apparently no reinforcements whatever, or hardly any, were assigned to textiles and food processing.

Graduates of training schools or courses were employed in large blocs. The chief of the Central Administration for Labor Reserves thus summed up the experience of five years of youth conscription:[128]

"The government preferred to allocate state manpower reserves in larger detachments, sometimes numbering hundreds or thousands of people. The Stalin Metallurgical Combine in Magnitogorsk and the Magnitostroi Trust were assigned 27,000 young workers. When the Donets Basin was liberated by the Red Army, student detachments comprising 20,000 people went there. In many plants, especially those evacuated or newly built during the war, graduates of training schools and courses number 30, 50, or even 70 per cent of the number employed."

The setup of training schools underwent some changes dur-

126 Piotr G. Moskatov, "State Labor Reserves," *Pravda,* October 1, 1945.
127 G. Zelenko [deputy chief, Central Administration for Labor Reserves], "State Labor Reserves in Five Years," *Izvestiya,* October 2, 1945.
128 See n. 126 above.

ing the war years. At first, two types of schools had been provided for, six-month courses with a limited curriculum for 16- and 17-year olds, and two-year courses with an enlarged program for 14- and 15-year olds. During the war special schools with a four-year course were created "for children of Red Army warriors and guerrillas, and for orphans whose parents gave their lives for the Motherland." In 1945 these special schools were attended by a total of 12,000 boys and girls. In addition, special institutions were established for the study of agricultural mechanization, one-year navigation courses and three-year schools for the commercial arts.[129]

The enlarged scope of training activities led to an administrative reorganization. The Central Administration of Labor Reserves was left only the direction of vocational training, while youth conscription for training, and the supervision and allocation of training school graduates were entrusted to a new CPC Committee for the Registration and Allocation of Manpower.[130] The division of functions was retained until after the war; in May, 1946, the two organizations were reorganized and merged in the Ministry for Labor Reserves.[131]

By the end of 1940, some 1,550 six-month and two-year schools had been put into operation. Many of them were destroyed during the war or evacuated to the eastern provinces. In the east new training schools were set up on a large scale, and from 1943 on, great efforts were made to rebuild such schools in liberated regions. In 1945, the total number of "labor-reserve" schools was 2,570, far above the 1940 figure.[132] In five years a total of approximately 12,000,000,000 rubles was spent on the training and allocation of manpower reserves.[133]

Far-flung activities for building up new reserves of juvenile workers began in 1945. Autumn conscription in 1945 had been envisaged on a relatively modest scale—155,000 students to enroll in two-year schools (and in assimilated one-, three and four-year schools) and 300,000 in six-month courses. Age regulations now were modified, six-month courses being opened to boys of 16 and

129 *Ibid.*
130 Interview with Piotr G. Moskatov, *Trud,* September 1, 1945.
131 *Pravda,* May 16, 1946.
132 See n. 126 above.
133 Vasily P. Pronin [Minister for Labor Reserves], "The Impending Draft of Youths for Labor Reserve Schools and Classes," *Pravda,* July 5, 1946.

17, and to girls of 16, 17 and 18, while schools with complete courses were to admit boys of 14 and 15, and girls of 15 and 16.

Special rules were issued for schools which were to train personnel for coal and ore mining, metallurgy and building trades. In peacetime only boys were to be admitted: 17-year olds to be trained in six-month courses, and 15- and 16-year olds in two-year schools. The original provision exempting students at institutions of higher learning from the draft was reenacted; exemptions might be canceled in emergencies, but not for students in the three higher grades of secondary schools.[134]

Efforts to widen the scope of vocational training continued in 1946. A special five-year plan for manpower reserves was worked out in connection with the Fourth-Year Plan (1946-1950). Vocational training schools were to become "the main source of reinforcements for the labor force in skilled and mass occupations," according to the chairman of the State Planning Commission.[135] It was contemplated that 4,500,000 young workers should graduate from training schools during the Five-Year-Plan period, including 1,200,000 graduates in 1950.[136] A detailed five-year program for labor reserves was still unfinished when the law on the Fourth Five-Year Plan, which set the goal, was passed by the Supreme Soviet of the USSR. Later the Minister for Labor Reserves, while still envisioning a total of 4,500,000 graduates in five years, insisted that 1,200,000 graduations a year must be achieved more quickly, "within two or three years." The estimated five-year expenditure for the training of manpower reserves was 27,000,000,000 rubles.[137]

As for the distribution of schools by industries, the program mapped out for 1946—1950 was to follow the pattern set in preceding years. Specific figures on the number of new workers to be supplied by the training schools were disclosed for only a few industries, during Supreme Soviet debates in March 1946. In five years, 660,000 training graduates were to go into coal-mining, assuring 80 per cent of the industry's recruitment; 570,000 graduates or 75 per cent of requirements were promised to iron and steel,

---

134 See n. 130 above.

135 Nikolai Voznesensky, presenting the draft of the Fourth Five-Year Plan to the Supreme Soviet of the USSR, cf. *Izvestiya*, March 16, 1946.

136 *Law on the Five-Year Plan for Restoring and Developing the National Economy of the USSR in 1946-1950*, OGIZ publications, Moscow, 1946, p. 51.

137 See n. 133 above.

and some 70 per cent to machine-building.[138] In July these preliminary estimates were revised and new data offered by the Minister for Labor Reserves:[139]

Industry	Estimated Number of Graduates, 1946-1950 (in thousands)
Metallurgy	150
Metal trades	1,860
Coal and ore mining	545
Railroad transportation	500
Construction	1,285

These figures, which entailed a substantial cut of manpower
supply to metallurgical plants, apparently were final five-year estimates.

Little was made public on the execution of this plan. The
annual economic-statistical summaries of the Central Statistical
Administration gave the following figures for juveniles graduat-
ing from the state labor reserve schools: [140]

1946	382,000
1947	790,000
1948	1,000,000
1949	723,000
1950	494,000

Altogether, the vocational schools for state labor reserves were
able to deliver 3,389,000 trained juveniles to the economy—i.e.,
75.3 per cent of the Plan figure. All that is known about the actual
distribution of the trainees is that in 1948 the coal-mining industry got eleven times as many young workers from the state labor
reserve schools as in 1946, the construction industry four times
as many, and the iron and steel industry 1.6 times as many.[141] It
is worth noting, too, that in the country juveniles were enlisted

---

138 See n. 125 above.
139 See n. 133 above.
140 *Izvestiya*, January 21, 1947; January 18, 1948; January 20, 1949; January
18, 1950; January 27, 1951.
141 E. Mochova, "State Labor Reserves—Main Source of Working-Class Recruitment in the USSR," *Voprosy Ekonomiki*, April, 1950, pp. 41-42.

mainly for the short-term courses, in the cities mostly for the schools with the two-year course.[142]

Preparations for a Planned Distribution of Manpower

From the early 1930's on, the recruitment of new workers on the farms and from urban manpower reserves was the primary concern of the Soviet labor planning. Another important objective was to perfect a system for compelling job seekers to take any work they were offered.

We briefly touched upon this problem in discussing the abolition of unemployment insurance. Job seekers were obliged to accept any kind of work—even if it had no connection with their trade, even if acceptance required them to move to another town or to the country. Sickness alone was held to justify refusal.

It proved impossible to enforce these rules in all their stringency. A decree of December 23, 1930, concerning the "registration and utilization of job seekers" [143] introduced more elastic rules. Under the new regulations an applicant had to accept any job offered within his own trade only, but distance from his place of residence remained no object. If there were no jobs in his trade, he had to accept vocational retraining if offered. Anyone who refused work or retraining "without valid reason" was to be dropped from the job seekers list for six months; but he still could be put to work on so-called "mass jobs," such as lumbering, logging, peat digging, etc.

The list of "valid reasons" for refusing work or retraining was broadened. There were now two acceptable grounds besides sickness: an offer of work involving a change of residence could be rejected if no appropriate "dwelling space" was supplied, and married women could refuse jobs that would force them to leave the locality of their husbands' residence. (Married men were not entitled to refuse jobs on this ground—apparently the first case in which the principle of equal rights for husband and wife was abondoned.[144])

---

[142] Ibid., p. 42.
[143] Ordinance of the People's Commissariat for Labor of the USSR, published in Izvestiya, December 29 and 30, 1930.
[144] Federal provisions issued on December 23, 1930, (see preceding note) superseded earlier regulations of the People's Commissariat for Labor of the RSFSR (of November 22, 1930, cf. Izvestiya Narkomtruda, 1930, p. 730) which

It must be kept in mind that these provisions came at a time when there were no more unemployment benefits in the Soviet Union. So the point was not to punish the unemployed worker's refusal to accept a job by depriving him of unemployment benefits, as under similar, though milder rules prevailing in other countries. There was more at stake here. The whole set of regulations was only one of many parts that went to make up the pragmatically developing organization of labor on the basis of compulsory labor service. But as the administrative setup of employment exchanges withered, the restrictive regulations of the rights of the unemployed came to an early, quiet, and unnoticed end. Other issues came to the fore.

As early as September 6, 1930,[145] the CPC of the RSFSR directed the People's Commissariat for Labor of the RSFSR to take steps to assure

(1) effective utilization of manpower in production;

(2) planned regulation of upgrading;

(3) efficient allocation of the existing labor force to individual industrial enterprises, industries, and regions;

(4) elimination of labor turnover.

These ideas were given more concrete expression in a decree of the People's Commissariat for Labor of the USSR of December 28, 1930, clarifying the duties of labor authorities (here called "administration of manpower") in the field of labor supply.[146] They were charged with the "recruitment and registration of labor," with the "systematic supply of manpower to industry, transportation, seasonal and other sections of the national economy," and in addition with "supervision of the efficient use of manpower in the establishment of the socialist sector, and transfer to other establishments of surplus manpower and skilled workers and technicians not employed in accordance with their qualifications." The point at issue was improved utilization not

---

treated husband and wife on an equal basis. Under the RSFSR regulations, not only married women but also married men were entitled to reject jobs in a different locality from the one where his or her consort worked or attended an institution of higher learning. The fact that a mere month after these provisions had been enacted federal legislation deprived married men of these advantages underscores the basic reversal of policy.

145 See n. 74 above.
146 *Izvestiya Narkomtruda*, 1931, No. 1-2.

only of the unemployed but of already employed manual and white-collar workers.

For the time being, this program was in the blueprint stage. Its realization was bound to transcend the limits of a manpower utilization policy and to lead to a fundamental change in the labor relationship—a change from a relationship resting on the labor contract to one resting on compulsion.

Accordingly, most of the problems broached in the framework of this program may best be dealt with under the broader aspect of the transformation of the labor relationship (see Chapter Three). The remainder—like "upgrading," the direction of manpower from lower levels of skill to higher ones—must be left to a separate treatise on vocational training. Here it should only be added that the program was never carried out in its entirety, that the shift to the principle of compulsory labor never went the whole way, with the result that the manpower policy of the 1930's presents a motley picture of diverse and partly heterogeneous elements existing side by side.

Chapter Three

TRANSFORMATION OF THE LABOR
RELATIONSHIP

*"Floating" Labor. — "Voluntary" Indenture. — Promoting Shop
Loyalty. — Curbs on Quitting. — On the Road to the Work
Book. — Tightening Work Discipline. — Labor Law Revision
of December 1938. — The "Reform" of June 1940: The End of
Free Labor Relations. — Criminal Courts Under Pressure. —
Beginning of Planned Manpower Allocation. — The War and
Postwar Years.*

"Floating" Labor

Around 1930 the labor market underwent a fundamental
change. Hundreds of thousands of new workers were employed in
production; real wages declined; the housing shortage seemingly
could get no worse. The result was extraordinary unrest in the
factories. Workers came and went in quest of better living and
working conditions. Labor turnover became the sore spot of the
economy, and the fight against "floating" came to dominate labor
policy and labor relations.

The rate of labor turnover had been high since the mid-
Twenties. From 1929 on it climbed steadily. Even annual average
figures, disguising seasonal peaks, show the accumulation of danger points. The following figures are for industry as a whole—
again concealing the particularly precarious conditions in some
vital industries: [1]

---

[1] *Socialist Construction of the USSR. Statistical Year-Book*, Moscow, 1936,
p. 531.

Year	Hirings	Discharges
	(Percentage of average annual number employed)	
1928	100.8	92.4
1929	122.4	155.2
1930	176.4	152.4

With total employment increasing rapidly, there may be nothing exceptional in the high rate of hirings. But the discharge rate was unquestionably alarming. A 50 per cent excess of a year's discharges over the average number employed means that each worker, on the average, changed jobs every eight months.

The trend was virtually disastrous in two key industries, coal and iron ore mining: [2]

Industry	Year	Hirings	Discharges
		(Percentage of average annual number employed)	
Coal mining	1928	140.4	132.0
	1929	201.6	192.0
	1930	307.2	295.2
Iron ore	1928	160.8	141.6
mining	1929	249.6	219.6
	1930	301.2	288.0

In these two industries, a worker's employment period in 1930 had fallen to about four months, with turnover more than doubled since 1928.

The effect on industrial production was ruinous, as the press kept emphasizing. From the monthly organ of the People's Commissariat for Labor of the USSR, June 1930, the following may be quoted: [3] "One of the most harmful effects of floating, in plants hardest hit by this disease, is deterioration of the qualitative composition of the labor force." Skilled workers, men who had spent many years in the plant, would quit to look for jobs in other plants, even in other industries:

"If the loss of skilled workers unfavorably affects work in individual plants, symptoms of a manpower exodus to other industries must be far more disquieting. In particular, this applies to the textile industry . . . Workers quit and change their occu-

---

[2] *Ibid.*
[3] Z. Mokhov, "Increase in Labor Turnover, 1929/30," *Voprosy Truda*, June, 1930, pp. 22 ff.

pation when reporting to employment agencies. Weavers, spin-
ners, dyers register as unskilled workers, and they do not return
to the textile industry but pass to the metal industry where unskilled work is paid considerably better than skilled work in the
textile industry."

Turnover was aggravated, the article went on, because
"plants looking for skilled workers engage in a peculiar kind of
overbidding which sometimes assumes the most repulsive forms
of pirating workers from other plants." Details were supplied:

"This pirating, often assuming grotesque terms, affects everyone from manager to simple worker. Sometimes even trust
directors participate. Thus the assistant general manager of the
Arma Trust, Comrade Vasil'yev, has found a singular way to
'solve the manpower problem.' He visits plants in the neighborhood, allegedly to find out how the orders of his trust are coming
along. Actually he is engaged in pirating labor. He accosts
skilled workers and foremen and offers them jobs; and as to
wages—'Don't worry, you'll be taken care of.'

"Labor piracy is getting to be literally an everyday occurrence and a subject of unabashed, rather good-natured discussion ... At a conference in the offices of the People's Commissariat
for Labor, the manager of the Dynamo Works actually bragged
of his successes. According to him, the Dynamo Works challenged
the AMO Works to a competition in improved labor piracy: 'The
AMO Works pirate our workers, and we repay them in kind.
They took our lathe operators. Well, the boys stayed for a while
and came back; five of them came back and brought a few others
with them.'

"We have not been able to establish whether the Dynamo
Works actually ordered its men temporarily to AMO, to get AMO
workers away from their plant. But in Leningrad we had a chance
to hear plant executives hurl such charges and reproach each
other for 'perfidious' methods of labor piracy.

"Even study tours through plants are used for such treacher-
ous Trojan horse methods. Plant managers have become suspi-
cious of all such tours; they point out that many participants visit
the plants only to pirate workers, for they observe that after
every such tour more men will quit their jobs. 'Our plant, particularly the tractor division,' we hear from the Red Putilov
Works, 'suffers from recruiters. They come as tour participants,
roam around, and ask the workers whether they would not like
to come over to another plant.' "

The spread of labor piracy[4] soon brought severe and partly successful counter-measures. On March 8, 1930, the Presidium of the Supreme Court of the RSFSR ruled that it constituted a criminal offense, to be punished as malfeasance in office.[5] True, this order specifically referred only to construction workers and regarded as a crime only mass piracy or piracy by means of fraudulent promises. Labor authorities were apprised of, and requested to observe, the ruling in a joint circular of the People's Commissariats for Labor and Transportation and the Supreme Economic Council of the USSR.[6] Again, only construction workers were mentioned. Nevertheless, the Supreme Court's opinion apparently took effect far beyond its original scope and contributed to the elimination of piracy in practice.

Stricter rules on compulsory hiring through employment exchanges[7] also helped. Laxity in enforcing this principle actually promoted floating and labor piracy. Hiring without recourse to employment exchanges increased enormously[8] until enforcement of institutionalized hiring was tightened.

However, piracy prosecutions and more stringent rules on hiring through employment exchanges struck at symptoms and side effects rather than at the root of the matter. The best way to check "floating" was certainly to improve wages and working conditions. In principle the authorities accepted the idea; in practice, however, they took another road—that of a gradual curtailment of worker's freedom to take a job and to leave it.

---

[4] For more details, cf. I. Zaromsky, "The struggle against Labor Turnover," *Voprosy Truda,* September 1930, p. 21.

[5] *Izvestiya Narkomtruda,* 1930, p. 413. The Court Presidium pointed out several sections of the Criminal Code which, it said, could establish standards for the punishment of piracy practices "until a new law is issued," although originally they were not aimed at pirating at all.

[6] *Izvestiya Narkomtruda,* 1930, p. 452.

[7] Decree of the CEC and the CPC of the USSR of December 15, 1930, in *Izvestiya,* December 17, 1930, Cf. Chapter Two, *supra,* to n. 32.

[8] For industry as a whole, the proportion of workers who had obtained jobs through the intermediary of employment exchanges had dropped to 60.5 per cent in the third quarter of 1930 as against 83.9 per cent in the same period of the previous year. The decline in individual industries was as follows: iron and steel, from 89.6 to 59.3 per cent; metals 86.1 to 61.3 per cent; textiles, 84.0 to 55.1 per cent; mining, from 85.0 to as little as 28.5 per cent. Data from Z. Mokhov, "Labor Agencies and Turnover," *Voprosy Truda,* May 1931, p. 40.

"Voluntary" Indenture

From early in 1930, strenuous efforts were made to check turnover by putting workers under "public pressure" without formally repudiating the legal guarantee of freedom of contract. "Among the measures applied," wrote one Soviet author, "these are worth mentioning: honor courts in the shop, pillorying of floaters on the bulletin board, use of factory newspapers." [9]

But the same source told of more drastic procedures: "The shop stewards of the Bela Kun factory passed a resolution to the effect that 'workers who quit the plant on their own, without having worked there for six full months, are to be expelled from the union as deliberate shirkers.' In several plants such deliberate shirkers were fired as well as expelled from their unions."

Local and plant organizations of the Communist Party and the Young Communist League[10] took pains to impress their members with the need to stay on the job. Violations were punished through the organization, and the punishment imposed could be expulsion from the Party or the *Komsomol*. As a rule, such directives applied to single plants only. But in July, 1930, for instance, the Mid-Volga Provincial Committee of the *Komsomol* generally forbade Young Communists to change jobs without valid reason; in every single instance the shift had to be sanctioned by the *Komsomol* cell.[11]

About this time a new procedure spread widely: workers voluntarily undertook to stay on the job for a certain length of time. In many instances the unions intervened openly, and the "voluntary" obligation turned into a union-imposed attachment to the plant. In 1930 the Moscow trade paper told of an agreement between the USSR Coal Trust ("Soyuzugol'") and the Agricultural Laborers Union of the Ukraine, in which the latter undertook to provide the Trust with 15,000 unskilled workers. The men were obliged to work in the mines for two years, and any member who quit without authorization was threatened with expulsion from the union as a "deserter." [12]

In the fall of 1930 the issue was taken up by the CC of the

---

9 Zaromsky, as quoted *supra,* n. 4, p. 22.

10 Membership in the Young Communist League is open to young people up to 23 years of age.

11 Z. Mokhov, "Effective Measures for Combating Labor Turnover," *Voprosy Truda,* March-April, 1931, pp. 72 f.

12 *Trud,* June 8, 1930.

CPSU. The CC manifesto on the tasks of the third Plan year still treated the indenture as formally voluntary, but at same time it urged the public to pressure the workers into taking the pledge. The manifesto said: [13]

> "To combat labor turnover, steps must be taken to assure the attachment of workers to production by a proper buildup of proletarian public opinion; by getting the workers to pledge themselves to the proletarian public to hold their jobs for at least a certain length of time;[14] by bringing to bear various means of public pressure, including a boycott of refractory production deserters; and by the introduction of different forms of bonuses and supply designed to make the workers stay in a plant."

The CC manifesto was followed by a lively public "campaign." By November 15, 1930, according to figures published by the People's Commissariat for Labor of the USSR and covering nine unions in Moscow province with a total membership of more than 200,000, no-quitting pledges had been signed by 37 per cent of all wage and salary earners and 66.4 per cent of the Communist Party members employed in the surveyed plants.[15] In the Ural province, within a few months, pledges were signed by from 35 to 59 per cent of the personnel of the individual trusts.[16]

Though voluntary in form, the pledge was frequently signed only after heavy pressure had been exerted by union, Party, and other authorities. This was made quite plain by the secretary of the Central Board of Technicians attached to the AUCTUC: [17]

> "We have made it our task to get every technical employee to bind himself voluntarily, before October 1, to the plant in which he is employed. We expect every technical employee to be ready

---

[13] *Pravda*, September 3, 1930. Cf. "The Turning Point: Tightening of the Labor Supply" in Chapter Two, *supra*.

[14] The CC of the CPSU, in a resolution of October 20, 1930, on "measures for a planned manpower supply of the national economy and for combating labor turnover" (*Pravda*, October 22, 1930) , recommended the duration of the Five-Year Plan as the desirable commitment period under the "no-quitting pledge."

[15] I. Troitsky, "Labor Turnover and the Fight against It," *Voprosy Truda*, February, 1931, p. 75. The author also cites data referring to individual plants. E.g., among the 1,600 workers of the Aviapribor factory in Moscow, the number of those who had taken the pledge was 470 by October 1, 1930; 568 by November 1; 757 by December 1.

[16] For details, cf. Mokhov, as quoted *supra*, n. 11, p. 74.

[17] *Trud*, September 16, 1930.

to go to the weaker industrial front sectors at the first call of
the Party and the Government."

What the "voluntary" commitment implied can be seen from
a dispatch from the Petrovsky Works in Dnepropetrovsk, where
the CC manifesto of September 3, 1930, caused "a considerable
invigoration of the activities of the technical employees' section."
The board of this section applied itself with special vigor to the
campaign. The report said. [18]

"Among the technical employees there were traitors to the
cause of industrialization and of the Five-Year Plan. Let the
whole country know their names; Engineer S. [the names, given
in full in the original text, are omitted here] of the rates and
standards office and commercial engineer M. of the open-hearth
department declined to sign the pledge to stay on the job. Their
bad example was followed by the following assistants and foremen . . . [seven names listed]

"The technical employees collectively denounce those who
refuse to follow the Party directive on combating labor turnover.
Only immediate signature of the voluntary pledge can expiate
this crime. The organized technical employees of Dnepropetrovsk
are in duty bound to launch an immediate large-scale campaign
to the end that not a single technical employee shall fail to
sign . . ."

Under such circumstances, the vast number of "voluntary"
pledges could hardly claim to be taken seriously. In fact, many
of the signers soon forgot about their obligation. But the campaign to promote "voluntary" indenture had paved the way for
new legislative steps in which the principles of compulsion showed
up more clearly.

Promoting Shop Loyalty

Before discussing the first steps to reconstruct the labor
relationship on the basis of compulsion, it may be worth noting
briefly the efforts made to combat personnel turnover by positive
measures.

The objective was to make the workers truly interested in

---

[18] *Za Industrializatsiyu,* September 16, 1930.

prolonged employment in one plant. In January, 1930, the CPC of the RSFSR directed the People's Commissariat for Labor and the Supreme Economic Council of the Republic to cooperate with the trade unions in providing wage and salary earners of high seniority with special advantages by means of collective bargaining. Upgrading of such "shop veterans" was to be facilitated; their children were also to profit in their education and vocational training from the parents' plant loyalty. The line was carried further by the CEC of the USSR in a directive of April 30, 1930, which suggested housing priorities for men who had been working in the same plant for a long time.[19]

The Party resolution of October 20, 1930, and the decree of December 15, 1930,[20] implemented this program. Workers and technicians (no mention was made of other categories of salaried employees) who had worked in one plant for a longer period of time were to get a number of privileges of the kind granted to those who distinguished themselves by superior efficiency, by inventions, or by useful suggestions: housing priorities, a higher education at the employer's expense, time in rest homes and sanitariums, extra rations of scarce goods, etc.

The phrasing, to be sure, remained very general, and no legal claims to preferential treatment were established. In only one respect was the decree more explicit: in a number of specifically listed industries, workers belonging to a plant for two years or more were allowed an additional paid vacation of three days annually, after November 1, 1930.

Other rewards for plant loyalty were provided shortly. When health insurance was reorganized under an AUCTUC resolution of January, 1931, sick benefits were linked with plant seniority. In subsequent years, similar lines of thought governed the whole social insurance system.

Soon all other devices to promote shop loyalty were overshadowed by the grading of social insurance benefits according to seniority (see Chapter Seven). Aside from this, the fight against "floating" turned more and more into progressive curtailment of labor's freedom of movement and decision.

---

[19] Z. Mokhov, "Incentives and Reprisals within the System of Measures to Combat Labor Turnover," *Voprosy Truda*, July, 1931, p. 31.

[20] For the Party directives, see n. 14, *supra*; for the decree n. 7, *supra*.

Curbs on Quitting

For a long time Soviet labor law, laid down in the Labor Code of 1922, tended to assure the freedom of employees to terminate their employment. Under Sec. 46 of the Labor Code, employment contracts entered into for an indefinite period [21] (the predominant type in Russia) could be terminated by the employee at any time, on one day's notice in the infrequent cases when the wages were paid weekly, and on seven day's notice in the case of the customary fortnightly or monthly pay.

This provision remained formally valid until 1940 and was confirmed repeatedly (as late as 1936 and 1937) by the Supreme Court of the RSFSR.[22] In practice, various special regulations soon tended to undermine the idea underlying Sec. 46.

The first step was the decree issued by the CPC of the RSFSR on September 6, 1930.[23] Quitting by an employee, even though in accord with Sec. 46, was now regarded as "arbitrary" termination of the employment contract and tantamount to an infraction of work discipline. The labor exchanges had to start maintaining separate lists of job seekers who had "arbitrarily" terminated their employment or violated work discipline, and to strike the men so listed from the relief rolls for a fixed period. "Stricter measures, including removal from the register of unemployed," were to be taken against "persons who keep changing their place of employment without valid reasons."

Within a few days, in an ordinance of September 13, 1930,[24] the People's Commissariat for Labor of the RSFSR went a step farther. Under this ordinance, employees who had "arbitrarily" terminated their employment lost their claims to unemployment benefits not just temporarily but permanently. They were not to get jobs, moreover, until every applicant on the regular waiting list was taken care of, and the employment exchange had to inform the prospective employer that the applicant had arbitra-

---

[21] Under Sec. 34, the duration of a contract running for a definite period could not exceed one year. On December 15, 1930, the maximum legal duration of an employment contract entered into for a definite period was extended to three years, by decree of the CEC and the CPC of the USSR.

[22] *Sovetskaya Yustitsiya*, 1936, No. 32, p. 22; 1937, No. 1, pp. 51 f.

[23] Decree of the CPC of the RSFSR "concerning regulations for supplying manpower for the national economy and for promoting the training of skilled labor," *Izvestiya*, September 8, 1930. Cf. Chapter Two, to n. 145.

[24] Issued in conjunction with the Supreme Economic Council of the RSFSR and the AUCTUC, cf. *Izvestiya Narkomtruda*, 1930, No. 26-27.

rily quit his last job. "Stubborn floaters" were liable to further punishment—including cancelation of their workers' food cards.[25]

Nation-wide rules were adopted by the CC of the CPSU on October 20, and promulgated by the CEC and the CPC of the USSR on December 15, 1930.[26] "Deserters" and "floaters" (wording of October 20) or "refractory disorganizers of production" (wording of December 15) were barred for six months from any jobs in industry or transportation. However, this did not apply to every employee who quit a job—only to termination of employment "under aggravating circumstances" to be more closely defined by the People's Commissariat for Labor of the USSR.

This definition was provided by the Commissariat on January 18, 1931, in an ordinance "determining the persons to be considered refractory disorganizers of production." [27] "Disorganizers" were now those, above all, who quit their jobs prior to the expiration of their contracts, or without giving the required notice—both still violations of contractual obligations. Yet even if due notice had been given and no contract violation was involved, a worker was branded a "disorganizer of production" if he had voluntarily changed jobs more than once in the course of twelve months. Additional "disorganizers of production" were all workers fired for infractions of work discipline (as specified in detail in the ordinance), particularly for unjustified absence from work.

All these restrictions of the worker's freedom of contract were put into effect without formally repealing Sec. 46 of the Labor Code—another indication of the empirical nature of developments. Perhaps those who made the rules were not even conscious of the fundamental import of this new departure.

On the Road to the Work-Book

While these measures were introduced, leading Soviet circles gave much attention to a different means of indirectly tying the workers to their jobs. In the fall of 1930, A. Tsikhon, People's Commissar for Labor of the USSR, disclosed: [28] "The People's

---

[25] Within the framework of rationing, workers received higher rations for certain foods.

[26] See n. 7, *supra*.

[27] *Izvestiya*, January 19, 1931.

[28] A. Tsikhon, "On Bolshevik Paths. Remarks on the Conference of Labor Agencies," *Voprosy Truda*, October-November, 1930, p. 8.

Commissariat for Labor is presently examing the question of whether to introduce a permanent work-book for all working people." In retrospect, many of the regulations issued in the late months of 1930 appear as preparatory steps to the introduction of the work-book.

On September 6, the CPC of the RSFSR directed the People's Commissariat for Labor to "work out precedures for entering the cause of discharge in the identification papers of any discharged employee." [29] Pursuant to this, the People's Commissariat for Labor of the RSFSR ruled on September 23, in open contradiction of the long-standing interpretation of existing law, that plant managers, in discharging a man, had to enter "the real cause of discharge (employee's request, expiration of contract, incompetence, absenteeism, etc.)" in his wage-book. If he had none (because of short-time employment or for other special reasons) the cause of discharge was to be noted in a special identification paper. On January 18, 1931, a decree of the People's Commissariat for Labor of the USSR extended this ruling from the RSFSR to the entire Soviet Union.

The wage-book was newly issued in every plant and was not a worker's permanent identification paper. Still, in registering an applicant for employment, the labor authorities were now obliged to call for his wage-book; this had been merely optional before. Now the reasons why a worker had left his last job were bound to come to the attention of the labor authorities and probably of his next employer.

This was the first step to prepare the public for the introduction of a permanent work-book that would accompany the worker from plant to plant. The second step was a propaganda "campaign" for the work-book. It was launched in January, 1931, with an "Open Letter" signed by workers of the Kalinin Machine Works in Moscow.[30] The purpose of the work-book was set forth as follows:

> "The present hiring procedure is wrong. A plant must know whom it hires; it must not hire people who are unknown. The picture of every new worker must be clearly discernible to management and proletarian opinion; not only his social origin but his production record must be public.

[29] See n. 23, *supra*.
[30] *Izvestiya*, January 14, 1931.

"This means that every worker must have an identification paper recording not only his personal data but his status in production; what he did on previous jobs, where he worked and why he left; what services he rendered to production, and how he assisted socialist construction; whether he is a disciplined worker or a money grabber or loafer; how much he earned; when and how he was promoted, etc. In short, everything favorable and unfavorable in the production record of a man must be put down in his identification paper.

"Thus it will be possible to have a clear picture of every worker in the plant. Floaters, money grabbers, loafers and wreckers will have no chance of getting into the plant. This identification paper must become a kind of production passport, without which it will be impossible to get work anywhere."

This Open Letter was the signal for the publication of numerous statements in favor of the work-book—and none against. Even so, within a few weeks the issue was tacitly shelved. Evidently the idea was still too unpopular, and for the time being other means would still do. Among them were tightening of general disciplinary rules, particularly in regard to absenteeism, and adaptation of the social insurance system to the requirements of production policy.

A kind of substitute for the work-book was soon introduced, anyway: a decree issued on December 27, 1932, obliged everyone to carry a passport.[31]

This — according to the text of the decree — was directed against "persons not connected with either production, administration, or education." Commenting on it, *Pravda* indignantly referred to "hundreds of people, class-alien or declassed, who pour into new industrial construction projects, dream of easy money, and seek to disrupt the iron discipline of socialist work." Passports were to help purge the giant industrial construction projects and government enterprises of "floaters" and "money grabbers."

The polemics could scarcely disguise the real objective, which was to tie the workers more firmly to their jobs. In fact, the passport turned into a labor passport. The decree of December 27, 1932, obliged every employee to show his passport in applying for work, and every employer to enter the bearer's place of

---

[31] Decree of the CEC and the CPC of the USSR, *Pravda*, December 28, 1932.

work in the passport. Seasonal workers got identification papers in lieu of passports, not valid for more than three months and only to be extended, under regulations issued on January 14, 1933,[32] upon application by plant managment—i.e., the employer.

The passport thus became an instrument for the control of workers' migrations and, indirectly, an efficacious device for binding workers to the plants. Its effectiveness was increased by the fact that it was introduced at the beginning of 1933, when cutbacks in employment were considered for the first time in ten years. Penalties for absenteeism were getting stiffer, and on the other hand, industrial management was empowered to handle the rationed food supplies for its employed personnel.

All this practically wiped out the worker's freedom to move from job to job. Indeed, labor turnover began to drop substantially. A few figures on discharges in industry as a whole, and in two industries particularly beset by "floating," may illustrate the decline: [33]

Discharges in Percentages of Average Annual Number Employed

Year	All Industry	Coal Mining	Iron Ore Mining
1930	152.4	295.2	288.0
1931	136.8	205.2	249.6
1932	135.3	187.9	198.7
1933	122.4	120.7	154.2
1934	89.7	95.4	111.5
1935	86.1	99.1	103.3

Several years passed without a reopening of the work-book issue. It was not until the end of 1938 that the idea was revived and put into effect, in connection with other measures to strengthen work discipline, as part of the sweeping revision of Soviet labor law in December, 1938. Its significance will be discussed later.

Tightening Work Discipline

The ground for the measures of 1938 was prepared by the tightening of disciplinary provisions. The most important of

[32] *Izvestiya,* January 15, 1933.
[33] *Socialist Construction* . . ., as quoted *supra,* n. 1, p. 531. For data on previous years, cf. *supra,* p. 178.

these concerned the "absence from work without valid reason,"— "truancy" (in Russian, *"progul"*).

It was shown earlier what happened to workers fired for "truancy" when they applied for other jobs. Much more significant for the transformation of the labor relationship, however, were the stringent provisions now introduced for the dismissal of "truants."

Originally, Soviet Labor law was very lenient toward absenteeism. Under Sec. 47, of the 1922 Labor Code, it was cause for discharge without notice (and, of course, without severance pay) only if the employee was absent without valid reason for three consecutive days, or for six days in the course of a month. This clause was revised in August 1927; thereafter discharge without notice was permitted if the employee failed to show up for three days in the course of a month.[34] "Valid reasons" justifying absence from work were later narrowed when the penal provisions of the Model Work Rules were revised on August 27, 1929, and again on December 17, 1930.[35]

This was soon not considered enough, especially in view of the increasing scarcity of labor. On November 15, 1932, Sec. 47 of the Labor Code was thoroughly revamped.[36] Employers were now obliged (not merely entitled as previously) to discharge "truants" without notice; and one day of unjustified absence sufficed. A discharged truant was to be relieved of the food cards and merchandise coupons (for rationed manufactured goods) issued to the employee in connection with his job, and he was to be evicted from any dwelling furnished to him by the plant. "Instantly,"— the People's Commissariat for Labor of the USSR added on November 26, 1932.[37] He was to be evicted with his family, regardless of a lack of other accomodation, "at any time of the year," and even "without providing transportation facilities."

The whole regulation evidently centered in the ruthless eviction clause. It was made even more stringent on June 27, 1933;[38] now the offender was to be evicted not only from buildings owned by his employer[39] but also from the property of construction or

---

[34] *Laws and Ordinances of the RSFSR,* 1927:577.

[35] *Izvestiya Narkomtruda,* 1929, pp. 577-581; 1930, pp. 750-753.

[36] *Laws and Ordinances,* 1932:475.

[37] Ya. Kiselev and S. Malkin, ed., *Collection of Labor Law Provisions,* issued by the People's Commissariat for Justice, 9th ed., Moscow, 1937, p. 252.

[38] *Laws and Ordinances,* 1933:244.

[39] Housing construction for personnel is carried out by Soviet industrial plants

housing cooperatives which had allotted him "dwelling space" under an agreement with his employer. There are few other housing facilities available for wage and salary earners in Soviet industry, especially in the new giant plants.

These Draconian provisions, coinciding in time with the changes in the labor market, did not fail to achieve the desired results. Truancy receded at once. Industry as a whole presented the following picture: [40]

Year	Man-Days Lost Through Truancy per Worker
1928	5.72
1929	4.09
1930	4.49
1931	5.96
1932	5.96
1933	.93
1934	.67
1935	.76

The new disciplinary provisions did not change the legal form of the relationship between employer and employee. But they did lay the groundwork for making unjustified absence from work a criminal offense, punishable under provisions of the Criminal Code. This was done by the legislation of 1938 and 1940, which indeed wrought a fundamental change in the labor relationship.

Labor Law Revision of December, 1938

The enactment of these "reforms" was preceded by a large-scale propaganda campaign. The opening shot was a letter to the editor of *Pravda*,[41] from a *stakhanovite* employed in the Ural Works for Heavy Machine building in Sverdlovsk. Thereafter, day in, day out, the entire Soviet press wrote of a horrifying breakdown of discipline in the plants, of "floaters," "truants," "loafers," etc.—as if Russian labor had become so utterly demoralized that nothing short of the most drastic measures could keep the workers on the job.

on a large scale. They retain ownership of the buildings and allocate dwelling space to their employees.
40 *Socialist Construction . . .*, as quoted *supra*, n. 1, p. 530.
41 *Pravda*, December 11, 1938.

Had this been true, no more serious indictment could have been returned against a system that had brought the workers' morale and their attitude toward their work to such a level. Actually, conditions were not half so bad. When *Pravda*, for instance, scathingly rebuked the Ural Works for Heavy Machine-Building, the birthplace of the "anti-truancy movement," for a loss of 7,978 man-days from January through November, 1938,[42] the figure seemed alarming, but in the giant plant it was equivalent to an annual loss of less than a work day per worker.

The obviously exaggerated picture of a breakdown of work discipline was designed to justify the new measures, which profoundly affected working conditions. They were enacted in two installments. The first was a decree of the CPC of the USSR "on the introduction of work-books," adopted on December 20, 1938;[43] the second, a decree promulgated jointly by the CPC of the USSR, the CC of the CPSU, and the AUCTUC on December 28, 1938,[44] "concerning measures to consolidate work discipline, improve the operation of social insurances, and combat abuses in this field."

The introduction of work-books was particularly unpopular. It was surely no accident that in the "campaign" they were not mentioned until they could no longer be passed over in silence— until the day the work-book law was published.

Under the act of December 20, 1938, work-books are issued by plant management and, once issued, accompany the employee from plant to plant. For the duration of employment they are in the safekeeping of management, which makes all entries.

In practice, this meant another considerable restriction of the worker's freedom, a new step along the road to compulsory labor. But even within the framework of this evolving system, the work-book managed to become only a means of pressure on wage and salary earners, not the basis for a comprehensive organization of labor. As there were then no more administrative agencies for the general regulation and supervision of what was once the labor market, the Soviet work-books, while fashioned in the Nazi-German pattern, could not perform the functions they performed in the Third Reich. The German work-book (introduced by a

---

[42] *Pravda*, December 22, 1938.
[43] *Izvestiya*, December 21, 1938.
[44] *Izvestiya*, December 29, 1938.

Reich law of February 26, 1935) was from 1938 on issued to every German on his graduation from grade school and automatically registered with the government labor office. It gave the German labor authorities constant control over all theoretically employable persons; it provided the basis for a comprehensive system of compulsory labor. The Russian setup differed in that no work-book was issued to the potential wage or salary earner until he actually took a job. Then only was he caught up in the intricate mechanism of manpower controls. As long as a Soviet citizen was not employed he retained a measure of freedom[45]—but even though the Russian worker and employee was in this way less bound, the whole system was at the same time shown to be purely oppressive, without even a semblance of constructive ideas.

The work-book was, so to speak, the prelude to the "reform" of December, 1938. It was completed in the decree of December 28, whose numerous clauses may be summed up as follows:

(1) employees had to give a month's notice of quitting, instead of seven days;

(2) penalties for tardiness and unjustified absence from work were greatly stiffened;

(3) vacation laws and social insurance were remodeled into devices to bind the workers more firmly to their jobs.

The longer notice required from an employee who wanted to quit needs no further elucidation. But quitting was not impeded by this provision alone. Under the decree of December 28, any employee who gave up a job of his own accord, even after a month's notice, lost all health and maternity insurance rights and was not entitled to sick benefits again until six months after start-

---

[45] In the wording of the Reich law of February 16, 1935, the introduction of work-books in the Third Reich was aimed at "securing an effective distribution of the labor force within the German economy." From its very inception it was intended to render possible the most complete utilization of manpower, both employed and unemployed. Writing on the motives underlying the introduction of the work book, Friedrich Syrup, one of the most authoritative spokesmen for German labor policy, said: "The consideration which determined the introduction of the work-book differed utterly from those, for example, which had led to issuing work-books to under-age industrial workers, in 1878, a measure which was intended to meet complaints then rampant about the deterioration of discipline and morals, the dwindling of parental authority, contract violations, etc. among juveniles." (Fr. Syrup, "Das Arbeitsbuch," *Soziale Praxis,* 1935, No. 22, p. 628.) The Russian work-book was to be used as a means of enforcing work discipline much more than as a device for nation-wide distribution and allocation of manpower. It resembles the German system of 1878 more than that of 1935.

ing a new job. This was spadework, so to speak, for the measures of 1940 which made job quitting generally a criminal offense.

The gist of the act of December 28, 1938, was a set of rigorous disciplinary provisions. Every instance of being late for work "without valid reason" was now punishable, every case of knocking off early for lunch or at closing time, every kind of "loafing" on the job, etc. The penalties provided were: warning; reprimand; severe reprimand coupled with a warning of further steps, especially dismissal; transfer to lower-paid work for a period of up to three months. The imposition of these penalties was not discretionary but mandatory on the plant manager.

If a worker incurred three such penalties within a month, or four within two consecutive months, he was liable—as in cases of truancy—to discharge without notice, with all the attendant consequences: eviction from home, if supplied on the basis of his employment, and loss of all sick benefit rights until he had put in six months on a new job.

Less than two weeks went by before even these provisions were stiffened further. A "clarifying decision" of January 8, 1939,[46] laid down the rule that being more than twenty minutes late for work constituted unjustified absence (whereas the law of November 15, 1932, required absence for at least a full working day). This was what gave the decree of December 28, 1938, its full repressive significance.

In the new vacation and social insurance rules all rights and claims were tied to the length of employment in one establishment. Full sick benefits (100 per cent of wages lost) were not to be due until after six years in a plant, and that only for union members. Between three and six years in the plant entitled employees to 80 per cent of full benefits; between two and three years, to 60 per cent; less than two years, to fifty per cent. Nonunion employees were to draw half the union rate, i.e., between 25 and 50 per cent of their lost wages.

A wave of reprisals engulfed managers and other plant executives who failed to apply the new rules with the necessary speed and vigor. Administrative penalties—reprimands, demotions, transfers, dismissals—were reserved for minor offenses; serious cases called for criminal prosecution. On December 31, 1938,

---

[46] Issued by the CPC of the USSR, the CC of the CPSU, and the ACTUC, cf. *Izvestiya*, January 9, 1939.

the Public Prosecutor of the USSR directed his subordinates to charge the guilty executives with malfeasance and dereliction in office—crimes punishable with imprisonment under Sections 109 and 111 of the Criminal Code.[47]

After mid-January, 1939, the major newspapers published almost daily lists of higher executives indicted for lack of firmness in carrying out the December laws. Soon the first jail sentence in such a case was announced: eight months for a department head of the Karl Liebknecht Works in Dnepropetrovsk who failed to discharge three truant workers on the spot.[48]

Imprisonment, usually of from eight to twelve months, then became the normal punishment for managerial violations of the law of December 28. In the first months of 1939 scores of such sentences were reported in the newspapers. As a result, plant officials, afraid of prosecution for "furthering truancy," began discharging employees without even so much as looking at the facts of a case. They soon acquired the nicknames of "reinsurers." The press carried many stories of unlawful firings by this type of men. Two Moscow courtroom reports may illustrate the point:[49]

> "The Moscow factory 'Moslastkozh No. 2' fired a woman worker, Kapustina, for absence from work without cause when she failed to report on a day which, according to the rotating shift schedule, was supposed to be her day off. Kapustina's shift had already gone home when the management announced a new schedule which would have required K. to report the following morning. K., who knew nothing about the change, could hardly be charged with violating work discipline; but the head of her department fired her, anyway, with the following consolation: 'You're fired now, but the moment the court acquits you I'll be glad to rehire you.' "

The other case was even more drastic:[50]

> "A woman worker, Comrade Fedyayeva, sued the Moscow Bread Factory No. 5 for reinstatement before the People's Court in the Proletarskii District. F. had been fired for being more than twenty minutes late for work. The court established that F. was pregnant and living outside the city. On her way to work

---

[47] *Sovetskaya Zakonnost'* 1939, No. 1.
[48] *Pravda*, January 26, 1939.
[49] *Trud*, February 16, 1939.
[50] *Trud*, February 10, 1939.

she was unable to get on the overcrowded train and so arrived at the factory ten minutes late. She lost fifteen more minutes in the crowed locker room of the bakery. The court decided in F.'s favor and ordered her reinstated."

In a matter of weeks there were thousands of dismissals for truancy. Complete figures were never released, but inferences can be drawn from data about individual plants. In the "Red Proletarian" factory in Moscow, 129 workers were punished with discharge in January, 1939, alone.[51] During the same month, punitive discharges from the Petrovsky Works in Dnepropetrovsk numbered 500.[52]

The dismissals as such affected only a minority, of course; but a constant fear of dismissal seized the masses of labor as a whole. The fear of being late became a nightmare to workers, many of whom had no watches or clocks, and sent them speeding to work in frantic haste. The same fear made them gulp their lunch as quickly as possible. "Lunch takes our workers from 15 to 22 minutes," boasted the canteen manager of the Moscow precision tool plant 'Tochizmeritel'.[53] And the assistant manager of the Kharkov Tractor Works stated that in their hurry to get back to work in time the men of his plant "sometimes don't get around to eating their lunch."[54]

The extent of intimidation may be glimpsed from other symptoms. In the early months of 1939 the press frequently reported on an extraordinary decline in visits to dispensaries and other treatment stations: "Decrease by 20 to 30 per cent or more," "marked a decline in cases of absence from work under the pretext to see a doctor."[55] Sickness certificates were reported to have dropped 50 per cent and more.[56]

The press attributed all this to a decline of malingering—obviously a gross overstatement. For example, it was reported that the number of sick cases among the personnel of the Tashkent Textile Combine had dropped by two-thirds.[57] Are we really to assume that two-thirds of those who reported sick prior to the new

51 *Trud*, February 2, 1939.
52 *Industrya*, February 2, 1939.
53 *Trud*, Februray 3, 1939.
54 *Trud*, February 2, 1939.
55 *Trud*, February 5, 1939.
56 *Trud*, February 3, 1939.
57 *Trud*, February 10, 1939.

measures were malingerers? — One way to reduce the number of sick cases was to pressure physicians into refusing to attest them.

Needless to say, all these open and disguised devices for the "consolidation of work discipline" were designed rather to increase pressure, than to create an efficient, well planned organization of work. But every repressive measure caused more discontent and begot new repression, demonstrating the essential weakness of the new labor policy. The legislation of December, 1938, had been in force for barely eighteen months when labor law and policy were "reformed" once more, in the same spirit.

The "Reform" of June 1940:
The End of Free Labor Relations

The new "reform" was introduced by decree of the Presidium of the Supreme Soviet of the USSR, on June 26, 1940. Again it went beyond mere disciplinary measures, as witness the title of the decree which dealt with "conversion to an eight-hour day and seven-day week, and prohibition of workers and employees from quitting their jobs of their own accord."[58] The new provisions, on the one hand, brought major changes in the rules governing working hours, and on the other, completely transformed the employment relationship.

The changes concerning hours will be taken up separately (see Chapter Five). Here it should only be noted that a special decree of the CPC of the USSR, of the same date, ordered steps taken to prevent the longer work week from resulting in higher weekly earnings. This was thoroughly indicative of the basic tendency of the "reform."

The second part of the decree of June 26, 1940, was far more important in principle. Its main provisions may be summarized as follows:

Sec. 3 forbade wage and salary earners to terminate employment of their own accord. Quitting a job, as well as taking a new one, was now unlawful unless approved by plant management.

Under Sec. 4, plant managers were empowered and obliged to approve termination of employment (a) if, in the judgment of a medical board, the employee was prevented by sickness or

---

[58] *Izvestiya*, June 27, 1940.

disability from performing his past duties and the r
could not assign him to other suitable work; or if
eligible for a pension desired to stop working in the planι,
the employee had to give up his work because of admission to a
special or higher institution of learning.

Sec. 5 provided for criminal prosecution of employees who
quit the plant of their own accord. Upon conviction, the People's
Court was required to impose prison sentences ranging from two
to four months. Truancy, i.e. unjustified absence from work, also
was made a criminal offense punishable with up to six months of
"corrective labor" at the place of employment, at wages reduced
up to 25 per cent.

With these provisions, employment ceased to be a free contractual relationship. As a rule—not always!—it began with an
employment contract; once begun, however, it became a relationship founded on the principle of compulsory labor (unless the
contract expressly specified a limited duration). Aside from a few
cases enumerated in the statutes, employment was no longer
terminable by the employee.

Unauthorized termination of employment and "truancy"
(lateness of more than twenty minutes in coming to work, without
valid reason) have since been offenses punishable by imprisonment or corrective labor under the Criminal Code.

Corrective labor at the place of employment[59] is a distinctive
feature of Soviet labor law. It means that the offender goes on
working where he is employed, but at reduced wages and subject
to more rigid discipline (with infractions treated somewhat like
violations of discipline in penal institutions).

Addtional teeth were soon put into these provisions. In
September, 1940, the AUCTUC issued an "interpretation" of the
law, to the effect that a sentence to corrective labor was to be regarded, for purposes of eligibility for insurance benefits, as an
interruption of employment.[60] An employee under sentence to
corrective labor was to be treated as newly-employed after having
quit of his own accord—meaning that he was not entitled to sick
benefits for six months after the start of his sentence.

Circles close to the Public Prosecutor of the USSR even took

---

[59] "Corrective labor in the plant without deprivation of liberty," as Sec. 20,
d of the Soviet Criminal Code puts it.

[60] *Pravda*, September 22, 1940.

the view not only that a term of corrective labor interrupted employment but that employment started to run afresh only after the corrective labor term had been served.[61] Whether this more rigorous interpretation of the law was accepted in actual practice could not be ascertained.

Other provisions enacted on June 26, 1940, also were stiffened through interpretation. The decree made truancy a criminal offense. But what was "truancy"?

Regulations issued by the People's Commissar for Justice and the Public Prosecutor of the USSR on July 22, 1940,[62] broadened its meaning to extend beyond lateness of over twenty minutes in coming to work. It now also meant being late after the lunch recess, or leaving early either for lunch or at the close of the work period. This was still in line with the measures of December, 1938, which no one had dared to implement in this way at the time, despite some admonitions in the press.[63]

Now another step was taken. The Supreme Court of the USSR, in the plenary session of August 15, 1940, ruled that the truancy provisions of June 26 were to apply to any "loafing on the job" ("*bezdel'nichaniye*") for more than twenty minutes.[64]

In practice, the point was to stretch the terms "truancy" and "loafing" by the broadest possible interpretation. The following quotation is from the periodical published by the Public Prosecutor's Office:[65]

> "Cases in which wage or salary earners report on time but are turned back because of intoxication must also be regarded as truancy."

The suggestion was followed and made law in new Model

---

[61] This view for example, was vigorously defended at a national conference of officers of the public prosecution by D. Shveitser, head of the civil law division of the Office of the Public Prosecutor of the USSR. The text of the speech appeared in print under the title, "The Struggle for Iron Discipline and for Bolshevik Order in the Plants as the Combat Assignment of the Prosecuting Magistracy," in *Sovetskaya Zakonnost'* October, 1940, esp. p. 30.

[62] *Sovetskaya Yustitsiya,* 1940, no. 13, p. 5.

[63] N. Aleksandrov, "Legal Problems of the Consolidation of Socialist Work Discipline," *Sovetsoye Gosudarstvo i Pravo,* 1939, No. 1, p. 78, insisted that being late for work after lunch should be treated as truancy. In actual practice, the "milder" interpretation prevailed at that time; only who were more than twenty minutes late at the beginning of the work period were considered truants.

[64] *Sovetskaya Zakonnost'* December, 1940, p. 7.

[65] Z. Vyshinskaya and V. Men'shagin, "Criminal Responsibility for Truancy and Unauthorized Termination of Employment," *Sovetskaya Zakonnost'* December, 1940, pp. 9 f.

Work Rules, adopted on January 18, 1941.[66] Nor was this all. The tendency to stretch the "truancy" concept found new forms of expression:[67]

> "Persons must be regarded as truants if they fail to comply with orders given by the management with regard to overtime work and to work to be done on days off . . . Today, when conditions often compel management to insist that workers put in overtime, non-compliance with such orders cannot be tolerated. The plant manager will be responsible for unlawfully scheduling overtime; the worker has no right to check on whether the conditions for permitting overtime work have been formally complied with. On the contrary, it is his duty to carry out the assignment; he is liable to prosecution as a truant if he refuses, leaves the job ahead of time, or fails to report for work on a Sunday or another day off."

Thus an employee who refused to work overtime was guilty of "unjustified absence from work," even though the overtime work had been scheduled in violation of the law. The Supreme Court of the USSR repeatedly upheld this view, and today it is the law throughout the Soviet Union.[68]

Even more fantastic cases occurred in actual practice. Absence from work with express permission from the management was subjected to criminal persecution if the leave, though requested and granted in good faith, was objectively illegal. Said the authors of the paper on the prosecution of truants:[69]

> "On September 11, the Moscow City Court dismissed truancy charges against the defendant B. The defendant had been sentenced by the People's Court for having left work well ahead of time, with permission from the management, to meet his wife at the railroad station.
>
> "The dismissal in this case can hardly be considered correct. We hold that in such and similar cases action must be taken against both the plant manager who permitted the employee to leave work ahead of time, and the employee who left it. The

---

66 *Laws and Ordinances*, 1941:63.

67 Shveitser, as quoted *supra*, n. 61, pp. 29 f.

68 N. G. Alexandrov, E. I. Astrakhan, S. S. Karinsky, G. K. Moskalenko, *Labor Legislation—Commentaries to the Labor Legislation of the USSR and to the Labor Code of the RSFSR*, I. T. Golyakov, ed., publ. by the Ministry of Justice of the USSR, Moscow, 1947, p. 60.

69 Vyshinskaya and Men'shagin, as quoted *supra*, n. 65, p. 10.

management's explicit permission to commit an act of absence from work without valid reason does not free the absentee from criminal liability."

It was a cruel policy. The authors of the decree of June 26, 1940, were well aware that it could not be enforced without tremendous pressure. Hence, Sec. 6 of the decree specifically called for criminal prosecution of plant managers who failed to press charges against all employees quitting their jobs of their own accord. The same rule applied to managers hiring employees who had quit their last jobs of their own accord.

On June 27, the day of the publication of the decree, the People's Commissar for Justice and the Public Prosecutor of the USSR directed their subordinates to start immediate proceedings under Sections 109 and 111 of the Criminal Code [70] against plant managers who failed to comply.[71]

Criminal Courts Under Pressure

An avalanche of indictments and jail sentences was loosed upon lax executives, to make them willing instruments of the new policy. Next in line were physicians, charged with being insufficiently "conscientious" in issuing sickness certificates and thus aiding and abetting delinquent employees. Essentially this was nothing more than a more rigorous repetition of measures tested in carrying out the "reform" of December, 1938.

Something new was added, however. It was no longer enough to punish workers for violating the decree of June 26, and managers and physicians for insufficient vigor. The judiciary itself became a target of prosecution. This new stage in the development of labor policy is important enough to be discussed in some detail.

Judges and other judicial officers were evidently not prepared to wield the criminal law as a weapon of labor policy. As a result, they themselves incurred ruthless reprisals, which were by no means confined to individual cases. Disciplinary punishment was imposed on hundreds of judges and ranking judicial officials, all the way up to the People's Commissars for Justice in several Soviet Republics. In not a few instances judges were put on trial.

---

[70] Sections dealing with malfeasance and dereliction in office. Cf. n. 47 above.
[71] *Sovetskaya Yustitsiya*, 1940, No. 11, pp. 6 f.

Typical was the case of a woman judge, B. Butskaya, of the Sixth People's Court in the Moscow District of Krasnaya Presnya. For allegedly showing consideration to "truants," she was removed from office and indicted. What was her crime? Judge Butskaya had sentenced 76 per cent of defendants accused of "truancy" to corrective labor terms of less than three months, with wage cuts of only 10 per cent in most cases[72]—in other words, she had acted entirely in keeping with the penal sections of the decree of June 26, which provided for a *maximum* of six months corrective work and a 25 per cent wage reduction.

The reprisals against magistrates and court officials took prompt effect. The periodical of the People's Commissariat for Justice and the Supreme Court of the USSR was soon able to note "some improvement in the organization of the fight against truants and floaters." From June 26 to October 15, 1940, the periodical stated, 70 per cent of the convicted "truants" were sentenced to corrective labor at the place of employment for terms exceeding three months; and 81 per cent of the convicted "floaters" went to jail for more than two months. In the first half of October the figures rose to 77.5 and 86.5 per cent, respectively.[73] The periodical concluded that a certain "optimism" was justified in regard to the future.

Action against judges and court officials did not suffice to assure the desired results. Soon the very foundations of the judicial structure were shaken.

The Soviet Constitution (Sec. 112) guarantees the independence of the courts. Judges can only be recalled by their constituency or removed after conviction and sentence by a criminal court. The imposition of administrative ("disciplinary") penalties on judges is incompatible with this constitutional safeguard, which was repeated in the Judiciary Organization Act of August 16, 1938, and still is considered an unshakable pillar of the judicial structure. The principle of the inviolability of judicial tenure, though frequently disregarded in practice, had some favorable effects on the general setup of the judiciary. But in the wake

---

[72] *Sovetskaya Yustitsiya*, 1940, No. 14. For a list of judges and judicial officials who incurred penalties, see my article, "The Routing of the Courts in the USSR," *Sotsialisticheskii Vestnik*, New York, 1941, No. 9-10.

[73] Editorial, "The Fight Against Truancy and Unauthorized Termination of Employment as the Most Important Task of the Courts," *Sovetskaya Yustitsiya*, 1940, No. 22, p. 1.

of the decree of June 26, even the imperfect guarantee of judicial independence was wiped out.

In direct violation of Sec. 112 of the Soviet Constitution, the Presidium of the Supreme Soviet of the USSR, on July 29, 1940, promulgated a decree concerning the "disciplinary responsibility of judges." [74] Even the form of an independent judiciary was thus abondoned.

Another basic principle of the Soviet courts had always been their composition of one career judge and several laymen sitting as "the people's assessors." [75] In the criminal courts, this principle was supposed to be observed with particular stringency; as late as 1938 the basic textbook of the Soviet constitutional law stated: [76]

> "The provision that people's assessors shall sit in all courts insure the achievement of two goals: (1) that the people be made to participate in administering the State, in performing the most important governmental functions . . ., and (2) that the administration of justice be imbued with genuine popular spirit, with the people's socialist sense of justice, with their beliefs, and their conscience. This court organization guar ntees true socialist democratism in the administration of justice, close cohesion of the judiciary and the people, the authority of the courts in the eyes of the people . . .
>
> "This requirement is grounded as a fundamental principle in the Stalin Constitution."

Pursuant to the decree of June 26, this "fundamental [constitutional] principle" also was overturned. In open conflict with Sec. 103 of the Constitution, a decree issued by the Presidium of the Supreme Soviet of the USSR on August 10, 1940,[77] kept the people's assessors from sitting on courts that were to try cases of absence from work without cause and unathorized changes of employment. Only career judges were to decide on "truants" and "floaters." But is it not precisely in those cases that the administration of justice should be imbued "with genuine popular spirit,

[74] *Sovetskaya Yustitsiya*, 1940, No. 17-18, p. 3.
[75] The People's Courts as set up under Soviet law are, in a way, successors to the provisional courts created by A. F. Kerensky in March 1917 when he was Minister of Justice. Cf. Judah Zelitch, *Soviet Administration of Criminal Law*, Philadelphia-London, 1931, p. 260.
[76] A. Ya. Vyshinsky [at the present writing Minister of Foreign Affairs of the USSR], ed., *Soviet Constitutional Law. Textbook for Law-Schools*, issued by the Law Institute of the Academy of Sciences, Moscow, 1938, p. 454.
[77] *Izvestiya*, August 11, 1940.

with the people's socialist sense of justice, with their beliefs, and their conscience"?

On August 15, the Presidium of the Supreme Court of the USSR issued an elaborate order "concerning deficiencies of court practice in cases involving unauthorized termination of employment by wage and salary earners, and absence from work without valid reason." [78] A few lines from this document may illustrate the effort made to turn the trials of "truants" and "floaters" into an assembly line for draconic punishment:

"If the court, in trying a case of truancy or unauthorized termination of employment, establishes the truancy or unauthorized termination of employment as fact, it is inadmissible and forbidden to the court to include in the sentence references to favorable attestations in which the delinquents are characterized as *stakhanovites*, exemplary workers, etc. Such attestations are issued with the obvious intention of easing the criminal responsibility of stubborn violators of work discipline who can never be *stakhanovites* or exemplary workers.

"It is the duty of the courts to institute action against plant managers who try to improve the situation of truants and refractory breakers of work discipline by giving them all kinds of attestations intended to exempt them from responsibility before the law or to ease such responsibility."

In practice, especially in the climate created by the heavy disciplinary pressure on judges, such directives were bound to disintegrate the administration of justice. We have previously encountered "reinsurers" among plant executives; now this type appeared among judicial officers. A few examples may illustrate their "reinsurance" operations:

"On August 30, the judge of a People's Court in the Bryansk district, Orel province, sentenced a man who had been absent from work because of illness and hospitalization. The accused was taken straight from the hospital to prison." [79]

"The defendant Zotova had fallen off the streetcar on her way to work and cut her legs. She reported for work on time, had her name taken down, and announced that she was going to the plant dispensary. There she was given a paper to the effect that medical treatment had been administered and that she had re-

[78] *Sovetskaya Yustitsiya*, 1940, No. 13, pp. 6-10.
[79] *Sovetskaya Yustitsiya*, 1940, No. 21, p. 9.

fused a sickness certificate although her condition rendered her unfit for work. The plant management and the judge of the People's Court for the 11th Moscow City district, to whom the evidence concerning Zotova's one-hour absence from work was submitted, found the above-mentioned facts immaterial. The People's Court sentenced Zotova to a four-month term of corrective labor at her place of employment." [80]

The magistracy's "reinsurance" efforts spread so fast that I. Golyakov, the Presiding Justice of the Supreme Court and presumable author of the order of August 15, was moved to intervene. In the December, 1940, issue of the periodical of the judicial authorities he published an article harshly criticizing the "liberal attitude" of numerous magistrates who abetted "truants" and "floaters" but at the same time violently denouncing the opposite extreme of judicial "reinsurance." Justice Golyakov wrote: [81]

"Besides inadmissible liberalism of court practice in the fight against infractions of work discipline, we observe another tendency: that of basing sentences on a mere formal finding of the facts of lateness or failure to report for work, and of omitting a careful examination of the facts and a finding of the defendant's material guilt. Court records frequently show sentencing of defendants who are not guilty at all of violating work discipline under the provisions of the decree of June 26, 1940.

"Such judges reduce court trials to the level of a formalistic evaluation of briefs submitted by the complainant plant management.

"Some judges, disregarding the law on judgment by default, proceed in truancy cases without a finding that the defendant actually refrained from appearing in court and that he was really served with a summons. Persons who failed to report for work because of illness and actually were in the hospital are known to have been sentenced to prison for truancy.

"Some judges forget that the decree of June 26 does not penalize every absence from work, but only absence from work without valid reason, and not every employee who quits his job, only an employee who quits of his own accord. Explanations

[80] *Sovetskaya Yustitsiya*, 1940, No. 22, p. 3.
[81] I. Golyakov, "The New Decrees of the Presidium of the Supreme Soviet of the USSR and the Tasks of Legal Science," *Sovetskaya Yustitsiya*, 1940, No. 23-24, p. 3.

by defendants, no matter how significant the facts they refer to, are frequently left uninvestigated and ignored."

Justice Golyakov's strictures against "liberal" judges left no doubt that his purpose was not to humanize court practice, nor to mitigate the fundamental severity of the provisions of August 15. He merely wished to put an end to glaring abuses detrimental to the prestige of the courts. In the same article, the Presiding Justice of the Supreme Court stressed emphatically that the general provisions of the Criminal Code on reduction of punishment (Sec. 51) and parole (Sec. 53) were inapplicable to cases involving "truancy" or "floating."

The ruling of August 15 remained in force. The leading Soviet law journal even ushered in the year 1941 with a series of articles discussing at great length "the procedural peculiarities" of criminal cases involving infractions of work discipline.[82] The process of remodeling Russian labor law on the basis of compulsory labor was continued, following the path of disciplinary punishment and criminal persecution rather than from those of planned labor policy.

Beginnings of Planned Manpower Allocation

To a much lesser degree, to be sure, the viewpoints of planned manpower organization also influenced the development of labor law in the 1930's. But they, too, helped to rebuild the employment relationship on the basis of compulsory labor.

As already mentioned, a decree of the CPC of the RSFSR of September 6, 1930,[83] directed the People's Commissariat for Labor and its subordinate agencies to supervise the distribution of the labor force and promote the most effective use of available manpower and its economically efficient allocation to the individual industries and plants. The CPC merely proclaimed the principle of overall allocation, leaving it to the Commissariat for Labor and the Supreme Economic Council to "work out methods and procedures for the adequate utilization of manpower in production" as well as "procedures for a planned allocation of manpower to plants, industries, and regions." Concrete plans

---

[82] B. Arsen'yev, "Procedural Specifics of Criminal Proceedings in Cases of Truancy and Unauthorized Termination of Employment," *Sovetskaya Yustitsiya*, 1941, Nos. 1, 2, and 3.

[83] See n. 23, *supra*.

were to be submitted within twenty and thirty days, respectively.

It was characteristic of the empirical nature of this policy that the People's Commissariat for Labor and the Supreme Economic Council not only did not complete their tasks within twenty or thirty days—they did not complete them at all.

The issue was revived, however, in the resolution of the CC of the CPSU of October 20, 1930,[84] a document of great importance for the future direction of labor policy. While treating the problem in more specific terms, the resolution narrowed down the scope of manpower allocation, confining it to the most effective use of the skilled workers and technicians.

The Commissariats for Labor of the USSR and of the Union Republics were empowered to order transfers of skilled workers and technicians from less important industries, plants, and regions to more important ones. The transfers had to be requested by the economic agencies—in practice, by plant management— and to be approved by the trade unions.

Detailed regulations were issued on December 15, 1930.[85] The Commissariat for Labor was given broad powers to "methodically distribute the labor force within the framework of production plans approved by the competent agencies." The rest of the legislation, however, did not express this general idea: it merely regulated two special problems: (1) the "combing-out" of surplus workers and skilled workers in the plants; (2) the procurement of technicians and skilled workers for particularly important industries and plants (especially the huge new industrial establishments) by taking non-surplus personnel, if necessary, from less important industries and plants.

The first problem had to do not so much with the efficient allocation of employed labor according to the needs of the national economy in general as with the elimination of waste and of the inefficient use of highly skilled labor. Instead of a general schedule of priorities, it involved only labor-saving and efficiency engineering within individual plants. Under this program, the transfer of "surplus" employees to other plants was merely a sideline. Only the second problem — the granting of manpower priorities to more important economic projects—reflected preoccupation with overall economic planning of the labor supply.

84 See n. 14, *supra.*
85 See n. 7, *supra.*

Subsequent legislation occasionally referred to the measures of December 1930, and to the resolution of the CC of the CPSU, but not one law or decree elaborated on the fundamental ideas of these documents. In legislation as well as in administrative practice, the planning of allocation and redistribution of the available labor force was reduced to "combing-out" operations.[86]

In the early 1930's, the campaign to comb out surpluses of skilled labor was carried out with energy and determination.[87] Yet the idea of planned overall allocation of manpower was tacitly shelved. It was not done officially, nor was the idea completely abondoned; the provisions of December, 1930, were neither rescinded nor developed further, and the legal situation remained confused.

There was, for instance, an ordinance of the People's Commissariat for Labor of the USSR of January 16, 1931,[88] directing skilled wage and salary earners who had held jobs in railroad transportation at any time during the five preceding years to report immediately for railroad work. The "mobilization" of ex-railroadmen was carried out virtually in the form of military conscription. Plant managers employing such men had to discharge and refer them to the local labor offices within ten days; the employees themselves had to report to the labor office within five days and were immediately put to work on a railroad, near or far.

A similar line was taken in a ruling handed down by the Presidium of the Supreme Court of the RSFSR on June 13, 1932.[89] Under this, specialists (skilled workers or technicians) who failed to comply with management orders assigning them to jobs in remote districts could be subjected to disciplinary punishment, or punished by "public opinion" (i.e., by trade union or shop meetings, etc.); those who refused to carry out similar orders of the labor authorities were to face court action for dereliction of duty.

---

86 In the "combing-out" of manpower surpluses the USSR showed less initiative than the RSFSR. The most relevant government act in regard to the problem emanated from the People's Commissariat for Labor of the RSFSR: an ordinance of January 23, 1931, "concerning fact-finding relative to manpower surpluses and the proper utilization of such surpluses"; cf. *Izvestiya Narkomtruda*, 1931, pp. 137 ff.
87 Cf. my article "The Five-Year Plan and the Regulation of the Labor Market in the USSR," *International Labour Review*, March, 1933, pp. 371 f.
88 *Izvestiya*, January 18, 1931.
89 *Izvestiya Narkomtruda*, 1932, p. 383.

These examples show how far the idea of compulsory labor had progressed even though the freedom of contract was still on the statute books. Up to the end of the 1930's, the official textbooks on labor law took the view that under Sec. 37 of the 1922 Labor Code no employee could be transferred without his consent from one plant to another, or, if the plant itself was moved, from one locality to another; that in cases of refusal on the employee's part, the employment was terminated through no fault of his, entitling him to severance pay on the terms that would apply if the employment were terminated by the employer.[90]

With respect to technicians, the law remained unclear up to the late 1930's. There were no general provisions formally tying technicians to their jobs or compelling them to obey transfer orders, nor were they free to leave at will. In the case of skilled workers (to say nothing of the unskilled who aroused much less interest) such formal rudiments of compulsory labor as had been seen in the early 1930's were gradually forgotten. Only compulsory transfer of "surplus" workers was carried on for some time.

The relaxation of formal compulsory service provisions was furthered by the disbandment in 1933 of the People's Commissariat for Labor and its agencies. Without labor supply authorities, a policy of planned manpower allocation could hardly be carried out. As the function of "combing-out" surpluses was transferred from the labor authorities to the economic administration and to plant management, it ceased being a means of planned manpower allocation and became simply another device for management to rid itself of employees considered superfluous.

This was the situation up to the end of the decade. The idea of planned compulsory manpower distribution did not reappear until after the decree of June 26, 1940, which legally bound wage and salary earners to their jobs. This decree did not contain provisions on the transfer of employees from plant to plant. The gap was filled by another decree issued by the Presidium of the Supreme Soviet of the USSR on October 19, 1940 [91]—"concerning the mandatory transfer of engineers, technicians, foremen, technical employees, and skilled workers from certain plants, offices,

---

[90] *Soviet Labor Law. Brief Textbook,* issued by the People's Commissariat for Justice of the USSR, Moscow, 1938, p. 22; *Soviet Labor Law. Textbook for Law Schools,* issued by the People's Commissariat of Justice of the USSR, Moscow, 1939, p. 64.
[91] *Izvestiya,* October 20, 1940.

and public institutions to others." The People's Commissars of the USSR were empowered to order the transfer of such qualified wage and salary earners from one place of work to another; the concept of technical "qualification" was broadly interpreted, and distance of transfer was no consideration.

As there were no labor authorities left in the Soviet Union a peculiar result ensued: compulsory transfers were ordered by the People's Commissariat under whose jurisdiction the trans-ferees were employed—which in practice meant by their employ-ers. There was no recourse against such decisions of the People's Commissariats; nor were they required to concur or even consult with the trade unions. It is not clear from the wording of the decree whether the Commissariats could only shift employees among plants within their jurisdiction, or whether they could cede them to other Commissariats. The latter, broader interpre-tation seems more in keeping with the intent of the decree.

Another important provision of the same decree of October 19, 1940, dealt with the termination of employment contracts. Under the terms of the decree of June 26, only employees work-ing under contract of indefinite duration were bound to their places of work. If the contract was for a limited term, the em-ployee was free to quit at the expiration of the time specified. The decree of October 19 changed this fundamentally. All employ-ment contracts signed for specific periods of time by skilled wage and salary earners were automatically turned into contracts for an unspecified period of time, and contracts of limited duration were henceforth permitted only in the case of unskilled workers. But it is in this very category that contracts for limited periods were extremely rare in the Soviet Union (except in seasonal oc-cupations).

With the decree of October 19, 1940, practically all elements of a system of compulsory labor were at hand. The only thing lacking was an administrative setup to make this system operate as a coordinated compulsory organization of work processes.

The War- and Postwar Years

The war did not cause any fundamental reversal in the labor policies of the Soviet Union. The inherent laws governing the development of a totalitarian dictatorship and manifested in the

Soviet-Russian labor policies had slowly permeated the whole organization of labor with the principle of compulsion even before the Soviet Union entered the war. The war brought the development to a logical conclusion.

Pointing the way, in this sense, were the measures which had been carried out already in peacetime, in the summer and fall of 1940. As has been shown above, they had legally sanctioned the freezing of wage and salary earners in their places of work and added harsher and more rigorous features to the disciplinary regime already in force. All this was reinforced in the sign of the war constellation.

On December 26, 1941, the Presidium of the Supreme Soviet of the USSR issued an act dealing with the "responsibility of wage and salary earners employed in war plants, in cases of unauthorized termination of employment." [92] The new decree aimed at "unconditional freezing of wage and salary earners in war plants." All manual and non-manual workers, regardless of sex or age, were pronounced "mobilized" and "tied for the duration of the war to the establishments employing them."

An employee who quit his job without specific authorization was a "deserter" liable to imprisonment of five to eight years (instead of from two to four months, as provided in the act of June 26, 1940, which had first made unauthorized termination of employment a criminal offense). The very concept, "war industry," received the broadest interpretation. As "other industrial establishments cooperating in supplying war industry" were put on the same footing as war industry proper, a great majority of all industrial plants was subject to the new legislation.

Judicial guarantees for the trial of wage and salary earners accused of unauthorized termination of employment, substantially restricted in 1940, were practically abolished. The act of December 26, 1941, placed all court proceedings in such cases under the jurisdiction of military tribunals.

Other measures followed in rapid succession. On February 13, 1942, the Presidium of the Supreme Soviet of the USSR enacted legislation "on wartime conscription of the employable urban population for work in production and construction." [93] Under this act all employables "from the ranks of those not em-

---

[92] *Izvestiya,* December 27, 1941.
[93] *Vedomosti Verkhovnogo Soveta,* March 5, 1942.

ployed in government institutions or government-owned plants,"
men from 16 to 55 and women from 16 to 45 (under provisions
issued seven months later,[94] even up to 50) years of age were subject to draft for industrial or construction work "at their places
of residence." Exemptions were granted only to students, to
mothers of infant children, and, if no other relatives could replace them in the house, to mothers of children under eight years
of age.

Soviet sources available in this country do not convey information on the handling of the labor draft in actual practice.
Most, if not all, of the urban employables were employed in government-owned plants or administrative and institutional establishments prior to conscription, and few remained to be drafted
under the act of February 13, 1942. But it evidently did not
remain a dead letter: in the following year, its provisions concerning women with small children were modified and general
exemptions granted only to women taking care of children under
four years; women with children of more than four but less than
eight years were made subject to draft, "provided that places in
nurseries and kindergartens could be secured, by the managers
of plants and construction projects, for the children of women
workers drafted." [95]

The industrial labor draft cannot possibly have been widely
applied, in spite of these strict regulations. More effective results
seem to have been achieved by the harvest conscription of city-
dwellers, first ordered on April 13, 1942, under a decree of the
CPC of the USSR and the CC of the CPSU concerning "regulation of the conscription of the employable population in cities
and rural communities for work in *kolkhozes, sovkhozes,*[96] and
MTS's." [97] [98]

Now many more men and women were made subject to
draft. Only those employed in industry and transportation were
exempt, while employees of the governmental and public services
were not; the act of April 13 explicitly required the latter to be

---

[94] Decree of the Presidium of the Supreme Soviet of the USSR of September
19, 1942, *Vedomosti Verkhovnogo Soveta,* October 10, 1942.
[95] Decree of the Presidium of the Supreme Soviet of the USSR of August 7,
1945, *Vedomosti Verkhovnogo Soveta,* August 23, 1943.
[96] Farms owned and operated by the government.
[97] "Machine-Tractor Stations," i.e., government-operated centers for farm machinery, etc., servicing the *kolkhozes.*
[98] *Laws and Ordinances,* 1942:60.

drafted insofar as it was possible without disrupting operation of the services. In contrast to the act of February 13, 1942, the draft further covered all school children from the sixth to the tenth grade, and all students of technical colleges and universities (except for students in the pre-graduation term).

The draft age was from 14 to 55 for men, and from 14 to 50 for women. In many places, drafting of schoolchildren (with teachers) for harvest work became the most widely applied form of conscripting city-dwellers for farm labor.

Though only temporary conscription was intended, the 1942 regulations failed to state the duration or amount of work required from a draftee. In 1943 the harvest labor to be performed by conscripts was specified: 50 to 60 daily quotas on state farms, or 40 to 50 "man-days" on collective farms. Reduced assignments were set for children: 20 to 30 daily quotas on state farms, or 20 to 30 "man-days" on collective farms. Having completed the assignment, conscripts could be "released from conscription at their request." [99]

Frequently—especially in cases of schoolchildren drafted for farm labor—the legal limits were exceeded. In 1943, conscripted schoolchildren of Moscow province worked 9,200,000 "man-days," an average of 71 "man-days" each. In 1944, a conference of students in Moscow province called on every student to do at least 75 to 80 "man-days" of harvest labor.[100] In the Bashkir Republic, 288,000 schoolchildren worked 14,000,000 "man-days" in 1944,[101] an average of about 49 each. The *per capita* number of "man-days" worked by schoolchildren in the Spasski district, Ryazan' province, in 1943 was 75; student bodies with the best work record issued an appeal to all students, promising that in 1944 every fifth-grade student (a group not even subject to draft) would put in at least 60 "man-days"; every student in the sixth and seventh grades, 75; those in the eighth grade, 100; and those in the ninth and tenth grades not less than 130.[102]

Conscription for harvest labor, under the act of April 13, 1942, also applied to villagers. The act made it possible both to get additional work out of the farm population, and to draft the

[99] Decree of the CPC of the USSR and the CC of the CPSU of July 17, 1943, "on 1943 harvesting," *Izvestiya,* July 18, 1943.
[100] *Sotsialisticheskoye Zemledeliye,* July 18, 1944.
[101] *Pravda,* December 2, 1944.
[102] *Sotsialisticheskoye Zemledeliye,* June 20, 1944.

non-farming rural population. Other provisions issued on the same day[103] raised the mandatory minimum amount of "man-days" a year per *kolkhoz* member by 50 per cent and more. In July, 1942, even children of *kolkhoz* farmers (from 12 to 16) were called on for compulsory work on the collective farm, with a minimum annual performance of 50 "man-days." [104]

Previous regulations limiting the number of mandatory "man-days" for members of collective farms were practically scrapped in 1944. All *kolkhoz* farmers and their dependents over 14 were ordered to take part in harvest labor, "regardless of past performance of their man-day minimum task." [105]

Harvest decrees for 1942 and the following years ordered the mobilization of all non-farming rural residents for harvest labor.[106] The press did not say how this was accomplished. Collective farmers worked much harder during the war than in peacetime, but apparently more often than not without special coercion.

Provisions aimed at an emergency supply of manpower for industry and agriculture were supplemented by a system of measures to stimulate industrial employment of adolescents and their vocational training which were discussed in Chapter Two. In addition, special rules dealt with the age limit of compulsory schooling and with the employment of disabled persons.

In August, 1943, the age at which school attendance became compulsory was reduced from eight to seven in many schools, with the proviso that in the future this would be the rule.[107] The innovation was highly desirable: in most countries where attendance of elementary schools is mandatory, compulsory schooling starts at an earlier age But the lowering of the entrance age did not add to the length of the curriculum which in most public schools still ranged from four to seven years; in the future, graduates were merely to be a year younger. The provision was to serve long-range manpower policy; in the postwar years, the ranks

103 Decree of the CPC of the USSR and the CC of the CPSU of April 13, 1942, in *Laws and Ordinances*, 1942:61.

104 Decree of the CPC of the USSR and the CC of the CPSU "on 1942 harvesting," *Laws and Ordinances,* 1942:108.

105 Decree of the CPC of the USSR and the CC of the CPSU of July 19, 1944 "on 1944 harvesting," in *Sotsialisticheskoye Zemledeliye,* July 20, 1944. For details on "man-days,' cf. source reference in Chapter Two above, n. 64.

106 See nn. 99, 105 above.

107 V. Potemkin [the People's Commissar for Education of the RSFSR], "Impending School Tasks," *Pravda,* August 24, 1944.

of adult employables would be heavily thinned by the ravages of the war.

Another provision aimed at immediate reinforcements. In August, 1942, social insurance agencies were directed to order "all disabled beneficiaries in Group 3" to go to work within three months. The bulk of permanently disabled persons (men under 55 and women under 45) were to take jobs in industrial plants, public services, or government offices.[108] Instructions issued to plant and service managers said that "recommendations from committees of medical and labor experts" were to be taken into account in giving jobs to the disabled, and that they should not be compelled to work overtime. Beneficiaries of disability pensions accepting new employment were to continue to draw their regular allowances, no matter how much they earned in their new jobs; those who refused employment were to be stricken from the pension rolls at once. I have not been able to find any information disclosing how many disabled workers were put to work.

For the nature of the system of labor law as it developed in wartime, the measures designed to lower the school age and to enlist invalids in the labor process are of slight significance. The decisive feature was the extension of the system of restraint, of binding workers to the plant. Cracks in this system appeared, however, even before the end of the war. Discipline slackened first in the plants which had been moved eastward in the first year of the war. In 1943, when the Red Army waged its great offensive and reconquered major areas, the workers generally expected the relocated plants to be restored to their original locations. But the government decided that, as a rule, relocated plants would remain in their new locations, to be replaced at their former sites with newly equipped plants manned partly with personnel that had stayed on under the occupation and partly with newly recruited crews.

The authorities had failed to reckon with the fact that, having waited so long and confidently for their return, the workers and employees of the relocated enterprises would spontaneously set out for home. By the time it turned out that many evacuees were on their way it was scarcely possible to use the punitive measures provided in the law. Homeward migration assumed

---

[108] Decree of the CPC of the USSR of August 28, 1942, quoted from *Labor Legislation,* issued by the *AUCTUC,* Moscow, 1945, pp. 7 f.

alarming proportions. In September, 1944, *Pravda* discussed the trend in an editorial under a title reminiscent of the early 30's: "Fight Floating!" The Party newspaper said: [109]

> "Plants with considerable numbers of workers, engineers and technicians had been evacuated to the Urals, to Siberia, to Central Asia. These plants remain in the east. The people who went there did not come to stay a day or two.
> That people from Moscow and Leningrad, Kharkov and Odessa feel the urge to return to their home towns may be understandable. But the interests of the socialist state require that the relocated plants be kept east."

"Floating" had reappeared, in defiance of all laws and statutes. But what caused it was more than just "homesickness" on the part of evacuees. In the east workers from invaded regions were exposed to severe hardships. The *Pravda* editorial explained:[110]

> "Every facility must be created for the evacuated wage and salary earners so that they may settle down at the new location, make their homes there and feel all right. We must not let facts go unheeded: evacuated workers at the time had been assigned living quarters where they had to double up with the original tenants and now are being evicted while the prosecuting magistracy actually sanctions such unlawful eviction orders . . . We must not permit a situation which arises when in numerous plants in the Urals or in the Volga area not even reduced housing construction programs are carried out."

It soon appeared that the "floating" disease was deep-seated; it was by no means limited to evacuees. Hardly three weeks had elapsed when *Pravda* returned to the painful subject in an editorial on "The Most Important Condition for Further Growth of Socialist Industry." The things labeled "most important" were once more "permanency of workers in our plants, overcoming fluctuation, tying the labor force to production." What caused— in spite of the war emergency—the high rate of turnover? The editors of the Communist paper said: [111]

> ". . . In recent years millions of new, young workers came

[109] *Pravda,* September 7, 1944.
[110] *Ibid.*
[111] *Pravda,* September 24, 1944.

into industry who have not yet acquired factory habits, who have not been sufficiently instilled with the spirit of consciously applied socialist discipline . . . Furthermore, hundreds of thousands of workers who during the war were evacuated to the east with their plants, manifest the urge to return to their home towns liberated by the Red Army from the German occupiers . . . Finally, not all economic executives and Party organizations pay due attention to the everyday needs of men and women workers . . .

"To put and end to turnover, plant managers, Party, union, and Communist Youth organizations must seriously improve the servicing of the workers' everyday needs, pay greater attention to their working and living conditions . . .

"Is it not a disgrace for the managers of the Zlatoust metallurgical plant that the roof of the dormitory for blooming mill workers is in ruins, that the ceilings leak in many rooms, and that on rainy days the water pours down on the beds? Is it not a disgrace for the plant that the prosecuting magistracy had no alternative but to institute court-action against Zubkov, assistant plant manager in charge of living conditions, and Oseyev, chief of the municipal housing department?"

Examples of the kind were many. By the end of the month—still September, 1944—the Board of the People's Commissariat for the Tank Industry deliberated on questions relative to "tying manpower to the plants." It heard the assistant manager in charge of personnel of the Kirov (formerly Putilov) plant in Leningrad which had been relocated in the Urals, and sternly reprimanded him for neglect of the workers' living conditions.[112]

In October, 1944, the following story was reported by an *Izvestiya* correspondent from Alma-Ata, capital of the Kazakh Republic.[113] "One of the nation's largest plants, whose output is of great importance," had been evacuated in 1941. After three years, labor turnover was rampant in the plant: "In the first half of the current year [1944] the plant had to let go 1,067 employees for different reasons. Turnover is still on the increase. In the third quarter, 583 persons were released from work, while 300 left their jobs of their own accord."

Who should be surprised that the workers made efforts to escape? "Only one-third of the workers now live in relatively well-

---

112 *Pravda,* October 1, 1944.
113 *Izvestiya,* October 27, 1944.

kept dormitories. Other plant employees to this day have been living in places which they had originally been assigned under doubling-up regulations," which meant "under unbearable housing conditions." The emergency housing program was not being carried out—"instead of eighteen dormitory barracks and twenty two-family houses, only nine barracks have been built." Even these had been erected on a remote site, at four and a half miles walking distance from the plant, and "some 600 workers have to walk daily to and from work," since "neither the plant manager nor the City Soviet have taken care to provide transportation for the workers."

The widespread discussion of "floating" in the newspapers ceased after a few weeks, as often happens in the Soviet Union. This did not mean that labor turnover was vanquished; for the time being, as far as we can judge from occasional references in the press, it hardly seemed to diminish. Twelve months after the situation in the Kirov Works in the Ural Region had been raised at the Board of the People's Commissariat for the Tank Industry, the representative of the State Planning Commission traveled through Chelyabinsk province (in the Central and South Ural region). He noted a high rate of turnover in all plants of the region and stressed especially the bad conditions in the Kirov Works: "This is no accident. In seven months, the year's plan for residential construction in the plant has been only 18 per cent fulfilled." [114]

Soon the trouble affected even the railroads with their traditionally low rate of turnover. In the summer of 1946, they registered "large fluctuations in the labor force." [115] The textile industry, suffering from a particularly severe labor shortage after the war (cf. Chapter Two) and with every reason to seek to remove causes of turnover, was painfully affected by floating. [116]

How labor turnover could rise to such an extent with the decrees of June 26, 1940, and particularly of December 26, 1941, remaining in force, was never discussed in the papers. The legal situation after the end of the war was rather confused, anyway. Immediately after the end of the war with Germany, when the Soviet Union—which took no part in the Japanese war until

[114] *Izvestiya*, October 13, 1945.
[115] *Trud*, July 31, 1946.
[116] Report of the Minister for the Textile Industry, I. N. Sedin, at the budget debate of the Supreme Soviet of the USSR, cf. *Pravda*, October 18, 1946.

August 1945—was in fact no longer at war, the leading Soviet circles apparently intended to drop the wartime labor laws. In particular, this intention seemed implicit in the decree issued on July 7, 1945, by the Presidium of the Supreme Soviet of the USSR, "concerning an amnesty in connection with the victory over Germany." [117] In this decree, persons convicted of unauthorized departure from war plants received strikingly special treatment.[118] These "demobilization" sentiments did not last, however. As early as August, 1945, the press carried an interview with the Public Prosecutor of the USSR, K. P. Gorshenin, "on the strengthening of work discipline," [119] in which the supreme guardian of law and justice came out for vigorous prosecution of "floaters" and "truants" and expressly called for strict compliance with the decrees of both June 26, 1940, and December, 26, 1941. In fact, the decree of December 26, 1941— the central piece of wartime labor legislation—remained in force for a long time and was commented upon as the law of the land in the Soviet textbooks on labor law.[120] The textbook published in 1949 was the first to pass over the December 26 decree in silence.[121]

The decrees of February 13 and April 13, 1942, governing compulsory labor service, do not seem to have been applied any more after the war's end. On occasion—possibly from force of habit—men were still drafted for work, though much less extensively than in wartime. In the fall of 1946, for instance, the papers reported that in the towns of the Novosibirsk region 28,000 persons had been drafted for harvest work.[122]

Even the enforcement of the decree of June 26, 1940, seemed

---

[117] *Pravda,* July 8, 1945.

[118] Persons convicted of general crimes or misdemeanors were pardoned if their punishment did not exceed three years in jail; longer terms were merely to be reduced, and only terms not exceeding one year were to be expunged from the penal record. In striking contrast to this, persons convicted of unauthorized departure from war plants and sentenced, under the decree of December 26, 1941, to at least five years in jail were granted full pardons, with all punishments expunged from the record, and all pending indictments were quashed. This would hardly have been done if there had been no intention of repealing the decree of December 26.

[119] *Izvestiya,* August 23, 1945.

[120] N. D. Alexandrov and D. M. Genkin, eds., *Soviet Labor Law,* publ. by the People's Commissariat of Justice of the USSR, Moscow, 1946, pp. 278 and 282; N. D. Alexandrov and G. K. Moskalenko, *Soviet Labor Law,* published by the People's Commissariat of Justice of the USSR, Moscow, 1947, p. 256. See also *Labor Legislation* (as in n. 68) , 1947, p. 57.

[121] N. D. Alexandrov, ed., *Soviet Labor Law,* publ. by the People's Commissariat of Justice of the USSR, Moscow, 1949, pp. 280-282.

[122] *Sotsialisticheskoye Zemledeliye,* September 15, 1946.

to be somewhat uncertain in 1945 and 1946. This, however, was merely a passing phase. The Soviet government and the CPSU strove hard to overcome the weakening of their rigid system—an unavoidable wartime phenomenon—in many fields. In the field of labor policy, too, they soon seemed ready for a consistent pursuit of the course that had been foreshadowed in the last years before the Soviet entry in to the war and strikingly expressed in the "reform" of June, 1940.

Chapter Four

WAGES AND LIVING STANDARDS, I
(Up to 1941)

On the Threshold of the First Five-Year Plan. — Projected and Actual Wage Trends under the First Five-Year Plan. — Partial Remedies Against the Decline of Real Wages. — "Wage Scale Reform of 1931": Intensified Differentiation of Wages.—Projected and Actual Wage Trends under the Second Five-Year Plan. — Additional Sources of Income. — Selective Income and Consumption Policy. — Wage Trends under the Third Five-Year Plan. — Purchasing Power of Hourly Earnings in 1938. — An International Comparison of Real Wages in 1938. — Trade Union Wage Policies. — Socialist Competition. — Appendices: 1. Socialist Competition and the Working Masses. — 2. The Stakhanov movement as an Instrument of Labor Policy.

On the Threshold of the First Five-Year Plan

The years of civil war and economic decay brought a substantial decline in wages and living standards. Recovery began in 1921, and by the end of the NEP period the prewar level had been regained and probably slightly exceeded.

Tsarist Russia did not favor labor statistics; data on wages and working conditions before the revolution are accordingly scarce, and Soviet living cost statistics are not too reliable.[1] Thus all comparisons with conditions before the First World War are subject to reservation. Nevertheless, the official Soviet calcula-

---

[1] On the cost-of-living index, cf. my *Der Arbeitslohn und die Lohnentwicklung in Russland*, Jena, 1924, pp. 66-82; also S. Zagorsky, *Wages and Regulations of Conditions of Labor in the USSR*, International Labour Office, Studies and Reports, Series D, No. 19, Geneva, 1930, pp. 202 ff.

tions, which place the purchasing power of the average weekly earnings of industrial workers in 1927/28 at 111.2 per cent of the 1913 standard, may not be far from the truth. Of course, there were large variations in different industries. In mining, real wages in 1927/28 averaged 86.6 per cent of the 1913 standards; in the metal trades, 96.6 per cent; in the chemical industry, 142.5 per cent; in the manufacture of food and beverages, 166.1 per cent.[2] Yet even aside from statistical uncertainties such comparisons mean little. In the long run, after all, the extremely low wage level of Tsarist Russia cannot serve as a yardstick for the trend in later years.

A somewhat clearer picture may be obtained by comparing Soviet data on wages and prices with similar data for other countries, as gathered over a period of years by the International Labour Office. As a rule the Soviet Union kept aloof from this statistical work of the ILO, but in one instance the People's Commissariat for Labor of the USSR overcame its usual reserve, supplying the ILO with data on wages and food prices in Moscow, for April, 1928. These figures, along with corresponding data for a number of cities in other countries, were reworked by the ILO into index numbers, with the British standard (city of London) taken as 100. The following table permits a comparison of the purchasing power of wages in different countries:[3]

Real Wages in Various Countries in April, 1928

City	Index Numbers of Real Wages (Real Wages in London = 100)
Philadelphia	185
Ottawa	155
London	100
Stockholm	88
Amsterdam	85
Berlin	71
Paris	56
Moscow	50
Prague	47
Warsaw	40

[2] M. Romanov [the People's Commissar for Labor of the RSFSR at the time], "Performance, Wages and Cost of Labor in State Industry," *Ekonomicheskoye Obozreniye*, March 1929, p. 125.

[3] *International Labour Review*, October-November, 1928, pp. 658 f.

There are three reasons why these figures still show conditions in Russia in too optimistic a light. First, the ILO data for other cities were largely taken from wage rates, while the Moscow figures were computed on the basis of actual weekly earnings, which are generally higher than wage rates. Secondly, the calculation was chiefly based on the wages of skilled and semiskilled workers; but the difference between the wages of skilled and semiskilled workers on the one hand and unskilled workers on the other is much larger in the Soviet Union than in other countries. Third, and most important: the Moscow wage level is much less characteristic of conditions throughout the country than that of the other cities. In fact, in 1928 the average monthly earnings of industrial workers were 90.60 rubles in Moscow, against a national average of 66.90 rubles. Thus nominal wages in Moscow were 35.4 per cent above the national average, while differences in prices were relatively insignificant. In terms of real wages, industrial workers in Moscow earned 19.2 per cent more than the national average.[4]

True, workers in the Soviet Union enjoy certain advantages — mainly free social insurance, unknown in other countries — which somewhat improves the picture. Yet these can hardly offset the low level of real wages.[5]

In an earlier article,[6] analyzing the comparative wage standards of the Soviet Union and Germany in 1928, I came to the conclusion that the ratio of Russian-German real wages was not 50:71 (i.e., 70.5:100) as in the ILO table. I found "real wages in Moscow about one-third below those in Berlin, even if the Russian worker's non-contributory social insurance, longer vacations, and lower income tax burden are taken into account." Considering further the higher level of wages in Moscow as compared with the rest of the country, I estimated average real wages in Russian industry to be estimated at "hardly more than 50 per cent of the German ones."

This was true of 1928. But the winter of 1928/29, the first under the First Five-Year Plan, was a turning point in Russian

---

[4] A. Rashin, "Wages in Large-Scale Industry in 1927/28," *Statistika Truda,* November-December, 1928, pp. 8 f.

[5] Cf. detailed discussion at the close of Chapter Five.

[6] Cf. my article "Ein Lohnvergleich: Moskau-Berlin," *Gewerkschafts-Zeitung,* weekly issued by the German Federation of Trade Unions (ADGB), Berlin, 1928, No. 51, pp. 802 f.

wage trends. Economic recovery from 1921 to 1928 had gone hand in hand with a corresponding rise in the wage level, but from that time on there was a marked divergence of industrial progress on the one hand, and wage trends on the other.

Projected and Actual Wage Trends under the First Five-Year Plan

The First Five-Year Plan envisioned an enormous increase in both nominal and real wages, "The wage problem occupies a central place in the Five-Year Plan," said the official commentary. "In the final analysis, wages constitute the basic category of economic planning in the Soviet state." This was said to distinguish the Soviet state from capitalist countries, "where wages constitute a subordinate category and are regarded, in addition to other factors of cost, as the one to be lowered in principle, as far as possible." [7]

Over the five-year period, nominal monthly earnings of wage and salary earners in all occupational divisions were to rise 44.1 per cent, and in industry proper, 42.0 per cent.[8] At the same time, the cost-of-living index was to drop 14 per cent,[9] so that the increase in real wages would amount to 67.7 per cent in all occupational divisions, and to 65.1 per cent in industry.

Nominal wage increases greatly exceeded Plan estimates. As mentioned before, the First Five-Year Plan was declared terminated nine months ahead of time, on December 31, 1932, and average annual earnings in 1932 came to 1,427 rubles in all occupational divisions, as against 994 rubles planned for the year 1932/33. The increase over 1927/28 was 106.8 per cent. In industry proper, nominal earnings in 1932 averaged 1,466 rubles as against a Plan estimate of 1,187 rubles for the year 1932/33— a gain of 75.4 per cent over the year 1927/28.[10] This was the result of an inflationary trend marked by soaring living costs and declining real wages.

To conceal the drop in real wages, the cost-of-living index

[7] *Five-Year Plan of Economic Construction of the USSR*, Moscow, 1929, Vol. II, 2, p. 185.
[8] *Op. cit.*, pp. 208 f.
[9] *Op. cit.*, p. 186.
[10] *Second Five-Year Plan for the National Economy of the USSR*, Moscow, 1934, Vol. I, pp. 504 f.

was first revised and then withdrawn from publication.[11] The press continued to report the nominal wage boosts as if they were taking place at a stable price level.[12]

A view of the actual trend, as it evolved from the outset of the Five-Year Plan policy, is hampered by the fact that from the late Twenties until the middle of the Thirties we have to deal with two (and often more) independent and widely divergent price movements. This peculiarity of the price trend already appeared on the eve of the Five-Year Plan policy, when a private retail trade with higher (in some cases lower) prices developed alongside the state and cooperative stores. For a time, the price differences between the private and "socialized" markets remained relatively slight, so that the two markets could exist side by side without rationing. Soon, however, this became impossible.

A few data may illuminate these developments. Price index figures computed for both "sectors" of retail trade by the Institute of Economic Trends, an adjunct of the People's Commissariat for Finance, are compared in the following table: [13]

Retail Price Index Figures
(1913 = 100)

	"Socialized" Trade	Private Trade	Per Cent Ratio
	(1)	(2)	(2:1)
1925/26	202	224	110.9%
1926/27	191	226	118.3
1927/28	184	244	132.6
1928/29	192	308	160.4

Index trends in both sectors did not begin to diverge sharply until halfway through 1927/28.

According to other statistics, which unfortunately go back no further than 1927/28, the price index for the private sector topped that of the "socialized" sector by 24.4 per cent in 1927/28; and by 49.5 per cent in 1928/29; in the first half of 1929/30 the difference rose to 99.9 per cent.[14] The ratios for 1927/28 and

---

[11] See below, especially n. 15.

[12] *Fulfilling the First Five-Year Plan for the Economic Development of the USSR*, Moscow, 1933, pp. 178 f.

[13] *Ekonomicheskoye Obozreniye*, November 1929, p. 180.

[14] A. Averbukh, "Conditions of Price Formation and Real Wages in 1929/30," *Planovoye Khozyaistvo*, June, 1930, p. 86.

1928/29, as given in this series, lag behind the figures of the institute of Economic Trends; the latter series, if continued in the same form, would probably have shown the price index for private trade in 1929/30 at substantially more than 100 per cent above that of the socialized sector.[15]

The swiftly increasing divergence of the price levels in private and socialized trade was a symptom of the growing scarcity of goods, particularly in the socialized market. Only consumers unable to fill urgent needs in the socialized market were willing to pay the much higher prices of private trade. Shortages soon made the rationing of food and various manufactured consumer goods inevitable.

In the first revolutionary years, the Russians had felt all the

---

[15] From 1926 on, two separate series of cost-of-living indexes were computed, one based on prices in the private market, the other on a "weighted" mean of "socialized" and private prices. The divergent curves of these two series did not fully reflect the discrepancy of prices in the two "sectors," as the second series was not exclusively based on prices in the "socialized" market but also included prices in the private market. The two series (according to *Ekonomicheskoye Obozreniye*, December, 1928, pp. 200 f.) show the following development:

Cost-of-Living Index of the Central Bureau of Labor Statistics
(1913 = 100)

	Weighted Prices (1)	Prices in Private Trade (2)	Per Cent Ratio (2:1)
1925/26	218.5	227.3	104.0%
1926/27	215.7	229.6	106.4
1927/28	217.3	244.7	112.6

Figures for both series were last released (*Ekonomicheskoye Obozreniye*, February, 1929, pp. 205 f.) as of January 1, 1929: weighted prices, 229.7; private trade prices, 274.3. The latter was already 19.4 per cent above the former. Thereafter publication of the cost-of-living index based on prices current in private trade was discontinued, and the index of weighted prices was remodeled (and lowered). But even in its revised form the living-cost index was no longer published after September 1, 1929 (last release in *Ekonomicheskoye Obozreniye*, September, 1929, p. 189). The revised index was still computed, though, for a while longer; in publications by officials of the economic administration, scattered figures were mentioned occasionally. The index seems to have been definitely discontinued in 1931, or perhaps as early as 1930.

Ekonomicheskoye Obozreniye itself, a monthly issued by the Supreme Economic Council, which regularly published the index series, was suspended in the spring of 1930 and merged with another monthly, *Planovoye Khozyaistvo*, issued by the State Planning Commission. After the merger, publication of statistical tables relative to economic trends was stopped. At the same time, *Planovoye Khozaistvo* absorbed *Statisticheskoye Obozreniye*, the monthly of the Central Statistical Office. Statistical tables regularly published by the latter concerning economic developments also were discontinued.

Earlier, *Statistika Truda* had been suspended without being incorporated with any other peridoical. Business trend reports of the Supreme Economic Council, which usually contained valuable material on the trends of labor, income and consumption, were no longer released after 1930, either (last release—on economic trends in October 1930—in *Za Industrializatsiyu*, November 23, 1930).

hardships of rationing. Economic recovery in the days of NEP made rationing unnecessary; it was abondoned and not resumed until the late 1920's. Some cities in Southern Russia and the Ukraine reintroduced bread cards in 1928, with Odessa starting in the spring. Leningrad followed suit in January 1929, Moscow in March. Cereals too were rationed in Moscow in March 1929, sugar, tea, butter, oil, macaroni, herrings, and soap in April, eggs and meat in September, potatoes and textiles in October.

By early 1930, most basic foods and many essential consumer goods were rationed not only in the big cities but almost everywhere in the country, in towns and sometimes in villages. The rationing setup was expanded and differentiated. In 1930, 26,000,-000 consumers held ration cards, in 1931, 33,200,000, in 1932, 40,300,000. In 1933, the lists were combed out and the total dropped to 39,000,000; in 1934, it rose again to 40,300,000.[16]

Only goods sold in the "socialized" sector were rationed; private trade remained exempt. The tacit assumption was that rationing would provide for the bulk of the workers' consumption. In fact, however, they could fill only a fraction of their needs with the rationed foods and consumer goods. From 1930 on the actual distribution of rationed goods shrank perceptibly in many places. In 1931 differential rules were established, with rationing reduced for large groups of consumers, including workers. In 1934, when differentiation was at its peak, only bread and sugar were rationed generally for all of the 40,300,00 consumers, while cereal cards were issued to only 11,500,000, meat cards to 6,600,000, butter cards to 3,300,000 and oil cards to 5,200,000.[17]

Even these figures applied only on paper. The number actually supplied with the goods to which their ration cards entitled them was substantially less. Many consumers were thus compelled either to shop in the private market or to cut down considerably on their consumption.

Even if prices had remained stable in both sectors of the retail trade, the shift of consumer purchasing from the socialized to the private sector would have forced up living costs. With

---

16 G. Zberzhkovsky, "A Transcended Stage," *Sovetskaya Torgovlya*, November—December, 1934, pp. 14 ff.; see also L. Hubbard, *Soviet Trade and Distribution*, London, 1938, pp. 29-35; Abram Bergson, *The Structure of Soviet Wages. A Study in Socialist Economics*, Cambridge, Mass., 1944, pp. 36-43.

17 Zberzhkovsky, *op. cit.*, p. 17.

prices soaring, particularly in the private market, the squeeze grew increasingly painful.

The cost-of-living index was last published in September, 1929. Scattered references in the press [18] indicate that in the fourth quarter of 1929 it was 7.9 or 9.8 per cent higher than in the same period of the previous year. In these calculations the shift of consumer purchasing from the socialized to the private sector seems to have been ignored; they were evidently based on the fiction that the consumers could buy almost everything they needed in government or cooperative stores.

Of greater interest are figures on the price trend based on consumer budget statistics which the periodical of the State Planning Commission published, as an exception, in the summer of 1931. From these data, living costs in October, 1930, the first month of the economic year 1930/31, may be computed as 144.8 per cent in excess of the average cost-of-living level in the year 1927/28.[19]

As prices really began to soar in the spring of 1931, the increase for the whole economic year ending on September 30, 1931, must

----

[18] Averbukh, as quoted supra, n. 14, p. 38; V. Bunimovich, "The Five-Year Plan and the Real Wage Level," *Na Planovom Fronte,* 1930, No. 7, p. 24.

[19] The data of the State Planning Commission are based on consumer budget inquiries and consist of two series of weighted price indexes wherein the figure for every quarterly period is computed as a percentage of the price level during the same period of the previous year, The first series compares current household expenditures at actual prices and at prices prevailing in the same period of the previous year. The second series compares household expenditures during the corresponding period of the previous year as it actually occurred with the cost of the identical quantity of goods at current prices, and the index number indicates the increase in cost which would have occurred were the same quantity of goods consumed in the period under investigation as had been consumed in the same period of the previous year.

The first series disguises the actual increase in the cost of living because it is based on a budget in which both quantity and quality of goods consumed are presumably no longer the same as they were a year earlier, the family budget having been adapted in the course of the year to changes in prices and availability of goods.

Yet the increase in living costs during a period of several years is not adequately reflected in the second series, either, for the latter's construction sets as a basis standard for the period under investigation the quantity and quality of goods consumed in the previous year. The increase in living costs over an extended period of time appears smaller than it was in actuality and than it would appear statistically if computed according to the quantity and quality of goods consumed during the initial period, *viz.,* in this particular case, in the course of the economic year 1927/28.

With these reservations, the data published in the periodical of the State Planning Commission (G. Polyak, "Contribution to the Problem of the Standard of Living of the Working Class," *Planovoye Khozyaistvo,* May-June, 1931, p. 68) may give some indications as to the incidence of living costs. These data are as follows:

have been considerably higher. During the first three years of the First Five-Year Plan, living costs rose certainly by 150, and perhaps nearly 200 per cent.

Did the workers' income increase correspondingly? The following date refer to annual *per capita* earnings: [20]

Price Index of Household Expenditure
(as percentage of expenditure in the same period of the previous year)

	Based on Items Consumed During the Period under Investigation	Based on Items Consumed During the Same Period of the Previous Year
4th quarter 1928	105.6	106.5
1st quarter 1929	109.0	110.5
2nd quarter 1929	116.7	118.1
3rd quarter 1929	115.1	116.7
Average for the year 1928/29	111.6	113.0
4th quarter 1929	114.5	115.5
1st quarter 1930	114.7	116.7
2nd quarter 1930	117.8	121.3
3rd quarter 1930	139.5	148.0
Average for the year 1929/30	121.6	125.4
October 1930	144.8	163.4

During 1928/29 prices according to the first series rose 11.6 per cent as compared with the annual average for the preceding year; and 13.0 per cent according to the second series. For the year 1929/30 the corresponding figures are 21.6 and 25.4 per cent, respectively. If one were to regard figures for October, 1930, as representative of the entire year 1930/31, the increase in this latter year would amount to 44.8 or 63.4 per cent, respectively. As prices continued rising and actually skyrocketed from the spring of 1931 on, this appears to be a definite understatement.

Price increases over the entire three-year period under review may best be measured by the second series which indicates yearly increases in the cost of living during the first three years of the First Five-Year Plan of 13.0, 25.4, and 63.4 per cent, respectively. Hence, according to this index, the cost of living during the year 1930/31 was 131.5 per cent above the level of the year 1927/28.

However, it was pointed out before that price increases for every individual year were computed on the basis of actual consumer choice a year earlier and failed to express previous changes in quantity and quality of household consumption as against the initial year. To eliminate this source of error, all index numbers must be recalculated on the basis of the actual consumer budget in the year 1927/28. This shows the total increase during the three-year period under review to have been 144.8 per cent. Since these figures did not take sufficient account of torrential price rises since the spring of 1931 (as only the monthly figure for October, 1930, was available), another correction has to be made. It will then appear that the actual increase in the cost of living in the first three years of the First Five-Year Plan period was higher than 150 per cent and perhaps 200 per cent.

[20] Data for 1927/28 from *Five-Year Plan* . . ., as quoted supra, n. 7, Vol. II, 2, p. 208. Data for 1930/31 were computed from figures discussed by V. Tsybul'sky, *Wage Policy in the USSR During Fifteen Years of Proletarian Dictatorship*, Moscow, 1932, p. 31. Average annual earnings of workers in all occupational divisions, according to Tsybul'sky, amounted to 933 rubles in 1930, and 1,096 rubles in 1931;

	Total Economy	Industry Proper
	(Rubles)	
1927/28	690	836
1930/31	1,055	1,115

In three years, the nominal earnings of wage and salary earners increased 63.6 per cent in the economy as a whole, and 33.4
per cent in industry proper—with prices climbing between 150
and 200 per cent. That is to say, real wages declined about 40 per
cent in the total economy, and some 50 per cent in industry.

To illustrate the trend, let us turn from index figures to
sober, everyday facts. Rationing, as introduced in 1928 and 1929,
was confined to the "socialized" sector of retail trade. Alongside
it, the private sector grew and thrived—not as a black market
but as a legal open market. In fact, from 1930 on the state and
the cooperatives themselves engaged in the so-called "commercial
trade," a retailing method outside the rationing system, at prices
approximating those of the private trade. Accordingly, the dis-
tinction between "socialized" and "private" sectors of trade was
dropped, in favor of one between "organized" (rationed) and
"unorganized" marketing. The former was carried on at relatively
low, fixed prices, the latter at the high inflationary prices.

Consumer purchasing was soon largely driven from the "organized" market into the "unorganized" one. For instance, in
drawing up the annual plan for 1929/30 it was estimated that
from 90 to 95 per cent of the workers' consumption would be
supplied at fixed prices, and the wage scales for the year were based
upon this assumption. But when the convention of the *Tsentrosoyuz* (Central Association of Consumer Cooperatives) met in
July, 1930, a spokesman for the People's Commissariat for Worker
and Peasant Control announced: [21]

> "Last year the share of private trade in the Ural province
> was 42 per cent; this year it has risen to 47 per cent of total
> sales. In the Kuznetsk Basin, Siberia, the share of private trade
> has risen from 27 to 44 per cent . . . The worker is compelled to
> patronize private trade."

The statement referred to regions where supply conditions

---

in industry proper, to 1,016 and 1,146 rubles, respectively. On this, estimates, as
indicated in the text for the economic year 1930/31, may safely be based.

[21] *Za Industrializatsiyu*, July 25, 1930.

were notoriously bad, but it permitted inferences on the general trend. Things grew worse in 1931. The official "commercial prices" were lowered a little, slightly depressing the price level of the private market, but the effects were offset by the rapid shrinkage of the "organized" sector. On the whole, real wages continued to decline.

The trend towards "unorganized" distribution was intensified and affected even Moscow and Leningrad, cities usually better supplied on the "organized" plane. The central trade union newspaper noted with concern that "a number of cooperatives and governmental trade organizations" had developed peculiar practices: "enthusiasm for commercial trade, removal of goods from the stocks earmarked for workers, and sale of these goods at commercial prices." [22] The newspaper of the industrial administration gave a colorful account of cooperative stores in Moscow in which commodities not available for rationed distribution were sold in large quantities at commercial prices.[23] The milk business of cooperatives in Moscow and Leningrad attracted particular attention: in the "organized" sector milk had then to be obtainable only for small children who were allowed half a liter[24] a day; in addition, it was distributed in factories, to employees engaged in work detrimental to health. But the plan for "organized" milk distribution in Leningrad was only 54 per cent fulfilled in September, 1931, and only 28 per cent in the first half of October; in Moscow, it was only 29 per cent fulfilled through July-September. Yet at the same time, the cooperatives, the pillars of "organized" marketing, sold milk and dairy products at "commercial" prices—for, while a liter of rationed milk cost 0.36 rubles in Leningrad, the same liter, sold in "commercial trade," brought the cooperative store 1.10 rubles.[25]

Curtailment of "organized marketing" began in 1932. On March 23[26] the CPC of the USSR decided to "continue food rationing only for flour, bread, cereals, meat, herring, butter,

---

22 *Trud,* November 26, 1931.
23 *Za Industrializatsiyu,* November 22, 1931.
24 A liter = 1.057 quarts, hence half a liter is somewhat more than a pint.
25 *Za Industrializatsiyu,* November 14 and 17, 1931.
26 The decision was not published until seven weeks after it was adopted (and actually became effective). As the curtailment of food rationing was bound to make a very unfavorable impression on the masses, it was evidently deemed expedient to keep the official news from the reader as long as possible.

oil, and sugar." [27] In most cities only bread and sugar remained on the list. The distribution of rationed bread became disorganized. Bread lines came to be an everyday spectacle as in the civil war years. From Moscow [28] and Leningrad,[29] and even more from other cities, came reports on "giant bread lines" in Kharkov;[30] "panic at bakeries," "endless bread lines" in Tiflis; [31] nighttime bread lines in Stalingrad,[32] etc.

When the new harvest was in, the acute crisis could be alleviated. But there was no rebuilding the rationed distribution of foods. It wasted away until it was abandoned in 1935.

The disparity in prices between the "organized" and "unorganized" sectors may be seen from the following table: [33]

Food Prices in Moscow, 1927-1932
(Kopecks per unit[x])

A: Prices in "organized" (in 1928, "socialized") supply
B: Prices in "commercial" (in 1928, "private") trade

		April 1928	November 1931	Average 1932
Rye bread	A	8	7.5	12.5
	B	8.4	...	250
Wheat bread	A	26[xx]	15	17.5
	B	30	...	400
Beef	A	87	100	212
	B	89.8	600	600
Milk	A	6.3	30	...
	B	8.7	200	85 to 100
Butter	A	243	410	466
	B	...	1800	1600 to 1800
Oil	A	...	...	170
	B	...	...	450 to 500
Sugar	A	62	58	95 to 125 [xxx]
	B	...	250	250 to 300 [xxx]

[x] Kilogram (equals to 2.2046 lbs.), except in the case of milk, where the price is for a liter (equal to 1.057 quarts).

[xx] Judging from the high price, and the price differential between rye and wheat bread, this refers to genuine white bread rather than the gray wheat bread of the later figures.

[xxx] The lower figure is for granulated sugar, the higher for cube sugar.

[27] Pravda, May 11, 1932.
[28] Za Industrializatsiyu, June 9, 1932.
[29] Za Industrializatsiyu, June 20, 1932.
[30] Snabzheniye, Kooperatsiya i Torgovlya, June 16, 1932.
[31] Snabzheniye, Kooperatsiya i Torgovlya, June 27, 1932.
[32] Snabzheniye, Kooperatsiya i Torgovlya, July 18, 1932.
[33] Data for 1928 from International Labour Review, October-November, 1928,

Workers and employees were severely affected by the dwindling "organized" supply and the sky-high prices of the "unorganized" market. As early as 1928/29, the first year under the Five-Year Plan, a "deterioration of the consumption pattern" was discussed in official publications. Still, while the calories consumed *per capita* in workers' families slowly declined from 1925/26 to 1927/28, the proportion of animal substances in the total calory intake increased, and the overall trend was not considered unfavorable. "1928/29 was the turning point"; now, for the first time, the drop in the caloric value of food consumed (from 2,392 to 2,338) was accompanied by a drop in the proportion of animal substance in total intake (from 17.2 to 16.2 per cent), although the calory intake of animal substances had been strikingly low from the start. The first five months of the economic year 1929/30 (October 1929 through February 1930) were again "characterized by an abrupt decline in the consumption of highly nourishing foods (meat, wheat bread, sugar and butter)." [34]

Similar reports soon followed for the whole year 1930. "Meat and dairy products play a much smaller part in 1930 nutrition." To make up for scarce animal foodstuffs, people ate more vegetable products, especially bread and potatoes. But bread consumption also showed a "deterioration of the pattern": less nourishing wheat and more rye. [35]

The decline in the *per capita* consumption of basic foods in 1929 and 1930, according to household surveys in workers' families is shown in the following table: [36]

(see table on page 143)

This was only the beginning. The deterioration of the workers' consumption continued throughout the First Five-Year Plan Period, although it was not as striking as the drop in real wages.

---

p. 659; for November, 1931, from a Moscow dispatch by Günther Stein in *Berliner Tageblatt*, November 29, 1931; for 1932, from *Byuleten' Ekonomicheskogo Kabineta*, published by S. N. Prokopovicz, Prague, No. 124 (October, 1935), p. 91. (Professor Prokopovicz had access to a number of Soviet sources which are not available in New York.)

[34] E. O. Kabo, "Problems of Nutrition," in *At the Latest Stage of Socialist Construction,* symposium published by the Economic Research Institute of the State Planning Commission, Vol. I, Moscow, 1930, pp. 281 ff.

[35] Polyak, as quoted *supra,* n. 19, p. 68.

[36] *Ibid.*

Annual Food Consumption in Workers' Families
Kilogram Per Capita

Food	1928/29 (1)	1929/30 (2)	Per Cent Ratio (2:1)
Rye flour and bread[x]	57.2	78.8	137.8%
Wheat flour and bread[x]	93.1	73.9	79.4
Cereals	15.7	16.7	106.4
Potatoes	114.7	154.7	134.8
Other vegetables	53.6	62.0	115.7
Meat and fats	51.0	40.7	80.0
Fish	11.0	16.8	152.7
Milk	77.7	79.5	102.3
Butter	2.4	2.2	91.8
Oil	3.8	3.4	89.5
Eggs	4.3	3.4	79.1
Sugar	15.6	12.8	82.1

[x] Bread in terms of flour content.

Partial Remedies against the Decline of Real Wages

Several factors counteracted the disastrous effect of reduced purchasing power. Two phenomena tended under the First Five-Year Plan to show the development of workers' living standards in a somewhat more favorable light than the trend of real wages would suggest: the vast extension of so-called "public feeding," and the increase in the number of gainfully employed members of working-class families.

Soviet "public feeding" means the sale of food (mostly hot food) in canteens of the "socialized" sector to which foodstuffs were supplied at low "standardized" rates, thus in turn enabling them to sell meals at prices that a worker could afford. With the rationed "organized" market dwindling and prices in private trade and in the government-operated "commercial" market climbing steadily, these public eating places were many a worker's only chance to feed himself somehow.

Under the First Five-Year Plan, the sales volume of the socialized sector canteens increased as follows: [37]

[37] N. Ryauzov, "Public Feeding in 1933," *Sovetskaya Torgovlya*, March-April, 1934, p. 48. Data refer to public eating places operated by the *Tsentrosoyuz* (Central Association of Consumer Cooperatives) or by the People's Commissariat for Food Supply, i.e. the overwhelming majority of public eating places within the "socialized sector." Other eating places (school canteens, cafeterias attached to large apartment buildings, etc.) were of secondary importance.

Year	Million Rubles	Year	Million Rubles
1928	102	1931	2,200
1929	207	1932	4,385
1930	800		

The increase in sales was partly due to rising prices, although in general the canteens did not shift the higher food prices to their customers in higher meal prices as much as in lower-quality meals. The second half of the First Five-Year Plan period brought especially vocal complaints about "public feeding." Yet for the bulk of the workers it remained the only chance to keep body and soul together.

Yet another development counteracted the decline in real wages: in workers' families, many members were now working for wages who had hitherto been living on the earnings of the head of the family. A few data may be added to underscore what has been said in Chapter Two. According to household surveys based on a large sample of workers' families, the number of persons gainfully employed per family unit rose from the inception of the Five-Year Plan—slowly at first, more rapidly later: [38]

	Gainfully Employed Per Family Unit
4th quarter 1928	1.23
1st quarter 1929	1.24
2nd quarter 1929	1.25
3rd quarter 1929	1.26
4th quarter 1929	1.28
1st quarter 1930	1.30
2nd quarter 1930	1.33
3rd quarter 1930	1.35
4th quarter 1930	1.43
1st quarter 1931	1.45

At first sight, it might appear that the trend reached its peak in 1931, with an average for the year of 1.45 employed per family unit; the number dropped to 1.44 in 1932, and remained at that level for the next two years.[39] Actually the trend continued—for the average family grew smaller and the total number of members in relation to the gainfully employed declined, as is apparent from the following figures: [40]

---

[38] Polyak, as quoted *supra,* n. 19, p. 66.
[39] *Labor in the USSR. Statistical Abstract for* 1934, Moscow, 1935, p. 266.
[40] Data for November, 1927, from G. Polyak, "Household and Family," *Eko-*

Economic Structure of Worker's Family (Yearly Averages)

Year	Size of Family	Providers	Dependents	Dependents for Each Provider
1927[x]	4.26	1.23	3.03	2.46
1930	4.02	1.32	2.70	2.05
1931	3.96	1.45	2.51	1.73
1932	3.93	1.44	2.49	1.73
1933	3.87	1.44	2.43	1.69
1934	3.83	1.44	2.39	1.66
1935	3.80	1.47	2.33	1.59

[x] November only.

If the newly-employed family members had earned as much, on the average, as the heads of the families, the *per capita* improvement in the workers' budget between 1927 and 1935 would have amounted to nearly 34 per cent, other things being equal. Actually, of course, the improvement was less; young workers seldom made as much as experienced older workers. Still, the increase in the number of gainfully employed members of working-class families, accompanied by a reduction in a family size, considerably cushioned the effects of lower real wages.

"Wage Scale Reform of 1931": Intensified Differentiation of Wages

Russian workers had experienced an inflationary decline in purchasing power before—on the eve of the Revolution and in the first revolutionary years. About the same time, similar phenomena appeared in other European countries. A certain leveling of wages is inherent in inflationary trends: any marked lowering of workers' living standards leads almost automatically to a tendency to make more extensive cuts in wages at the higher income levels of labor than in wages that do not even guarantee a bare subsistence.

In the Soviet Union, such leveling of wages was deliberately promoted in the first revolutionary years.[41] But the First Five-

---

nomicheskoye Obozreniye, March, 1930, p. 85; for later years, from *Labor in the USSR. Statistical Abstract for* 1935, Moscow, 1936, p. 342.

[41] Cf. my *Der Arbeitslohn . . .,* as quoted *supra,* n. 1, pp. 19-25.

Year Plan featured the opposite policy: from 1931 on—with inflation at its peak—there were conscious, methodical efforts to carry wage differentiation to the most far-reaching extremes.

The slogan was: "Fight petty-bourgeois egalitarianism!" A superficial reader of Soviet newspapers could indeed get the impression that wages in the USSR had largely leveled off in the late 1920's. The real picture was different. Inequality of wages had been marked in Tsarist Russia, where skilled workers were few and unskilled ones glutted the labor market; widely graduated wages become a sort of tradition which was not actively countered until the first revolutionary years. But with the inauguration of the NEP the leveling idea was abandoned and a new, intensified wage differentiation was begun.[42]

Its ultimate effects were so anti-social that by 1927 the trade unions were obliged to come out against its excesses. A revision of union wage scales, carried out in 1927/28, actually succeeded in narrowing the gap between the wages of skilled and unskilled workers. But the difference in pay remained great.

For the purpose of determining pay, the Russian union collective contract divides employees into "wage classes" for which different index figures are set, starting with 1.0 for the lowest class (Class 1). The pay agreed upon in wage negotiations for Class 1 is then automatically multiplied for the higher classes with the index figure set for each. The result is a wage scale (termed "wage net" in Russian). The typical scale after the reform of 1927/28 fixed the multiplying factor for the top class (usually Class 8) at 2.8—in other words, wages in the highest class were 180 per cent above those in the lowest. Higher differentials were set for individual industries: in mining wages in the highest class were three times those of the lowest, in textiles, 3.5 times as much.[43] These rates were for manual work; special scales were set for managerial, clerical, and technical employees.

Metal workers, for example, were paid according to the following scale:

---

[42] *Op. cit.*, pp. 61-66.

[43] V. Radzyminsky, "Planning of Wages," *Voprosy Truda,* November-December, 1931, p. 46.—Concerning the reaction in 1927 against the growing differentiation of wages, see Abram Bergson, as quoted n. 16, *supra,* pp. 186-189.

Class	Index Figure	Wage Increase over Preceding Class
1	1.0	—
2	1.2	20.0%
3	1.45	20.8
4	1.7	17.2
5	1.95	14.7
6	2.2	12.8
7	2.5	13.6
8	2.8	12.0

The differentials increased absolutely, from lower to higher brackets, but the relative increment decreased in the upper brackets—i.e., earnings of a top employee did not exceed those of his immediate inferior by the same percentage as did those of the lower wage "classes." [44] A few years later, such scales were *ex post facto* condemned as "sliding down an inclined plane" [45] and branded as "opportunistic deviationism," if not indeed a crime: [46]

> "Because of the opportunists in the trade unions and in the People's Commissariat for Labor, the wage scale reform of 1927/28 became the starting point for an intensive unfolding of petty-bourgeois egalitarianism.

[44] To give the reader a clear picture of the actual extent of wage differentiation, we may note here the proportion of wage earners in different wage rate brackets. By industries, the following percentages were recorded by A. Rashin, "Differentiation of Wages in Industry in March 1929," *Statistika Truda*, October-November, 1929, p. 3, (by that time the "reform" of the rate schedules introduced in 1927/28 was in full operation) :

Per Cent Workers in Different Wage Categories

Wage Bracket	Electrical Appliances and Equipment	Special Machines	Transportation Machinery	Iron and Steel	Printing and Allied Trades	Rubber
1	10.3%	8.5%	6.2%	8.9%	1.3%	4.7%
2	31.4	23.6	24.8	15.9	13.3	22.3
3	20.2	28.2	25.7	24.7	12.7	43.6
4	14.5	15.3	19.7	20.3	14.6	16.8
5	12.1	11.7	13.0	15.3	15.3	8.9
6	7.8	7.9	7.1	8.6	22.0	2.5
7	3.5	4.0	2.9	4.9	14.6	1.1
8	.2	.8	.6	1.4	6.2	.1
Total	100%	100%	100%	100%	100%	100%

[45] Tsybul'sky, as quoted *supra*, n. 20, p. 19.

[46] R. Vladimirov, "Workers in the USSR over a period of 15 years," *Voprosy Truda*, November-December, 1932, p. 29.

"The unionist theoreticians of that period zealously pro-pounded petty-bourgeois, anti-Party, egalitarian theories. In his *ABC of Wage Theory and Practice,* Gurevich wrote that 'the main task of the working class in our country and of its trade unions is the gradual elimination of the distinctions created by capitalism in the remuneration of workers.' The Eighth Trade Union Convention [in December, 1928] gave a political founda-tion to this rightist-opportunistic tendency and was pleased to note, after Ginzburg's report, that 'the gap between the earnings of skilled and unskilled workers has narrowed.' "

Thus "opportunistism" was still in full sway in December, 1928. In 1932, the AUCTUC reported to the Ninth Trade Union Convention: "It is only thanks to the direct, specific intervention of the CC of the Party and of Comrade Stalin that the trade unions have begun to tear down the old system and expunge egalitarianism. Pursuant to instructions of Comrade Stalin, the AUCTUC, in the second half of 1931, initiated the revision of wage scales. This revision was first carried out in the most impor-tant industries." [47]

The first scales set in accordance with the new principles were jointly approved by the AUCTUC and the SEC of the USSR [48] for the coke industry (on September 5, 1931), for the iron and steel industry and for coal mining (on September 20), and for iron and manganese mining (on September 28). These deci-sions no longer set index figures but directly determined pay rates for the various wage classes. In addition, special scales were set for time and piece work in the coke industry and in ore mining. In all cases the gap between the lowest and highest rates was con-siderably widened:

Bottom-to-Top^x Ratio

	Coke Industry	Iron and Man-ganese Mining
In time work	1:3.3	1:3.7
In piece work	1:3.2	1:3.75
Time-work low to piece-work high	1:4.4	1:4.5

x Class 7 in the coke indutry, Class 8 in iron and manganese mining.

In the iron and steel industry, and in coal mining, wage dif-

---

[47] *Material to the Report Submitted by the AUCTUC to the Ninth Trade Union Convention,* Moscow, 1932, p. 47.
[48] *Izvestiya Narkomtruda,* 1931, pp. 682-691.

ferentials were in part even more drastic. In coal mining, the provision of September 20 established a single scale for 11 classes, with daily wages ranging from a low 1.60 rubles in Class 1 to a high of 7.00 rubles in Class 11, or 1:4.4. Iron and steel mills were divided into three groups, and within each group not two but three different scales were set for manual workers: for piece work in metallurgical departments, for piece work in other departments, and for time work. Actual wages in plants in the highest wage group were as follows: [49]

Daily Wages in Rubles

Class	Piece Work in Metallurgy	Piece Work in Other Departments	Time Work
1	3.50	3.05	2.30
2	4.25	3.70	2.78
3	5.10	4.45	3.36
4	6.20	5.40	4.07
5	7.50	6.53	4.90
6	9.00	7.90	5.95
7	11.50	10.08	7.60
8	13.00	---	---

For piece work in the metallurgical departments the bottom-to-top-class ratio was 1:3.7, for piece work in other departments and for time work it was 1:3.3. But the ratio of the lowest time rate (time work, Class 1) to the highest piece rate (piece work in metallurgy, Class 8) was 1:5.5; the daily wages (without overtime, progressive piece-work premium, or bonuses) of the highest-paid worker were 450 per cent above those of his lowest-paid co-worker at the bottom of the pyramid.

From the data in the table, we can also compute relative increases.[50] In absolute figures, the differentials rose enormously

---

[49] *Ibid.*

[50] From the table in the text the following schedules of rate increases may be computed:

Increase in Daily Wage Rates over Preceding Class

Class	Piece Work in Metallurgy		Piece Work in Other Departments		Time Work	
	Rubles	Per Cent	Rubles	Per Cent	Rubles	Per Cent
2	.75	21.4%	.65	21.3%	.48	20.9%
3	.85	20.0	.75	20.3	.58	20.9
4	1.10	21.6	.95	21.3	.71	21.1
5	1.30	21.0	1.13	20.9	.83	20.4
6	1.50	20.0	1.37	21.0	1.05	21.4
7	2.50	27.8	2.18	27.6	1.65	27.7
8	1.50	13.0	---	---	---	---

from class to class; but even the percentage of each increment no longer decreased at the top of the scale. It remained relatively stable (between 20.0 and 21.6 per cent) in Classes 2 to 6 and rose steeply in Class 7 (Class 8 in metallurgical departments—piece work—was practically a subdivision of Class 7).

Differentiation of wage rates was but one of many weapons against "egalitarianism." Greater results were to be obtained with incentive wages, especially in the form of progressive piece rates, as emphasized in the "wage scale reform" of 1931. Stress on piece work had by then characterized Soviet wage policy for years. Since the late 1920's, premium wages, too, had been fairly widespread. What was new in the measures of 1931 was the general tendency to base wages on piece rates rising with the increase of the individual worker's actual output.

The most elaborate progression scales were devised. Leading trade union circles especially favored a wage system which would raise or cut piece rates by percentages corresponding to output above or below an established "performance quota." If, for example, a worker's actual output exceeded his quota by 20 per cent, the basic piece rate for his total output, not only for that in excess of the quota, would be raised 20 per cent. Conversely, if he fulfilled only 80 per cent of his quota, the basic piece rate would drop 20 per cent.

As the tendency was to base quotas upon the performance of the "shock-brigade worker," if not the "best shock-brigade worker," such a system was bound to have a painful effect on the workers in general.[51] Fortunately, this extreme idea was dropped when the new wage schedules were worked out in 1931.

A unified system of progressive piece-work rates did not emerge at all. Even in the joint decisions of the AUCTUC and the Supreme Economic Council, which introduced new wage scales for individual industries in September, 1931, piece-work rates were based upon two different principles.[52]

In the coke industry the following incentive system was set up: base pay for output up to 50 per cent of the quota; 120 per cent of base pay for the next 30 per cent of the quota; 150 per

---

[51] More about these tendencies in my article "At the Labor Front" in *Sotsialisticheski Vestnik*, Berlin, 1931, No. 10, p. 6.

[52] See n. 48 *supra*.

cent of base pay for the last 20 per cent of the quota; and 180 per cent of base pay for all output exceeding the quota.

Similar scales were introduced in the iron and steel industry: base pay for output up to one-third of the quota; 20 per cent more for anything between one and two-thirds; 50 per cent more for the last third; and 80 per cent more for all output above the quota.

A different system prevailed in coal, manganese and iron mining. Here the base rate applied to all output within the quota, with graduated extra pay for excess production only. In iron and manganese mining the first 10 per cent above quota was paid at 120 per cent of the base rate; the next 10 per cent at 150 per cent of the base rate; and all output exceeding the quota by more than 20 per cent at 180 per cent of the base rate. Similarly in coal mining: 125 per cent of base pay for the first 10 per cent above quota, 140 per cent of base pay for the next 10 per cent; and 180 per cent of base pay for anything further.

The disadvantages of a piece-rate system with differentials for below-quota performance were soon apparent. A joint decision of the People's Commissariat for Heavy Industry and the AUCTUC of October 26, 1932,[53] abolished such differentials in the iron and steel industry and set a uniform piece-rate bonus of 50 per cent for all output in excess of quota. The abolition of differentials within the quota became general in a short time.

However, there appeared a tendency to expand the system of differential bonuses for performance in excess of quota. In particular, the two fundamental decisions of the CPC of the USSR and the CC of the CPSU on revisions of the wage system in Donets coal mining (May 21, 1933) and railroad transportation (July 8, 1933)—decisions which strongly influenced the general trend of wage policies—developed the idea of progressive premium pay for additional output.[54]

The new wage rules for the Donets coal mines provided for a 100 per cent bonus for the first 10 per cent of production in excess of quota. But if output exceeded 110 per cent of the quota, all output above the quota (not only that exceeding it by more than 10 per cent) was to receive a 200 per cent bonus—i.e., three times the base rate. This applied to jobs classified as "most im-

[53] *Za Industrializatsiyu,* October 27, 1932.
[54] *Laws and Ordinances,* 1933:183 and 242.

portant." For other jobs, premium pay was scheduled differently: 150 per cent of the base rate for output between 100 and 120 per cent of quota, and 200 per cent of the base rate for all output beyond quota in case this was exceeded by more than 20 per cent. Bonus pay for railroad workers was scaled along similar lines.

Only the main trend has been pointed out here; a detailed discussion of the graduated piece-work scales and supplementary bonus systems would exceed the scope of this book. It is enough to say that all of them were intended to increase output, and that their effect was an extreme disparity in actual earnings.

Projected and Actual Wage Trends under the Second Five-Year Plan

As we have seen, the balance of wage developments under the First Five-Year Plan was very unfavorable. Nominal wages (or, to be precise, nominal earnings) greatly exceeded Plan estimates, but a much greater inflationary rise in living costs considerably depressed the level of real wages.

This was not officially admitted. On the contrary, government spokesmen time and again pointed out that wages had risen far more than had production. They ignored the fact that the wage boosts were nominal while the increase in output was real (whether measured in quantities of goods or in "stable 1926/27 prices"). The official version, expounded even in textbooks, went like this: [55]

> "Despite the undoubtedly enormous success achieved in rais- ing the productivity of labor in industry, transportation, and the socialist sector of agriculture during the four-and-a quarter years of the First Five-Year Plan, it must be stressed that in this very respect the Plan has been only about one-half fulfilled. In regard to wages, on the other hand, it was overfulfilled two-and-a-half time. The average output per worker rose 41 per cent, while average annual earnings rose 103.6 per cent. According to the Five-Year Plan, the productivity of labor was to rise 2.4 times as

---

[55] M. M. Krivitsky, ed., *Labor Economics. Textbook,* published by the Institute for Economics of the Communist Academy, Moscow-Leningrad, 1933, Vol. I, p. 135.

fast as wages; the actual result was that wages rose 2.5 times as fast as productivity."

Such a view of the results of the First Five-Year Plan was bound to make the planners very cautious about further wage increases. Early in 1933, at a conference of union and industry leaders called by the AUCTUC to discuss problems of labor policy, the head of the wage division of the AUCTUC, Kuritsyn, took the view that there would be "no mechanical wage increases at all this year, except maybe in coal mining," and that higher earnings could only be considered as a concomitant of increased productivity. Even in this case wages should lag behind the increase in output per worker—in other words, piece rates were to be reduced.[56]

The annual plan for 1933, approved late in January,[57] contemplated a 6.7 per cent increase of (nominal) earnings in all occupational divisions, and a 9.3 per cent increase in industry proper, while the (real) productivity of labor in industry was to be raised 14.0 per cent.

This proved illusory. Average nominal earnings in all occupational divisions rose 9.8 per cent, rather than the contemplated 6.7; earnings in industry rose 10.0 per cent, rather than 9.3; and output per worker increased 10.7 per cent.[58]

The annual plan for 1934 redoubled the effort to slow down the rise of nominal earnings. Productivity was to be raised 13.5 per cent in industry, 10.0 per cent in railroading, 24.8 per cent in water transport, etc. But the level of earnings in all occupational divisions was to rise only 3.7 per cent.[59]

In the spring of 1934, the Second Five-Year Plan was approved in its final form. Here, too, the question of wage rises was cautiously handled. From 1932 to 1937, average earnings were to rise 23.0 per cent in all occupational divisions and 26.9 per cent

---

[56] For details, cf. my article "On the Eve of the New Collective Bargaining Campaign," *Sotsialisticheskii Vestnik*, Berlin, 1933, No. 3, pp. 10 f.

[57] *Pravda*, February 1, 1933.

[58] B. Markus, "Problems of Labor in 1933 and in the Plan for 1934," *Planovoye Khozyaistvo*, May-June, 1934, pp. 148, 159; cf, the anonymous article "Foundations of the Plan for the National Economy for 1934," *op. cit.*, p. 199.

[59] Markus, as quoted in preceding note, p. 149; "Foundations . . ." as quoted there, p. 199. According to Markus, p. 159, an increase of only 2.8 per cent had been contemplated originally.

in industry proper.[60] Output per worker was to increase much more rapidly: 63 per cent in industry, 43 per cent in railroading, 86 per cent in water transport, 75 per cent in the building trades, etc.[61] After the sad experience of the First Five-Year Plan, a reduction in living costs was no longer mentioned; it was planned however, to "double real wages" in the course of the Second Plan.[62] How this was to be done was not explained.

The actual trends of real wages under the Second Five-Year Plan elude exact analysis, even more than those under the First Plan. Not only had the last remnants of a cost-of-living index disappeared; the facts themselves were complicated and obscured by the contradictory price movements in the "organized" and "unorganized" markets and the simultaneous shift of consumer purchasing from the first to the second. Prices of rationed commodities were systematically raised, while most of the state "commercial" prices were at first slowly reduced and from 1934 on abruptly slashed—depressing prices on the private market.

The object of this policy was to bring the price levels in the two spheres of supply closer together and thus to facilitate the abolition of rationing. Rationing of bread, flour, and cereals was ended on January 1, 1935; [63] that of meat, fish, butter, oil, sugar and potatoes on October 1, 1935.[64] From that time until the war there was no food rationing in the Soviet Union.

The following table may illustrate price trends from 1932, the last year of the First Five-Year Plan, to October, 1935, the first month after the termination of food rationing: [65]

---

[60] *Second Five-Year Plan* . . . , as quoted *supra,* n. 10, vol. I, pp. 504 f.

[61] *Op. cit.,* p. 325.

[62] *Ibid.*

[63] Pursuant to decisions of the CC of the CPSU of November 26, 1934 (*Pravda,* November 29, 1934) and of the CPC of the USSR of December 7, 1934 (*Pravda,* December 8, 1934).

[64] Pursuant to a decision of the CPC of the USSR and the CC of the CPSU of September 25, 1935 (*Pravda,* September 26, 1935).

[65] From data published in official Soviet publications, partly inaccessible in New York, as assembled by Professor S. N. Prokopovicz in his *Byuleten' Ekonomicheskogo Kabineta,* Prague, No. 124, October, 1935, p. 91.

Food Prices in Moscow, 1932-1935
(Kopecks per Unit[x])

A: Ration-prices

B: Prices in state "commercial trade" (after de-rationing, so-called "uniform state prices")

		1932 Average		1934 Average	1935 January	1935 October
Wheat flour	A	19		72	—	—
(96% grind)	B	—		—	260	180
Rye flour	A	14		66	—	—
(95% grind)	B	—		—	250	160
Wheat bread	A	17.5		60	—	—
(from 96% flour)	B	400		300	110	100
Rye bread (from	A	12.5		50	—	—
95% flour)	B	250		150	100	85
Buckwheat	A	25		32	—	—
	B	100 to	110	700	500	430
Potatoes	A	...		25	25	—
	B	...		125	60	30
Beef, first grade	A	212		328	328	—
	B	600		570	1400	760
Pork, first grade	A	303		460	460	—
	B	...		900	1600	...
Milk	A	...		...	...	—
	B	85 to	100	80	180	160
Butter (unsalted)	A	466		800	800	—
	B	1600 to	1800	2700	2600	1650
Sunflower oil	A	170		270	270	—
	B	450 to	500	2400	2400	1350
Eggs	A	100		180	180	—
	B	...		350	...	...
Sugar, granulated	A	95		200	200	—
	B	250		1000	650	450
Sugar, lump	A	125		250	250	—
	B	300		1200	750	490

x Kilogram, except for milk (1 liter) and eggs (10 eggs).

The complex developments immediately preceding the abolition of food rationing need not be related in detail. Summing up, I should like to repeat some conclusions I drew at the time, from day-to-day observations of the movement of wages and prices: [66] "Due to rising prices and to changes in the food supply organization, the level of real wages dropped from year to year from the beginning of the First Five-Year Plan period until mid-1931; then, for nearly two years, it oscillated at about the level attained, with a tendency to decline further. Not until mid-1933 did the workers' living standard register some improvement, interrupted by a new wave of price rises in the spring of 1934."

The new wave was so painful for the average citizen that the government took emergency measures. In May 1934, departing from the previous policy of systematic wage differentiation, the CPC of the USSR and the CC of the CPSU issued a decree "to raise the wages of low-paid wage and salary earners in connection with the rise in standardized bread prices." [67] The monthly payroll ("wage fund") of the whole economy was increased by 95,000,-000 rubles. The annual plan for 1934 had fixed the aggregate payroll for the year at 38,124,600,000 rubles[68]—an average of 3,177,000,000 rubles a month; so the decree increased the monthly payroll by 3 per cent. Out of the total of 23,000,000 employed, however, only the lowest income groups, some 9,000,000 wage and salary earners, were to benefit; so that for them the increase in monthly wages may have amounted to a little over 10 rubles per person, i.e., somewhat more than 10 per cent.

The lowest-paid sections of labor were thus more or less recompensed for the rise in bread prices; but the general price spiral set off by the bread-price movement was not offset for these sections, either.

In retrospect, the sudden rise decreed for standardized bread prices in the spring of 1934 appears as a mere preparatory device for the de-rationing of bread. Once lowest-grade bread was sold by the government at .50 and .60 rubles a kilogram, the jump to the new "uniform" state prices which followed on the abolition of rationing seemed no longer audacious. And once bread ration-

[66] Cf. my article "New Difficulties Ahead," *Sotsialisticheskii Vestnik*, Paris, 1934, No. 12, p. 4.

[67] *Pravda*, May 28, 1934.

[68] "Foundations . . . ," as quoted *supra*, n. 58, p. 223.

ing was gone, de-rationing of other foods was no longer a problem.

As mentioned, de-rationing was carried out in two stages. Rationing of bread, flour, and cereals ended first, on January 1, 1935. Transitional hardships were lessened by a new wage increase and a reduction in the "commercial prices" of several other foods. But in October, when all foods were de-rationed, there was no second wage increase and only a slight cut in the new uniform state bread prices, to ease consumer distress.

The wage increase of January 1935 was not limited to the lowest income classes, as in May, 1934. The same decree of the CPC of the USSR which eliminated bread rationing on December 7, 1934, appropriated an amount of 4,200,000,000 rubles for raising wages, salaries, scholarships, and pensions; another 100,000,-000 rubles was added later. Of the whole appropriation, 270,000,-000 rubles were earmarked for scholarships and pensions; left for the wage fund were 4,030,000,000 rubles plus an additional allotment of 337,500,000 rubles for wage rises in lumber and rafting—a total of 4,367,500,000 rubles.[69]

In comparison with average annual earnings in 1934, this meant a wage increase of about 10 per cent. However, wages were not raised evenly but differentiated regionally in each jurisdiction. For example, in favored Moscow, the wages of manual workers and technical employees hitherto enjoying the same rationing privileges, in plants under the People's Commissariat for Heavy Industry, were raised 21 and 25.50 rubles a month, respectively; the wages of construction workers under the same Commissariat, 19 and 21 rubles; those of employees not enjoying the same rationing privileges as manual workers (i.e., the bulk of lower and medium employees) 15 rubles.[70]

The average monthly wage increase for all wage and salary earners in the country amounted to approximately 15 rubles, giving the average working-class family of 1.44 gainfully employed members an additional monthly income of some 22 rubles. But de-rationing of bread (according to calculations by Weinberg, the AUCTUC secretary in charge of wage policy) put the average

[69] *Plan for the National Economy of the USSR for* 1935, 2nd ed., Moscow, 1935, p. 643.

[70] *Za Industrializatsiyu*, December 29, 1934.

working-class family to an additional monthly expense of some 31 rubles.[71]

Thus, despite the wage increase, the food supply reorganization lowered the standard of living of an overwhelming majority of wage and salary earners. Only those in the higher income brackets, who before de-rationing had filled an important part of their household needs in the private market, benefited perceptibly by the new policy.

Moreover, the whole extra wage increase of January, 1935, was somewhat dubious. In part, it simply represented a raise that was due and could not be avoided, anyway. Including the extra raise, the aggregate yearly payroll was set at 49,800,000,000 rubles in the annual plan for 1935, as against 41,6000,000,000 rubles in 1934—an increase of 19.8 per cent. The number of employed had to rise 4.9 per cent.[72] Hence, the planned *per capita* increase over 1934 was 14.2 per cent—or 4.1 per cent after deduction of the January raise.

But the 1934 annual average, taken as a basis of comparison, was a thing of the past in the late months of 1934. Soaring prices had made an upward adjustment of nominal earnings inevitable; the annual plan merely stabilized wages at the general level attained during the last quarter of 1934. The official commentary on the 1935 plan made no bones about it: "The plan for 1935 is essentially based on the idea of maintaining the wage level reached during the last quarter of 1934." [73]

The economic authorities were thus faced with the task of halting any wage raises by increasing production quotas.

The task was insoluble. It rested on the erroneous assumption that de-rationing of bread and later of all other foods would have no significant effect on actual living costs. The opposite happened. For years, the entire wage system had been built on the idea that the ruble was but slightly depreciated—an idea which in the sphere of "standardized" prices was indeed not too far from the truth. But in the meantime inflation had progressed by leaps and bounds in the free market as well as in the sphere of "commercial" prices (and of the subsequent "uniform" state prices). Even though de-rationing was followed by a cut in free market

[71] *Trud*, January 15, 1935.
[72] *Plan . . . for 1935*, as quoted *supra*, n. 69., pp .640 ff.
[73] *Op. cit.*, p. 329.

prices and a slight upward movement of wages, the disparity of wage and price levels remained enormous.

Figures to document this will be given below. Here we need only say that a gradual adjustment of the wage level to a currency far more depreciated than the wage fixers had assumed appeared now inevitable.

Adjustment of wages was slow in coming, and the transition was painful. The most dramatic example was the crisis experienced by public eating places.

As long as the public canteens based the price of a meal on "standardized" food prices, millions of wage and salary earners unable to afford the prices of the "unorganized sector" could feed themselves somehow in the public canteens. But when the "standardized" prices were raised in 1934, and especially when rationing was abolished, the public eating places were forced to charge more, and they simply priced themselves out of the reach of large masses of workers. At the same time prices in the free market declined slightly, and a tendency to eat at home appeared in the better-paid sections of labor.

"The engineers' and technicians' canteen in the Stalin Machine Works in Leningrad charge 2 to 3 rubles for a mediocre lunch, and many married engineers and technicians who have thrifty and capable wives or domestics think it better nowadays to take their meals at home," said a report from Leningrad, published shortly before bread went off the rationing list.[74] According to the same report, the sales volume of "open"[75] eating places in Leningrad declined rapidly after the summer of 1934: they sold 951,000 courses in August, 837,000 in September, 736,000 in October.

The newspaper of industry, which published these data, added a warning: with "housewives placed in the same situation as public canteens," there might soon be a danger that "home-cooking will replace public feeding, and housewives who have worked in factories in the past years will return to the kitchen stove."[76]

While the industry organ viewed this trend with alarm

---

[74] Za Industrializatsiyu, December 12, 1934.

[75] "Open" eating places are those open to the general public, as distinguished from plant and shop canteens admitting only personnel employed in the respective plants and shops.

[76] Za Industrializatsiyu, December 12, 1934.

mainly from the point of view of a decreasing supply of female labor—the mass of the workers was concerned with another side of the same story. Again and again in the early months of 1935, reports leaked out mentioning the bad food and the high prices charged in the public canteens.

The secretary of the Public Restaurant Employees Union attacked the widespread practice of concealing price increases by reducing portions.[77] The plenary session of the Central Board of the Aircraft Workers Union heard numerous complaints of "short-weighing on portions served, and price raises accompanied by cuts in the caloric value of the food." At the plenary session of the Central Board of the Non-Ferrous Metal Workers Union the public canteens were charged with "unbearable price boosts," etc.[78]

Almost everywhere, attendance fell off rapidly. In the district of Vasil'yevski-Ostrov in Leningrad, where many metal plants and shipyards are located, the number of customers in public canteens dropped 30 per cent from November-December, 1934, to January, 1935. In the canteen of the North-Cable Works in Leningrad the number of courses sold daily fell from 10-12,000 in December to 7,000 in January.[79] The picture was the same in Kharkov and Stalingrad,[80] Gor'ki[81] and Yaroslavl,[82] Tambov[83] and Novosibirsk,[84] etc. Gor'ki reported a slump in school canteens: by the end of February, the number of students taking hot meals had dropped from 80 per cent to 25, and in working-class neighborhoods to 20 per cent.[85]

The number of courses sold dwindled even faster than the number of customers. Many workers were not able to eat at home; but their income did not suffice for complete meals in the public canteens. A report from the Kharkov Locomotive Works said: "Many workers have ceased eating two courses for lunch because of the rise in prices."[86] The manager of heavy-industry canteens in the district of Vasil'yevski-Ostrov in Leningrad took comfort

[77] *Trud*, February 22, 1935.
[78] *Trud*, February 28, 1935.
[79] *Za Industrializatsiyu*, February 20, 1935.
[80] *Trud*, March 6, 1935.
[81] *Za Industrializatsiyu*, February 20, 1935.
[82] *Za Industrializatsiyu*, February 28, 1935.
[83] *Za Industrializatsiyu*, March 6, 1935.
[84] *Trud*, January 12, 1935.
[85] *Trud*, March 4, 1935.
[86] *Trud*, January 18, 1935.

in the "virtually undiminished attendance of public canteens, with a decline marked only [sic!] in the number of courses sold."[87]

The fact was that the purchasing power of money wages kept dwindling, but the economic planners failed to take it sufficiently into account. Payroll estimates, then, were naturally exceeded, year in and year out. That the Second Five-Year Plan had con- templated 1,755 rubles average annual earnings for 1937 was soon forgotten; this figure was surpassed as early as 1934, a few months after the Plan had been approved. Substantially higher figures in the plans for the subsequent years still underestimated the rise of nominal earnings. How greatly their authors mis- judged the real course of development may be seen from the fol- lowing data for the last three years of the Second Five-Year Plan period: [88]

Annual Per Capita Earnings of Wage and Salary Earners

	1935	1936	1937
	All Occupational Divisions		
Annual plan figure, in rubles	2,046	2,546.7	2,976.1
Actual earnings reported, in rubles	2,273.7	2,770.2	3,047
Plan figure exceeded by . . . per cent	11.1	8.8	2.4
Per cent increase over previous year:			
Plan figure	10.4	12.0	7.4
Actual	22.7	21.9	10.0
	Industry [x]		
Annual plan figure, in rubles	2,129	2,487	2,908
Actual earnings reported, in rubles	2,285	2,715	3,005
Plan figure exceeded . . . per cent	7.3	9.2	3.3
Per cent increase over previous year:			
Plan figure	16.4	8.8	7.1
Actual	25.0	18.8	10.7

x In addition to so-called "big industry," the term "industry" here includes also small shops and handicraft.

---

[87] *Za Industrializatsiyu,* February 20, 1935.
[88] Data from *Plan . . . for* 1935, as quoted *supra,* n. 69, p. 641; *Plan for the National Economy of the USSR for* 1936. Vol. I, Moscow, 1936, p. 458; "Foundations

While the Second Five-Year Plan had envisaged a 23.0 per cent increase in *per capita* earnings in five years, earnings actually rose 113.5 per cent. But this increase was nominal. What, in the same period of time, was the change in Russian labor's real wages?

In statistical terms it is hard to give an exact answer. Comparing the purchasing power of nominal wages in fixed prices for 1932 and in "uniform" prices for 1937 would produce a devastating result. Price increases would appear to range from 250 to 1,600 per cent, and the average rise in the price level would have to be estimated at 400 to 500 per cent,[89] as compared with a nominal wage increase of 113.5 per cent. This would mean that under the Second Five-Year Plan real wages were cut in half or less.

This conclusion would not be correct, however. Ration-prices were largely meaningless in 1932, as many food items had disappeared from the "organized" market and the bulk of labor had to pay substantially more for them. As a matter of fact, real wages were already so low at the end of the First Plan that further drops of the suggested magnitude would inevitably have caused a complete disintegration of economic life.

---

of the Plan for the National Economy for 1937," *Planovoye Khozyaistvo*, March, 1937, pp. 223, 242; *Results of Fulfilling the Second Five-Year Plan*, Moscow, 1939, p. 105. Wherever later sources differed from earlier ones, the former were used and percentage changes computed accordingly.

[89] Based on the table on "Food prices in Moscow, 1932-1935" given above in the text, price trends (controlled prices) between 1932 and October 1935 may be summarized as follows:

	1932 (ration-prices)	October 1935 ("uniform government prices")	Per Cent Increase October 1935 over 1932
	Kopecks per Kilogram		%
Wheat flour	19	180	847
Rye flour	14	160	1,043
Wheat bread	17.5	100	471
Rye bread	12.5	85	580
Buckwheat	25	430	1,620
Beef	212	760	258
Butter	466	1,650	254
Sunflower oil	170	1,350	694
Sugar, granulated	95	450	374
Sugar, lump	125	490	292

Reduction of "uniform government prices," which was to clear the way for de-rationing of food, was pretty well completed by October, 1935. Further price-cuts ordered in the course of the following months did not significantly modify the price level. Hence, the general level of controlled prices in 1937 may be assumed to have been very near that of October, 1935, and the price increases shown in the table may be taken as approximately representative of conditions in 1937.

As far as can be judged from day-to day observation of economic trends (always hazardous, due to the peculiarity of Soviet statistics) the living standards of labor at the end of 1935, after de-rationing, cannot have been much lower than at the close of the First Five-Year Plan. In 1936 and 1937 prices remained relatively stable, while nominal *per capita* earnings increased over 30 per cent, as shown in the above table.

Money wages had partially adjusted themselves to the reduced value of the ruble; by the end of the Second Five-Year Plan real wages must have been some 20 per cent higher than at the beginning. Still, this first real improvement since the inception of the Five-Year Plan policy did not suffice to make up for the havoc wrought under the First Five-Year Plan. On the average, the real earnings of Russian labor remained far below the level of 1928.

Additional Sources of Income

Under the Second Five-Year Plan, as under the First, there were elements counteracting the decline of purchasing power and helping to maintain living standards.

We have discussed above the reduction in the size of workers' families and the increase in the number of wage and salary earners per family unit in the early years of universal planning. The data quoted above until 1935, inclusive, were not released for subsequent years, possibly indicating that the trend had almost run its course and could not go much farther. However that may be, it is certain that under the Second-Five-Year-Plan the strain on family budgets could not be eased to the same extent as under the First by *new* family members taking up gainful employment.

Insofar, however, as the number of gainfully employed per family unit had already increased under the First Five-Year Plan or at the beginning of the Second, the effects were now felt much more. The newly-employed workers who had started in the lowest brackets were upgraded and earned more. Not many data are available on this problem, either, but family budget inquiries in 1934 and 1935 show at least that the annual *per capita* earnings of heads of families in 1935 were 24.7 per cent above those of 1934, and that *per capita* earnings of other family members (who scarcely increased in number per family) had risen 39.7 per cent.[90] There is every reason to assume that this trend did continue.

More important was another source of additional income which under the Second Five-Year Plan (and under the Third) had effects similar to those of "public feeding" under the First Plan. The regular food supply was supplemented by "individual vegetable gardening" and private breeding of sheep, goats, and fowl. This "self-supply" had been vigorously promoted since the last years of the First Five-Year Plan. It spread rapidly, particularly in medium and small cities, and above all in mining districts. According to the household surveys of 1933 and 1934, this "individual sector" yielded on the average the following annual quantities of food for each family surveyed:

	Industry as a Whole		Mining	
	1933	1934	1933	1934
Potatoes, kilogram	49.1	105.5	127.8	227.7
Vegetables, kilogram	17.8	27.6	31.5	36.9
Milk, liter	23.2	39.3	41.0	55.8

By 1934, according to the same source, coal miners were raising 42 per cent of their potato consumption, 12 per cent of their vegetables, 43 per cent of their milk, 8.7 per cent of their cereals, etc.[91] There are no comparable data for later years, but numerous press reports indicate that small-scale farming and vegetable gardening as part-time occupations of industrial workers made substantial progress under the Second and Third Five-Year Plans.

Of course, in view of the enormous discrepancy between the wage and price levels, the offsetting factors described here were not too significant. An adjustment of the wage level to the price level remained unavoidable; and indeed, it gradually came about, although in peculiar fashion.

Selective Income and Consumption Policy

From the late 1920's on, the idea of fostering differentiation of wages found increasing acceptance in Russian economic policy.

---

[90] S. Kheinman, "The Toilers' Standard of Living in the USSR," *Planovoye Khozyaistvo*, August, 1936, p. 112.

[91] All data from Kheinman, *op. cit.*, pp. 109 f.

It was now given an even more important part to play in the process of adjusting the wage level to the new price conditions. Progressive piece rates and premium wages were expanded more and more—not only to boost output but also for the deliberate purpose of using plant payroll funds mainly to improve the condition of the "leading groups" of workers and employees essential to production.

From the mid-Thirties on, wage strategy in the plants was focused on raising the standard of living of these "leading groups," workers and employees on whom the government relied most for the fulfillment of production plans. As mentioned before, a major part of the payroll increases approved in 1934 and 1935 was absorbed by this "elite." The considerable increase in their earnings figured largely in the increases in aggregate payrolls and overall *per capita* earnings; wage and salary earners in the middle and lower brackets participated to a far lesser extent in the upward movement.

In the absence of comprehensive statistics, this selective distribution of wage incomes can only be illustrated by scattered samplings. A characteristic instance was furnished—perhaps unintentionally—by the Moscow trade union newspaper in a report from the famous Tsentralnaya Irmino coal mine in the Donets Basin, the birthplace of the Stakhanov movement.[92] From September to December, 1935, the payroll of the mine had risen from 340,000 to 500,000 rubles, and the miners' average monthly earnings from 235 to 320 rubles. Of the 1,560 wage and salary earners employed in December, 60 were in the 1,000-2,500 bracket, 75 in the 800-1,000 bracket, and more than 400 in the 500-800 bracket. This left more than 1,000 wage and salary earners in groups with monthly earnings of less than 500 rubles.

The correspondent of the trade union newspaper was enthusiastic about the high wages paid in the upper brackets at Tsentralnaya Irmino. But what were the earnings of the more than 1,000 employees in the lower groups? Assuming that the average monthly income of the top group was only 1,200 rubles, that of the second group 850 rubles, and that of the third group 600 rubles; assuming further that the latter group numbered not "more than 400" but exactly 400 employees, the three groups

92 *Trud*, January 20, 1936.

together amount to 535 employees with aggregate earnings of 375,750 rubles—about one-third of the personnel, accounting for three-quarters of the payroll. What was left for the remaining two-thirds would barely allow employees in the lower brackets to average 125 rubles a month.

In view of the prices prevailing at the end of 1935, this is so incredibly little that one wonders whether in his excess of enthusiasm the trade union correspondent may not have overestimated the number of employees in the higher income brackets. Possibly, *per capita* earnings of a majority of workers employed in the mine exceeded 125 rubles. But even in that case the distribution of income among the personnel would suggest that practically the entire payroll increase from September to December was used to raise the earnings of the top groups.

The extensive differentiation of living standards which resulted from this selective distribution of wages was warmly welcomed and strongly promoted by the government. One of the leading experts on labor statistics proudly deduced from household survey data that in the last quarter of 1935 *per capita* consumption in working-class families in the lowest and highest income brackets differed in the following ratios: [93]

	Ratio of Lowest to Highest Income Group
Meat	1 to 5.7
Butter	1 to 17.0
Fish	1 to 1.9
Fruit	1 to 6.7
Pastry	1 to 3.4

The differentiation of earnings became more acute at the close of the Second Five-Year Plan, and again under the Third. As average earnings increased and prices remained relatively stable from 1935 to the beginning of the Third Five-Year Plan period, a numerically rather considerable and constantly growing upper stratum of wage and salary earners actually received a substantial rise in real wages.

The majority of wage and salary earners drew little benefit from the increase. The worst distress, to be sure, was relieved by a decree of the CPC of the USSR of November 1, 1937,[94] specifi-

---

[93] Kheinman, as quoted *supra,* n. 90, p. 116.

cally providing for raises in the lowest wage categories. In industry and transportation (not, however, in other occupational divisions, and particularly not in retail trade where low income prevailed), wages in the lowest brackets were brought up to 110-115 rubles a month. A monthly payroll increase of 50,000,000 rubles was granted, probably intended for no less than two or three million wage and salary earners. The mere fact that such steps were necessary is indicative of the condition of large strata of workers at the close of the Second Five-Year Plan period.

Wage Trends under the Third Five-Year Plan

Only summary data have been published on the movement of wages projected under the Third Five-Year Plan. No details and officially explained programs were issued. Most of what we know about wages and earnings planned was contained in V. M. Molotov's report to the Eighteenth Convention of the CPSU in March, 1939, and in the resolution which the Convention subsequently adopted. This said that annual *per capita* earnings in the total economy were to reach 4,174 rubles in 1942, a 37 per cent gain over 1937. No mention was made of changes in purchasing power.[95]

This time, actual developments do not seem to have strayed too far from the Plan. In 1938, annual *per capita* earnings were 3,467 rubles.[96] No data were released for 1939.[97] As for 1940, the chairman of the State Planning Commission, Voznesensky, speaking at the Eighteenth Conference of the CPSU in February, 1941, mentioned an aggregate payroll of 123,700,000,000 rubles in the total economy which was said to be employing 30,400,000. According to Voznesensky, the annual plan for 1941 contemplated an

[94] *Izvestiya*, November 2, 1937.
[95] *Eighteenth Convention of the CPSU, March 10 to 21, 1939. Stenographic Transcript of Proceedings*, Moscow, 1939, p. 664.
[96] I. Sautin, "Raising the Material and Cultural Standards of Toilers in the USSR," *Planovoye Khozyaistvo*, May, 1939, p. 11.
[97] Only the figure for the aggregate payroll in all occupational divisions is available, 116,500,000,000 rubles in 1939, according to N. Voznesensky, "The Economic Results of the Year 1940 and the Plan for the Economic Development of the USSR for 1941. Report to the Eighteenth Conference of the CPSU," *Bol'shevik*, 1941, No. 3-4, pp. 38, 53, and 67 (published in the United States under the title, *The Growing Prosperity of the Soviet Union*, New York, 1941, pp. 9, 39 f., and 45). The above figure for 1939 compared with 96,000,000,000 rubles for 1938, according to Sautin, as quoted *supra*, n. 96, p. 11.

increase of 14,000,000,000 rubles in the aggregate payroll and an increase of 1,200,000 in the number of employed.[98]

From these figures it is easy to compute annual *per capita* earnings in 1940 and 1941. We get this approximate picture for the years 1938-1941:

	Annual Per Capita Earnings (rubles)	Per Cent Increase over Previous Year	Per Cent Increase over 1937
1938	3,467	13.8%	13.8%
1939	. . .	. . .	. . .
1940	4,069	. . .	33.5
1941 (planned)	4,358	7.1	43.0

The Third Five-Year Plan figure probably would have been considerably exceeded in 1942. Certainly, however, the extreme discrepancy between planned and actual developments under the First and Second Five-Year Plans would not have marked the Third.

The quoted figures give a general idea of the trend of nominal wages under the Third Five-Year Plan. What happened to real wages? The answer to that has been facilitated by the diligent work of the U.S. Embassy, which for several years noted food and clothing prices in the government stores of Moscow.[99]

The prices recorded for the main food items remained relatively stable from 1936 to mid-1938. Bread, flour, and sugar prices were unchanged as late as 1940, while macaroni, noodles, etc. started going up early. Meat, fish, and meat and fish products rose sporadically in the second half of 1938, and later generally. Milk went up slowly but steadily from the beginning of the period; dairy products followed much later. The development of vegetable and fruit prices was particularly unfavorable to the consumer.

Of the total of 83 food prices recorded on July 1, 1936 and 1938, 24 remained unchanged, 35 rose, and 24 declined. Added up, all 83 prices show a total increase of 7.0 per cent in two years. Clothing prices gave the consumer a better break. Of 17 times re-

[98] Voznesensky, *ibid.*, cf. preceding note.
[99] Embassy data refer to January 1 and July 1, 1936; July 1, 1938; January 1 and July 1, 1939; January 1 and 24, April 10 and July 1, 1940; and January 1, 1941. Cf. *Monthly Labor Review*, November, 1939, pp. 1276 ff.; May, 1940, pp. 1272 ff.; August, 1940, pp. 500 f.; February, 1941, pp. 474 ff.; May, 1941, pp. 1292 ff.

corded for July 1 of 1936 and 1938, 10 went up while 7 went down; added up, however, the 17 items became 4.5 per cent cheaper. Thus, it may seem that the general level of food and clothing prices changed hardly at all from 1936 to 1938.

The real picture was less favorable. The selection of merchandise in government stores declined visibly: for July 1, 1936, prices were recorded for 107 food items in Moscow government stores; on July 1, 1938, 83 remained on the list. The trend was even more evident in clothing: of 39 items of clothing for which prices were noted on July 1, 1936, only 17—less than half—were still for sale in 1938.

Things became worse from 1938 to 1939. Of the 107 food items offered on July 1, 1936, only 66 had prices listed three years later. Of these 60 were comparable with price listings of July, 1938: 24 prices had risen over the year, 3 had dropped. Added up, the 60 items together had gone up only 5.4 per cent, but as the increase affected low-priced foods in particular, it was painful nonetheless.

Again the situation was more complicated in clothing: there were only 13 items with comparable price listings for July, 1938, and 1939, and of these 11 went up and none went down. Added up, prices for the 13 items of clothing rose as much as 38.2 per cent.

The variety of merchandise for sale was not all that declined. Stocks also dwindled. The U.S. Embassy report on developments up to July, 1939, adds:[100] "Bread lines and the long lines for the purchase of various consumers' goods have been accompanied by an increase of underground private trade prohibited by the Government. It was disclosed, for instance, that private traders were selling sugar for a price twice as high as they had paid in the Soviet stores and that they were demanding 6 rubles for a cake of laundry soap which they had bought for 1.50 rubles in the Government stores."

This was just the beginning. Almost all prices soared in the following year. On July 1, 1940, prices comparable with July, 1939, were recorded for only 39 foodstuffs and 23 items of clothing. 30 foodstuffs and 22 items of clothing had gone up over the year, and not one price had dropped. Added up, food prices had

---

[100] *Op. cit.*, November, 1939, p. 1277.

risen 54.9 per cent, clothing prices 83.5 per cent. (Here the arithmetical average of food-price rises overstates the trend felt by the average consumer; if 4 luxuries—the two best candy and caviar brands—are taken off the 1940 list, the average increase in the price of food items from July 1, 1939, to July 1, 1940, would not be 54.9 but 39.5 per cent.)

All this referred to government stores. But the consumer in those critical years had to depend more and more on the private market, where prices rose much higher than in government stores. The digest of U.S. Embassy data on the situation of January, 1940, says:[101]

> ". . . The shortage of goods has become more pronounced than at any time since the introduction of the card rationing system in 1930, which was later discontinued.
>
> "There were 129 items available in the State stores in Moscow in 1936, but this figure had fallen to 88 by January 1, 1939, to 83 by July 1, 1939, and to only 44 by January 1, 1940. Furthermore, according to the Embassy report, only a few of these 44 items are readily available in Government stores at present, and such essential commodities as milk, butter, eggs, sugar, potatoes, and various others listed in the table as 'available' are on sale only very irregularly, and apparently in insufficient quantities. This results in long queues of customers who wait for hours in front of the stores. Under such circumstances the State-store prices quoted often become only nominal or at best of secondary importance, since the existing situation considerably restricts the actual consumption of foodstuffs by the population.
>
> "Furthermore, the acute shortage of essential commodities in the State stores has caused the open-bazaar market prices to soar to abnormally high levels."

The same report quotes some private market prices prevailing in Moscow, as of January 1, 1940. For 10 food items (meat, vegetables, milk, eggs) there were comparable prices charged in government stores, and on the average the private prices were 77.2 per cent higher.

Prices kept rising through the second half of 1940, but their ascent was no longer as steep as it had been from mid-1939 to mid-1940. Newspapers of the period after January 1941 contain only scattered references, too scanty to be appraised here. For a gen-

---

101 *Op. cit.*, May, 1940, p. 1272.

eral view of the trend of real wages under the Third Five-Year Plan the above data may suffice.

They show that the process of raising real wages, having started at the end of 1935, continued into 1938. In the summer of 1938, or perhaps a little earlier, the trend reversed itself, with nominal earnings lagging far behind the price level. By 1941, real wages had taken a new plunge, and on the eve of the Soviet Union's entry into the war they cannot have been much higher, by and large, than at the end of the First Five-Year Plan period.

Purchasing Power of Hourly Earnings in 1938

What does all this mean in practice? The actual purchasing power of wages in 1938, the peak year of real wages in the Thirties, is worth closer scrutiny. In that year the average employed Russian earned 3,467 rubles, i.e., 289 rubles a month. These averages represented actual earnings computed from plant payrolls and including all piece-rate and premium payments, as well as overtime; they covered all branches of the economy and administration and all groups of wage and salary earners, including industrial executives and high government officials but also including the poorly paid apprentices, farm laborers, and service personnel in factories and offices.

Until recent times, average wages were higher in industry proper than in the total economy. The Second Five-Year Plan envisaged no change: in 1937, *per capita* earnings in industry—not just industry proper but industry in the broader sense, including small shops and handicraft—were to exceed the average for the total economy.[102]

---

[102] This was illustrated by the following figures (from *Second Five-Year Plan* . . . , as quoted supra, n. 10, vol. I, pp. 504 f.) :

	Annual Per Capita Earnings in Rubles	
	1932 (Actual)	1937 (Plan)
All occupational divisions	1,427	1,755
Thereof:		
Industry incl. small-scale and handicrafts	1,410.10	1,778.50
Industry proper	1,466	1,860.60
Thereof: manual workers	1,385	1,736.20
technical employees	3,634	4,361
other salary earners	2,076	2,353
maintenance workers	888	1,074.50
apprentices	474	594

However, as mentioned, it did not work out that way. From the mid-Thirties on, the wage-differentiation policy favored the managerial and administrative machine and to some extent discriminated against manual workers. The same tendency prevailed in industry proper.[102a]

Therefore, if the average annual income in all occupational divisions was 3,467 rubles in 1938, the *per capita* income of manual workers in industry may be estimated at no more than 3,300 rubles a year, or 275 rubles a month. On the basis of a "six-day week" (five work days and one day off—cf. Chapter Five below), i.e., 24 work days per month, and a seven-hour day this would mean hourly earnings of 1.65 rubles.

At the official exchange rate 1.65 rubles equaled 31 cents.[103] But by then the official rate had long been fictitious, and in purchasing power a ruble was worth a good deal less than 19 cents.

What it meant in 1938 to make 1.65 rubles an hour can best be seen if the amount is viewed in relation to commodity prices. To this end, the government store prices noted by U.S. Embassy officials on July 1, 1938, are listed below. Of course, the rate of 1.65 rubles an hour was a national average and earnings in Moscow were a little higher; but the Moscow government prices scarcely differed from the national average and will serve very well in judging the purchasing power of nation-wide hourly earnings.

The following table is a near-complete reproduction of the prices listed by the U.S. Embassy, omitting only a few luxury items:[104]

[102a] The last known data on the average earnings of different groups of industrial employees refer to the year 1937. According to these, the average annual earnings of wage and salary earners had reached 3,038 rubles in the total economy and administration, and 3,005 rubles in the industry. Within the industry, however, technical employees earned on the average 6,533 rubles a year, other white collar employees 3,471 rubles, workers 2,820 rubles, the lower service personnel 1,662 rubles, and apprentices 1,002 rubles (Draft of the Third Five-Year Plan—see *supra* Chapter I, n. 75—p. 228). Thus, the average annual earnings of workers in industry proper were 6.2 per cent below the average earnings of all industrial employees, and 7.2 per cent below the average earnings of employees in all economic and administrative divisions.

[103] $1 = 5.30 rubles. Conversely, 1 ruble = about $0.19.

[104] *Monthly Labor Review,* November, 1939, pp. 1277 f.

Prices in Moscow Government Stores, July 1, 1938

Commodity	Unit ˣ	Price (Rubles)
Bread, black, rye	kg.	.85
Bread, white, wheat	kg.	1.70
French loaf	200 g.	1.20
Flour, 72 per cent	kg.	2.90
Flour, 30 per cent	kg.	4.60
Vermicelli	kg.	5.50
Macaroni	kg.	5.00
Noodles	kg.	5.30
Wheat, meal	kg.	4.50
Barley grits, fine	kg.	1.30
Shelled oats, grits	kg.	1.20
Rolled oats	kg.	.57
Buckwheat grits	kg.	3.50
Shelled millet grits	kg.	2.10
Rice	kg.	6.50
Milk, fresh	l.	1.60
Cream, fresh	l.	6.80
Cream, sour	l.	8.00
Cheese, Swiss	kg.	24.80
Cheese, American	kg.	22.20
Cheese, Holland	kg.	14.80
Butter, first grade	kg.	20.00
Butter, second grade	kg.	17.50
Eggs	10	6.50
Sunflower oil	kg.	15.92
Sugar, granulated	kg.	3.80
Sugar, lump	kg.	4.10
Honey	kg.	4.50
Tea	400 g.	36.00
Cocoa	250 g.	14.75
Pepper, black, ground	100 g.	8.00
Salt	kg.	.05
Potatoes	kg.	.40
Cabbage	kg.	1.50
Sauerkraut	kg.	.57
Carrots	kg.	.80
Chives	kg.	.60

ˣ It may be helpful to recall that one kilogram equals 2 pounds and 3.3 ounces; one liter, 1.06 liquid quarts; and one meter, 3.28 feet. Conversely, one pound equals 454 grams; one quart, .95 liters; and one foot. 30.5 centimeters.

Prices in Moscow Government Stores (Continued)

Commodity	Unit	Price (Rubles)
Lettuce	kg.	1.00
Cucumbers	10	5.00
Lemons	kg.	17.50
Walnuts	kg.	9.00
Almonds	kg.	15.00
Raisins	kg.	8.00
Dried apples	kg.	8.00
Dried prunes	kg.	12.00
Dried mixed fruits	kg.	7.50
Canned goods:		
Pork and beans	500 g.	2.11
Tongue	400 g.	7.10
Corn	500 g.	1.00
Sardines in oil	250 g.	3.25
Fish in tomato sauce	500 g.	6.20
Beef chops	kg.	11.50
Beef steak	kg.	12.50
Beef roast	kg.	9.60
Beef for soup	kg.	7.60
Veal	kg.	10.00
Pork chops	kg.	10.60
Pork roast	kg.	9.50
Ham, fresh	kg.	10.00
Ham, smoked	kg.	18.00
Bacon	kg.	16.00
Salt pork, fat	kg.	22.00
Lard, second grade	kg.	13.00
Mutton chops	kg.	9.60
Mutton	kg.	8.00
Chicken, first grade	kg.	13.00
Geese, first grade	kg.	11.00
Duck	kg.	13.00
Turkey	kg.	13.00
Sausage, ordinary	kg.	10.00
Sausage, Vienna	kg.	12.00
Sausage, Hamburger	kg.	16.00
Sausage, Cracow	kg.	14.00
Salami	kg.	30.00
Perch, frozen	kg.	5.40
Herring, salted	kg.	5.50

Prices in Moscow Government Stores (Continued)

Commodity	Unit	Price (Rubles)
Laundry soap	kg.	3.10
Glycerine soap	cake	1.55
Matches	box	.02
Kerosene	l.	.47
Ladies' stockings, rayon	pair	4.50
Ladies' stockings, cotton	pair	4.00
Men's shoes, leather	pair	163.00
Men's rubber overshoes	pair	18.70
Ladies' rubber overshoes	pair	18.70
Shirt, cotton	piece	35.00
Tablecloth, linen	piece	25.00
Towel, linen	piece	17.50
Necktie, rayon	piece	18.80
Hat, felt	piece	40.00
Cap, woolen	piece	25.70
Fur cap, Astrakhan	piece	250.00
Cloth, woolen, heavy	m.	125.00
Flannel, cotton	m.	7.50
Calico	m.	3.32
Crepe de Chine	m.	75.00
Cotton shirting	m.	8.90

I need not compute here what average earnings of 1.65 rubles an hour would buy, or how many hours and minutes a Russian worker had to work for each item listed. The table offers the reader every opportunity to make all desired comparisons.

An International Comparison of Real Wages in 1938

Available data on the purchasing power of wages in the Soviet Union do not easily submit to comparison with conditions elsewhere. A worker's family budget does not depend on wages and prices alone. Custom, tradition, education, technological development, household techniques, the organization of retailing, and many other factors make for profoundly different living standards. No "weighted index" considering all these elements has ever been devised, and even if there were one, the scant statistical

evidence would prevent its computation for the Soviet Union. At
best, international comparisons can be made by spot checks—as,
for instance, by calculating the amount of work required for the
purchase of certain commodities, foodstuffs or other essentials in
different countries.

The tables below are compiled from the international wage
and price data regularly published by the International Labour
Office.[105] The wages used for comparison are actual earnings—not
wage rates—for the Soviet Union and all other countries except
France and Great Britain. Where the ILO quotes two sets of figures for a country—as in the case of the United States—the lower
was used (for the United States that the Bureau of Labor Statistics: $0.639 for 1938).

In a few instances, the Moscow figures refer to food items of
lower quality than those used for computing purchasing power in
other countries. Thus butter data for almost all countries had to
be based on the price of the best quality product, while the price
of second-grade butter was used for Moscow; likewise, figures for
Latvia and Poland are based on a meat price calculated from quotations for prime beef. These discrepancies make the differences
in purchasing power between the Soviet Union and other countries seem somewhat less than it was, but for a summary comparison—and nothing else can be made here— they are of slight significance.

Now let us view the results of the comparative calculations:

[105] Wage data (1938 average) from *International Labour Review,* February,
1940, pp. 203 ff.; for Great Britain, from *Year-book of Labour Statistics,* 1939, Geneva,
p. 126. Price data (October, 1938) from the last mentioned sources, pp. 176 ff.

Instead of the national average, ILO data for France are average figures for
male workers in Paris (10.50 francs), male workers in cities other than Paris (6.19),
and female workers in cities other than Paris (3.42), referring in all cases chiefly to
skilled workers. An estimated average of 5.50 francs was used for computing the
table, which possibly is too low.

ILO statistics for Great Britain do not give average wage figures for all industries. Instead, data referring to individual categories of workers in different industries, males only, are supplied, ranging between 49 and 76 shillings weekly. Based
on these data, an estimated average hourly wage of 1 shilling 2 pence for all
industries was used for workers of both sexes.

For Poland the average wage of industrial workers, male and female, was .78
zloty according to *International Labour Review* (February, 1940, p. 208). This
obviously was an error. According to the *Year-book* . . . , p. 107, this figure referred
to male workers only, whereas hourly wages of female workers averaged .53 zloty.
On the basis of average figures for both sexes indicated in the *Year-book* . . . for
previous years, an estimated .69 zloty was used as the average figure for 1938.

Purchasing Power of Wages in 1938

Average minutes of work required to earn the price of a food unit (kilogram for solids; liter for milk; 1 egg for eggs)

Country	Wheat Bread	Wheat Flour	Beef 2nd grade	Milk	Butter 2nd grade
USSR	62	106[x]	276	58	636
Denmark	39	15	61	15	131
Estonia	93	61	97	18	275
France	34	47	110	21	303
Germany	54	33	125	17	237
Great Britain	20	18	67	26	146
Latvia	65	64	121	24	286
Poland	55	39	128	23	296
Sweden	41	21	78	12	150
United States	17	8	47	12	70

Country	Eggs	Potatoes	Sugar Granulated	Macaroni
USSR	24	14	138	181
Denmark	5	6	22	...
Estonia	8	11	74	146
France	10	8	60	97
Germany	9	6	57	59
Great Britain	9	7	23	49
Latvia	14	10	80	145
Poland	10	7	87	122
Sweden	7	6	20	34
United States	3	4	11	30

[x] Seventy-two per cent flour. Work time necessary to earn the price of one kilogram of 30 per cent wheat flour was 167 minutes.

Only in the cases of bread and potatoes is the difference between the Soviet Union and other countries less than tremendous; indeed, the bread price comparison partly favors Moscow. But the Moscow price used for the calculation—1.70 rubles per kilogram of wheaten bread—was the price charged for bread made of 85 per cent wheat flour. White bread of higher-grade flour was much more expensive, as evident from the previous table of Moscow prices on July 1, 1938—when a kilogram of "French loaf" cost the average worker 3 hours 38 minutes of work, not 1 hour 2 minutes.[106]

---

[106] For several years bread prices in Moscow remained unchanged as fixed

Let us disregard this, however, and add up the prices for all nine foods as given for each country. We find that, in order to buy one liter of milk, one egg, and one kilogram each of bread, wheat flour, beef, butter, potatoes, sugar, and macaroni, the average industrial worker in the various countries had to work:

	Minutes		Hours and Minutes
USSR	1495	=	24:55
Latvia	809	=	13:29
Estonia	783	=	13: 3
Poland	767	=	12:47
France	690	=	11:30
Germany	597	=	9:57
Sweden	369	=	6:9
Great Britain	365	=	6:5
United States	198	=	3:18

Denmark is not listed here because there are no Danish data on macaroni. Making a comparison only in regard to eight foodstuffs, excluding marcaroni, the working time required to earn the eight totals 294 minutes for Denmark, as against 1314 minutes for the Soviet Union. For what a Danish worker could buy in 1938 after working 4 hours 54 minutes, the Russian had to work 21 hours 54 minutes.

Even in such low-wage countries as Estonia, Latvia, and Poland, 1938 real wages, expressed in nine food items, were nearly double those of the Soviet Union. In France real wages were 2.2 times as high as in the Soviet Union; in Germany, 2.5 times; in Great Britain and Sweden, 4 times; and in the United States, 7.5 times.

---

in the winter of 1935/36 (except for highest-grade French loaf, which soon was raised from 5.40 to 6.00 rubles per kilogram). A general increase in bread prices was ordered much later, in October, 1940. The following are prices for different grades, according to the price schedule of 1935/36 (rubles per kg.):

Rye bread	95 %	.85	French loaf	85 %	2.75
do.	87 %	1.00	do.	75 %	3.60
do.	65 %	1.50	do.	30 %	5.40
Wheat bread	96 %	1.00	Twist (wheat bread	85 %	2.50
do.	85 %	1.70	made with yeast)	75 %	4.00
do.	75 %	2.80	do.	30 %	5.80
do.	30 %	4.20	"Sitnyi" (Russian	75 %	3.50
			raisin bread)	30 %	5.30

Price data from *Laws and Ordinances*, 1935:421 and 427, 1936:43.

For these comparisons purchasing power was computed from *per capita* earnings—but the great differentiation of wages in the Soviet Union makes this more a statistical than a real figure. To bolster the productivity of the "leading groups" despite the low level of average wages, differentiation was given more and more drastic forms. Speaking at the Eighteenth Convention of the CPSU, N. M. Shvernik—then leader of the Soviet trade unions and now chairman of the Presidium of the Supreme Soviet of the USSR—evoked storms of applause by praising a coal-cutting machine operator named Besedin who had earned as much as 3,549 rubles a month in 1938.[107] The trade union newspaper commended another mine-worker, Mizin, for making 31,217 rubles in 1938, a monthly average of more than 2,600 rubles.[108] These, of course, were exceptional cases. But there were many thousands employed in 1938 at wages in excess of 1,000 rubles a month. The statistical average did not remain uninfluenced by their incomes.

An example may illustrate this. At the Eighteenth Convention of the CPSU, L. M. Kaganovich, People's Commissar for Transportation, put the average monthly earnings of railroad employees in 1938 at 287.90 rubles, those of freight locomotive engineers at 846 rubles, and those of passenger locomotive engineers at 1,042 rubles.[109] The salaries of railroad executives and technical experts also were far above average. How much could be left for the bulk of workers and lower employees?

We have seen that annual earnings of workers and employees in all branches of the Soviet economy and administration averaged 3,467 rubles in 1938, or some 289 rubles a month. Supposing that the most highly-paid 5 per cent averaged three times the average wage, and that another 10 per cent earned twice the average wage—two modest estimates—what remained for 85 per cent of all workers and employees was 65 per cent of the total payroll. This means an average of not 289 but 221 rubles a month, corresponding to an hourly wage of not quite 1.32 rubles. In order to buy the nine food items listed above, 85 per cent of all wage and salary earners had to work an average of 1869 minutes or 31 hours rather than the previously computed 25.

[107] *Eighteenth Convention* . . . , as quoted *supra*, n. 95, p. 155.
[108] *Trud*, January 16, 1939.
[109] *Eighteenth Convention* . . . ,as quoted *supra*, n. 95, p. 263.

Trade Union Wage Policies

To understand how a wage trend like the one described could set in at all, one has to consider the wage policy of the unions which provided the trend with ideological cover. As it is known, in the summer of 1929—under direct pressure from the CC of the CPSU—all trade union activities in the Soviet Union underwent a fundamental realignment. In particular, the new orientation profoundly influenced the union wage policies. Their purpose, henceforth, was no longer to maintain and raise wages; instead, they were to serve primarily as instruments for increasing output.

It has been shown that the First Five-Year Plan period was characterized by particularly unfavorable wage developments. Inflationary increases in the cost of living outran the rise of nominal earnings and resulted in declining real wages. Quite a few plant managers, aware of the intimate connection between wages and performance, tended to grant workers higher wages than permissible under the estimates of government plans bent on ignoring the soaring flight of prices. Such managers frequently met with union opposition. The unions, considering themselves guardians of "financial discipline," strongly objected to payrolls in excess of plan estimates. They went so far as to bring charges against plant executives for "exceeding payroll limits." They insisted on raising the performance quotas set by the plants and their time-keeping and standard departments ("rates and standards bureaus," or "TNB" after the Russian initials), submitting "counter-quotas" under which more production per unit of time was required to earn the base rate of pay.

A few examples may illustrate this. In Tula a general increase in quotas was ordered in 1930. In the spring of 1931 the Moscow union newspaper carried a Tula dispatch saying: "Among plant executives here there is a tendency to refrain from revising quotas this year." In other words, management did not intend to raise quotas. But—"the unions conducted their campaign in exemplary fashion . . . Under pressure from the Union Council, the revision of quotas was begun. A flood of counter-quotas, greatly in excess of TNB schedules, made plain the vast possibilities existing."[110]

[110] *Trud*, April 12, 1931.

It was the same story in the Ukraine. There the unions set up "counter-quotas" everywhere:[111]

> "Miners, metal workers, chemical workers; workers of the black coal pits of the Donets Basin and of the red manganese mines of Krivoi-Rog; workers in iron and steel and in metal and machine-building plants, submitted counter-quotas far in excess of plan estimates."

The central union agencies and the union newspaper *Trud* took pains to make the locals proceed with the necessary firmness. *Trud* was indignant because "many economic executives, with the obvious connivance of union organizations, took the road of unjustified wage increases."[112] The Central Board of the Union of Machine-building Workers exposed conditions in machine-building, attacking "wage increases far in excess of the approved payroll, while neither the production plan nor the plan for increasing productivity were fulfilled." The union asked the Public Prosecutor to institute criminal action against a number of plant managers who had raised wages![113]

Nor did central union headquarters remain inactive. At a meeting of the Presidium of the AUCTUC in May 1932, Gavrill D. Veinberg, AUCTUC secretary in charge of wages, stated:[114]

> "In many plants there is a tendency to exceed approved payrolls. We must keep in mind that the unions are held responsible for surpassing payroll allotments. We must take measures to remedy the situation as speedily as possible. Union interests today must center on completion of the reform of wage rates, strengthening of wage discipline, and elimination of raises in excess of payroll allotments."

A special conference on wage policy was called by the AUCTUC in January 1933. It was attended by delegates from the AUCTUC, from union central boards, and from local union councils of the most important industrial centers; also by representatives of the various People's Commissariats in charge of industry. The official union position again was stated by G. D. Veinberg. He said:[115]

[111] *Trud,* April 9, 1931.
[112] *Trud,* January 14, 1932.
[113] *Trud,* February 16, 1932.
[114] *Trud,* May 21, 1932.
[115] *Trud,* January 24, 1933.

"We must take to task any unionists who tolerate distortions of the Party line in wage questions, proceeding with the same severity as does the Party against opportunists in its own ranks who obstruct the delivery of grain or other operations in the front lines of socialist construction. You sometimes hear whispering in union ranks, like this: 'Does it behoove the unions to oppose concessions which industrial executives grant in wage questions? If we do that, how can we face the workers?' This is the most shameful misconception of union tasks. It is 'trade unionism' pure and simple . . . We must actively combat this kind of 'defense' of labor's interests!"

Henceforth, no "shameful misconceptions" were tolerated. The unions had been charged with preventing pay increases, and anyone who failed to carry out the assignment was guilty of "trade unionism" of the prohibited, proscribed, outlawed "opportunistic" variety.

With the unions no longer interested in the goals which characterize the essence of union activities all over the world, their participation in the fixing of wage rates and performance quotas became irrelevant. The institution of collective bargaining was doomed. Collective agreements became inconsequential and gradually extinct. Their decline and eventual disappearance had been foreshadowed by the directive of the AUCTUC and the Presidium of the Supreme Economic Council of September 28, 1929,[116] which had made the collective agreement just another device for carrying out the government's production plan. What this implied in everyday practice came to light within a short time.

The new directive was first put into effect when contracts were drawn up for the year 1929/30. It clearly appeared that unions had no say in the matter. *Trud*'s coverage of the "contract renewal campaign" contained inadequate and colorless information, but the daily of the Supreme Economic Council, *Torgovo-Promyshlennaya Gazeta*, the organ of industrial management, was well-informed and able to discuss the new collective agreements with skill, vitality, and interesting details. It could even afford to attack union editors in an "Open Letter" which scolded them for their passive attitude toward the renewal of collective agreements.[117]

---

116 *Pravda*, September 29, 1929.
117 *Torgovo-Promyshlennaya Gazeta*, October 25, 1929.

Useless for the protection of wage and salary earners, collective agreements were left only one function—to help increase production. It was only as tools of the government's production policies that collective agreements could become indirectly instrumental in promoting the welfare of the working people. But then why bother with such agreements at all? Would not agreements on "socialist competition" serve better?

In 1929 there was still a marked tendency to put off the decision. "Before the end of this year," *Pravda* said,[118] "a number of stipulations included in agreements on socialist competition will be transferred to collective agreements. This will be repeated and extended every year, with the ultimate aim of merging the two types of agreements in one document, which will deal with the fulfillment of the production plan and will be signed by workers and industrial executives."

Formally, collective bargaining agreements still were entered into in the early 1930's, but their content was increasingly determined by the government's economic goals. An ordinance issued in the spring of 1933 provided that collective agreements might no longer contain any clauses assuring wage and salary earners of any rights or advantages beyond those guaranteed by existing legislation. This was almost the end. When contracts drawn up for 1933 came up for renewal, most of them were automatically extended for another year without review or change. For 1935, new collective agreements were negotiated under orders of the CPC of the USSR for persons employed in water transportation, commercial establishments, lumber, and rafting; apart from these, collective bargaining agreements withered away unnoticed.[119]

In 1937, when discussions centered on the so-called "trade union crisis," it was decided to reintroduce collective agreements, but this decision was not carried out.

As collective bargaining agreements lost in importance, the unions and their representatives in the plants, the plant committees, were increasingly barred from taking any hand in fixing wages. Originally the plant committees had played an important role in wage negotiations. With piece rates the dominant form of

[118] *Pravda*, October 24, 1929.
[119] *Soviet Labor Law. Textbook for Law Schools,* published by the People's Commissariat for Justice of the USSR, Moscow, 1939, pp. 60 f.

wages in the Soviet Union and specific rates usually being set for every plant, a special mechanism was required to establish rules and specifications.

Wages were, and as a rule still are, determined in two consecutive stages. The rate schedule determines wage rates (monthly, in most cases) for different categories of wage and salary earners. These, however, are but one factor in computing actual piece rates. Another factor is the performance quota. It is not included in the collective agreement and is fixed separately in every plant. The piece rate then is computed as the ratio of the hourly wage rate to the quota.

Participation is setting quotas used to be one of the main tasks of labor representatives in the plants. Under Sec. 56 of the 1922 Labor Code "the performance quota shall be determined by agreement between the management of the plant and the union agency." For this purpose, joint labor-management bodies functioned in the plants, the so-called piece-rate and grievance committees, abbreviated RKK (the Russian initials). If no unanimous decision was arrived at in the RKK, the final decision was made by an arbitration board also functioning within the plant. Labor representatives on RKK and arbitration bodies were appointed by the plant committees.

From the early 1930's, there was a noticeable tendency to fix quotas and piece rates without RKK participation. Quotas, as a rule, were set by TNB, the management's rates and standards department, and the RKK merely had to approve TNB suggestions. The workers' participation in the determination of working pace and performance had become highly illusory. Later the determination of job standards was officially declared to be the exclusive domain of management, although Labor Code provisions to the contrary were not repealed.

This was done formally in January, 1933, in a ruling emanating from neither the CPC nor the People's Commissariat for Labor but from the unions themselves—from the Presidium of the AUCTUC. The decision, unpretentiously confined to "changes in the operational activities of the RKK," provided that piece rates and quotas were to be determined by management and no longer required RKK approval. Only in the event that the quotas set by management were "faulty," or not in line with collective agreements, were labor representatives permitted to institute grievance proceedings through RKK machinery. The only regular task left to labor on the joint labor-management committees was to familiarize the personnel with the quotas and piece rates decided upon by management, and to spur the workers on to fulfill their quotas. This is still the law of the land.[120]

The new regulations, decided upon January 2, 1933, were first put into effect surreptitiously and not made public until four months later.[121] Even under the conditions prevailing in the Soviet Union in the early 1930's, it evidently seemed wise to let so radical a change become an accomplished fact before taking public responsibility for it.

Of course, the new system required some "theoretical" justification. At the plenary session of the AUCTUC in July 1933, AUCTUC secretary G. D. Veinberg obliged:[122]

> "To set up the wage system and the establishment of job standards correctly, in accordance with specific conditions in individual industries and specific features of individual production processes, it is necessary that the responsibility for such decisions be imposed directly upon plant administrators and technical managers. This also is dictated by the necessity of assuring one-man management and commercial accounting in the plants . . . No one but management shall be primarily responsible for technical standardization, for wage scale, quotas, piece rates, etc. Today quite a few comrades in the plants share the idea that the union should have as much to say about wages as management. That is a fundamental error. It would imply that the union takes the place of management. It is a 'leftist' opportunistic distortion, undermining of one-man management, interference with the operational functions of management. This must be stopped."

It is true that minor improvements followed in later years. Under the terms of a decree of the CPC of the USSR of January 14, 1939,[123] general directives concerning the establishment of quotas must be approved by the central economic agencies immediately concerned and by the secretary of the AUCTUC, or by the chairman of the central board of the respective union. But this did not change the actual establishment of rates; once the

---

120 A. E. Pasherstnik, *Legal Questions Concerning the Remuneration of the Labor of Wage and Salary Earners,* (Russian) , publ. by the Law Institute of the Academy of Sciences of the USSR, Moscow-Leningrad, 1949, p. 242.
121 *Trud,* May 9, 1933.
122 *Trud,* July 8, 1933.
123 *Laws and Ordinances,* 1939:38.

directive from "high up" is issued, quotas and piece rates are still set by management, with unions and plant committees barred from even so much as discussing them.

With the essential function of labor unions abolished, their authority dwindled fast. The new union policy met with resistance on the part of the workers—mute but appearing spontaneously in various places. Tension increased; "wildcat" labor disputes developed.

The unions, in turn, did not hesitate to use the strongest measures against discontent in the plants. A start was made during the 1929 "collective bargaining campaign." Of course, repressive measures were initiated not by the unions or the Communist Party; the pattern developed for years by the CPSU was followed and action called for by a group of "production workers." *Pravda* prominently displayed an appeal to all workers of the Soviet Union, signed by 42 workers of two Dnepropetrovsk metal plants. A new battle cry was born: [124]

> "When collective agreements come up for renewal, backward groups of workers, stirred up by counterrevolutionary Trotskyites, rightist opportunists, kulakophiles, and initiators of whispering campaigns, will start presenting their non-proletarian and greedy demands . . .
> "We appeal to all workers of the Soviet Union to put up the most active resistance against the sorties of grabbers and whisperers, and actively to fight the class enemy who has infiltrated our plants."

Whenever possible, the press suppressed any news of labor disputes; but occasionally the facts leaked out. A few illustrations may suffice.

In the GEZ plant in Kharkov several fitters employed in the tool-making department insisted on lower quotas, "threatening to stop work unless their demands were granted within five days." They succeeded in gaining support from a few union officers and even of "some Young Communists." Thereupon "public opinion in the plant" was mobilized against the "shameful behavior of the fitters." A resolution was adopted which called for "further increases in productivity and further cost reduction." The fitters promptly dropped the subject.[125]

---

[124] *Pravda*, October 22, 1929.
[125] *Trud*, April 13, 1931.

In the Kirov Works in Leningrad, workers transferred from another plant voiced dissatisfaction with "allegedly low piece rates" and asked for a raise. The demand was rejected, and the union harshly rebuffed the culprits. Yet the "grabbers" (among them several CP members) were not appeased. Unrest spread. Finally the objectors were fired and the union paper blacklisted their names in an appeal addressed "to all plants," which were requested "to refrain from hiring these grabbers, and to place them in public quarantine." [126] It was never revealed how much of a raise had been asked for by the blacklisted men.

Meanwhile, management kept setting higher and higher quotas, and friction increased, especially in the spring of 1933 when labor representatives were not even consulted any longer and plant officials first used their newly-acquired right to fix quotas at their discretion. A *Trud* report said: [127]

> "The revision of quotas met with considerable resistance from class-hostile elements, grabbers, and loafers. Numerous sorties of class enemies have been recorded, directed at hampering fulfillment of the plan to increase productivity. These sorties were of various kinds: now threats against TNB employees, now clever slowdowns, sabotage of timekeeping, propaganda against quota revision, attempts to organize resistance by individual groups of workers."

The reported facts were characteristic enough; even more so was the language of the union paper.

The decisions and official unionist statements just quoted laid down the line on union wage policy, which came to be the alpha and omega of Soviet union leaders. Later there will be a chance to consider the concrete forms which this policy assumed in the post-war years. The principle has never changed.

Here we may only take up the beginning of a special manifestation of this unionist wage policy—or rather, perhaps, of unionist production policy: the so-called socialist competition.

---

[126] *Trud,* September 7, 1931.
[127] *Trud,* April 6, 1933.

"Socialist Competition"

The "mass movement" created early in 1929 around the slogan of socialist competition aimed specifically at higher output, cost reduction, and improved quality of production. "Socialist competition" had been conceived as a near-permanent contest between individual plants or plant departments vying with each other for better production results. Soon, however, it became a device to further competition among individual workers.

In the spring of 1929 the Sixteenth Conference of the CPSU issued an appeal "to all workers and toiling peasants of the Soviet Union." [128] "Competition and the Five-Year Plan," it said, "are indissolubly linked." It called for "competition in cutting production costs, in increasing productivity, in consolidating work discipline, in increasing planted acreage and yield, in drawing more peasants into *kolkhozes* and cooperatives, in streamlining the government machine and bringing it nearer to the masses, in improving the work of cultural and social institutions serving the needs of the toiling masses." A new universal remedy for all social and economic ills.

First of all it was introduced in industry. As the physical strength, the skills and intellectual abilities with which individuals are endowed are by no means equal, such a "competition" compels all workers to strive for the speed and performance of those who have "smashed the record." Anyone who wants to take part in the contest must strain himself to the utmost, exhaust his strength, and endanger his health. In a socialist economy, aiming by definition at the protection of the human being, competition among individual workers, if it is to take place at all, should be focused mainly on quality, not quantity, of performance. And it goes without saying that it should be subject to the most stringent and minute control by organizations of workers themselves, by unions of their own choosing.

"Socialist competition," as it spread in the Soviet Union after 1929, had nothing in common with such concepts. Competition among plants might still have approximated the notion of a stimulating factor in a socialist economy, had it not been for the lack of managerial, technological and plain operational pre-

---

[128] Dated April 29, 1929, the appeal was printed in *Pravda*, May 4, 1929.

paration. Actually, Soviet plants were not geared to maximum efficiency, and the attempt to stimulate maximum efforts through competitive incentives often resulted in uncoördinated work and operational chaos.

Moreover, "socialist competition" was carried out under conditions which precluded the safeguarding of the workers' interests. It was not left to the workers whether or not to participate in production contests—they had to. Nor were they free to determine the objectives of the contest, or to limit the competitive effort in regard to individual performance. In reality, "socialist competition" became a matter of extracting the highest performance possible, of spurring men to unlimited exertion. It was used by management, especially in the first year, as a device to increase production at any cost, whatever the effect on working conditions.

Competition among individual workers or workers' teams rapidly became the essence, of the new "movement," with maximum quantity of output per worker, along with "voluntary" reduction of piece rates, as the objective.

Workers who agreed to engage in competition usually called for the establishment of higher quotas, and thus for lowering piece rates. The underlying motives were varied. Some workers, particularly of the younger generation, were animated by enthusiasm for socialist construction—or else prompted by a sporting spirit. Others were guided by the desire for advancement, by the hope to be upgraded from "common laborers" to higher-classed "excellent" workers; the Moscow union paper had openly suggested that "initiators" of competition would be given higher-paid jobs.[129] In other cases, workers acted from fear lest they lag behind speedier co-workers and lose their jobs (unemployment still was considerable in 1929).

In most instances, the results of "socialist competition" were unfavorable to a majority of workers. The "competitors" could directly ask for reduction of piece rates only for themselves. But this was enough to exert heavy indirect pressure on the general wage level. Quite often the initiative shown by the participants in competition was used by management to cut piece rates generally, even below the rates set by the "competitors."

In a letter printed by the Moscow union paper, workers of an

---

[129] *Trud*, July 19, 1929.

industrial plant in Tula complained about their manager: after a group of workers reported for competition at reduced rates, he had said: [130] "So you've raised the quota? Then it was too low. O.K., let's raise it another 20 per cent." Another dispatch stated: [131] "In a number of plants in the Ukraine several groups of workers expressed the desire to have the quota raised 10 per cent. This induced the management in those plants to raise the quota for all workers 15 or 20 per cent."

Increased effort was paralleled by a deterioration of general working conditions. Reports about worsened conditions were so frequent that the AUCTUC had to adopt a special resolution warning of a "bureaucratic degeneration of socialist competion." It pointed to a number of deplorable results, such as "longer hours, work on holidays, all-round revision of wage rates and quotas," also "attempts to violate labor laws or rates and standards set in collective agreements, and thus to depress the workers' condition." [132]

To elicit such statements from the new union leadership, conditions must have become frightening indeed. Only a few months earlier, the old AUCTUC leadership had been severely upbraided for its coolness to "socialist competition." [133] And only three weeks earlier, several locals which suggested that unions exercise some restraining control over "challenges to competion" [134] had been sharply rebuked.[135] Now the AUCTUC itself viewed the results or "socialist competition" with marked uneasiness.

At the AUCTUC session which deliberated on the results of the campaign for "socialist competition," Akulov, the rapporteur, said: [136] "It is time to approach the problem of shifting emphasis in competition from increases in the individual worker's output to improved utilization of plant and equipment through divers efficiency-engineering measures." However, this was only a short moment of irresolution for the AUCTUC. The Central Council

---

[130] *Trud*, May 30, 1929.
[131] *Trud*, August 6, 1929.
[132] *Trud*, August 2, 1929.
[133] *Trud*, May 12, 1929.
[134] A challenge to competition usually consisted in some statement like this: "I, So-andSo, declare my intention of increasing my quota by . . . per cent, and challenge So-and-So to join me." Was it not reasonable to ask for union supervision of such challenges? This, however, had been branded as "rightist opportunism."
[135] *Trud*, July 10, 1929.
[136] *Trud*, July 25, 1929.

of the Trade Unions soon regained its composure and thereafter showed no wavering in its energetic promotion of the new "movement."

Clearly, the "competition" movement had become synonymous with a novel sweating system. It aroused bitter resentment, particularly in the beginning.[137] Tensions between workers and unions ensued, causing friction and trouble. The socialist competition itself created obstacles to production. The resulting difficulties were taken into account. The speed-up and other excesses of "socialist competition" were somewhat restrained.

The most varied methods of spurring the worker on to increase his productivity soon arose on the basis of "socialist competition," the best known of which is the Stakhanov movement.[138] In principle, however, the "competition" system remained unchanged, and it has become an organic part of the entire Soviet organization of labor, with a far-reaching influence on the wage structure.

APPENDIX 1:

"Socialist Competition" and the Working Masses

For the Soviet press, 1929 was a year of constant attacks on the "greed," "raffishness," and "backwardness" of the workers who showed a lack of understanding for the "socialist competition." In particular, "backward workers from the countryside were the target. The newspapers said that their only purpose in coming to the city was to grab as much money as they could. Did they not constantly display *kulak* attitudes? Were they not reactionaries and enemies of socialist construction?

The real basis of the tension was pointed out in a *Trud* report on conditions in the railroad repair shops in Tver':[139]

"Even in the most advanced departments, ['socialist'] com-

---

[137] Some illustrations will be found in Appendix to this Chapter.

[138] It is impossible to give a systematic description of the Stakhanov movement within the framework of this book. The author was therefore forced to limit himselm to picturing the development of the movement, which shows its character as a means of spurring the worker on to greater productivity, in Appendix 2 to this chapter.

[139] *Trud,* July 2, 1929.

petition takes place in an atmosphere of silent struggle. At first, even many Communists looked askance at the shock brigades . . .

" 'What good is this competition? You drive yourself, you wear yourself out, and it does the work no good, either.' Behind this sly reasoning flares fierce anger at competition. And why shouldn't people be furious, since the factory plan destroys their personal plans for getting rich, since they have no strength left after work in the plant to work in the village?"

Ironical depreciation of the workers' interest in their village property was hardly suited to kindle enthusiasm for "socialist competition." In an astounding letter from a metal worker, named Goshev, which *Trud* printed at the time, the true motives of the opponents of "competition" were stated with unusual sincerity and frankness: [140]

"Comrade Editor [Goshev wrote]: Why is it that your newspaper says so much about workers who are enthusiastic about socialist competition, and nothing about the doubts that fill many workers? Why do you grant space to stories about productivity and remain silent about the price that has to be paid for it? Let me tell you my opinion.

"In the Shagov Factory, Ivanovo-Voznesensk province, 800 weavers refused to participate in socialist competition. They acclaimed that there was no chance to increase production, since the work day was filled up to the limit, anyway, and the quotas had already been raised. Present-day working conditions are called 'sweating,' anyway; and now socialist competition—it just smells of capitalist exploitation!

"As any old worker I share this view, and that is why I don't take part in the competition and don't try to outdo the other fellows' performance.

"A cheap thing, comrade, the achievements that those records brag about! Supposing a man like that gets more work done per day and then suggests raising the quota. Well, then who are these record workers? Young-Communists, youths full of strength and zeal. With that, of course, you can move mountains. And their example is imitated by reckless oldsters who may once in a while succeed in a record performance. But how long can this last? One month, two months, maybe six months you can bear up under these conditions: you don't have the stamina for more. But we are just ordinary workers and have to work our jobs for years to come."

The fact that such a letter could appear in *Trud* indicated the

---

[140] *Trud*, July 3, 1929.

degree of tension, the amount of pent-up resentment in the plants. Discontent had spread so widely that it had to be given an outlet. Of course, the editors of *Trud* dissociated themselves from the tenor of the letter, gratuitously supplying the broad hint: "The class enemy lurks behind his [the letter-writer's] back." [141] A few days later the warning was repeated and underscored. The letter, *Trud* said, had been "slanted politically." [142] That was a clear threat, an attempt to intimidate workers who had the courage to speak up against "socialist competition"!

During the summer of 1929 threats and admonitions were added for the benefit of those who, instead of admiring the pacemakers of "competition," insulted them as "carreerists," "bootlickers," "spies," "stoolpigeons," "informers," etc. The newspaper of the Young Communist League, coming out in defense of "informers," had to admit: "Squealing sometimes serves the purpose of settling personal accounts; it has become a hideous phenomenon." Nevertheless, "informers are very valuable to socialist competition . . . On the whole, I believe in informers." [143] This profession of faith was surely a slip of the tongue. But even so, it gave some idea of the climate prevailing in Soviet industrial plants in 1929.

APPENDIX 2:

The Stakhanov Movement as an Instrument of Labor Policy

The Stakhanov movement had its origin in the record set by Alexei Stakhanov, a coal miner who, on August 31, 1935, cut 102 tons of coal in six hours. The way had been carefully prepared for the record by the management of the mine; Stakhanov had been allowed to concentrate exclusively on the cutting operation and had had the help of a group of assistants. However, this was revealed only later; at the beginning, Stakhanov's achievement was represented as a heroic individual deed which should serve as a model for all.

All the machinery was immediately set in motion to set off a record-hunt such as had never been seen before. Reports on the fulfilment of daily work norms by 500, 600 and 1,000 per cent were, for a short while, a daily occurrence. At the end of October, the coal miner Makar Lashtoba fulfilled his work norm by as much as 2,274 per cent and cut 311 tons of coal in one day.[144] Having begun in coal

---

[141] *Trud*, July 4, 1929.
[142] *Trud*, July 12, 1929.
[143] *Komsomol'skaya Pravda*, July 28, 1929.

mining, the movement quickly spread to other industries and to transportation, and in many places set off a veritable fever, Take, for example, the report in the leading industrial newspaper containing a
description of the work of the brigade in the Gorki automobile works
led by the famous metal-forger, Busygin:[145]

> ". . . The entire brigade is in the grip of a tremendous work
> fury. It is simply impossible to conceive of going up to one of
> these people to distract him for a minute. No one smokes, no
> one talks. I have visited many plants, but nowhere have I seen
> such an ecstasy of work."

What this deliberately unleashed "tremendous work fury" was to
mean in a socio-political sense was soon enunciated very clearly. When
the first All-Union Conference of Stakhanovites met in the latter part
of October 1935 and one of the conference participants attempted to
define the term "Stakhanovite," the chairman, Deputy Commissar for
Heavy Industry Yuri Pyatakov, interrupted him impatiently: "Why
should we rack our brains over the definition of a Stakhanovite? A
Stakhanovite is a worker who overthrows all our work norms." [146] And
in his concluding address to the conference, Pyatakov formulated the
same thought even more sharply:[147]

> "The essence of the Stakhanov movement lies in the fact that
> the Stakhanovite—actually, with his own hands, not just in theory
> but in practice—overthrows all so-called technical work norms
> . . . . Technically based norms represent a phantom that served to
> intimidate us, a brake that held us back."

One might be inclined to think that Pyatakov, in this offensive
against technically based norms, was attacking only the *"so-called
technical norms,"* which had been improvised without serious analysis
of the work process or were based on already outdated technology.
However, the principal organ of heavy industry, in its lead articles
before and during the conference, left no room for doubt that the
attack on the technical norms aimed much further: "No attention is
to be paid to the technical performance norms, even if they have been
checked three times, or to the projected production capacities." [148]
"Down with the phantom of the projected production capacities!" [149]
And Pyatakov himself, in his above-quoted speech, virtually talked
himself into a state of delirium:

144 *Trud,* November 1, 1935.
145 *Za Industrializatsiyu,* October 15, 1935.
146 *Za Industrializatsiyu,* October 22, 1935.
147 *Za Industrializatsiyu,* October 24, 1935.
148 *Za Industrializatsiyu,* October 10, 1935.
149 *Za Industrializatsiyu,* October 21, 1935.

"We will smash the devil himself and attain unheard-of production results of which no one has ever dreamed . . . . One must simply shout: 'The devil take it!' "

Not much good could be expected of this sort of morbid whipping oneself on.

We cannot go into the production-political results of this policy here. Needless to say, they were not very satisfactory.[150] As for the effect the policy had on the working and living conditions of the broad masses of workers, it was often extremely unfavorable.

As was to be expected, the development of the Stakhanov movement brought about in numerous cases a raising of the performance norms and hence a lowering of the piece-work rates, and produced a feeling of insecurity among the workers. The discontent was intensified when—as often happened—especially favorable conditions for full activity and high earnings were created for the Stakhanovites at the expense of the other workers. Thus, the official trade-union *Trud* reported that in the great "Skorokhod" shoe factory in Leningrad, at a time when there was a shortage of materials, the Stakhanovites were deliberately—and openly—kept fully supplied so that they could show a high work record, while the other workers had to stand about with nothing to do. The chairman of the factory employees' committee wrote in *Trud*: [151]

> ". . . What is actually the moral position of a Stakhanovite when he is fully occupied while his neighbor is idle? Shura Dmitrieva, a woman Stakhanovite in the children's shoe section, came to me:
>
> " 'It is unpleasant for me, Maximova. See to it that enough work is found for everyone or that the personnel is reduced. Otherwise I will stop working.'
>
> "Serious conclusions had to be drawn from this and they were drawn."

What sort of "conclusions" these were the report does not mention. That they did not improve relations between the Stakhanovites and their less fortunate fellow-workers is obvious. These relations were not very friendly anyway, as the same report from the "Skorokhod" factory illustrates with an example:

"The backward workers M. and S. made fun of Martynova,

---

[150] In this connection, see my articles in *Sotsialisticheskii Vestnik*: "Under the Banner of Rationalization" (1936, No. 6/7), "One Year of the Stakhanov Movement" (1936, No. 18/19), "Joyless Anniversary" (1937, No. 17/18).

[151] *Trud*, October 25, 1935.

one of the best Stakhanovites. During the work, they came up to Martynova several times, stroked her back as though to show sympathy, and asked:

" 'Isn't your blouse damp, Madame? Aren't you tired?' "

Here the tension between the Stakhanovites and the other workers still assumed relatively harmless forms. The workers' hostility toward the Stakhanovites was also expressed in other ways—and often much more clearly. In the Uritsky works in Smolensk, the famous Stakhanovite machine-fitter Likhoradov actually felt "hounded." [152] The colleagues of the equally famous Stakhanovite locomotive engineer Krivonos refused to shake his hand.[153] In the "Red Iron-Presser" works in Rostov-on-Don, a dirty broom with the inscription, "A bouquet for fulfilling three work norms," was laid on the machine tool of a woman Stakhanovite.[154] There were also worse cases, in which threats and even violence were employed against Stakhanovites.[155] Even though these cases may often be exaggerated by the Soviet press, their symptomatic meaning is unmistakable.

Stakhanovism soon became a euphemism for the utter straining of every bit of energy. If a plant manager found himself unable to overcome malpractices in his plant, he tried to extricate himself in one fell swoop with the aid of "Stakhanov days" (more properly, Stakhanov 24-hour periods, *"Stakhanovskiye sutki"*). The director of the big Petrovsky works in Dnepropetrovsk once reported with pride how his plant, despite severe deficiencies in raw materials supply and in internal plant organization, had set a record by introducing Stakhanov days: [156]

". . . All this was achieved through exertion of a kind that cannot be stood uninterruptedly. The section chiefs cannot, after all, work continuously day and night. Nor can the plant management spend day and night in the various sections. One also cannot expect every brigade to report for work voluntarily several hours before the beginning of its shift and remain at work several hours after the end of the shift. . . . This literally required insane exertion."

That the economic results of this sort of industrial practice were found to be unfavorable in the long run is obvious, and the fact was

---

[152] *Pravda*, October 31, 1935.
[153] *Pravda*, October 16, 1935.
[154] *Trud*, November 1, 1935.
[155] *Pravda*, October 16, 22 and 29, 1935; *Trud*, October 23 and 27, 1935; *Za Industrializatsiyu*, October 3, 15, 20 and 26, 1935.
[156] *Za Industrializatsiyu*, January 18, 1936.

often openly acknowledged in the Soviet press. Regarding the effect of these practices on working conditions, the press was much more reserved, but it could not completely ignore it. It was soon reported that the record-hunt had caused the danger of accidents in the mines to increase and had led to major disasters, whereupon reprisals had been carried out against the responsible engineers, who had, it so happened, warned against the dangers.[157] It was stated that the Stakhanov record-hunt had led to "gross violations of the labor laws," including the practice of having juvenile laborers work in two successive shifts.[158] Other facts were also brought out.[159]

This had a further unfavorable effect on economic development and brought the internal organization of work in the plants to a virtual state of crisis, as well. The low-point in this respect seems to have been reached in the years 1936 and 1937. Thus, for example, a report from the State Watch Factory No. 1 stated that the performance norms in the factory had been raised in the spring of 1936 on the initiative of the Stakhanovites, on condition that a series of "demands" were met, whereby the workers "are provided with good tools and with a sufficient number of measuring instruments, the entire equipment [of the factory] is put in good condition," etc. The report declared: [160]

> "Many of our demands were adopted in the plan for organizational-technical measures. But not one of the demands was fulfilled. The equipment was not put in good condition; it is more run down today than it was before. The work tools are of even worse quality today. . . . All this has led to deplorable results. In our section, the established performance norms are fulfilled by only 58 per cent. . . . The earnings of Stakhanovites, to say nothing of the other workers, have declined. The turnover in personnel has reached extreme proportions. More and more Stakhanovites are leaving the plant. . . ."

Some Stakhanovites tried to arrest the process of distintegration by presenting their case in the press. Busygin—the best-known of the Stakhanovites after Stakhanov himself—complained in the organ of heavy industry that, in the Gorki automobile works, the personnel turnover had spread to the Stakhanovites: The best Stakhanovites were leaving the plant and writing letters to the plant newspaper; "every one of these letters tells of the outrageous behavior [of the

157 Regarding these trials of engineers, which in some cases resulted in death sentences, see my articles in *Sotsialisticheskii Vestnik* (with exact references to Soviet sources): "The Stakhanov Movement and Protection of Labor" (1936, No. 4) and "The Trial in Novosibirsk" (1936, No. 23/24).
158 *Trud*, March 14, 1936.
159 See further Chapter VI below.
160 *Trud*, September 9, 1936.

plant administration] toward the workers." [161] On the same day, it was reported in the central trade-union organ from a large textile factory in the Moscow region: "Of the 3,000 female weavers, almost 1,000 were Stakhanovites; today, half of them no longer fulfil the performance norms." [162] A number of similar cases were mentioned in the lead article in *Bolshevik* dedicated to the first anniversary of the Stakhanov movement, and the following over-all picture was given for three major areas of the textile industry:[163]

> "The work of the cotton and linen industries in the Moscow, Leningrad and Kalinin regions is assuming particularly disgraceful forms. Thousands of Stakhanovites, who in these regions had switched to stretch-out work, no longer fulfil their performance norms. In July, only 25 per cent of the female spinners and 15 per cent of the female weavers in the cotton industry of these regions fulfilled the new norms."

In the spring of 1937, it became known that even the famous Central Irmino mine, in which Alexei Stakhanov had set his record, "is no longer fulfilling the Plan," [164] that "the largest mines, famous throughout the entire Donets Basin, have been operating very irregularly lately and lag behind more and more frequently," [165] that the famous metal-forgers Busygin and Faustov of the Gorki automobile works had not fulfilled the performance norms for 1936 on the average,[166] that even "workers who the year before were awarded the honorary title of 'Master of Socialist Labor' are no longer fulfilling the Plan." [167]

These malfunctionings were, to be sure, not attributable to the Stakhanov movement alone. This was just the time of the "Great Purge" of 1936-38, which shook the entire economic and governmental apparatus of the Soviet Union in the severest way. The painful concomitants of Stakhanovism were now also officially attributed to the "wrecking" activities of "enemies of the people" and "foreign agents." Not until 1938, when the "Purge" had begun to wane and a certain modicum of order was gradually restored to economic organization, was some degree of tranquillity also imparted to the Stakhanov move-

---

[161] *Za Industrializatsiyu*, August 5, 1936.
[162] *Trud*, August 5, 1936.
[163] "Anniversary of the Stakhanov Movement" (lead article), *Bolshevik*, 1936, No. 17, pp. 17-18.
[164] *Pravda*, April 10, 1937.
[165] *Za Industrializatsiyu*, March 9, 1937.
[166] *Za Industrializatsiyu*, April 8, 1937.
[167] "Spearhead the Stakhanov Movement and Go Forward!" (lead article), *Bolshevik*, 1937, No. 16, p. 6.

ment. Toward the end of the Thirties, the movement became a normal element in the everyday policy of raising work productivity. The extraordinary interest in Stakhanovism which had been displayed only recently in official circles slackened off perceptibly. That is how it has remained. The Stakhanov movement is still promoted today, but it is no longer regarded as a panacea as when it was inaugurated in 1935.

Chapter Five

WAGES AND LIVING STANDARDS, II
(Since 1941)

Wage Trends in War-Time.—Post-War Policies.—Wages Trends under the Fourth Five-Year Plan.—Prices during the War.—The De-Rationing.—Lowering the Price Level.—Reintroduction of Union Contracts.—The Development of Real Wages: 1928-1938-1940-1951.—International Wage Comparison: 1950/51.—"Socialized Wages."—Appendices: 1. The Wage Fund Mystery.—2. Contradictions in the Analysis of Post-War Wage Trends.

Wage Trends in Wartime

The priciple of recent Russian wage policies has been to block any "mechanical" rise in the wage level. It was already well defined before the war: as a rule, a worker could increase his earnings only by increasing his performance (either quantitatively or, in the case of upgrading, qualitatively). In the last year before the Soviet Union entered the war, the tendency to hold down the wage level was manifested on one occasion in a way that was glaring even for Soviet conditions. In June 1940 (cf. Chapter VI, below, for details), the order to change from the seven-hour day to the eight-hour day and to the 48-hour week was accompanied by a directive not to raise daily and monthly wage rates in lengthening hours (i.e., to lower hourly rates) and to raise the performance quotas for piece work (i.e. to lower piece-work rates). Longer hours were not to result in higher earnings. In this case, the negative attitude toward a possible rise in the wage level went far beyond the rejection of "mechanical" wage increases.

After the Soviet Union's entry into the war—when the rules

governing working hours were changed again and overtime was introduced so extensively (Chapter VI) that the eight-hour day was in fact replaced by a ten- or eleven-hour day—the government refrained from a freeze of earnings. Overtime pay was reduced but not abolished: henceforth, overtime pay was to be generally time-and-a-half (instead of time-and-a-half and double time, as before). The result was bound to be a substantial increase in average earnings: by 37½ per cent if working hours were increased from eight to ten a day, and by 56 per cent if they were increased from eight to eleven a day.

Published information about actual wage trends during the war is very scanty. It took Voznesensky's book (repeatedly quoted above) to reveal that average earnings in industry rose 42 per cent between 1940 and 1944, and 53 per cent in the industries directly subordinate to the government of the Soviet Union.[1] This corresponds approximately to the lengthening of hours (plus overtime pay). In part it may also have reflected the increased importance of war industry proper, with its higher wage rates. Beyond that, a *de facto* freezing of wages—despite the extremely unfavorable changes in the price level (see below)—was vigorously enforced.

This policy, to be sure, did not preclude wage increases in special cases for particular groups of workers and employees. Such exceptions were few in number. The only one of any importance, cited again and again by Soviet authors dealing with wartime wage policies, was the raise granted to teachers and other employees of elementary and higher schools under a decree of the Council of People's Commissars of the USSR and the CC of the CPSU of August 11, 1943.[2] In their practical scope the exceptions were strictly limited.

On the other hand, the efforts to hold down the wage level did not reverse the trend toward the most extensive differentiation of earnings, with higher pay for wage and salary earners of special importance to production. This trend even was intensified. Wage scales in a number of occupational divisions were revised for the purpose, with incentive wages and performance bonuses climbing higher and higher. The stated reason was the need to provide the greatest possible differentiation of wages a firm basis in the everyday application of wage rules, a principle

---

[1] Voznesensky (see Chapter I, N. 60), pp. 117-118.

proclaimed as "socialist," as opposed to the "capitalist" principle of wage leveling. On the eve of war, this almost incredibly distorted concept was even introduced into Soviet textbooks. "The characteristic feature of wage dynamics in capitalist countries," said the textbook of Soviet labor law published in 1939 by the People's Commissariat of Justice, "is the leveling of wages of skilled and unskilled workers. . . Petty bourgeois leveling [uravnilovka] in the remuneration of labor is socialism's worst enemy. For years leveling has been relentlessly combated by Marxism-Leninism." [3]

In wartime, these wage-political ideas were carried farther. A learned Soviet author characterized the trend as follows: [4]

> "The measures taken in the field of wages from 1942 to 1944 were an important step forward in the fight against leveling and in the application of the socialist principle of labor remuneration to all sections of the national economy.
>
> "The decrees concerning wage questions were only partly linked to specific wartime conditions, and only partly reflected these conditions. Such, for example, were the rules issued in 1942 for the duration of the war and providing for the differentiation of wages of railroad train and dispatch crews according to the railroads' proximity to the front. Basically, the content of these decrees was determined more by the general laws of national economic development and expressed general principles of wage policy in the USSR which have proved fruitful and effective not only in peacetime but also under war conditions.
>
> "Never perhaps was a revision of wages, to say nothing of revision handled by the rates and standards departments of plant management, carried out in a relatively short time in so many and so diverse occupational divisions as during the war. Under wartime conditions, complete and consistent application of the socialist wage principle was of exceptional importance to the fulfillment of the tasks which the war imposed on the economy: increasing the productivity of labor, stepping up war production,

---

2 Laws and Ordinances, 1943: 197.

3 Soviet Labor Law, textbook for law schools, published by the People's Commissariat of Justice of the USSR, 1939, pp. 123-124.

4 A. E. Pasherstnik, "Legal Problems of Wage Control in the Circumstances of the War for the Fatherland," Izvestiya Akademii Nauk SSSR, Otdeleniye Ekonomiki i Prava, 1945, No. 2, pp. 13-14.—English ("Problems of Legal Wage Regulation in Wartime") in The American Reviews on the Soviet Union, 1946, May, pp. 61-62.

and assuring the smooth and coördinated functioning of the administrative and economic machinery."

The "socialist" wage principle amounted here to incentive wages pure and simple, with a huge difference between base pay and the top of the scale. Fantastic rates for record and shock workers—"front-line fighters of production," as they are styled in the Soviet state—were to accomplish what the wretched standard of the broad masses made impossible otherwise. While the bulk of labor lacked sufficient food and decent housing and was accordingly not too efficient at work, the record compensation of the "front-line fighters" was to conjure up everything at once: smooth production, increased output, a properly functioning administration and economy.

Another Soviet author put it somewhat more plainly, without referring to the "principles": [5]

> "In a number of industries, wage rates were revised in such a way as to assure skilled workers a higher pay. Likewise, problems of supply (of manufactured goods, supplementary food, etc.) are being regulated so as to satisfy the front-line fighters of production to the largest possible extent."

The result was a more glaring differentiation of earnings than had come to prevail before the war (see Chapter IV above). The top wages of the "front-line fighters" increased enormously (for some strange reason, all cases discussed in the newspapers refer to mining). In October 1943, miners Ivan Bazhenov and Afanasy Kedya (both employed by the Bryansk Coal Trust, Voroshilovgrad province) made 4,152 and 6,600 rubles, respectively. "Already hundreds and thousands of Donets miners earn such Stakhanov wages," the trade union paper reporting these facts added with enthusiasm[6]—an overstatement, no doubt, and yet peak earnings of this kind were no longer as infrequent as before the war. A year later, the same newspaper published the names of fifteen outstanding record-smashers in Donets mines, each of whom was able to take home 4,- to 6,000 rubles a month from January through September 1944; the most successful, Mikhail

---

[5] P. A. Khromov, "The Productivity of Industrial Labor during the War," *Izvestiya Akademii Nauk SSSR, Otdeleniye Ekonomiki i Prava*, 1945, No. 1, p. 41.
[6] *Trud*, December 25, 1943.

Afonin, had reached an average monthly income of 10,000 rubles.[7] In the Bakal' iron ore mines in the Southern Urals drill operator Grigorj Onufriyenko made 93,000 rubles from January through September[8]—10,333 rubles a month. Miner Aleksandr Selyutin of the Bryansk Coal Trust made 112,375 rubles in 1944 [9] —an average of 9,364 rubles monthly.

These figures are so scarce, and perhaps so accidental, that a comparison with data for the preceding years can only be made with reservations. Still, it is worth noting that while the average wage level rose about 75 per cent between 1938 and 1944, according to these figures, the top figure of monthly earnings published in the press nearly tripled (rising from 3,549 rubles in 1938 to 10,333 rubles in 1944).

This development of nominal earnings during the war was accompanied by an extremely unfavorable price trend. The result—inevitable in the tragic circumstances prevailing in the Soviet Union in those years—was a substantial wartime drop in real wages. This phenomenon will be taken up later, in connection with postwar developments.

Postwar Wage Policies

The ten- and eleven-hour day could not work out in the long run. A sporadic return to the eight-hour day set in before the end of the war. The movement was begun by isolated plants which could hardly influence the total picture, but the situation rapidly changed once the war was over. From mid-1945 on, reconversion to the hours in force before 1941 proceeded apace (see Chapter VI).

If conversion to the ten- and eleven-hour day—with higher pay for time worked above eight hours—had substantially increased earnings (see above), the return to the eight-hour day, nowhere accompanied by raises in wage rates, substantially reduced them. With wage rates, as a rule, unchanged during the war, the resumption of pre-war hours, other things being equal, was bound to bring earnings back to the prewar level. But in many, if not in most cases, other things were not equal. The

---

[7] *Trud*, September 9, 1944.
[8] *Izvestiya*, October 11, 1944.
[9] *Pravda*, January 1, 1945.

physical and mental exertions of the long, only recently ended war years and the lowering of living and above all of nutritional standards inevitably impaired working efficiency, while the inferior professional composition of the working class as compared with 1940 was bound to do the same.[9a] It can be assumed, therefore, that the level of earnings in the first postwar year was slightly below 1940: If a monthly average of 339 rubles was calculated for 1940, the corresponding figure for early 1946 can be estimated at from 300 to 339 rubles.

This was the starting point of most recent developments.

With data on the latest wage trends extraordinarily scarce even for Soviet conditions, special attention must be paid to the analysis of the official wage-political attitude after the war. This permits us to draw certain conclusions regarding the wage trend.

Late in March 1945, after an interval of more than a year, the AUCTUC met for its thirteenth plenary session. The end of the war was near at hand, and the plenary session was to prepare the unions for the tasks immediately following. Beside the effort to increase productivity, which remained the principal task of the unions, their interest during this period was to be focused on "care" for the workers' and employees' "every-day needs." This meant that union activity was to concern itself mainly with members' interests outside the plant, with the satisfaction of their needs as consumers and citizens—in other words, not with work-

---

[9a] For "a number of industries," the decline in labor productivity "after the war" was admitted by AUCTUC Chairman Kuznetsov in his report to the Fifteenth Plenary Session. He explained it "primarily by the difficulties connected with the reconversion of plants to peace-time production," although emphasizing that output had "also declined in some industries turning out the same products as in wartime, as for example in coal and copper mining and in the oil and textile industries." There, the decline was said to be "chiefly due to poor organization of machinery, and to frequent interruptions of production" (*Trud*, April 13, 1946).— Incidentally, it is characteristic of the mentality of Soviet union leaders that in discussing the causes of the postwar decline of labor productivity the chairman of the central union council completely ignored the human element.

On the extent of the decline the Soviet press contains only desultory statements, if any. The report of the Central Statistical Administration for the year 1946 does not mention the productivity of labor at all—surely not a good sign. The report for 1947 says that "in industry the productivity of labor increased 13 per cent over 1946." From the 1948 report we learn further that "the productivity of labor in industry increased 15 per cent over 1947 [i.e. 30 per cent over 1946] and exceeded the prewar level." (Cf.*Izvestiya*, January 21, 1947, January 18, 1948, and January 20, 1949.) —If the prewar level was not exceeded until the 1946 level had risen 30 per cent, the productivity of labor in 1946 was considerably below that of 1940.

ing conditions and not with the interests of union members as producers and party to the labor relationship.

This was the basic tendency of the major speech delivered by AUCTUC Chairman Vasily V. Kuznetsov, as well as of the debates of the plenary session which lasted for several days.[10] The editing of the voluminous resolutions seemed to meet with some difficulties, for they were not published until six weeks after the session ended.[11] These resolutions visibly corrected the original text, went beyond the debates of the plenary session and, although timidly, dealt also with the theme of "improvement of working conditions." The resolution on Kuznetsov's report demanded "that management and union fully expand the funds appropriated for the purpose and use them in the first place for the repair of existing ventilation systems and the installation of new ones, as well as for the installation and improvement of showers, locker rooms, washrooms, drying appliances for work clothes, drinking fountains, and lighting plants." It further obliged the unions "strictly to supervise the enforcement of laws for the protection of pregnant women" and "laws for the protection of juvenile workers." This timid attempt to go beyond the union members' daily consumer troubles was the extent of the unions' concern with the "improvement of working conditions." The central question of wages was not touched upon with one word even in this improved resolution.

This could not suffice for long. In a lengthy resolution of September 1945, the Presidium of the AUCTUC dealt with the enforcement of the decisions of the Thirteenth Plenary Session.[12] This time wages were at least mentioned. The Presidium told the unions "to insist that managers quickly draft and apply organizational and technological measures" to increase the productivity and *with it* the earnings of labor. At the Fourteenth Plenary Session in December the same idea was elaborated on by AUCTUC Chairman Kuznetsov:[13] "Union organizations must insist on the elimination of conditions impeding increases in productivity and, *consequently*, in wages."

In April 1946, at the Fifteenth Plenary Session devoted to

---

10 *Pravda*, March 28-31, 1945.
11 *Trud*, May 11 and 12, 1946.
12 *Trud*, September 7, 1945.
13 *Trud.* December 7. 1945.

"tasks of union organizations in fulfilling the Five-Year Plan for the Reconstruction and Development of the National Economy in 1946-1950," Kuznetsov once more declared:[14] "All organizing activities of the union must be directed toward assuring the workers of all requisites for an uninterrupted increase in the productivity of their labor, and, in consequence, of their wages." And the resolution of the Fifteenth Plenary Session repeated:[15] "The central, regional, and local union bodies and the shop committees must . . . eliminate conditions which prevent the workers from increasing their productivity and *thus* raising their wages." Raising wages *only* by increasing productivity had become a creed by this time. Other ways of raising wages had ceased to exist.

This is the way things remained. In drafting the Fourth Five-Year Plan the idea was made law: the plan provided for rises in the wage level only "simultaneously with increases in the productivity of labor."[16] In other words, as chairman of the State Planning Commission, Nikolai Voznesensky, explained it: "The average yearly earnings of workers and employees in the national economy rise together with the increasing productivity of labor."[17]

This is still the basic tenet of the new Russian wage policy— with one essential qualification: the earnings of labor are to rise only with increasing productivity, but their upward movement must lag behind that of productivity.

The principle is not new to Russian wage policy. Its history can be traced back a quarter of a century, to the decree "On Wage Policy" of the CC of the CPSU of August 19, 1924.[18] But what characterizes the most recent policy is the vigorous stress placed upon two ideas: the exclusive dependency of wage rises on increased productivity, the urgent necessity of keeping the scope of wage rises below that of increases in productivity.

In practice, the lag is enforced by frequent revision of production quotas. This in turn is prescribed by law: the Fourth Five-Year Plan ordered "the expanded application in industry of technologically based quotas, considering advances in technology

---

[14] *Trud*, April 13, 1946.
[15] *Trud*, May 5, 1946.
[16] *Supreme Soviet of the USSR, 1st Session* (March 12-19, 1946), *Minutes*, p. 395.
[17] *Ibid.*, p. 67.
[18] A. E. Pasherstnik (see Chapter IV, n. 120), p. 187.

and the development of labor saving devices." [19] The formula sounds somewhat vague and almost innocuous. But its meaning has been expressed much more plainly in special publications: the quoted provision of the Five-Year Plan "makes periodical revision of production quotas compulsory." [20] Periodical revision—invariably upward—is a drastic measure.

The Five-Year Plan formula implies even more. It underscores the significance of the "technologically based" production quotas. In Soviet literature, "technologically based" quotas are contrasted with "empirical-statistical" quotas calculated on the basis of data regarding production averages actually achieved. "Technologically based production quotas, unlike empirical-statistical ones, take into account the present level of modern technology, the most efficient technological processes, the best order of equipment, and the most perfect organization of the place of work, excluding any possibility of a loss of working time. In the determination of technological quotas, the actual performance of a given job is analyzed, all unnecessary, superfluous operations are excluded, and the most perfect, most progressive Stakhanovite working methods and new, efficient, technological processes inducing workers to increase the productivity of their labor are taken into account." [21]

A production quota corresponding to these ideal technological and organizational conditions—which can exist only in extremely rare exceptional cases—is practically impossible to fulfill. Actual quotas are set hardly anywhere in this perfect form. But the idea is of decisive importance to the whole development of wages, and it serves in fact as a permanent spur in quota determination.

There is one additional factor. Previously (in Chapter IV) it was shown that the idea of incentive wages in the form of a "progressive premium pay" had begun to influence the Russian wage system since the early 1930's. In wartime this trend was promoted with special vigor. In 1940 bonuses already made up $4\frac{1}{2}$ per cent of the aggregate workers' payroll of industry as a whole; among technical employees in industry they amounted to 11 per

19 *Minutes*, etc., (as in n. 16) , p. 396.
20 A. E. Pasherstnik, p. 245.
21 V. Zasetzky, "Technologically Based Quotas," *V Pomoshch FSMK* (*For the Shop Stewards*) , a fortnightly published by the AUCTUC, 1947, No. 14, p. 25.

cent of the payroll. These figures rose considerably until 1944: to 8 per cent for industrial workers, and to 28 per cent for industrial technical employees.[22] Nor did the Fourth Five-Year Plan order a halt, much less an alleviation; what it ordered was a "systematic extension of the importance of bonuses in the remuneration of labor."[23] The decision did not remain a dead letter; the Council of Ministers of the Soviet Union worked out special bonus pay statutes for all branches of industry, principally for engineers and technicians, but often for workers, too. Wage practice has been profoundly influenced by these provisions, as may be seen from a few instances: in the first quarter of 1948 bonuses, for executive personnel in automobile and tractor plants amounted to from 47 to 78 per cent of the payroll (including bonuses); in the Kaganovich Ball Bearing Works in Moscow, in the same quarter, bonuses made up 28 per cent of the foremen's pay.[24]

This wage policy must be considered as a whole: no "mechanical" wage raises; the wage level to rise only as a delayed consequence of increased productivity; and high bonuses to reward success. These are the foundations of a wage policy which, in effect, tends to retard a rise in the wage level for the bulk of wage and salary earners, and simultaneously, by extensive differentiation of pay, to promote a privileged stratum of workers and employees.

Wage Trends Under the Fourth Five-Year Plan

The Fourth Five-Year Plan, for the period from 1946 until 1950, was approved by the Supreme Council of the USSR in March, 1946. It contained only scant references to the expected wage trend: with the total number of wage and salary earners in all economic and administrative branches scheduled to rise to 33,500,000 by 1950, the wage fund in the same year was to amount to 252.3 billion rubles, and the average of annual earnings (including all overtime pay, bonuses, etc.) to 6,000 rubles.[26] The wage fund mentioned in the Plan is substantially larger than the

---

22 Voznesensky (as in n. 1) , p. 117.
23 *Minutes*, etc., p. 296.
24 E. Manevich, "Wages and New Motivations of Labor under Socialism," *Voprosy Ekonomiki*, 1949, No. 10, p. 32.
26 *Minutes*, etc., pp. 395-396.

sum of wages and salaries: that sum, with the average annual earnings envisioned for the stated number of workers and employees, would come not to 252.3 billion, but only to 201 billion rubles. Russian economic statisticians have for some years been working with two kinds of wage funds—the wage fund in a broadened sense and the wage fund proper—using for the term wage fund without defining the difference between both the two funds in their publications. This practice, resulting in frequent confusion and hampering the analysis of events, will have to be taken up later (in the Appendix to this chapter). Here we can only stress—and this is doubted by no one in the Soviet Union or abroad—that in 1950 the average earnings of labor were supposed to be 6,000 rubles, i.e. 500 rubles a month, or, as Vosnezensky put it in his report on the Five-Year Plan, 48 per cent more than in 1940.[27]

We have seen that the average earnings of labor had greatly increased in wartime but dropped again, early in 1946, to the level of 1940, if not somewhat farther. What happened in subsequent years?

The annual reports published by the Central Statistical Administration for the several years of the Plan period tell us about the most important economic developments.[28] Wage figures, to be sure, remained exceedingly scarce in these reports; so the trend cannot be studied without some hypothetical assumptions. The author's results are questioned in particular by many American experts on Russia—a fact which compels me to analyze the fragmentary data in greater detail than would otherwise be advisable here.

The wage trend in *1946* was marked by an extraordinary event completely at odds with customary Soviet developments. On September 15, 1946,—in connection with a great increase in prices of rationed goods (bread, meat, sugar and others)—the wages of lower and middle groups of workers and employees were raised.[29] Supposedly a preparation for the abolition of rationing, which will be discussed in detail below, this "mechanical" increase added from 80 to 110 rubles a month to the incomes of

[27] *Ibid.*, p. 67.
[28] Cf. *Izvestiya*, January 21, 1947, January 18, 1948, January 20, 1949, January 18, 1950, and January 27, 1951.
[29] *Pravda*, September 16, 1946.

those earning not more than 900 rubles a month—i.e. to the over-whelming majority of workers and employees. The whole development will be taken up later, in discussing the price trend; here it should only be stressed that the level of monthly earnings, calculated on the average of all workers and employees, went up about 95 and perhaps close to 100 rubles.

Decreed from September 16 on, the raises were to affect the last three-and-a-half months of 1946. As a result, the average of annual earnings rose by 335-350 rubles, the annual average of monthly earnings by 28-29 rubles. If, as we have seen, the level of average monthly earnings was between 300 and 339 rubles at the beginning of the year, their average for the whole year, even assuming a slight upward movement of the wage level independently of the September raises, was bound to reach about 350, perhaps close to 370 rubles—or, to stick to annual figures in view of the approximate character of our data, about 4,200-4,400 rubles a year.

It is significant that the 1946 report of the Central Statistical Administration made no mention of wage trends at all, aside from citing the September increases. This reserve is understandable, for even if these increases are taken into account, average monthly earnings had probably declined in 1946, as against 1945.

In *1947* the picture was different. It was only then that the raises of September 1946 exerted their full effect on the annual averages. If, as just mentioned, they amounted to some 95 or almost 100 rubles a month, on the average of all employment categories, and already raised the annual average of 1946 by 28-29 rubles, there still remained a reserve of almost 70 rubles a month to increase the 1947 annual average. This meant a rise of at least 800 rubles in the annual average—a rise to some 5,000-5,200 rubles,[30] or an 18.2 to 19.0 per cent increase over 1946.

This partly hypothetical calculation is borne out by the report of the Central Statistical Administration for the year 1947.

---

[30] This result is in striking contrast to the figures of the economic plan for 1947, as published by *Pravda* on March 1, 1947. This plan, the only annual one made public after the war, puts the number of workers and employees at 31,600,000 and the wage fund at 280 billion rubles—an enormous figure even for the wage fund in its broader sense. If (following the usual method based on Abram Bergson's "A Problem in Soviet Statistics," in Harvard University's *Review of Economic Statistics*, November 1947), we reduce it by 20 per cent to find the wage fund proper, the stated employment figure would indicate average annual earnings of 7,090 rubles. This, if correct, would mean a thorough revision of the newly ap-

This report is more eloquent than the preceding one. It tells us that the national wage fund increased 23 per cent over the previous year, simultaneously with an increase of 1,200,000 in the number of wage and salary earners. This amounts to a 4 per cent increase in employment, which with the stated wage-fund increase enables us to calculate the rise of average monthly earnings: 18.2 per cent.

The striking similarity of the results obtained by the two calculations is one more sign that the hypothesis used in the first is in line with actual facts.

The report for *1948* mentions a 10 per cent increase in the wage fund, with the number of workers and employees rising by 2,000,000. This meant a 6.4 per cent increase in the number of wage and salary earners, and an increase in average annual earnings of about 3.4 per cent, to 5,200-5,400 rubles.

For *1949* and *1950* the reports of the Central Statistical Administration are even scantier than before, and not without good reason. From 1949 on, the Soviet government embarked upon a rigid price reduction policy which has already met with notable success (s. below). A rise in the wage level would be in direct conflict with this deflationary policy. In some plants and industries, such as coal mining and the building trades, average earnings may have risen slightly, partly due to increased productivity and to the improved qualitative makeup of the labor force. In other plants and industries a certain decline is likely. The average level seems to have remained unchanged, at best; the chances are that it declined a little.

Another indication of this is the curious tricks employed by the Central Statistical Administration in composing its reports for 1949 and 1950. The wage fund and average earnings, were not mentioned even indirectly any more. Instead, there were references to percentage gains in the "income" of workers and employees (in the 1949 report) or of workers, employees and peasants (in the report for 1950). The "income" comprised not only the actual earnings of workers and employees and the money and goods received by peasants; it also included all "services ren-

dered to the population at the expense of the state." Besides—
and this was what counted—the lowering of the price level was
taken into account in calculating "income." According to this
calculation, the per capita income of workers and employees had
risen 12 per cent in 1949, while the income of workers, employees
and peasants as a whole—not per capita—supposedly increased 19
per cent in 1950. Even if these figures corresponded to the facts,
they would hardly indicate a rise in average money earnings, in
view of the greatly lowered price level (see below). At best, therefore, average earnings—i.e. the level of nominal wages—in 1950
may be estimated at the approximate level previously calculated
for 1948. They were hardly higher, at best, than 5,200-5,400
rubles a year, or 435-450 rubles a month.

In contrast to the more optimistic calculations of the average
earnings of Russian labor which characterize in particular the
more recent American and British publications,[31] Soviet authors
never claim that average earnings in the Soviet Union exceeded
500 rubles a month, or 6,000 a year. If they had—even as early as
1948 or 1947—the Soviet press would surely say so. Even apart
from this silence, the Soviet treatment of the subject is extremely
significant. Late in 1949, for instance, the Economic Institute of
the Academy of Sciences of the USSR published a book[32] which,
to prove that earnings had risen in the Soviet Union, recalled that
"according to the postwar Five-Year Plan the average earnings of
workers and employees *will* rise to 6,000 rubles in 1950, far exceeding the level of 1940" (italics mine). Another example is an
article on the rise of the laboring masses in the August 1950
issue of the Economic Institute magazine. Intended as a source of
material for speakers ("Lectures and Discussions"), this article
contains a mass of data on the most diverse questions, but on the
wage trend it gives only annual averages up to and including
1940, plus the Five-Year Plan figure for 1950.[33] How could this
be—particularly in a pointedly apologetic article—if that level,
by then, had been considerably exceeded?

Nor does the Central Statistical Administration's report on

---

[31] Cf. Appendix 2 to this chapter.
[32] N. S. Maslova, *The Productivity of Labor in Soviet Industry*, publ. by
the Economic Institute of the Academy of Sciences of the USSR, Moscow, 1949,
p. 121.
[33] Ya. Zhukovsky, "The Rise of the Material and Cultural Level of the
Toilers—the Law of the Development of Socialism," *Voprosy Ekonomiki*, August
1950, p. 69.

the fulfillment of the Fourth Five-Year Plan, published in April 1951,[34] contain a word about equaling—much less exceeding—the level of earnings planned for 1950. We are forced to the conclusion that the level of annual earnings envisioned in the Five-Year Plan for 1950——6,000 rubles—has not been achieved.

By themselves, of course, these figures do not tell much. A correct appraisal of their significance requires a closer examination of the price trend in the 1940's.

Prices during the War

As we have seen in Chapter IV, a rapid price spiral, which painfully cut the purchasing power of wages, had made itself felt in Russia since the outbreak of World War II, long before the Soviet Union got into it. It is true that food rationing, reintroduced when the Soviet Union entered the war, slowed down the depreciation of the ruble. Prices of rationed food were stabilized at the then prevailing level of government prices, substantially below the price level of the private market; they remained unchanged throughout the war,[35] and for a while after—until September, 1946. But the sale of food under the rationing system was limited and did not meet minimum requirements.

Consumers had to resort to the private market where food was offered for sale by *kolkhozes* and individual *kolkhoz* members. When they brought their produce to the cities, the farmers were free to sell to any buyer without restrictions and to charge whatever prices they choose. Determined by supply and demand prices in this seller's market rose constantly. The government itself participated—from the Spring of 1944 on—in the non-controlled market. In a number of cities, so-called "commercial" stores were set up. There the government sold food, including rationed items, without putting any restrictions on sales to individual consumers. It charged prices many times higher than those fixed for food distributed on ration cards, keeping close to the price level of the private market. The intention was to influence prices in the private market through competitive sales and to put

---

[34] *Pravda*, April 17, 1951.
[35] Aleksandr V. Lyubimov [People's Commissar for Trade of the USSR], "Remarks on the Next Tasks in Expanding Sales," *Planovoye Khozyaistvo*, 1945, No. 4 p. 22.

a brake on inflation by draining the market of the consumers' "surplus" money.

Non-controlled prices climbed steadily up to 1946. Though no official data were published on the movement of free prices throughout the war years, some indications are available from the material gathered by foreign correspondents and visitors from abroad, particularly Walter Graebner, Henry C. Cassidy, Walter Kerr, Edgar Snow, William L. White, and Edmund Stevens.[36]

In 1942 and 1943 prices in the private market and in government stores (chiefly Moscow) fluctuated as follows (per kilogram): black rye bread, 100 to 150 rubles; butter, about 800 rubles; meat, 200 to 500 rubles; honey, 500 rubles; potatoes, 50 to 70 rubles; cabbage, 25 to 80 rubles, and so forth. In the summer of 1944 the price level in the free market still was extremely high, but several items dropped considerably. Obviously, the worst was past.

The trend crystallized more clearly after the war, in the second half of 1945. To a certain extent prices in the private market went down more rapidly than they did in "commercial" stores. Thus, "sharp reduction in prices" of meat, milk, potatoes, etc., was noted in the private market practically everywhere.[37] A new trend, characteristic of postwar conditions, had come to the fore.

How did workers make ends meet during the war? Prices in the non-controlled market, of which quite a few were cited above, were prohibitive. Rations—except for bread—were inadequate.[38] Moreover, quite a few of the food items which made up the rations were unavailable. More often than not rationed distribution of food was confined to bread and—less frequently—potatoes.

---

[36] Data from Walter Graebner, *Round Trip to Russia*, Philadelphia-New York, 1943, pp. 166 f.; Henry C. Cassidy, *Moscow Dateline*, Boston, 1943, pp. 319 f.; Walter Kerr in the *New York Herald Tribune*, May 18, 1943; Edgar Snow, *People on Our Side*, New York, 1944, p. 167; William L. White, *Report on the Russians*, New York, 1945, pp. 148 f.; Edmund Stevens, *Russia Is No Riddle*, New York, 1945, p. 59. While retail prices in the Soviet Union usually are per kilogram, most of the authors quoted list prices per pound, without specifying whether lb. (454 grams), old Russian pound (409 grams usually taken as equal to 400 gram), or metric pound (500 grams) is meant. To render comparison possible between wartime data and those indicated in Chapter IV for earlier years, I had to reconvert the former to the kilogram basis (one kilogram equaling 2.2 lb., 2.5 Russian pounds or 2.0 metric pounds), assuming in most cases that lb. was referred to.

[37] I. Lukashev (deputy People's Commissar for Trade of the RSFSR), *Izvestiya*, September 8, 1945.

[38] A recent well-documented *Survey of Soviet Russian Agriculture* by Lazar

Meat, butter, sugar, etc., though included in the rationing schedules, were supplied irregularly or not at all.

Rationed food failed to provide the minimum diet. Only a
few wage and salary earners could afford to buy in the private
market. Additional sources of supply had to be opened up. Canteens and cafeterias attached to plants and offices assumed major
importance. In 1944 the network of public eating places accounted for 25 per cent of all food sales in government retail
trade,[39] a highly impressive figure. To judge from fragmentary
information scattered in newspapers, meals served in public eating places were poor, but to millions they provided at least the
basic nourishment.

Next to the public eating places, vegetable gardening, operated by workers either individually or collectively, became a
considerable additional source of food. Even prior to the war
many manual workers (and, less often, non-manual workers as
well) had grown vegetables on plots of their own. Since 1942, cultivation of vegetable plots was given strong government support
and it developed into a broad "movement" under the direction
of the trade unions.

In addition to plots cultivated by individual wage and salary
earners, there appeared "collective" vegetable gardens, i.e., either
quasi-cooperative enterprises run by the workers themselves, or
—more often—ancillary farms organized and operated by indus-

Volin, published by the U. S. Department of Agriculture, Washington, 1951, cites
the following data (p. 175):

Food Rations in Moscow, December 1942 and 1943
(in grams)

Month and category	Bread Per day	Groats Per month	Meat and Fish Per month	Fats Per month	Sugar Per month
December 1942					
1st category	800	2,000	2,200	800	500
2nd "	600	2,000	2,200	800	500
3rd "	500	1,500	1,200	400	300
4th "	400	1,000	600	200	200
5th "	400	1,200	600	400	300
December 1943					
1st category	650	2,000	2,200	800	500
2nd "	550	2,000	2,200	800	500
3rd "	450	1,500	1,200	400	300
4th "	300	1,000	600	200	200
5th "	300	1,200	600	400	300

The first category comprised heavy workers; the second, ordinary workers;
the third, employees; the fourth, dependents; the fifth, children under twelve years.
[39] Lyubimov, as quoted supra, n. 25.

trial plants and offices of the administration and cultivated by the latter's employees. Of the produce of these "collective" gardens, a certain proportion was set aside for those who did the work, while the rest served to supply public eating places; this was changed in 1944 when all crops raised in "collective" vegetable gardens were reserved for public eating places.[40] To a considerable extent the spread of collective gardening must have permitted the expansion of the network of canteens and cafeterias in the plants.

The importance of individual and collective vegetable gardening is apparent from the growing number of wage and salary earners participating in the "movement": in 1942, there were 5,000,000; in 1943, 11,600,000; in 1944, 16,500,000; and in 1945, 18,500,000, embracing the bulk of manual workers and probably also the majority of non-manual workers. Planted acreage was 500,000 hectars in 1942, 770,000 in 1943, 1,400,000 in 1944, and 1,600,000 in 1945. Potato and vegetable crops in 1945 totaled some 10,000,000 tons; also, for the first time, some 500,000 tons of grain and legumes were harvested in 1945.[41] To what extent this success was due to individual and cooperative cultivation, as distinguished from ancillary farms set up by industrial management, was not disclosed.

The Soviet workers' "victory gardens" spread widely during the war years; they not only assured the supplies of potatoes and vegetables to large numbers of wage and salary earners and their families but also contributed toward reducing potato and vegetable prices in the urban private market.[42] Still, the nutritional budget did not balance. Scarcity of food and inadequacy of wages called for other sources of food supply. In many places, notably in smaller towns and barely urbanized workers' communities around industrial sites, where rationed food was issued even less regularly and less frequently than in large cities, numerous workers resorted to a new expedient, raising poultry and livestock.

By 1945, wage and salary earners already owned some 5,000,-000 head of cattle (mostly cows), some 4,000,000 sheep and goats, and some 1,000,000 hogs.[43] More recently, after the war, the gov-

---

40 *Trud*, September 2, 1944.
41 *Trud*, December 2, 1943; December 27, 1944; December 29, 1945.
42 *Trud*, January 16, 1946.
43 *Trud*, December 27, 1945.

ernment initiated a new "movement" to foster livestock and
poultry raising by wage and salary earners, following the model of
the campaign for individual and collective vegetable growing. On
November 23, 1945, the government issued a decree dealing with
appropriate measures to further this "movement," and on January 17, 1946, another decree followed, designed to sponsor live-
stock- and poultry-raising cooperatives of wage and salary earners.[44] Again the campaign was headed by the central bodies of
the trade union movement.

Yet all this—public feeding, individual and collective vegetable gardening, livestock and chicken raising by workers and
employees—fell far short of balancing the enormous discrepancy
between wage and price levels. The living standard of wage and
salary earners declined vastly in the war years. Raising of real
wages turned into one of the most important problems of economic policy. While this problem remained unsolved, the economic reconstruction of the country after the war devastation
seemed scarcely possible.

The Soviet government attacked the problem chiefly in the
sphere of prices. It regarded as its primary task closing the gap
between the prices of rationed food and those on the free market; this in turn was to make it possible to abolish rationing.

The De-Rationing

The impending abolition of rationing was first announced
by Stalin on February 9, 1946, in a campaign speech[45] on the
eve of supreme Soviet elections. The announcement was welcomed as a promise of salvation, as the first tidings of the imminent alleviation of suffering and privations.

Although food was scarce, and in spite of the abyss between
wages and prices, rationing had grown to be highly unpopular.
Equipped with ration cards, the consumer had to stand in line
for hours on end in front of food stores; he never knew whether
he actually would obtain his ration and the food finally supplied
often was of poor quality. It is true that to most consumers commodities offered at fancy prices in the private market were no
more than a mirage. Precisely this, however, made the people ex-

---

[44] *Trud*, December 11 and 27, 1945; February 21, March 6 and 14, 1946.
[45] *Pravda*, February 10, 1946.

pect that along with the end of rationing prices on the free market would be brought down.

The Fourth Five-Year Plan, as approved in March, 1946, specifically announced de-rationing of bread, flour, grits, groats and macaroni, "effective by the fall of 1946"; all rationing was to end in 1947.[46] But late in August the newspapers sprang the news that "due to drought in a number of provinces of the USSR and to reductions in government stocks," de-rationing of bread and other grain products was postponed till 1947.[47] The disproportion between non-controlled prices and the wage and salary earners' purchasing power was still too substantial to permit de-rationing, even on a minor scale. The groundwork had to be laid beforehand.

Some steps had already been taken during the early part of the year. By order of the People's Commissariat for Trade "commercial" prices of many important food items (bread, sugar, meat, fish, and others) had been reduced in February, 1946.[48] According to an American press dispatch, "commercial" prices of milk and dairy products were reduced in June.[49] Early in July cutbacks were ordered for shoes, clothing, textiles, etc.[50]

However, even after all those reductions had been effected, private and "commercial" prices remained very high. John Strohm, an American correspondent who visited the Soviet Union in 1946, during the late summer, i.e., after food prices had been lowered in government stores in February and June, recorded the following prices charged in Moscow in the private market or in "commercial" stores: butter, 250 rubles a kilogram; sugar, 300 rubles a kilogram; milk, 10 rubles a quart (perhaps a glass?); eggs, 10 to 11 rubles apiece.[51] De-rationing still was far off.

Then, in September, 1946, the government in one single ef-

[46] *Minutes*, etc., p. 400.
[47] *Pravda*, August 29, 1946.
[48] *Izvestiya*, February 26, 1946.
[49] Associated Press dispatch in *New York Times*, June 13, 1946. Strange though it may seem, this price cut was not mentioned in *Pravda, Izvestiya* or *Trud*.
[50] *Izvestiya*, July 2, 1946.
[51] *New York World-Telegram*, October 7 and 8, 1946. Prices listed by Strohm are per pound. What pound? In this case it seemed more likely that the metric pound was used, and I so assumed. If lbs. were meant, 10 per cent must be added to the figures I have indicated. Some more data supplied by Strohm (*op. cit.*, October 10, 1946) are worth mentioning. In Moscow bazaars a two-pound chicken (lean) sold at 250 rubles; for a five-cent chocolate bar Moscow "commercial" stores charged 30 rubles; a pound of tomatoes in urban bazaars in the Ukraine cost 25 rubles, a quart of milk 15 rubles, an egg 6 rubles.

fort ordered a batch of measures which brought de-rationing much nearer. The purpose of the legislation was to bridge the gulf which separated market prices from fixed ration prices.

According to the official press release,[52] the decree issued by the Council of Ministers of the USSR on September 15, 1946, dealt with "measures aiming at drawing closer together the high commercial and low rationing prices by further lowering commercial prices, in order that commercial prices may be abolished and the new rationing prices made uniform government prices when the time comes to eliminate the rationing system." Simultaneously, "taking into account the hardships imposed upon low- and medium-paid wage and salary earners by the increase in rationing prices," the Council of Ministers decided to raise all wages and salaries not exceeding 900 rubles monthly.

The wording of the decree was not made public, and only with respect to the increase in wages were details given in the daily press. On the increase in prices of rationed goods and the lowering of "commercial" ones, however, an interesting publication of the U. S. Department of Labor[53] contains ample data, utilized below.

All three groups of measures together formed a single program, but each must be briefly taken up by itself.

(1) The increase in prices of rationed goods is illustrated by the following table:

Ration prices in Moscow before and after September 16, 1946
(in Rubles per Kilogram, for Milk per Liter)

	September 1, 1946	October 1, 1946	Ratio
Rye bread	1.00	3.40	3.4:1
Wheat bread	3.80	11.25	3.0:1
Wheat flour (30 per cent)	4.60	13.00	2.8:1
Sugar (lump)	5.50	15.00	2.7:1
Butter (1st quality)	28.00	66.00	2.4:1
Beef	14.00	30.00	2.1:1
Mutton	14.00	34.00	2.4:1
Pork	12.00	34.00	2.8:1
Bacon	27.00	55.00	2.0:1
Chicken	14.00	37.00	2.6:1
Milk	2.50	8.00	3.2:1

[52] *Pravda*, September 16, 1946.
[53] "Soviet Union: Trends in Prices, Rations and Wages," prepared by Irving B. Kravis and Joseph Mintzes, in *Monthly Labor Review*, July 1947. This study

An unweighted average for all eleven foodstuffs yields a
2.7:1 ratio of new prices to old—a near tripling of costs. If we
consider the especially sharp rise in the price of rye bread, the
burden of the increase on the bulk of consumers looms even
heavier.

The study by the U. S. Department of Labor also calculated
the cost of monthly rations before and after September 16 (according to the composition of rations in August 1946).[53a] The costs
of a monthly ration in Moscow (if fully drawn) would show the
following for different ration categories:

*Changes in cost of rations in Moscow, August to October, 1946,
weighted by quantities in August food rations
(in Rubles)*

	August 1946	October 1946	Increase
Heavy worker	99.85	281.53	181.68
Worker	91.30	255.88	164.58
Employee	59.60	169.43	109.83
Dependent	36.30	104.00	67.70
Child under 12	49.25	139.13	89.88

In this calculation, too, the costs are shown as having almost
tripled in September.

(2) To narrow the gap between the two worlds of rations
and "commercial" prices, the increase in the former was further
combined with a substantial reduction of the latter. A few examples may illustrate these reductions:

*Changes in selected food prices in Moscow commercial stores
(in Rubles per Kilogram)*

	Before September 16, 1946	After September 16, 1946	Decrease in %
Wheat flour	35	24	31
Sugar (lump)	150	70	53
Sugar (granulated)	120	60	50
Butter (salted)	400	240	40
Beef	140	90	36
Smoked ham	470	220	53
Chicken	200	195	3

seems to rest on the U. S. Embassy reports which already supplied valuable data
for the analysis of price trends in the last years before the Soviet Union entered
the war (see Chapter IV).

[53a] In several instances rations were reduced on September 16, so that some
foodstuffs which before that date could be bought, though not always obtained,

On the average, the level of "commercial" food prices had probably declined more than one-third. But even after this decline, and despite the considerable simultaneous increase in ration prices, the gap between the two price worlds remained wide. This may be illustrated by a table taken from the Department of Labor study and showing the gradual narrowing of the gap from July, 1944 to October 1946:

Reduction in gap between Moscow commercial and ration prices
for 4 food items, July 1944 to October 1946
(Prices in Rubles per Kilogram)

	July 1944	July 1945	January 1946	August 1946	October 1946
Lump sugar					
Ration price	5.5	5.5	5.5	5.5	15
Commercial price	750	500	250	170	70
Commercial price as multiple of ration price	136	91	45	31	4.7
Butter					
Ration price	28	28	28	28	66
Commercial price	800	540	400	400	240
Commercial price as multiple of ration price	29	19	14	14	3.6
White Bread[x]					
Ration price	2.8	2.8	2.8	2.8	8
Open-market price	140	...	50	30	60
Open-market price as multiple of ration price	50	...	18	11	7.5
Beef					
Ration price	14	14	14	14	30
Commercial price	320	220	170	140	90
Commercial price as multiple of ration price	23	16	12	10	3.0

[x] For white bread, open-market prices are used in place of commercial prices because of the lack of data on commercial prices.

Whereas in the summer of 1944 the level of "commercial" prices was generally more than twenty times, and in exceptional cases over a hundred times, above the level of ration prices, this

at prices for rationed goods were from now on only purchasable at considerably higher free prices. Therefore, the calculation of the cost increase according to the rations in force before September 16 shows the result of the comparison in attenuated form.

ratio dropped to somewhat over ten by August, 1946, and to an average of about 3 to 5 after September 16.

Lest this presentation be overburdened with detail, we omit an analysis of the prices of non-food commodities, where the ratio of the two price levels—ration and "commercial"—was approximately the same as for foodstuffs, after September 16. For details, the reader may be referred to the Department of Labor study.

As can be seen from these figures, the "commercial" prices were practically out of reach for a vast majority of wage and salary earners even after their reduction in September 1946. The reduction did not compensate the bulk of workers and employees for the stiff rises in ration prices. A simultaneous upward revision of the general wage level became an unavoidable necessity.

(3) In fact, the decree of September 15 caused an almost general rise in wages and salaries from September 16 on. Workers and employees earning less than 300 rubles a month got a raise of 110 rubles; those earning between 300 and 500, one of 100 rubles; those earning between 500 and 700, one of 90 rubles; and those earning between 700 and 900, one of 80 rubles. Beyond that, no raises were granted. Workers and employees earning more than 900 rubles a month were assumed—probably rightly—to be sufficiently compensated for the rise in ration prices by the reduction of the "commercial" ones. The higher a man's income, the more this reduction of "commercial" prices helped to raise his living standard. For the top strata of workers and employees the reform of September 15 meant indeed a considerable improvement of their material situation.

Not so for the great majority, to whom the free market remained virtually closed even after September 16. As previously mentioned, the wage rises ranged from 80 to 110 rubles a month—but the cost of a single worker's or employee's monthly ration rose by 110 to 182 rubles (cf. the table above). Thus the raises offset only part of the additional expense, and in cases of workers providing for families only a small part.

If we consider the measures of September 15, 1946, as a whole, we find that once again—despite the raises for the lower and middle groups—the tradition of promoting inequality was followed. Real earnings of the top strata of workers and employees were augmented by these measures, while those of the great majority were reduced.

All this was obviously designed as a preparatory step for doing away with the rationed distribution of goods. This final problem was tackled at the end of 1947. The Soviet government's decree of December 14, 1947,[54] abolished rationing and simultaneously carried out a currency reform with markedly anti-social features, a discussion of which would exceed the scope of this work.[54a] The end of rationing ended the dual system of state prices. Instead of "standardized" and "commercial" prices, "uniform state prices" were fixed—for foodstuffs, by and large, of the level of the former "standardized" prices, for most other commodities considerably higher, though on the average about two-thirds lower than the former "commercial" prices.

In retrospect, this appears as the first decisive step in the direction of restoring the prewar level of real wages. The goal was still far away. The new "uniform" prices were still much too high to enable the bulk of workers to satisfy their most pressing needs from the set wages. The reader can see this for himself, if he will compare the above-mentioned ration prices, in force after September 16, 1946, with the average earnings of some 450-465 rubles a month (i.e. about 2 rubles 20 kopecks an hour, at a 48-hour week). Thus a restoration of the prewar level of real wages required either a substantial increase in nominal wages or a sharp reduction in prices. The Soviet government, in the years that followed chose the second course.

Lowering the Price Level

Real wages immediately after the abolition of rationing were extraordinarily low even for Soviet conditions. To give the reader a general idea, we shall compare data on the prices of some essential foodstuffs with data on average earnings. The months selected for comparison are April, 1928 and July, 1938, the peaks of the curve of real wages in the Twenties and Thirties; also July 1940, to characterize the pre-war level of real wages, and January 1948, the first month after the abolition of rationing. Foodstuffs were not rationed in any of these month.[55]

54 *Pravda*, December 15, 1947.
54a At the time, I analyzed the abolition of rationing and the accompanying currency reform in *The New Leader* of December 20, 1947, and January 17, 1948, and—in greater detail—in *Sozialisticheskii Vestnik*, December 1947, and January 1948.
55 Sources for the data until 1940 were listed in Ch. IV; for the prices in January, 1948, see *Pravda* Dec. 15, 1947.

Earnings and prices of important foodstuffs
in the free state trade (in rubles)

		April 1928	July 1938	July 1940	January 1948
Average monthly earnings in the USSR[x]		59.5	289	339	450-465
Prices in Moscow					
Rye bread	kg	0.08	0.85	0.85	3.00
Wheat bread	kg	0.26	1.70	1.70	4.40
Butter	kg	2.43	20.00	28.00	64.00
Meat	kg	0.87	7.60-12.50	14.00-20.80	30.00
Sugar (granulated)	kg	0.62	3.80	5.00	15.00[xx]
Milk	liter	...	1.60	2.10	3.00-4.00
Eggs	10	...	6.50	8.50	12.00-16.00

* Monthly average in the corresponding year.
** Price for lump sugar; in July 1940 it was 5.50 rubles.

The table clearly shows 1948 prices far ahead of wages even in comparison with 1940, not to mention 1938, much less 1928.

This situation could not be allowed to continue. The people responsible for Soviet policy were aware, however, that any substantial rise in the level of nominal wages would aggravate the inflation that was far advanced, anyway. Under these circumstances, a policy of lowering prices, in particular as regarded mass consumer goods, had become urgently necessary, and after some vacillation it was adopted.

The first price reduction after the abolition of rationing occurred in April 1948.[56] For the bulk of workers and employees, however, it was only of limited importance. A 10 to 20 per cent cut in the price of passenger cars, motorcycles, field glasses, cameras, radios, or even bicycles, sewing machines, pocket watches, hunting rifles and the like—all this was not for the millions living in misery but almost solely for the privileged upper stratum. It is significant that the only food price reduced at that time was that of caviar. The mass of consumers got some relief only from the reduction in the price of cigarettes (10 per cent) and of alcoholic and non-alcoholic beverages (20 per cent).

Almost a year went by before a methodical price reduction policy was introduced. Since then, the price level (in state trade)

---

[56] *Pravda*, April 10, 1948.

has been lowered three times—in 1949, 1950 and 1951, each time on March 1 [57]—and the trend does not yet seem to have run its course.

The cut of March 1, 1949, chiefly affected a majority of foodstuffs. To name but the most important: bread, flour, cereals, meat and meat products, fish and fish products, and butter came down 10 per cent, cheese 20 per cent, and the exorbitant salt price of 1.40-1.60 rubles a kilogram 30 per cent. Alcoholic beverage and cigarette prices were cut once more (25-28 and 10 per cent, respectively), while the price of sugar, milk, eggs, vegetable oils remained unchanged.

Much greater reserve was shown in lowering the prices of manufactured products. Of these, only a relatively small number became cheaper. In particular, the prices of wool and silk fabrics were cut 10 per cent; but those of cotton fabrics—of primary importance for mass consumption—remained the same. And once again prices of motorcycles, field glasses, pocket watches, etc., were reduced.

All in all, at a very rough guess, the price cuts of March 1, 1949, probably added almost 10 per cent to the real wages of the vast majority of wage and salary earners.

Yet this was only a beginning. March 1, 1950 brought the second price reduction, the most important ever undertaken in the Soviet Union. This time, there was a more or less general drop in state retail prices, for the most part far more than in the previous year. Bread and flour prices came down 25-30 per cent, cereals 15-20 per cent, sugar 12-15 per cent, meat and meat products 24-35 per cent, fish and fish products 10-30 per cent, milk 10 per cent, butter 30 per cent, vegetable oils 10 per cent, eggs 15 per cent, etc. At a rough guess, the overall level of food prices probably dropped 20 per cent—a drop which in turn increased the purchasing power of money, i.e. real wages, 25 per cent.

The Soviet press, to be sure, never mentioned such a real wage increase in 1949. Whenever the question was touched upon, incidentally and vaguely, lower figures were given. We may infer that the price cuts were combined with some wage cuts.

The third price reduction, on March 1, 1951, was more modest in scope. Whereas the preceding one had been virtually

---

[57] Cf. the decisions of the Council of Ministers of the USSR and the CC of the CPSU as reported by *Pravda* on March 1, 1949, 1950, and 1951.

general, with many prices slashed 20-25 per cent, some as much as 35 per cent, and only a few as little as 10 per cent, the 1951 cuts did not, as a rule, exceed 10-15 per cent, and even these were by no means general. The prices of such essential foodstuffs as sugar, potatoes, vegetables, fruits and such industrial products as fabrics, clothes, and shoes remained unchanged. By and large, the purchasing power of money probably increased little less than 10 per cent.

Still, as the third successive price cut this was a noteworthy event. Yet its meaning, as well as the results of the price reduction policy as a whole, can be properly judged only against the general economic trend after the war. The pre-war level of industrial production had then been exceeded, just as the pre-war levels of agricultural production, transportation, and national income had been reached or exceeded. All this applies not only to the calculation "in current prices" but also to a *real* calculation in goods. So, after all these price cuts, have real wages also reached their pre-war level?

No figures have been made public for the prices in force after the most recent reduction, but we can calculate them on the basis of prices announced on December 15, 1947, when rationing was abolished, and on the basis of the successive cuts. The following table (showing also corresponding prices for July, 1940, insofar as they are available, and the price ratio of March 1951 to July, 1940) may throw light on this trend.

The table shows that, even after the vigorous price reduction, prices remained considerably above 1940, and that real wages did not reach the level of 1940, much less that of 1938. Even if we assume that the level of (nominal) earnings was not affected by the deflationary policies of recent years and that average earnings in 1951 remained about 2.20 rubles an hour, as in 1948, the comparison of 1951 and 1940, not to mention 1938, yields an unfavorable result.

Average hourly earnings increased from 1.63 rubles in 1940 to 2.20 rubles in 1951: about 35 per cent. In calculating the general price increase, we shall use all comparable figures from the table except the salt price, which went up exorbitantly—nearly tenfold—but does not count for so much in a worker's household. A rough calculation (of arithmetical averages) shows that the prices of the 14 foodstuffs increased 48 per cent (51 per cent without counting coffee and tea) between 1940 and 1950.[58] Thus, even in comparison with 1940, the real wages of 1951 had dropped some 10 per cent.

Food prices in Moscow: 1940 and 1948 to 1951
(In rubles per kilogram, milk per liter, eggs ped 10)

	Prices in July 1940	Jan. 1948	Cumulative price reductions from 1948 to 1951 in %	Prices in March 1951	Price ratio to July 1940 March 1951
Rye bread	0.85	3.00	43	1.70	2.00:1
Wheat bread					
2d quality	1.70	4.40	46.5	2.35	1.38:1
1st quality	...	7.00	46.5	3.75	...
Rye flour	...	4.80	43	2.75	...
Wheat flour					
2d quality	...	6.20	46.5	3.30	...
1st quality	...	8.00	46.5	4.30	...
Maccaroni	6.10	10.00	43	5.70	0.93:1
Buckwheat grits	4.30	12.00	39	7.30	1.70:1
Lump sugar	5.50	15.00	12	13.20	2.42:1
Meat					
1st quality	(17.60)*	30.00	42	17.40	0.99:1
Perch, frozen	(7.00)**	12.00	27	8.75	1.25:1
Herrings, salted	8.00	20.00	27	14.60	1.83:1
Butter, salted	28.00	64.00	46.5	34.20	1.22:1
Vegetable oil	15.65	30.00	10	27.00	1.73:1
Milk	2.10	3.00-4.00	19	2.40-3.25	1.34:1***
Eggs	8.50	12.00-16.00	23.5	9.20-12.25	1.26:1***
Salt	0.05	1.40-1.60	67	0.46-0.52	9.80:1***
Tea	100.00	160.00	19	129.60	1.30:1
Coffee	49.00	75.00	10	67.50	1.38:1

  * Average between prices of beef for soup (14.00), for roast (18.00), and for steak (20.80).
  ** Average between prices in January, 1939 (5.40) and January, 1941 (8.50).
  *** According to the mean, between the higher and the lower price.
1934, No. 12, p. 4.

---

  58 In view of the particularly stiff increase in the prices of rye bread, buckwheat, vegetable oil, and herrings, it may be assumed that the results of a more precise calculation would be even more unfovorable to the middle and lower strata of labor.

We will return to these developments in our concluding discussion of the wage trend since the start of universal planning. First, however, we have to discuss another event in the sphere of wage policies—an incident regarded by some people, notably in foreign union circles, as a turning point in most recent Soviet wage policy.

Reintroduction of Union Contracts

Above (in Ch. IV) we saw the withering of collective labor contracts in the Soviet Union in the mid-Thirties. Leading Communist circles were well aware of the glaring light this fact cast on the deterioration of unionism and the decline of the working class. Nothing was left undone to convince the rest of the world that collective bargaining was still practiced in the Soviet Union, with the purpose of safeguarding the interests of the employees, as in the 1920's or abroad. One could read in a pamphlet published in New York, in 1942, by a Communist "front" organization:[59]

> "Collective agreements are entered into both between the national union and the managing boards of an industry and between each local union and the local factory management.
>
> These agreements fix time and piece rates for all operations. They provide the conditions for overtime work, sometimes allowed only with the consent of the union. They guarantee the maintenance of earnings in cases of temporary transfer to lower paid jobs and for a trial and guarantee period pending the setting of piece rates on new or changed operations. They specify the bonuses to be paid for production in excess of norms and for inventions and improvements in technique. They deal with such matters as the employment of new workers, safety, sanitary and job-training facilities and the amounts to be set aside by management for workers' housing, sport and cultural activities. On the other hand, they set forth the obligations of the union for the maintenance of proper labor discipline."

This "line" was strictly adhered to.[60] Even the trade union delegations visiting the Soviet Union during or shortly after the war—from the U.S. and Great Britain especially—invariably re-

[59] *The Trade Unions of our Soviet Ally*, by Clifford T. McAvoy, publ. by the American Council on Soviet Relations, New York, 1942, pp. 13-14.
[60] See also *Organized Labor in the Soviet Union*, by Edwin S. Smith, publ. by the National Council of American-Soviet Friendship, New York, 1943. pp. 24-26.

ported what they had learned about the current practice and tremendous importance of collective bargaining in the Soviet Union.[61]

In the long run, it was evident that this legend would be impossible to maintain. And it seemed equally impossible to give the unions abroad a satisfactory explanation of the Soviet abolition of collective contracts. In particular, this fact seemed to impede the realization of the new trade union international that was being planned in Moscow toward the end of the war.

On February 19, 1947, it was reported in the Soviet press that "the Council of Ministers of the USSR, following the example of previous years, agreed to the proposal of the AUCTUC for collective bargaining in 1947." The "example of previous years" was a euphemism, of course, as collective contracts had not been signed in the Soviet Union for more than ten years. Much more important than this phrasing, however, is the fact that the union contracts, as signed again in the Soviet Union since 1947, are fundamentally different from such contracts as known abroad, or as signed in the USSR in the first decade of the Revolution.

Today, collective bargaining in the Soviet Union is consciously not designed to defend the interests of wage and salary earners. As stressed by *Trud,* the official trade union paper, in an editorial dedicated to the reintroduction of collective contracts: "As the guardian of workingmen's interests we have the socialist state." Therefore the purpose of collective agreements consists not in the protection of labor, but "in guaranteeing the fulfillment and overfulfillment of the state production plan for the given establishment." Hence "the main stipulation of the contracted obligation must be an increased demand from every worker. Without strengthening labor discipline and without ruthless struggle against the violators of state and labor discipline— grabbers and loafers—there can be no real fulfillment of obligations laid down in the collective agreement."[62]

And how should the wage problem be dealt with, in collective bargaining? It used to determine the fundamental content of collective agreements, but in the Soviet Union this has long been an obsolete view. The chairman of the AUCTUC had this to say on the subject, immediately after the reintroduction of union con-

---

[61] See in particular *Report of the C. I. O. Delegation to the Soviet Union,* Washington 1945, p. 21.
[62] *Trud,* February 19, 1947.

tracts was announced:[63] "Any change in the system of labor pay can take place only upon a decision of the government. This rule remains valid even when collective agreements are concluded. This does not mean, however, that management and labor are not concerned with wage problems. Their duty consists in creating conditions for the increase of labor productivity, and as a consequence, for a rise in wages."

The raising of wages—or, rather, of earnings—as a mere concomitant ("as a consequence") of the rising productivity of labor is, as we have seen, an essential part of the most recent Russian labor policy.[64] The reintroduction of collective agreements did not alter that. Rather: since 1947 it is precisely in connection with the conclusion of collective agreements that production quotas have been revised in a manner on which the Soviet press is exceedingly frank. Just one example:[65] "Alongside the conclusion of collective agreements, a revision of norms will take place. This will require special attention on the part of management and trade unions, since our plans must be based not on average-arithmetic norms already reached in production, but on average-progressive norms, which must be oriented toward the achievement of the best workers."

There is no need here to take up this emphasis on the "best" in setting performance quotas valid for all. Its significance has been shown earlier, in analyzing union wage policy. The reintroduction of collective agreements did not change the foundations of a wage policy which was rigidly laid down in 1945/46 and resulted in constant pressure on the wage level. It has not become a factor which might influence the wage trend so as to favor the workers and employees.

The Development of Real Wages: 1928-1938-1940-1951

Based on our detailed discussion of the several phases of the wage trend since 1928, we can now try to obtain a comprehensive view of the trends since the Soviet Union's adoption of a policy of universal planning, i.e. the Five-Year Plan policy. Shortly be-

---

[63] *Pravda*, February 21, 1947.
[64] Cf. Sec. "Union Wage Policies" in Ch. IV above.
[65] *Izvestiya*, March 6, 1947.

fore this policy was adopted, the pre-war level of real wages—i.e. the level prevailing before World War I—had for the first time been exceeded in the Soviet Union. This was to be the starting point of a further upward movement, which was supposed to raise real wages substantially under the very first Five-Year Plan.

The nominal increase in wage and salary earners' income under the first and subsequent plans was indeed considerable. Annual earnings, calculated on the average of all categories, amounted to 690 rubles in 1927/28—or, to use the calendar year, 703 rubles in 1928—and around 5,200-5,400 rubles in 1951, increasing almost eight times, or according to some optimistic calculations (see Appendix 2 to this chapter) perhaps as much as eleven times. At the same time, however, the purchasing power of money greatly declined, as may be seen from the comparison of prices in the tables on pp. 141 and 228. To cite but a few instances, rye bread in 1951 cost 21 times as much as in 1928, beef 20 times as much, butter 14 times as much, sugar 20 times as much, etc. In fact, an increase of nominal earnings to almost eight times (or even eleven times) the 1928 level meant an exceedingly painful decline in real wages.

It was not a continuous development. In the years of the First Five-Year Plan, from 1928 to 1932, real wages.dropped about 50 per cent. They fluctuated at about that level until 1935; then, until about the middle of 1938, they rose again, but without ever reaching the real wage level of 1928. As previously shown, their 1935/38 increase may be estimated at about 20 per cent. The middle of 1938 brought the beginning of a new drop in the real wage curve—a drop continuing until 1946, at varying rates of speed. Not until the end of 1946 was there a new upward movement, which has not yet come to an end. Yet not only the peak of real wages in the Twenties (1928) and the considerably lower peak of the Thirties (1938) remain unequaled, but today's real wage level is still noticeably under that of 1940. If I am wrong about the latest level of nominal wages and the more optimistic view is correct, the real wage level of 1940 has been exceeded, but the 1938 level, not to mention that of 1928, would still be far from attained.

An attempt to calculate the Moscow living cost index from the food prices from 1928 to 1940, and on that basis to reconstruct the development of the real wages of industrial workers in

Moscow, has been made by S. N. Prokopovicz.[66] According to this, the real wages of industrial workers in Moscow dropped from 100 in 1928 to 33.9 in October 1935—a result even less favorable than the above estimate—and rose to 46.4 (i.e. 36.7 per cent) by 1938, only to drop again to 35.7 in April, 1940.

The same method was used by Kravis and Mintzes for the calculation of Moscow cost of living indices from 1936 to 1950.[67] Combining the figures of Prokopovicz and Kravis-Mintzes we arrive at the result that living costs, equaling 1 in 1928, appeared to have reached 29.5 in January 1948, 26.6 in March 1949, and 20.7 in March, 1950.

Harry Schwartz, the best-known exponent of the relatively optimistic view of recent Russian wage trends, assuming average annual earnings in 1948 to have been 7,400 rubles, calculates on the basis of the Prokopovicz and Kravis-Mintzes index figures that the real wages of the Russian worker (not of Prokopovicz's industrial worker in Moscow, but of a country-wide average of all groups of wage and salary earners) had declined "in terms of 1928 'Food Rubles'" from 703 rubles in 1928 to 404.1 by 1938, and to 250.5 by 1948.[68] Thus, the real wage index would have dropped from 100 in 1928 to 57.5 in 1938 and 35.6 in 1948.[69] According to the living cost index of Kravis-Mintzes, assuming that the level of nominal wages remained unchanged since 1948, this would amount to 50.5 for 1950, and for 1951, after the most recent price cuts, to about 55—scarcely more than half the real wages attained on the threshhold of the First Five-Year Plan.

66 S. N. Prokopovicz, *Russlands Volkwirtschaft unter den Sowjets*, Europa-Verlag, Zürich-New York, 1944, p. 306.

67 Irving B. Kravis and Joseph Mintzes, "Food Prices in the Soviet Union, 1936-1950," in *The Review of Economics and Statistics*, May, 1950, p. 167.

68 Harry Schwartz, *Russia's Soviet Economy*, Prentice-Hall, New York, 1950, p. 461.

69 Another author, approaching Harry Schwartz's relatively optimistic views in his appraisal of recent Russian wage trends, arrives at similar results: "The weighted prices of all consumers' goods in 1948 were probably close to, perhaps above, 30 times their 1926/27 base . . . The average nominal wage in 1948 was about 11 times the 1926/27 base" (Naum Jasny, "The Soviet Price System" in *The American Economic Review*, December, 1950, p. 849). According to this, real wages would have dropped from 100 in 1926/27 to a mere 36.7 in 1948—Average annual earnings were 624 rubles in 1926/27 and thus, according to Jasny, about 6,900 rubles in 1948.

International Wage Comparison: 1950/51

We have already had occasion to compare real wages in the USSR and a number of other countries. Those comparisons applied to 1928 and 1938, the two peak years of real wages in the Twenties and Thirties. A similar attempt should be made for the present.

This undertaking is facilitated by two detailed studies made in the U.S. Department of Labor,[70] comparing the purchasing power of hourly earnings in different countries, measured by the price of food. It was calculated how many minutes the average worker must work in different countries to be able to buy certain quantities of various foods. On that basis, index figures were then calculated for real hourly earnings, taking into account the relative importance of different foodstuffs in a worker's household and the resulting variations from country to country.

From the comparison of prices in minutes of work we can get a good picture of the relative level of real hourly earnings in the countries in question. The American study bases its figures for the Soviet Union on the assumption that in 1950 average (nominal) earnings in the USSR had reached 2 rubles 94 kopecks an hour. This would equal average annual earnings of some 7,300 rubles, i.e. about one third more than calculated above. If our view of the most recent nominal wage trend is correct, the American tables must be revised by adding one third to the work-time prices quoted for foodstuffs in the Soviet Union.

But let us stick to the American figures, for the time being. In the following table, to simplify the picture, we show only data for eight countries (out of a total of twenty in the American source) and for 16 foodstuffs (out of a total of 52, and of 25 from the Soviet Union):

---

[70] Irving B. Kravis, "Work Times Required to Buy Food" and "Work Time Required to Buy Food, 1937/50" in *The Monthly Labor Review*, November 1949 and February, 1951.

Prices of foodstuffs calculated in minutes of work
(per pound, for milk per liter, for eggs per dozen)

	United States	Great Britain	France	West Germany	Italy	Sweden	Hungary	USSR
Bread	6	6	9	10	15	10	11	19
Wheat flour	4	7	17	11	17	7	17	36
Maccaroni	9	18	30	...	23	...	...	62
Meat (average)	28	...	...	...	118	39	...	182
Pork chops	29	...	90	88	120	49	100	304
Bacon	25	44	...	...	...	...	...	458
Chicken	18	...	...	...	...	39	120	228
Butter	31	37	169	129	183	60	160	373
Oleomargarine	12	18	67	53	...	...	93	198
Milk	8	15	20	16	23	8	21	52
Eggs	22	66	96	105	102	54	106	291
Potatoes	2	3	9	4	8	3	4	11
Cabbage	3	...	15	10	...	4	...	16
Onions	3	17	...	16	...	13	...	28
Sugar	4	9	25	26	43	9	40	122
Tea	54	77	...	...	...	...	...	1,334

The work-time prices do not always apply to the same type
of merchandise. This tends to make the comparison somewhat
vague for some foodstuffs, especially bread. The comparative calculation is always based on the price of the type of merchandise
most widely sold in the particular country, and the bread types
in particular vary greatly from country to country. In the United
States, as in France and Italy, the most common bread is white
wheat bread, while in the USSR it is the plainest rye bread (containing plenty of water). In the case of bread, therefore, the table
above presents the unfavorable Soviet position in a rather mild
light. To be sure, if a comparative calculation of the purchasing
power of wages is based on the prices of a large number of goods,
the disturbing influence of this factor is largely offset.

With the work-time prices as a starting point, the index figures for the purchasing power of hourly wages—i.e. of real hourly
wages in different countries—can be calculated (by means of a complex procedure which we cannot discuss here).

In the U.S. Department of Labor tables, real hourly wages
(or, rather, hourly earnings) in the United States were put at

100. To give a clearer picture of Soviet conditions, we take real hourly earnings in the USSR as the starting point of our comparison, putting them at 100 and accordingly recalculating the figures of the Labor Department table. The Labor Department calculated index figures for 1936/38, 1949, and 1950, while our table has been simplified by drawing only on the 1936/38 and 1950 data (for all countries mentioned in the American study except two, Czechoslovakia and Israel, for which the calculated index figures were clearly exaggerated): [71]

Indices of real hourly earnings in 1936-38 and 1950

	1936-38	1950
USSR	100	100
Italy	108	171
Hungary	121	193
Austria (Vienna)	158	200
France (Paris)	283	221
Chile	108	264
West Germany	213	271
Netherlands	188	271
Finland	204	279
Ireland	183	329
Switzerland	204	329
Great Britain	193	443
Sweden	250	450
Denmark	304	521
Canada	358	557
Norway	283	600
United States	417	714
Australia	383	764

The Soviet figures for 1936/38 refer to July 1936. If available data for July 1938 were used for the USSR—perhaps raising the Russian index figure by 15 per cent—the picture would look somewhat more favorable for the Soviet Union. But even then, in most cases, the difference between the real wage level in the Soviet Union and abroad would be striking. As far as the 1950 data are concerned, the table shows the Soviet Union in a rather too favorable light. As mentioned before, the calculations of the U.S. Deparement of Labor rest on the assumption that average annual earnings in the USSR amounted to some 7,300 rubles in 1950;

---

[71] For Czechoslovakia, the 1950 index figure was allegedly 329; for Israel, 450.

so, if my less optimistic judgement of the nominal wage trend is correct, the 1950 relationship of real wages in the Soviet Union and in other countries was even worse than it appears from the table.

Of course, we have seen that in 1950 the USSR was vigorously engaged in restoring the pre-war level of real wages—an operation not yet completed today. It would be better, therefore to use 1951 data for the Soviet Union, raising the Soviet index figures by some 10 per cent. In part—but not entirely—this would offset the error due to the assumption of excessively high nominal wages in the Soviet Union. On the other hand, if average annual earnings in 1950 in fact reached the level assumed in the American study, the Russian figure for 1951 would have to be about 110 (or else all others would have to be reduced accordingly). Even in this case, however, real hourly wages in the Soviet Union would seem exceedingly low in comparison with the wage level of even such impoverished countries as Italy, Austria, or Hungary.

The table reveals still another important fact. In every case —with the single exception of France—the difference between the real wage level in the USSR and in other countries increased from 1936/38 to 1950; in most cases it increased a great deal. If we consider that—as just shown—the table presents the Soviet position as slightly worse than it was in 1936/38 and slightly better than it was in 1950/51, the deterioration of the relative Soviet position between 1936/38 and 1950/51 is even more extensive.

The approximative character of all such calculations makes it impossible simply to compare their results with the results obtained by other methods. In particular, they diverge—sometimes considerably—from the results of the wage comparison for 1938, obtained (in Chapter Four) on the basis of rather scanty material and by a rough calculation.[72] To discover a trend, one must, if possible, use the same method for the different periods, as was done for 1936/38 and 1950 in the American study.

As for the 1928 wage comparison offered at the beginning of Chapter Four, those figures were obtained by methods similar to, if not identical with, those employed by the U.S. Department of

---

[72] If the figures of the table on p. 299 are recalculated into index figures (with USSR = 100), we get these results: France 217 (as compared with 283, according to the American study), Germany 250 (213), Sweden 405 (250), Great Britian 420 (193), United States 751 (417).

Labor. Thus they may—although with some reservations—be compared with our latest ones. A reconstruction of the index figures quoted in the table on p. 131 to conform with those in the last table yields the following picture:

Indices of real wages: 1928, 1936-38 and 1950

	1928	1936-38	1950
USSR	100	100	100
France	112	283	221
Germany	142	213	271
Netherlands	170	188	271
Sweden	176	250	450
Great Britain	200	193	443
Canada	310	358	557
United States	370	417	714

As previously emphasized, these figures are based on the assumption that the average annual earnings of Soviet workers in 1950 reached the relatively high level of about 7,300 rubles. If this is not the case, the gap between the wage level in the Soviet Union and in other countries has widened even more, since the adoption of the policy of universal planning, than appears from the above table.

"Socialized Wages"

For an appraisal of labor's standard of living, real wages provide the most important though not the only criterion. Some developments countering the depreciation of wages have already been mentioned. In addition, there is the major fact that Russian labor has not known any mass unemployment since the early 1930's. On labor's overall balance sheet this certainly counts as an important asset.

Another asset is pointed out by Soviet authors when they enthusiastically write of "socialized wages." They insist that neither nominal nor real wages are an adequate measure of the standard of living of wage and salary earners in the Soviet Union; that the overall picture is seen in a much more favorable light when "socialized wages" are taken into account.

What are socialized wages? They are the benefits and advantages for wage and salary earners, which the individual employee does not have to pay for either directly or by deductions from his wage or salary. These direct and indirect social benefits encompass social insurance[73] (including health services), education, housing, and special welfare funds in the plants.

If the general course of wages is to be properly evaluated, two questions concerning socialized wages need to be answered. First, what effect do socialized wages have on the workers' standard of living? And second, what is the relationship between the trends of individual and socialized wages? Does the development of socialized wages tend to outdistance that of individual wages and improve the trend of living standards beyond what can be seen from the development of the individual wage? Or is it the other way around: do socialized wages lag behind individual wages?

There is a third question that also needs to be considered. If socialized wages are to be viewed in correct perspective, we must establish whether or not their role in the Soviet Union differs basically from that of similar phenomena in other countries.

1. Social insurance and public health services are the most important element in socialized wages. In 1927/28, on the eve of the First Five-Year Plan, all benefits paid out from insurance funds for sickness, maternity and unemployment, and all disability and old-age pensions, constituted an 8.5 per cent addition to the aggregate payroll. Corresponding percentages in 1928/29 and 1929/30 were 8.8 and 6.5, respectively. As there was no large-scale unemployment, and no unemployment relief in subsequent years, when comparing these percentages with those of later times unemployment payments should be deducted from them, in which case they are reduced to 7.0, 7.2 and 6.1, respectively.[74]

In a few years' time this ratio had rapidly declined, and in 1932, at the end of the First Five-Year Plan period, relief and benefit payments added a mere 3.9 per cent to the aggregate payroll.[75] This was more or less the percentage in subsequent years. After the war, however, the large increase in the number of disability and old-age pensions being paid out caused the percentage

---

[73] Social insurance in the Soviet Union does not require contributions from the insured wage and salary earners. Cf. Chapter Seven below.

[74] Polyak, as quoted *supra*, Chapter IV, n. 19, p. 85.

[75] *Labor in the USSR . . . .*, as quoted *supra*, Chapter IV, n. 40, pp. 21, 344.

to rise again, and in 1950, 7.2 per cent of the aggregate payroll
went for social insurance.[76]

Similarly, the cost of public health services (including major
investments) declined in the course of the First Five-Year Plan
from 5.0 per cent of the aggregate payroll of all occupational divisions in 1927/28 to 4.4 and 4.3 per cent, respectively, in the two
following years.[77] Later years showed a slight increase and in 1936
the percentage was 4.6.[78] Data for calculating this percentage are
not available for the subsequent years, as funds for the health
services ceased to be provided for by the budget for social insurance and instead were included in the government's general
budget.

2. The sums spent by the government on education, including not only vocational training but also general education insofar as it benefits wage labor, constitute another factor in socialized
wages, according to Soviet thinking. Statistically, money spent to
educate wage and salary earners and their children cannot be
separated from money spent to educate the population at large. All
official estimates generally overstate the proportion to be counted
as part of socialized wages.

Indeed, it is doubtful if expenses for education should be
included in wages at all, whether individual or socialized. If they
are included, then why not include other public expenditure, particularly those of municipalities? After all, most of the funds
distributed by urban municipalities in the Soviet Union and almost everywhere in the world are aimed at raising general living
standards; and to a large extent this is true of the national budget.

Educational expenditures increased very considerably in the
last two decades. But only that part of these expenditures should
be included in socialized wages which was spent on scholarships
and stipends granted to students from the ranks of labor. To be
sure, educational grants were of great importance, and enabled
hundreds of thousands of wage and salary earners and their children to attend high school and college.

---

[76] If the average annual wage in 1950 was 7,400 rubles, and not 5,200-5,400
rubles as assumed in this work (see Appendix II to this chapter), then the percentage was 5.1.

[77] Polyak, as quoted *supra*, Chapter IV, n. 19, p. 85.

[78] Budget data for social insurance from *Laws and Ordinances*, 1936: 404;
data on aggregate payrolls from "Foundations . . . for 1937," as quoted *supra*,
Chapter IV, n. 88, p. 242.

What is the importance of the educational item in labor's "budget"? In the beginning, it was moderate—1.3 per cent of the aggregate payroll in 1927/28; 1.4 per cent in 1928/29; 2.1 per cent in 1929/30.[79] This ratio increased slowly but steadily till the middle of the Second Five-Year Plan period. Educational grants to students of high schools and colleges totaled 1,778,000,000 rubles in 1935.[80] Of the recipients, 75 to 80 per cent were wage or salary earners, or children of wage or salary earners; thus, an estimated 1,400,000,000 rubles was spent in 1935 on scholarships for students from the ranks of labor (including non-manual labor). This was some 2.5 per cent of an aggregate payroll of approximately 56,200,000,000 rubles.[81]

Yet the proportion of workers and workers' children among high school and college students was by this time on the decline. A large number of grants were given to the children of medium- and high-bracket non-manual workers; the proportion of grants to manual workers must have been substantially below the 2.5 percentage given above. This came more clearly to the fore in the late 1930's. Finally, in October 1940, free education was abolished in high schools and institutions of higher learning, and scholarships and stipends were restricted to students winning the highest scholastic grades.[82]

3. Housing ranks third among the items included in socialized wages. Huge amounts were invested in housing construction after the inception of the Five-Year Plan policy. But the housing shortage, already acute at the beginning of the period, grew steadily worse when accelerated industrialization—the essence of the Five-Year Plans—caused the urban population to mount faster and faster. The number of city dwellers, approximately 27,900,000 on October 1, 1928, increased to 55,900,000 by January 17, 1939, according to census data. If housing construction is to be considered as a supplement to individual wages, it must then be asked to what extent the housing shortage was reduced by new construction.

Urban dwelling space available on October 1, 1928 (i.e., on

[79] *National Economy of the USSR. Statistical Yearbook*, issued by the Central Statistical Office, Moscow-Leningrad, 1932, p. 418.
[80] *USSR—Country of Socialism. Statistical Reference Book*, Moscow, 1936, p. 82.
[81] "Foundations . . . for 1937," as quoted *supra*, Chapter IV, n. 88, p. 242.
[82] See chapter II above.

the eve of the First Five-Year Plan) totaled 160,200,000 square meters for a population of 27,900,000,[83] or 5.7 square meters per inhabitant.[84] ("Dwelling space" in Soviet statistics include all residential space, but exclude entrance halls, corridors, bathrooms, toilets, and kitchens other than living-room-kitchen combinations.)

The following table shows Plan estimates as well as actual achievements in providing new dwellings:[85]

Housing Construction under the Five-Year Plans
(Million square meters)

	1st Five-Year Plan	2d Five-Year Plan	3d Five-Year Plan
Dwelling space at the beginning of the period	160.2	185.1	[200.8]
New construction			
Plan	62.5	[72.5]	36.0
Actual	[32.9]	26.8	...
Dwelling space at the end of the period *			
Plan	213.0	246.5	[223.8]
Actual	185.1	[200.8]	...

* Allowing for natural losses from deterioration.

The figures reveal a substantail falling-off in housing conditions. The First Five-Year Plan had anticipated an increase in the urban population from 27,900,000 to 34,700,000;[86] housing construction was to enlarge the dwelling space available per person to 6.1 square meters (as compared with 5.7 square meters prior to

---

[83] *Five-Year Plan* . . . , as quoted *supra,* Chapter IV, n. 7, vol. I. p. 129; vol. II, 2, p. 292.

[84] One square meter equals 1550 square inches or 10.76 square feet. Hence, the space available per person approximated 61 square feet.

[85] Official data on available "dwelling space," new construction, loss through destruction, and net gain in housing capacity, are incomplete. To a certain extent gaps had to be filled by computing approximate figures on the basis of an estimated "mortality rate." Data for the First Five-Year Plan refer, as usual, to the period ending September 30, 1933 for plan estimates, and to the period ending December 31, 1932 for what was actually achieved. Figures calculated by the author are given in the table in brackets; unbracketed data were taken from the following sources: *Five-Year Plan* . . . , as quoted supra, Chapter IV, n. 7, vol. II, 2, pp. 292 f.; *Fulfilling the First Five-Year Plan* . . . as quoted supra, Chapter IV, n. 12, p. 186; *Second Five-Year Plan* . . . , as quoted *supra,* Chapter IV, n. 10, vol. I, p. 533; *Results of Fulfilling* . . . , as quoted *supra,* Chapter IV, n. 88, p. 63; *Eighteenth Convention* . . . . , as quoted *supra,* Chapter IV, n. 95, p. 665.

[86] *Five-Year Plan* . . . , as quoted *supra,* Chapter IV, n. 7. vol. I, p. 129.

the Plan). In reality, aggregate dwelling space increased only by 24,900,000 instead of the envisaged 52,800,000 square meters, which means that the Plan was executed only to the extent of 47.2 per cent. But the urban population had meanwhile risen to 39,700,000[87]—a gain of 11,800,000, not 6,800,000. Instead of increasing, dwelling space per person dropped to 4.7 square meters.

Under the Second Five-Year Plan, aggregate dwelling space was to increase by 61,400,000 square meters; new construction, however, increased it by only 26,800,000. Assuming that the loss in residential space from deterioration did not exceed 6 per cent in five years[88] (which probably is too low an estimate), aggregate dwelling space at the end of the Second Five-Year Plan period must have approximated 200,800,000 square meters—a net increase in five years of only 15,700,000 square meters, or 8.4 per cent (the Plan thus being fulfilled only to the extent of 25 per cent). Yet the urban population at the end of the planning period (as estimated on the basis of the 1939 census figure) approximated 53,-000,000, which represented a gain of 33.5 per cent.

Dwelling space in the cities must have fallen below 4 square meters per person by the end of 1937; it had thus declined about one-third since 1928. As the new construction envisaged by the Third Five-Year Plan was small, there is no reason to assume that conditions have improved up to the outbreak of the war.

It is probable that these summary data do not take into account the enlargement of housing capacity resulting from the urbanization of rural settlements. In the twelve years that elasped between the census of December 17, 1926 and that of January 17, 1939, about 5,800,000 inhabitants of rural localities became city dwellers through reclassification.[89] But even if it is assumed that the enlargement of dwelling space resulting from this has been left completely out of account in the statistics given above, and that the dwelling space per person in the new urban localities was approximately the same as it was in the cities on the eve of the First Five-Year Plan (5.7 square meters)—which would mean a total of 33,000,000 square meters,—nevertheless, the amount of available dwelling space is still seen to be extremely meager: about

[87] *Second Five-Year Plan* . . . , as quoted *supra*, Chapter IV, n. 10, vol. I. p. 427.
[88] The authors of the First Five-Year Plan assumed a rate of deterioration of about 6 per cent—5.8 per cent for the "socialized sector" and 6.3 per cent for the "private sector."
[89] S. Sul'kevich, *The Population of the USSR*, Leningrad, 1939, p. 15.

233,800,000 square meters for a population of approximately 53,-000,000, or about 4.4 square meters per person. This represents a decline of almost 25 per cent from the amount of dwelling space available per person at the beginning of the First Five-Year Plan period.

This is such a poor showing after a whole decade of industrial expansion, that one is tempted to assume that the so-called "individual" housing construction was not included in the statistics. During these years the government encouraged workers who needed apartments to build themselves small, often inadequate houses, free grants of land being assured to such builders. The most optimistic estimates would not claim that more than twenty or thirty million square meters were produced by such makeshift building. Nevertheless, if it is true that some such figure must be added to the total amount of available dwelling space, the space per person at the end of the Second Five-Year Plan was still less than 5 square meters. And since that time there has certainly been no improvement in this ratio.

Urban wage and salary earners, the overwhelming majority of the urban population, are living today in much more crowded conditions than prior to the inauguration of the Five-Year Plans.

Moreover, the figures cited are statistical averages, and again do not express the privileges enjoyed by the upper strata. Inequality of housing accommodations has gone farther than differentiation of income, and one or two million executives, officials and highly paid workers live in residences far above the standards of some twenty years earlier. The improved housing accommodations enjoyed by these upper strata have greatly impressed a number of observers, especially visitors from abroad, and have led to their overestimating the general level of Soviet housing. But the better the residences occupied by the few, the more average figures are misleading, the more do statistics disguise the fact that large masses of workers are forced to live in substandard dwellings.

Under these circumstances, it is scarcely possible to consider the sums spent for the construction of dwellings as increasing the amount of "socialized wages" received by the worker. If the building of new houses were in fact expanded to such an extent that a marked amelioration of the conditions under which the working class is housed took place, then one would perhaps be justified in regarding a part of the cost of construction as a kind of socialized wage. Present conditions in the Soviet Union, however, provide no such justification.

In this connection there is one more aspect of the housing problem that needs to be considered. Outside of the Soviet Union the assumption is widespread that rent does not figure as an important item in the worker's budget, since it is so low that much of what the worker has to spend on rent in other countries he can use in the Soviet Union for buying other things; in other words, his wages have an added purchasing power.

Rents are in fact relatively low—but this is only half the truth. In the Soviet Union rent is paid in return for the provision of much fewer facilities and services to the tenant than is the case in most other countries. It represents merely the price charged for "dwelling space," and does not entitle the tenant to be supplied with light, water, and facilities for drainage and disposal of garbage; in many cases ordinary repairs are at the tenant's expense.

This is of considerable importance. Rent proper is computed according to "class principles," i.e., in proportion to the tenant's income, so that one tenant in a building may pay five times the rent paid by another tenant for the same amount of dwelling space. However, all other housing expenses are usually apportioned according to the amount of dwelling space occupied or to the number of family members; these expenses, then, are not apportioned according to "class." If in addition to the basic rent, these unavoidable additional expenditures are taken into account, total expenses of Russian workers and employees for housing are comparable to those borne by workers and employees in other countries.

Only once, so far as I know, have Soviet officials ever made public statistics on the housing expenses borne by Russian wage and salary earners which were computed to include all additional charges. A report was submitted to the Thirteenth Convention of the International Institute of Statistics by USSR delegates which calculated expenditures by Soviet wage and salary earners for housing in the manner current in the rest of the world. These data referred to 1928 and revealed that expenses for rent, heat, light, etc. amounted to 15.5 per cent of the total outlay of the average Russian wage or salary earner's budget.[90] The table below

---

[90] *International Labour Review*, November 1933, p. 654.

shows how this compares with the situation in other countries:[91]

Expenditure for Housing, Including Heating and Lighting

Country	Year	Percentage of Total Outlay of	
		Manual Workers	Non-Manual Workers
Belgium	1928-29	11.4	17.6
Czechoslovakia	1931-32	12.3	14.0
Denmark	1931	19.0	21.2
Estonia	1937-38	16.3	16.1
Finland	1928	17.1	19.8
Germany	1927-28	14.4	16.7
"	1937	18.2	...
Latvia	1936-37	14.9	14.7
Netherlands	1935-36	21.5	18.2
Norway	1927-28	18.0	17.6
Poland	1929	8.9	...
Sweden	1933	19.1	21.1
United States	1935-36	24.7	...

At the beginning of the First Five-Year Plan, housing expenses were approximately as large an item in the budget of Soviet wage and salary earners as they were in the budget of the workers of other European countries. They were larger for the USSR than for Poland, Belgium or Czechoslovakia, and smaller than for the Scandinavian countries or the Netherlands, with their superior housing facilities. They were, of course, substantially lower for the USSR than for the United States, where high rent is in a sense the obverse of low expenditures for food.

How things developed in later years cannot be stated with the same degree of accuracy. Rent proper increased at a slower pace than did nominal earnings, and as a result the percentage of a family's budget devoted to rent declined. In 1928/29, rent (excluding other housing expenses) is said to have comprised 7.5 per cent of the total outlay of single workers; 8.8 per cent in working-class families with one provider; and 8.1 per cent in working-class families with two or more providers.[92] For later

[91] *Year-Book of Labour Statistics*, ILO, Montreal, 1943, p. 177.
[92] *Labor in the USSR, Statistical Abstract for 1931*, Moscow, 1932, pp. 157 f.

years, data are available only for all types of households together.
Of all household expenses, rent proper comprised, in 1931, 6.8
per cent; in 1932, 6.3; in 1933, 4.9; in 1934, 4.8; and in 1935,
4.5.[93] However, other housing charges not included in rent rose
substantially, so that the percentage of the individual's income
used to defray all housing expenditures presumably remained
more or less unchanged.

From the mid-Thirties on, it was repeatedly suggested that
the system of computing basic rent according to "class" be modified, if not eliminated entirely. The way for this was prepared
by a reorganization of the Housing Fund Administration in October 1937.[94] But this "reform" was abandoned for the time being
because of the obvious decline in the purchasing power of low-
paid wage earners.

4. According to Soviet thinking, socialized wages also include
the funds set aside in industrial plants to improve the living conditions of the plants' personnel. Up to 1936 there existed several
categories of such plant funds, of which the most important were
called "Funds for Improving the Living Conditions of Workers"
(FUBR in the Russian abbreviation).

By law, 75 per cent of such funds were to be used for housing
construction, and the remainder for other improvements. These
funds, however, were quite small and exercised no significant effect
on the standard of living of the general working population. Aggregate amounts were as follows:[95]

Year	Million Rubles	Year	Million Rubles
1927/28	28.8	1932	61.0
1928/29	32.1	1933	65.0
1929/30	43.8	1934	100.0
1931	66.0	1935	112.0

This added no more than one-third of one per cent to the
aggregate payroll at the beginning of the period, and about one-

[93] *Labor .... for* 1936, Moscow, 1936, pp. 342 f.
[94] Cf. my article "Housing Reform," in *Sotsialisticheskii Vestnik*, Paris, 1937, no. 20, pp. 5ff.
[95] Data to 1931 inclusive, from Polyak, as quoted *supra* Chapter IV, n. 19, p. 113; for the following years, from *USSR—Country of Socialism*, Moscow, 1936, p. 53.

fifth of one per cent at the end of the period. Of course, the FUBR did not benefit all wage and salary earners, but industrial workers for the most part; hence the addition to industrial payrolls alone were greater. But even here it was insignificant. Moreover, the major part of these funds was spent on housing. We have seen that housing conditions under the first two Five-Year Plans did not improve at all, so that the scant influence of these funds on the workers' living standards is obvious.

On April 19, 1936, all FUBR and similar plant welfare funds were replaced by uniform "Plant Managers Funds."[96] These were to be financed by contributions to the extent of 4 per cent of the net profits of individual plants as scheduled in their financial operation plans, plus 50 per cent of the additional profits realized outside the plan. Accordingly, these funds assumed a fairly large size as early as 1936; in establishments within the jurisdiction of the five People's Commissariats in charge of industry they totaled 950,000,000 rubles and added 6.3 per cent to the aggregate payroll of these establishments.[97] Of the amounts accumulated, 50 per cent was to be devoted to building construction; the remaining 50 per cent was to be used for "individual premiums" and other extra benefits. In the first year of operation the authorities found out that amounts allocated to housing construction had been used for other purposes. Of the total of 950,000,000 rubles, only 55,000,000 rubles, or less than 6 per cent, were spent on housing, while more than double that amount—117,000,000 rubles—went for "individual premiums," i.e., rewards granted for the most part to plant executives and highly paid employees.

The source[98] from which these data are taken does not indicate what payments from Plant Managers' Funds were used to promote the welfare of the rank-and-file of wage earners. It did emphasize, however, that "serious infractions of the law concerning Managers' Funds were noted in a very large number of establishments, where Funds were used to finance large-scale investments not envisaged by the Plan." Up to the Soviet Union's entry into the war, such complaints were frequently voiced in the press. Plant Managers' Funds never really made any significant contribu-

---

[96] Act of the CEC and CPC of the USSR, *Laws and Ordinances*, 1936: 169.
[97] G. Polyak, "In Re Funds of Plant Managers," in *Planovoye Khozyaistvo*, April, 1938, pp. 6of.
[98] *Op. cit.*, p. 66.

tion towards raising the living standards of the majority of wage and salary earners.

During the war the regulations governing the operations of Plant Managers' Funds were suspended. After the war, they were put in force again for industry, by a decree of December 5, 1946.[99] Subsequently, a series of special decrees made these regulations valid also for a number of other branches of the economy.[100] However, the operations of Plant Managers' Funds in recent years seem to have been no more successful than those before the war.

Other items sometimes referred to by Soviet economists as adding to the amount of socialized wages are altogether insignificant and need not detain us.

From this general survey of "socialized wages," it can hardly be concluded that they outdistance "individual wages" or make up for the latter's decline. They do not require us to modify in any way the analysis we have made of the dynamics of the living standards of Russian labor.

Of course, the Soviet press tries to give special importance to the role played by socialized wages and likes to represent them as something characteristic of and known only to the Soviet Union. In the work by Voznesensky to which we have frequently referred, this is stated with patricular emphasis:[101]

> "To the money wages paid workers in the Soviet Union one must at least add state sickness and maternity benefits, paid vacations, payments from Plant Managers' Funds, free schooling and scholarships, the state-borne cost of improving work skills through vocational training, free medical care and rest homes, state-supported institutions for the care of children, and the benefits granted to large families. All these things, in contrast with capitalist countries, increase the average money wages of workers in the Soviet Union by 38 per cent."

All these benefits do indeed raise the workers' standard of living. Where real wages are as low as we find them in the Soviet Union, many needs more or less provided for in this way would otherwise go completely unsatisfied; so that socialized wages acquire an importance in the Soviet Union which they otherwise

---

99 *Laws and Ordinances*, 1946: 272.
100 *Laws and Ordinances*, 1947: 61, 62, 90, 91, 151 and 152.
101 Voznesensky, *op. cit.*, pp. 118-119.

would scarcely enjoy. But it is very doubtful whether they add 38 per cent to the workers' money wages. Since the appearance of Voznesensky's book this "38 per cent" has of course been constantly cited in the Soviet Union, but no attempt has ever been made to show concretely on what it is based.

The assertion that no such state-supported system of social security and welfare exists outside the Soviet Union is completely unfounded. Almost all the benefits enumerated by Voznesensky (as well as by many others) exist in one form or another in every modern state, where they perform an important function. But no one thinks of finding in them—as do Soviet economists—a justification for an inadequate level of wages.

APPENDIX 1

The Wage Fund Mystery

As mentioned in the text, the term wage fund has a double meaning in Soviet economic statistics. This was frankly expressed for the first time in February 1941, at the 18th Conference of the CPSU. Chairman Voznesensky of the Gosplan, reporting on the economic results of 1940 and the economic plan for 1941, stated that in 1940 the wage fund had reached 123.7 billion rubles. Then, in the concluding part of the same report, he mentioned that in 1941 the wage fund would reach 175 billion rubles, 14 billion above 1940 [102]—implying a 1940 figure of 161, not 123.7 billion rubles. Was the 37.3 billion difference a mistake? Or were there two wage funds?

In 1946, the mystery cropped up again. The Fourth Five-Year Plan, approved by the Supreme Council of the USSR in March of that year, envisioned total employment in 1950 as 33,500,000 and average earnings as 6,000 rubles. This would mean a wage fund of 201 billion rubles. But the 1950 wage fund announced in the plan was 252.3 billion rubles [103]—i.e., 51.3 billion more.

The Soviet textbooks on economic statistics are silent on the discrepancy. Outside of the Soviet Union, various explanations have been advanced. Most observers are inclined to use the lower figure for the wage fund in the proper sense of the word—i.e., for the sum of all wages and salaries, including overtime, bonuses, etc.—and the higher figure

---

[102] *Bolshevik*, No. 3/4, 1941, pp. 38 and 53.
[103] *Minutes*, etc., pp. 395/396.

for the wage fund proper *plus* the so-called social services (expenses for public health, social insurance, education, etc.). However, no shred of evidence to support this assumption has been discoverable in the Soviet press; nor would it be justifiable from a finance-technical point of view, as Abram Bergson has convincingly shown.[104] Bergson himself is inclined to explain the difference between the two wage funds mainly by the fact that in the Soviet Union the number of (normally employed) wage and salary earners is larger than appears in the statistics of the Central Statistical Administration (or TSUNKHU, the Central Administration of Economic Accounting, as the Central Statistical Administration was called for years). The smaller wage fund is supposed to correspond to this incomplete census of workers and employees, and the larger one to cover the total number. Yet this explanation is all the less justifiable since—for once—the double meaning of the term "wage fund" has been explained in Soviet literature itself. In the reference book published by the Central Statistical Administration in 1944, we read [105]:

> "Wages are carried on the books not only for free workers and employees, and cooperative artisans [*kustari*] but also for the military personnel and for other categories which are not free wage and salary earners [*nye yavlyayutsya vol'nonayemnymi*]. Labor statistics, in centralized procedure, calculate the so-called *full wage fund* [*polnyi fond zarabotnoy platy*], comprising all payments carried on the books as wages, whether made to workers, employees, and cooperative artisans or to other individuals (military personnel et al.)." (Italics in the original.)

The significance of this reference to "individuals" who "are not free wage and salary earners" was indirectly underscored by the fact that by 1948, when a second, enlarged edition of the same *Dictionary and Handbook* was published, the slightest hint of the "full wage fund" had been deleted.

The double meaning of the term is thus quite easily explained. The smaller wage fund is the wage fund as such, the wage fund proper, the sum of the wages and salaries of all workers and employees (and their actual equals, the "cooperative artisans"). In the larger wage fund—the "full wage fund"—the term is broadened to include the money earnings of the military personnel and, counting for a great deal more, the *unfree* workers and employees: of the millions of Soviet slaves in labor camps and elsewhere.

---

[104] Abram Bergson (as in N. 30), p. 241.
[105] *Dictionary and Handbook for Socio-Economic Statistics*, publ. by the Central Statistical Administration of the USSR, Moscow 1944, p. 213. See also Harry

The double meaning of the term "wage fund" has created extensive confusion in the analysis of recent wage trends. This will be discussed in detail below, in Appendix 2. The confusion started with the publication of the economic plan for 1947 [106]. In this, the only annual economic plan made public in the Soviet Union after the war, total employment was set at 31,600,000 and "the wage fund" at 280 billion rubles. If this was the wage fund proper, the average earnings of a worker or employee were to rise to about 8,860 rubles according to plan—obviously an impossible assumption. The 280 billion clearly meant the "full" wage fund. Yet even for this, the figure was extraordinarily high—with the Fourth Five-Year Plan, approved barely a year earlier, envisioning a considerably smaller full wage fund (252,3 billion rubles rather than 280) and a considerably larger number of wage and salary earners (33,500,000 rather than 31,600,000) in 1950.

Evidently there were to be special reasons for an extraordinary growth of the full wage fund in 1947. What were they? The answer seems obvious. In 1947 the number of Soviet slaves was unusually large: millions of men and women returning and "repatriated" from Germany, Austria, and elsewhere were sent to labor camps, and the same fate probably overtook millions of people from the Soviet territories which had been under German occupation during the war. Moreover, large numbers of German, Japanese and other war prisoners were still working in the Soviet Union at that time and contributing to the growth of the "full wage fund."

In 1947 (perhaps already in 1946) the difference between the wage fund proper and the "full" one seems to have been larger than ever before.

APPENDIX 2

Contradictions in the Analysis of Post-War Wage Trends

The above view of post-war wage trends in the Soviet Union is considerably at variance with what might be described as *communis opinio doctorum,* the consensus of the experts—or, to be exact, of Western experts. In the circles of those American, British, and French statisticians and economists who show interest in Russian social and economic development, the post-war Soviet wage level—we refer to the nominal wage level—is all but generally assumed to have been,

---

Schwartz, "A Critique of 'Appraisals of Russian Economic Statistics,'" in *Review of Economic Statistics,* February 1948, p. 40.

[106] *Pravda,* March 1, 1947.

and to be, much higher than this book puts it. According to our cal-culations the average annual earnings of workers and employees amounted to 4,200-4,400 rubles in 1946, to 5,000-5,200 rubles in 1947, to 5,200-5,400 rubles in 1948, and either remained on that level or—more probably—declined somewhat in 1949 and 1950. Prevailing opinion in the United States, on the other hand, is characterized by the figures advanced by Professor Harry Schwartz of Syracuse Univer-sity, according to whom the average annual earnings in the Soviet Union reached 6,000 rubles in 1946, 7,100 rubles in 1947 and 7,400 rubles in 1948 [107], and continued slowly rising. Even higher figures have lately been mentioned in the British press. G. R. Barker of Birmingham University's Department of Economics and Institutions of the USSR calculated average earnings in 1948 as 9,000 rubles, and in 1949 and 1950 as 9,300 and 9,550 rubles, respectively [108] In France, too, the Soviet wage level was estimated at considerably higher figures than the facts seem to warrant. The statistical bulletin of the Federa-tion of French Industrialists, for example, recently put average month-ly earnings in Soviet industry at 573 rubles in 1946 and 660 rubles in 1949 [109]—which would mean annually (in round figures) 6,900 rubles for 1946 and 7,900 for 1949.

In the press, all these figures were supported only by cursory evidence, if any; the only serious attempt to justify them was made by Harry Schwartz. Often they are quoted without any attempt to prove them—which does not mean, of course, that no arguments for them exist. In private correspondence and personal discussion with a number of American experts I have tried to find the arguments in favor of the higher figures. These arguments did not convince me; nor, so far, have I been able to make my opion prevail. I readily admit the fragmentary nature of my reasoning; the data accessible to us are insufficient for conclusive deductions, and accordingly mine are partly hypothetical. Nevertheless, they seem to me more solidly founded than the customary, more optimistic view of recent wage trends in the Soviet Union. To facilitate the reader's orientation in this controversy, I shall try to state here the salient features of the deductions which I question.

The differences are chiefly rooted in the *method* of analyzing the incomplete and partly contradictory data of Soviet statistics. What we

---

[107] Harry Schwartz, "Soviet Labor Policy 1945-1949" in *The Annals of the American Academy of Political and Social Science*, May 1949, p. 80, and in his latest work, *Russia's Soviet Economy*, New York, 1950, p. 460.
[108] G. R. Barker, "Soviet Labour," in *Bulletins on Soviet Economic Develop-ment*, June, 1951, p. 21.
[109] *Bulletin du Conseil National du Patronat Français* (CNPF), No. 63, Feb-ruary 20, 1951.

have are average wage figures for 1940 and 1944, a few vague statements on changes in the wage level in subsequent years, the Plan figure for 1950, as well as the general line of the wage policies carried out in these years. On the basis of this *direct,* if incomplete, information on wage trends and wage policies, the Soviet wage trend in the years of the Fourth Five-Year Plan and the wage level in 1950 can be approximately determined. This is the method employed in this book.

But there is also another method. One can try to determine the wage trend on the basis of *indirect* information throwing light upon the economic trend as a whole (state budget, extent of consumption, sales tax yield, etc.). The tacit assumption is that, by and large, the wage fund expands in proportion with the national economy (below, it will be shown to what extent this is correct). To back up the reasoning, there is the analysis of data on social insurance receipts and on the so-called full wage fund—i.e., more material which supposedly throws indirect light on the wage trend.

The two methods—which may be somewhat inexactly called *inductive* and *deductive*—need not exclude one another. Rather, the results of the inductive method can be checked against data on the development of the economy as a whole, and if a discrepancy should appear in the process it would call for explanations. On the other hand, the results of the reconstruction of wage trends on the basis of indirect data must be able to stand the test of actual available data on the wage level (and wage policy).

* * *
*

As a matter of fact, *one* figure was apparently decisive for the optimistic calculations of Soviet wage trends: the figure given for the wage fund, i. e., the full wage fund, in the economic plan for 1947. Thus Harry Schwartz writes in *The Annals:*

"... The data for 1946-48 are estimated in the following fashion: It is assumed that the wages fund goal of 280 billion rubles for 1947 set by that year's plan was actually achieved. The 1946 and 1948 wages funds can be calculated on the basis of percentages showing their relationship to the 1947 fund. . . . It is further assumed that the pay roll received by workers and employees in the national economy was about 80 per cent of the wages fund calculated above. This assumption is based on the constancy of the percentages calculated by Professor Bergson in his article in the *Review of Economic Statistics,* Nov. 1947, p. 236."

The "constancy" of the percentage ratio of full wage fund and wage fund proper has become a virtual credo—a sort of *lex Bergsoni*—among American students of Russia. However, as shown in Appendix 1 on the basis of that very economic plan for 1947, this constancy is a fiction. Yet the argument quoted from Harry Schwartz is the core of the reasoning of all experts who agree with the optimistic appraisal; their other arguments play a subordinate role in all discussions of the subject and are intended mainly to bear out a view taken on the strength of the 1947 payroll argument.

These arguments, by themselves, are not unimportant and deserve a critical examination. As mentioned before, most of them are based on the idea of a certain parallelism in the growth of the wage fund proper and of the economy as a whole. This parallelism, however, can only be assumed with reservations. Indeed, the total economy rests on labor, but by no means on wage labor alone. Besides the economic sector resting on wage labor, there is the peasant sector and —especially important to the Soviet economy—a third sector resting on slave labor. The three sectors by no means grow at the same rate; in particular, the one resting on unfree labor played an unusually large role in the Soviet economy of the first post-war years.

There is also this to be considered: the economy, even the economic sector resting on wage labor, can expand without a corresponding upward movement of the wage fund proper. This happens when real wages decline, or when the development of the real payroll lags behind that of the economy. These considerations carry special weight if conclusions on the wage fund ratio before and after the war are drawn from a comparison of the economic level in 1940 and in the first post-war years.

All this must be considered in trying, for example, to deduce the dynamics of the wage fund proper from the dynamics of the state budget. The fact that the state budget grows faster than the wage fund is partly explained by the increasing role of the state in the economic life—a process which has not quite reached its end even in the Soviet Union. Yet the difference in growth between state budget and wage fund is much too large to be explained by this alone: after all, the state budget grew 130 per cent between 1940 and 1948, while the wage fund proper, if my calculations are correct, less than 50 per cent [110]. This difference may be largely due to the above mentioned general reasons.

---

[110] In 1940, the state income of the USSR totaled 178.1 billion rubles, in 1948, 410.5 billion—i.e. 2.3 times as much as in 1940. (Cf. the reports of Finance Minister Zverev in the Supreme Soviet of the USSR—*Pravda*, April 1, 1941, and June 14, 1950). The wage fund amounted in 1940 to 123.7 billion rubles; in 1948

In this context it is worth noting that in 1950, for the first time since the war, the state budget decreased: from around 437 billions in 1949 to around 422 billions[111]. This may have to do with the deflationary policies of the Soviet government which we discussed before[112]. This fact makes it seem likely that in 1950—with employment on the increase—the upward movement of the wage fund proper came to a halt and the level of average earnings was correspondingly lowered. Further indications of this are the data of the development of sales tax receipts, the real basis of the Soviet state budget. In 1949, sales tax receipts remained almost on the level of the previous year; in 1950 they declined not only below the level of 1949 and 1948 but below that of 1947 [113]. This falling off of sales tax receipts without any announced change in the tax rates, and with total employment continuing on the increase[114], is one more sign that the curve of average earnings began to drop toward the end of the 1940's.

These are the main arguments for the more optimistic appraisal of recent wage trends in the Soviet Union. The social insurance argument, which will be taken up in Chapter Seven, plays only a minor part.

Surprisingly, the "optimists" never attempt to check their figures against the direct data on wage trends and policies. In particular, they completely ignore the sharply restrictive wage-political tendencies, vigorously stressed again and again since early 1945 and bound to be especially manifest in the transition from the long wartime working hours to the 48-hour week.

For this is where we must seek the root of the entire controversy. The wage level in 1946, before the increases of mid-September, is the starting point of all calculations. To justify the higher figures for the most recent trend, it is first necessary to prove—or at least to show with some probability—that the average monthly earnings of Soviet workers and employees previous to September 1946 were at least 35-40 per cent higher than in 1940. Thus far, no one has seriously attempted this; nor has any one tried to explain why, if the higher figures for the

---

with employment at 33,450,000 (see Chapter I) and average annual earnings 5,200-5,400 rubles, it amounted to 173.9-180.6 billion, i.e. 1.41 to 1.47 times as much as in 1940.

[111] See Zverev's reports to the Supreme Soviet of the USSR, *Pravda*, June 14, 1950, and March 8, 1951.

[112] See pp. 224 ff. ff.above.

[113] Sales tax receipts totaled 239.9 billion rubles in 1947, 247.5 billion in 1948, 250.3 billion in 1949, and 236.1 billion in 1950. See Zverev's reports in the Supreme Soviet of the USSR, *Pravda*, February 1, 1948, March 11, 1949, June 14, 1950, and March 8, 1951.

[114] The number of wage and salary earners rose 6,000,000—i.e., 18 per cent—between 1947 and 1950. See Chapter One.

average earnings of Soviet workers and employees were in line with the facts, the Soviet press has never mentioned them, preferring—as shown above (p....)—to confine itself to speaking of the relatively modest figure envisioned for the end of the Fourth Five-Year Plan *in the future tense.*[115]

---

[115] This book was in print when I received two recent studies of Naum Jasny (*The Soviet Price System* and *Soviet Prices of Producers' Goods.* Stanford University Press, Stanford, Calif., November 1951 and February 1952, respectively). In the first of them an attempt is made—for the first time, as far as I know—to present "optimistically" the post-war development of nominal wages in the USSR, basing the analysis on the "inductive" method, and to confront Jasny's conclusions with my appreciation of the development. "Solomon Schwarz is certainly in the wrong," writes Jasny, "he assumes for the beginning of 1946 a wage level lower than in 1940, in spite of the evidence of substantial wage raises for large groups of workers during the war . . ." (p. 29). Jasny himself calculates "the average paid-out wage of all workers and employees in the first half of 1945" as "around 5,500 rubles"; "by the end of 1945 or the beginning of 1946 it may have declined to, say, 5,000-5,250 rubles" (p. 24). The latter figure is the point of departure for Jasny's calculations of wage levels in the following years.

It may be approximately correct to accept Jasny's figure of 5,500 rubles a year for the level of earnings at the beginning of 1945, or—more exactly—for the time immediately before the general transition from the ten-hour-day to the eight-hour-day. However, Jasny's figure of 5,000 to 5,250 rubles for the beginning of 1946, *i.e.* for the time immediately after the transition to the eight-hour-day, is highly arbitrary, and the author does not even attempt to prove it. The transition from the ten-hour-day (with pay for 11 hours) to the eight-hour-day could in fact be accompanied by a decline in earnings of only 4.5 to 9 per cent (as in Jasny's assumptions) if at the same time wage rates would be boosted and/or the productivity of labor would highly increase. The raising of wage rates was, however, at that time out of question. And the productivity of labor showed in the period immediately after the end of the war a significant decline. It is, thus, simply impossible that the transition from the ten- to the eight-hour-day caused a decline in earnings by only a few per cent. The decline by at least 25 to 30 per cent is more likely, a decline not to the level of 5,000-5,250 rubles, as it is accepted by Jasny, but rather to approximately 4,000 rubles.

Taking as his point of departure a much too high figure for the beginning of 1946 Jasny calculated the average for 1947 at 6,813 rubles, for 1948 at 7,056 rubles (p. 23). In his second book mentioned above he corrected the figure for 1948 to 6,775 rubles and accepted for 1949 7,000 rubles, for 1950 7,250 rubles, for 1951 7,500 rubles (p. 10). Yet, if, as shown above, the figure of 5,000 to 5,250 rubles for the beginning of 1946 is erroneous—Jasny's figure for 1947 to 1951 also are much too high.

Chapter Six

HOURS AND WORKING CONDITIONS

General Attitude. — The Seven-Hour Day. — Continuous Work Week. — Labor Protection on the Wane: (a) Breakdown of the General Limitation of Hours; (b) Deterioration of Protection of Female Labor; (c) Decline of Safety Standards; (d) Ineffecutal Labor Inspection. — Curtailment Measures of 1940. — Wartime and Postwar Development. — Appendix: Conflict Between Unions and Economic Authorities Over Protection of Labor, 1935.

General Attitude

Limitations of hours; protection of the worker's life and health from occupational hazards; special protection for working women and children; safeguards established by law, adopted by administrative practice, supervised by free labor organizations of the workers' own choosing; labor inspectors to enforce legislative and administrative codes—this is the traditional program for the protection of labor, the objective which organized labor and many non-labor champions of social reform have been fighting for ever since "factory laws" appeared on the horizon of modern industrial society.

It is in this sense that "protection of labor" had been one of the main objectives of Soviet labor policy from its early days. It is impossible within the scope of this book to describe the system in its entirety, or to relate its evolution. That would call for a major study of its own. Here we can only deal with the characteristic changes that have occurred in the Russian system of working conditions since the initiation of the Five-Year Plan policy.

When maximum production came to be the guiding principle and the essence of all social and economic endeavors, the

HOURS AND WORKING CONDITIONS   259

accepted system of the "protection of labor" was reduced—like all labor policy—to secondary importance. Social considerations were subordinated to economic motives. Changes of substance or organization in this field were no longer actuated by a desire to raise the social, economic, and cultural levels of labor, or to improve labor's working and living conditions. They were primarily part of the effort to increase production—regardless of whether the working and living conditions of labor might suffer damage.

Since the late 1920's Soviet social policy has been based on the assumption that anything that helped production would ultimately result in the betterment of working-class life. In the conditions of the Soviet state, production policy was said to be the best social policy.

The Seven-Hour Day

The introduction of the seven-hour day was the most momentous event in the realm of Russian social policy during this period. It has been widely noted as such even outside the Soviet Union.

The idea of a seven-hour day turned up for the first time in an official statement in October, 1927. On October 15, on the occasion of the imminent tenth anniversary of the October Revolution, the CEC of the USSR, the legislative assembly of the Soviet state, issued a manifesto,[1] introduced and explained before the CEC by the then head of the Soviet Government, A. I. Rykov, chairman of the CPC of the USSR. First among the measures of labor, farm and educational policy announced in this document was the introduction of the seven-hour day:

> "On the threshold of the Tenth Anniversary of the October Revolution, the CEC of the USSR resolves:
> "(1) To assure production workers in industrial establishments of a change-over to the seven-hour day in the course of the next few years, without reduction in earnings; and to this end to charge the Presidium of the CEC and the CPC of the USSR with initiating, a year hence at the latest, the gradual execution of this resolution in several industries, in accordance with the progress made in reorganizing the plants and increasing efficiency and productivity."

---

[1] *Laws and Ordinances*, 1927:613.

It was clear that there was no intention of introducing the seven-hour day at once, yet even so, the announcement came as a complete surprise to the Soviet public. Prior to the publication of the manifesto, not the slightest mention had been made of the issue.[2] The decision to include the announcement in the anniversary manifesto was made by the Politburo just a few days before the CEC was convened for the anniversary session;[3] today there can be no doubt that the purpose was to play off the new reform against the leftist opposition within the CPSU.[4]

---

[2] After the publication of the manifesto, the press took pains to present the reform as carefully planned in advance. On October 18, 1927, a *Pravda* editorial, "On the Seven-Hour Day," tried to refute the charge that announcement of the seven-hour day had been an "intra-Party maneuver": The reform, it said, had been seriously discussed in an article in the *Planovoye Khozyaistvo* of May, 1927, and in the State Planning Commission's original draft of the Five-Year Plan.

Both references were unfounded. The Five-Year Plan draft (the document referred to can only be *The Prospects of the Expansion of the National Economy of the USSR for* 1926/27–1930/31, Moscow, 1927) did not touch on the problem at all. And V. Zaitsev's article, "The Work Day and the Prospect of Shortening It," in the May, 1927, issue of *Planovoye Khozyaistvo*, was a purely theoretical discussion of the possible effects which introduction of the six-hour day "in 1940/41" might have on production and wages, with the author concluding that, other things being equal, the result would be a 10 per cent cut in production and wages. The article evoked no echo, and was completely ignored in both general and economic and union papers.

According to an item in *Pravda* of October 25, 1927, a *Pravda* reporter was told in the Labor Division of the Supreme Economic Council of the USSR that "the problem [of the seven-hour day] had been discussed in industrial circles for a year and a half and had already been raised by the late Comrade F. Dzerzhinsky" (who died on July 20, 1926). Not even a semblance of proof was ever furnished for this statement, nor was it ever repeated.

[3] Plenary sessions of the CC of the CPSU and of the AUCTUC were held shortly before the CEC session. Judging by press reports, the seven-hour day was not even mentioned in the debates of either body. The question apparently came up in the Politburo of the CC in the first half of October. That the initiative had come from the Politburo was stressed in the official Party manual, *The CPSU in the Decisions of Its Conventions, Conferences, and Plenary Sessions of the CC*, 6th ed., Vol. 2, Moscow, 1940, p. 195. Before a larger audience, the issue was first dealt with by N. I. Bukharin, in his address on the tenth anniversary of the October Revolution at the Moscow Provincial Trade Union Convention on October 12, 1927. However, the press did not report this address until October 18, after publication of the manifesto of October 15.

[4] It was repeatedly stated in the Soviet press that the leftist opposition (i.e., the group led by Trotsky and Zinovyev) had voted against the manifesto and especially against the seven-hour-day provision at the session of the CEC of the USSR. This charge was brought up for the first time in a *Pravda* editorial of October 26, 1927. In the previously mentioned editorial of October 18, which severely castigated the opposition, there was not a word about oppositionist votes being cast against the seven-hour day, much less against the manifesto as a whole; and press reports on the CEC session of October 15 (cf. *Pravda* and *Izvestiya* of October 16) specifically emphasized that the manifesto had been adopted unanimously.—I regret to say that in earlier publications (particularly in the *Internationales Handwörterbuch des Gewerkschaftswesens*, Vol. 2, Berlin, 1932, p. 1463)

The idea was promptly taken up by industrial leaders, who saw in the introduction of the seven-hour day a means of extending the three-shift system to plants which had hitherto been working in one or two shifts. Here the reform was consciously regarded as a measure of production policy, to which important social-political interests were to be sacrificed if necessary.

During the first year that the seven-hour day was in practice, new working schedules were introduced almost exclusively in textile plants. Why there? "The immediate change-over to the seven-hour day in textile plants was determined by economic considerations," wrote the leading labor expert of the Supreme Economic Council:[5] "To promote grain deliveries, the textile industry was to raise production and to make maximum use of available plant equipment." Similar reasons for the seven-hour day were advanced in the best Soviet study on the subject:[6]

> "By the end of 1927 difficulties in meeting the growing demand for textile goods became acute, with execution of the grain supply program increasingly dependent on the industry's ability to turn out enough merchandise for the peasants. The textile industry in general and the cotton industry in particular are among those in which machinery reserves have been working under great stress, for the most part in two shifts. The need to throw a mass of extra textile goods on the rural market in the

---

I myself accepted the Communist press version of the oppositionists' vote against the seven-hour day.

The fact is that (not in the CEC session of October 15, 1927, but in the preceding caucus of the Communist CEC delegation of the same day) the oppositionists came out against the manner in which the issue was brought up for discussion. In the caucus, Zinovyev and Trotsky stressed that the issue was suddenly raised after the wording of the manifesto had been decided upon, and not even at a formal Politburo session but "through a telephone poll of Politburo members." They pointed out that the promised introduction of the seven-hour day was in obvious contradiction to the policy of relaxing the safeguards on working conditions, particularly in regard to working hours, as it had been systematically pursued in the preceding years. Instead of the vague promise to introduce the seven-hour day they suggested including a clear-cut program of urgently needed improvements in the manifesto, and considering shorter hours only after this program had been carried out. Trotsky's and Zinovyev's speeches at the Communist caucus of October 15 were published in the Left-Communist *Die Fahne des Kommunismus*, Berlin, No. 35, November 11, 1927, pp. 197 ff.

[5] A. Rabinovich, "The Seven-Hour Day," *Ekonomicheskoye Obozreniye*, August, 1928, p. 43. Nearly identical formulations will be found in an article by B. Markus, then the leading exponent of the government's labor policy: "Notes on the Practical Operation of the Seven-Hour Day," *Bol'shevik*, 1928, No. 8, p. 42.

[6] Ya. Kvasha and F. Shofman, *The Seven-Hour Day in the Textile Industry*, Moscow, 1930, pp. 5 f. (Cf. also an article by these authors, "Seven-Hour Factories in the Transition Period," *Planovoye Khozyaistvo*, October, 1928, pp. 303 f.)

shortest possible time, and at any cost, made it imperative to speed up production. But production could only be raised by introducing an additional [third] shift."

Reduction of hours was only a subordinate factor in the introduction of three-shift schedules—which soon turned out to be highly detrimental to the working and living conditions of labor. Even V. V. Schmidt, the People's Commissar for Labor, was moved to say in his report to the AUCTUC in October, 1928:[7] "The introduction of the seven-hour day must increase production. But our task is to keep the resulting burden from being placed exclusively [sic!] on the workers' shoulders."

As pointed out before, the first plants converted to the shorter work week were almost exclusively textile plants. Conversion started in January, 1928. By October 1, 28 plants employing 131,-000 workers had adopted the seven-hour day; 24 of them, employing 121,000 workers, were textile factories.[8]

Increased production was to be assured primarily by combining the seven-hour day with considerable intensification of labor mainly by a "stretch-out," i.e., by giving each worker more machines (looms, spindles, etc.) to operate. To cite but one example: in the cotton mills, which had introduced the seven-hour day early in 1928, the grouping of weavers according to number of looms operated in December, 1927, directly before the seven-hour day was introduced, and in September, 1928, some months after conversion to the new schedules, was as follows:[9]

	December 1927	September 1928
Tending two looms	67.5%	36.6%
Tending three looms	29.3	35.6
Tending four looms	1.4	24.6
Tending automatic looms (Northrup)	1.8	3.3

The stretch-out is still slightly concealed in these figures, since plants converting to the seven-hour day had to hire new workers, who had to be trained first and so, as a rule, were not immediately given more than two looms to operate.

The seven-hour day brought up the problem of scheduling,

---

[7] Trud, October 31, 1928.
[8] Control Figures for Labor for 1929/30, published by the People's Commissariat for Labor of the USSR, Moscow, 1930, p. 107.
[9] Kvasha and Shofman, as quoted supra, n. 6, pp. 27-38.

which led to agitated discussions between management and unions. The main issue in the textile negotiations was the institution of the so-called "split shifts"—putting each worker on two daily three-and-a-half hour shifts, separated by a seven-hour recess. The usual schedule was like this: the first shift worked from 4:00 to 7:30 A.M. and from 2:30 to 6:00 P.M.; the second, from 7:30 to 11:00 A.M. and from 6:00 to 9:30 P.M.; the third, from 11:00 A.M. to 2:30 P.M. and from 9:30 P.M. to 1:00 A.M. The three remaining hours were to be used for maintenance, ventilation, and cleaning.

Such schedules were hard on the workers. The Textile Workers Union opposed the introduction of split shifts, and the question had to go to the People's Commissar for Labor who, in January, 1928, decided for the union and definitely against "split shifts."[10] But this formally binding decision remained a scrap of paper, and the press, including the trade union paper, took care not to recall it.

"All year," the central union organ wrote nine months later, "the fight against the split-shift system which endangers the workers' health has been waged in the textile factories that introduced the seven-hour day. But we are making no progress; almost everywhere split shifts remain in effect."[11] In 1929, a survey of the textile industry by the State Planning Commission showed that in the so-called "seven-hour factories" 23.9 per cent of the workers worked split shifts in the cotton industry, and 20.0 per cent in the wool industry, while the remaining personnel was working uninterrupted seven-hour shifts—another extremely unfavorable type of schedule.

The disadvantages of such time schedules were aggravated by the pernicious effects of night work, now largely extended to women (and, in smaller measures, to juveniles). The ban on night work for women, under Sec. 130 of the Labor Code, was forgotten.

In introducing the seven-hour day and the three-shift system, preservation of the ban had at least been contemplated for pregnant women and nursing mothers. Early in 1928 the government's Committee on the Seven-Hour Day, presided over by the People's Commissar for Labor, had issued an ordinance forbidding night work for women after five months of pregnancy, and for nursing

10 *Trud*, January 12, 1928.
11 *Trud*, October 1, 1928.

mothers for seven months after delivery.[12] A year later, the second prohibition was reduced to six months after delivery.[13]

In actual practice, however, both regulations seem to have been largely ignored. The mass employment of women in the textile industry raised so many difficulties that women themselves frequently rebelled against the ban. In the Rodnikovskaya factory (Ivanovo-Voznesensk province), one of the largest of the early "seven-hour plants," a meeting of pregnant and nursing women was held to discuss the issue, and only seven of the fifty participants favored exclusive assignment to day shifts. The Ivanovo-Voznesensk local of the Textile Workers Union thereupon decided to maintain the ban only for work on certain machines tended exclusively by pregnant or nursing women and operating for only one day shift. As for the rest: "For the present, pending regulation of the issue, night work by pregnant women and nursing mothers shall be permitted."[14]

Of course, this union decision was valid only in one province, and formally only until the CEC of the USSR issued its decree of January 2, 1929, "on the seven-hour day" (see below). But actually conditions changed hardly anywhere after enactment of the new rules. To quote the aforementioned study published in 1930: [15]

> "There were numerous instances where shop meetings rejected special provisions barring pregnant women and nursing mothers from the night shift, and where the women in question objected strongly to such an arrangement. Pregnant women and nursing mothers vigorously opposed working constantly on the same shift, either because they feared their earnings might drop as a result of the change of loom, or because they wanted to work on the same shift with their husbands, or sometimes because of an erroneous concept of solidarity ('Why should I be working by day if others have to replace me on the night shift?'). Quite often women workers try to conceal their pregnancy so as not to be taken off the night shift."

Working conditions in general deteriorated wherever seven-hour day and three-shift schedules were introduced without the

---

[12] *Trud*, January 7, 1928.
[13] *Laws and Ordinances*, 1929: 30 and 133.
[14] I. Belen'ky and A. Kucherov, *Seven-Hour Factories. Three Months of Operations*, published by the Ivanovo-Voznesensk Trade Union Council, Ivanovo-Voznesensk, 1928, p. 35.
[15] Kvasha and Shofman, as quoted *supra*, n. 6, p. 141.

necessary pre-arrangements. The labor expert of the Supreme Economic Council wrote:[16]

> "In introducing additional shifts the plants have shown themselves unprepared in regard to the most elementary conditions of normal work (lighting, ventilation). The plants practically operate around the clock, and there is no chance to cool or ventilate the premises as used to be done by night before the third shift was introduced. As a result, the rooms get too hot for the night shift, especially toward the end of the week. In many factories the temperature during the third shift rises to 40° centigrade [104° Fahrenheit]."

Unlike the usual experience with shorter hours, the seven-hour day under these circumstances was inevitably accompanied by a higher sickness and accident rate, as revealed by the People's Commissar for Labor.[17] In fourteen cotton factories converted in January, 1928, the accident rate in the second quarter of 1928 was 35.7 per cent above that recorded for the fourth quarter of 1927.[18] At a special conference for the protection of labor, called early in December, 1928, by the Moscow Trade Union Council, delegates stated that the new time schedule impaired the workers' health.[19]

Worse, if possible, was the impact of the seven-hour day on general living conditions. New schedules with increased night work affect the worker's life under any circumstances; in the housing conditions prevailing in Russia, they literally turned it upside down. This was particularly true among the textile workers, many of whom live to this very day in huge dormitories called "factory barracks."

A vivid picture of these conditions was presented in a report to the Young Communist newspaper:[20]

> "The three-shift schedule has completely upset the accustomed pattern of life in the factory barracks. Day and night the barracks buzz. In the extremely crowded conditions (3.7 people to a room) where about 40 per cent of the families lack rooms separated from others by tight partitions and two and more

---

16 Rabinovich, as quoted *supra*, n. 5, p. 45; similarly Markus, as quoted *supra*, n. 5, p. 45.
17 Report to the AUCTUC, see n. 7, *supra*.
18 Report of the Deputy People's Commissar for Labor, I. A. Tolstopyatov, *Trud*, November 7, 1928.
19 *Trud*, December 12, 1928.
20 *Komsomol'skaya Pravda*, February 28, 1928.

members of most families go to work, frequently on different shifts, there is no chance for the worker to get normal rest."

Both the introduction of the third shift and the "stretch-out" of labor were to serve a single purpose: higher output. The results were much more modest than expected,[21] and in the early 1930's official enthusiasm for the seven-hour schedules began to fade. Meanwhile, however, the seven-hour day had come into wide-spread use and had generated laws of its own. Multiple shifts were considerably reduced, which in turn lessened the ill effects noted in the first two years of seven-hour schedules.

Originally, in 1928, the seven-hour system was confined mainly to the textile industry. In the very next year, however, it was extended to other industries. A decree of January 2, 1929,[22] obliged all "production plants" in industry, transportation, communications, and the communal economy to convert to the seven-hour day by October 1, 1933; only seasonal trades were exempted. All newly-built plants in heavy industry and all newly-built large-scale plants in light industry were to operate in seven-hour shifts from the start. The limitation to "production plants" was another birthmark revealing the system's origin in considerations of production. Eight-hour schedules were retained in the building trades, in transportation (except for the production plants of this branch of the economy), in commerce, in agricultural work, etc.

In accordance with the decree of January 2, 1929, a detailed program for the gradual extension of the seven-hour day was mapped out in the First Five-Year Plan. The percentage of industrial workers on a seven-hour day was to rise as follows in the course of the five-year period:[23]

	Heavy Industry (Group A)	Light Industry (Group B)	All Industry
1928/29	13.4%	23.8%	18.3%
1929/30	40.0	40.0	40.0
1930/31	58.8	53.5	56.3
1931/32	81.6	80.1	80.9
1932/33	100.0	100.0	100.0

[21] For details cf. my paper "The Seven-Hour Day in Soviet Russia," *International Labour Review*, September, 1930, pp. 338-346.

[22] Decree of the CEC and CPC of the USSR "on the seven hour-day" of January 2, 1929, in *Izvestiya*, January 10, 1929.

[23] *Five-Year Plan of Economic Construction of the USSR*, Moscow, 1928, Vol. II, 2, p. 182.

In the beginning, actual developments closely followed this pattern. But toward the end of the Five-Year Plan period the trend slowed down, as the Soviet leadership's interest in the seven-hour day waned because of the disappointing economic results of continuous three-shift operations.

In 1932 the Central Statistical Office (TsUNKhU) released data showing that on January 1, 1931, 1,581,400 or 58.7 per cent of all industrial workers were employed on seven-hour schedules (Group A, 57.4 per cent; Group B, 59.7 per cent).[24] Later issues of the TsUNKhU summaries of labor statistics (published in 1935 and 1936) contained no more data on the scope of the seven-hour day, nor did the general *Statistical Yearbook of the USSR*, after 1932. The report submitted by the AUCTUC to the Ninth Trade Union Convention (in April, 1932) maintained complete silence on the seven-hour day and its significance in the system of Russian social policy, and so did the official report on the execution of the First Five-Year Plan.

[24] Details may be gathered from the following table, condensed from data of the Central Statistical Office published in the latter's *Labor in the USSR. Statistical Abstract for* 1931, Moscow, 1932, p. 129:

Workers On Seven-Hour Schedules
as of January 1, 1931

Industry	Number Employed on Seven-Hour Schedules (in thousands)	As Percentage of Total Employed
Fuel	216.2	60.9%
Coal	178.0	58.7
Oil extraction	21.3	66.4
Oil refineries	7.1	88.8
Iron mining	35.4	36.9
Salt	1.2	19.4
Glass, enamel, cements	67.0	49.5
Metals	497.1	58.6
Iron and steel	149.0	62.7
Metal trades, machine-building	251.9	51.6
Electric appliances and apparatus	60.6	79.1
Power generation	10.4	69.3
Textile industry	343.6	59.5
Cotton	272.3	74.7
Wool	36.0	53.8
Clothing	98.5	64.0
Leather	63.5	49.1
Chemicals	78.3	68.7
Woodworking	60.6	45.1
Printing	28.4	68.6
Paper	20.6	60.3
Grand Total	1,581.4	58.2
Total Group A (heavy industry)	1,004.7	57.4
Total Group B (light industry)	576.7	59.7

Yet a possible repeal of the seven-hour day was never mentioned in those years, and until the end of the decade the bulk of industrial labor worked on the basis of a seven-hour day, although the prevalence of overtime work often brought actual working hours far above the limit. The seven-hour day was not generally discarded until June, 1940, when all rules on hours of work underwent a fundamental revision (see below).

Continuous Work Week

Conversion to seven-hour operations was still under way when a new rearrangement of time schedules was launched. Plants were converted to continuous operation without idle machinery—i.e., without days of rest. Like the seven-hour day, this reorganization came suddenly; and this time the motivation by considerations of production was frankly proclaimed.

The idea was first put up for discussion by Yurii M. Larin, a well-known Soviet writer, in the course of the debate on the report submitted by CPC Chairman A. I. Rykov[25] to the Soviet Congress of May, 1929.[26] The Congress did not take up the suggestion; it was mentioned by none of the delegates speaking after Larin, nor by Rykov in his concluding remarks.[27] The plenary session of the AUCTUC, which met after the Soviet Congress and remained in session until June 1, did not consider the problem, either.

Early in June, however, Larin evidently succeeded in winning over the Politburo of the Communist CC. A few days completely changed the scene. Every paper suddenly placed unusual emphasis on "the great socialist idea" of continuous production. As early as June 8 the press could report that the Supreme Economic Council of the RSFSR had directed its efficiency experts "to

---

[25] *Pravda*, May 23, 1929.

[26] After the idea of continuous operations had won out, the economic press sought to deny that Larin had fathered it. It was said to have been discussed in newspapers several weeks before Larin's speech by engineers and industrial executives (cf. *Torgovo Promyshlennaya Gazeta*, June 5 and 6, 1929). The fact is that this discussion had no effects, while Larin managed to convince government agencies of the advantages of continuous operations and to give wide publicity to the project. In the public eyes Larin undoubtedly retained the credit for the initiation of the project.

[27] *Pravda*, May 28, 1929.

submit in two weeks a master plan for the introduction of continuous production in the several industries." [28]

A week later, the Supreme Economic Council of the USSR ordered all its subordinate agencies to give immediate consideration to "practical measures" for the introduction of continuous operations and to submit a "comprehensive report" to the Presidium of the SEC by July 15.[29] On August 26, the CPC of the USSR issued a decree "on the change-over to continuous production in plants and institutions of the USSR," [30] ordering "systematic conversion" on a national scale. Many plants hastened to introduce continuous schedules without awaiting regular orders. The enthusiasm for continuous production seemed to be almost universal. Only from circles around the People's Commissariat for Labor came timid objections, which were promptly and publicly rebuked.[31]

Conversion was carried out at a feverish pace. In the first half of June, Larin estimated the number of workers on continuous schedules at 15 per cent of the total employed in the industry (oil, iron and steel, paper, etc.). This may have been an overestimate. He also suggested extending the system to 20 per cent of all industrial workers in 1929/30, to another 20 per cent in 1930/31, to 10 per cent in 1931/32, and to 35 per cent in 1932/33. By the end of the first planning period all industrial workers were to be on continuous schedules.[32]

But at the close of 1929 orders went out to extend the continuous week to 43 per cent of all industrial workers by April 1, and "at least two-thirds of industry" by October 1, 1930. Even these figures were soon surpassed. By April 1, 1930, 63 per cent of all industrial workers were reportedly engaged in continuous production.[33] And in June 1930 it was further decreed that the conversion of industry to continuous operations be completed in

---

[28] *Trud*, June 8, 1929.
[29] *Torgovo-Promyshlennaya Gazeta*, June 15, 1929.
[30] *Izvestiya*, August 27, 1929.
[31] Cf. my paper "The Continuous Working Week in Soviet Russia," *International Labour Review*, February, 1931, p. 161.
[32] *Trud*, June 8, 1929.
[33] *Pravda*, December 14, 1929; June 25, 1930. Data in the abstract of labor statistics issued by the State Planning Commission, *Labor in the USSR. Reference Book for 1926–1930*, Moscow, 1930, pp. 22 f., differ slightly. There the following figures are indicated for April 1, 1930: all industry, 61.0 per cent; heavy industry (Group A), 71.6; light industry (Group B), 46.5. For data on individual industries, cf. my paper, as quoted *supra*, n. 31, p. 164.

1930/31; only the textile industry was exempted because of shortage of raw materials.[34]

Originally the continuous work week was considered for industry only. Soon, however—in the August 26 decree[35]—efforts were made to extend it to stores, offices, government agencies, etc. To what extent stores actually went over to a continuous work week cannot be ascertained: such figures never seem to have been published.

The idea of introducing continuous operations was to assure continuity of plant utilization without infringing on the workers' leisure time—not quantitatively, at least. This objective could only be achieved by a radical revision of time schedules.

The legal guarantees of shorter working time on the eve of Sundays and holidays—by two hours under the eight-hour day, and by one hour under the seven-hour day—could no longer apply. Most of the traditionally numerous Russian holidays had to be abolished. Plants were now to work around the clock for 360 days a year, with only five annual holidays (six in a leap year). But the scrapping of most holidays, and extension of work hours on the eve of Sundays and holidays, had to be made up for somehow. At first, it was planned to extend the annual vacations and at the same time to cut the "week" from seven days to six (five work days and one day off). The idea of longer vacations was soon dropped, however, and there was introduced a "five-day week" (four work days and one day off) with rotation of day schedules to guarantee continuous operation. Thus this "five-day week" differed basically from the one widely called for and widely introduced in the United States[36] and in some European countries (five work days followed by a prolonged two-day weekend).

Work schedules based on the Soviet "five-day week" hardly affected the individual worker's annual working time. On an eight-hour day, it amounted to an increase in his yearly working hours from 2,196 to 2,208, i.e., by only 0.5 per cent; on a seven-hour day it meant a drop from 1,962 to 1,932, or 1.5 per cent.[37]

Rules for the new time schedules were laid down on Sep-

---

[34] *Pravda*, June 25, 1930.

[35] See n. 30 *supra*.

[36] The American five-day week was known at that time in the Soviet Union as the "Ford week."

[37] L. Berezansky, *Conversion to the Continuous Work Week*, issued by the AUCTUC, Moscow, 1930, p. 80.

tember 24, 1929.[38] They provided for the general introduction of the five-day week, but without requiring literal observance of the five-day rhythm of work and leisure time. From the outset, "summary computation of work time" over longer periods (up to a month) was permitted, with hours worked during any such period not exceeding a five-day average of 32 (on eight-hour schedules) or 28 days (on seven-hour schedules).

Yet the five-day week did not have to be applied generally even as a mere computational quantity. Building and seasonal trades were exempted and put on a continuous six-day "week" (five work days and one day off).[39] Industrial establishments which regularly had to halt production for one or two days out of work every month for maintenance were to change over to continuous production on a six- or seven-day "week" (five or six work days, respectively).

In addition, many plants converted only partially and kept the remainder of their men on the "interrupted work week," as it was now officially termed. Assigning workers to shifts and drawing up rotation schedules and time charts became an intricate business and compounded the confusion. The setup varied not only from plant to plant but often within a plant, from department to department and from team to team.

"According to very incomplete data, about 50 different time schedules were counted in plants converted to the continuous work week," said an article published in December, 1929, in the periodical of the People's Commissariat for Labor.[40] "Shifts rotate at intervals ranging from four to thirty-seven days. The number of shifts worked in succession, without a day off, varies between four and thirty. Leisure time per week fluctuates between 24 and 84 hours. Frequently a worker's rest period between two shifts is no more than eight hours." Elsewhere in the same issue, the Labor Commissariat periodical said:[41] "There are plants converted to the continuous work week where the workers have to work thirty days and sometimes thirty nights in a row, and then get seven days off."

---

[38] *Izvestiya*, September 25, 1929.
[39] Decision of the government commission for converting plants and institutions to the continuous work week, of October 23, 1929, in *Izvestiya Narkomtruda*, 1929, p. 786.
[40] A. Sorkin, "Time Schedules in Plants with Continuous Production," *Voprosy Truda*, December, 1929, p. 47.
[41] *Op. cit.*, p. 121.

The continuous week was expected to yield economic results, such as increased production, etc. That more efficient use
of industrial equipment may help to raise output is self-evident;
whether it really does depends on whether the establishments in
question are able to cope with new, complex organizational problems. But this very ability was often lacking. In the summer of
1930, the organ of the Supreme Economic Council summarized
the picture as follows: [42]

> "The economic organizations under the Supreme Economic
> Council [industrial boards, "trusts," "combines," etc., administer-
> ing individual groups or combinations of plants] have not paid
> sufficient attention to the continuous work week. No steps were
> taken to concentrate production in the best plants and to in-
> crease their capacity. The experience gathered by plants which
> introduced the continuous week at an earlier date were hardly
> drawn upon. A great majority of plants failed to make organi-
> zational and technical preparations for conversion to the continu-
> ous week. At best, they confined themselves to drawing charts
> and making advance calculations—hardly warranted, to boot—
> of the economic yield of the continuous work week."

As a result, the economic benefits of continuous operation
turned out to be much less than had been hoped for. There were
even cases of declining production after plants had been converted to continuous schedules. Still, in the long run, the additional effort exerted on multiple shifts probably took effect
despite these difficulties, and the vast industrial expansion which
took place under the First Five-Year Plan may to some extent be
creditable to continuous operations.

The social implications of the continuous week were more
obvious. Its introduction necessitated far-reaching changes in the
regulation of leisure time. Continuous production meant, first,
that the simultaneous days of rest so far applying to most of
Russian labor had to go, and second, that the days off had to be
staggered evenly around the year.

Loss of their chance to rest on the same days would strike
the workers as a backward step under any circumstances. How
much more so in Russia, where housing conditions that often
force families to crowd into one apartment—plus the fact that

[42] *Za Industrializatsiyu,* May 22, 1930.

frequently several family members go to work—make common days of rest especially precious!

When the continuous work week was introduced, managers were ordered to consider family relationships in scheduling the various shifts, so that, if possible, members of one family would have their days off together. In practice this provision remained virtually inoperative—nor, in view of the jumble of work-time arrangements, could it be otherwise.

Employees on the whole resented the innovation. "What do we have our families for?" workers in Moscow told a *Pravda* reporter,[43] "Are we to get no rest at all? What are we to do at home if the wife is in the factory, the children in school, and no one can come to see us? What is left but to go to the public tea room? What kind of life is that—when holidays come in shifts and not for all workers together? That's no holiday, if you have to celebrate by yourself?"

The fact that the removal of simultaneous days of rest also removed the Sabbath, thus possibly hurting the workers' religious feelings, was less important in Russia than it would have been elsewhere, especially in countries with an overwhelmingly Roman Catholic population or in Great Britain. If official propaganda nevertheless kept stressing that the workers' discontent with the continuous work week was exclusively due to religious motives and therefore to be fought as "reactionary," this was done for transparently political reasons: any criticism of the continuous week was to be discredited from the outset.

To the superficial observer, the more evenly spaced distribution of working and leisure time over the whole year, as achieved by the removal of numerous holidays and by the correspondingly more frequent insertion of regular ("weekly") days off, might appear as an advance in the sense of a more efficient arrangement.

It is true that some rudiments of a more efficient ratio of working and leisure hours are inherent in the "arithmetics" of continuous operation; but even these were nullified in practice. The more regular distribution of working and leisure time remained a paper plan; its widespread "estimated calculation," along with the multiplicity of prevailing schedules, impaired even

---

[43] *Pravda*, October 1, 1929. For more corroborating evidence see my paper, as quoted *supra*, n. 31, pp. 175 f.

such relative uniformity of leisure time as had previously existed.

Moreover, the more frequent days off were due mainly to the annulment of shorter hours on the eve of the regular rest days. In this respect the new setup ran frankly counter to the basic trend of all progressive work-time doctrines which regard precisely the longer weekend as a significant cultural improvement.

In the end, these consequences of continuous operations were bound to affect performance and production. And as the general economic results fell short of expectations, anyway, and management every day ran into new technical troubles, a distinct reaction set in against the continuous week.

As early as May 1930 the newspaper of the Supreme Economic Council mentioned returns from continuous schedules to the old "interrupted week." [44] At this time the continuous week was still advancing, but by fall it had clearly reached its peak. On October 1, 1930, 72.9 per cent of all industrial workers were employed on continuous schedules.[45] Then their proportion dropped to 68.5 per cent as of January 1, 1931 (from 86.5 to 79.1 per cent in heavy industry, and from 52.2 to 49.4 per cent in light industry).[46]

Increasing confusion and operational difficulties speeded the decline. The periodical of the People's Commissariat for Labor of the USSR stated in February, 1931: [47]

> "Experience has shown that the main advantage of the continuous week, the continuous operation of machinery, is not only not utilized in a number of cases but is replaced, contrary to the real purpose of the continuous week, with continuous operation of the plant as a whole."

If part of the workers are idle, the author emphasized, the machines which cannot be operated by others are idle, too, and there is no continuity. The article continued:

> "In the very nature of things, the disproportion between the number of workers on continuous schedules and the number of machines in continuous use is the most sensitive barometer in-

---

[44] See n. 42 *supra.*

[45] B. Falk, "The Continuous Work Week, Industry's Greatest Reserve," *Voprosy Truda*, February, 1931, p. 37.

[46] *Labor in the USSR . . .*, as quoted *supra*, n. 24, p. 129.

[47] Falk, as quoted *supra*, n. 45, p. 37.

quently, the change from the continuous five-day week resulted in twelve additional working days per year (300 instead of 288).

The return to the non-continuous week was officially declared a temporary measure, to be abandoned when conditions were ripe for efficient operation of continuous schedules. But in practice the decline of the continuous week was regarded as definitive. In fact, its scope narrowed rapidly. The last comprehensive data published indicate that 74.2 per cent of all industrial workers were employed on non-continuous schedules ("six-day week" in practically all cases) by July 1, 1935, and only 25.8 per cent on continuous schedules.[52] The continuous week was finally eliminated along with the non-continuous six-day week, and the normal seven-day week with Sunday as the regular day off reinstituted, when all work-time regulations were revamped in 1940 (see below).

Three-shift schedules also fell into disfavor, because of their bad economic effects. Applied on a rapidly increasing scale up to 1932, they were largely discontinued in subsequent years. The last (1936) yearbook of labor statistics published by the Central Statistical Office showed an increase of the "shift coefficient"[53] from 1.50 in 1928 to 1.73 in 1932 for all occupational divisions; the coefficient dropped to 1.70 in 1933, 1.61 in 1935.[54] No later comprehensive data have been released as far as can be ascertained. Partial data occasionally leaking out indicated that the decline in multiple shifts continued. It may be assumed that by 1940 time schedules based on multiple-shift operations were not much more widely accepted than at the inception of the Five-Year Plan policy.

Labor Protection on the Wane

(a) Breakdown of the general limitation of hours

The exclusive emphasis which Russian economic and social policy from the late 1920's on placed upon production had drastic effects in all fields of labor policy. One of its decisive conse-

---

[52] *Labor in the USSR. Statistical Abstract for 1935*, Moscow, 1936, p. 80.

[53] Ratio of total number of man-days to number of man-days on the most numerous shift (the first day shift).

[54] See n. 52, *supra*, p. 96. This source (p. 79) also supplies data on the number of man-days on the first, second, third, and fourth shifts in July, 1935, for all occupational divisions, heavy industry (Group A), light industry (Group B), and

quences was the far-reaching breakdown of the limitation of working hours.

On paper, the eight-hour day—and soon, in many plants, the seven-hour day—remained the rule, with overtime work subject to rigid restrictions. The law laid down explicit prerequisites for over-time, including specific approval by officials of the labor inspecto-rate (Sec. 104, Labor Code). Without previous approval over-time work could be ordered only in emergencies, by joint labor-manage-ment committees in the plants, but such emergency decisions were to be immediately communicated to the labor inspectorate.

Overtime was strictly limited to four hours in two consecu-tive days or 120 hours for the year (Sec. 106 Labor Code) and absolutely prohibited for juveniles under 18 years of age (Sec. 105) and pregnant women and nursing mothers (Sec. 131). Clear-cut provisions governed overtime pay: at least time and a half for the first two hours, and at least double time for any additional hours as well as for work on days off (Sec. 60).

In practice, the tendency from the late 1920's on was to ignore the legal restrictions on overtime. The manpower short-age of the early 1930's made this trend increasingly prevalent. Overtime was now mostly scheduled by management regardless of the provisions of the Labor Code. Besides—a new phenomenon

individual industries; in addition, the "shift coefficient" is indicated. From these data, it is easy to compute percentages of workers employed on different shift schedules:

Workers on Different Schedules
As Percentage of Total Number Employed

	One Shift	Two Shifts	Three Shifts	Four Shifts	Shift Coefficient
All industry	38.2%	22.8%	35.4%	3.6%	1.61
Group A	40.4	19.4	36.6	3.6	1.58
Group B	33.1	30.4	33.3	3.2	1.66
Power	43.4	4.8	41.4	10.4	1.61
Fuel	28.8	16.4	48.0	6.8	1.83
Coal	11.4	11.2	66.6	10.8	2.38
Oil	37.8	6.0	54.6	1.6	1.68
Peat	60.9	28.8	9.9	.4	1.27
Iron ore mining	18.2	11.6	70.2	—	2.11
Chemical	42.1	10.4	37.5	..10.0	1.61
Iron and steel	25.5	11.6	59.7	3.2	1.93
Metal trades, machine-building	51.7	22.4	25.5	.4	1.40
Woodworking	37.0	23.6	39.0	.4	1.62
Paper	29.7	12.2	48.9	9.2	1.84
Textiles	22.3	36.0	40.5	1.2	1.85
Cotton	22.2	40.2	36.0	1.6	1.83
Wool	18.8	30.6	47.4	3.2	1.97

—employees working overtime were often kept on the job for two consecutive shifts, sometime even for three.

Whenever these practices became particularly blatant they were more or less gently criticized in the press; but these strictures were not taken very seriously by management. A few examples may be cited.

In the spring of 1930 the widely read newspaper of the Young Communist League indignantly reported that the "October Siren" factory in Nizhni-Novgorod had substituted a continuous "ten-day week" for the five-day week. In other words, workers did not get a day off until they had worked for nine days in succession. In the Kerch Metal Works the ten-day week was combined with a ten- or eleven-hour day; in a coal mine in the Kuznetsk Basin the workers had foregone all claims to days off; and so on.[55]

The Young Communist newspaper's indignation was not too profound. On the front page of the same issue it carried a paean in praise of the overtime records in the Stalin Metal Works in Leningrad in assembling a large turbo-generator. The British engineering consultant, in line with European experience, had suggested ten months for the job, but the plant decided to do it in four months and set off a veritable record fever for the purpose:[56]

> ". . . For three days in a row, the men worked overtime without pay, with scarcely two or three hours' sleep. Workers Shilov and Naukonin worked more than three successive shifts, the Young Communist Zabaluyev worked 72 consecutive hours. The Trifonov gang (16 men) stayed on the job 34 hours. . . Finally, the test day came. The night before, three Vickers rotors were installed. Three rotors in one night! And at Vickers' in England the best they can do is to install two in 24 hours!"

Record-breaking was promoted everywhere. Frequently the men themselves were made to adopt overtime resolutions at plant meetings. In fact, some workers, especially the younger ones, were impressed with the show of energy, efficiency, and skill manifested in these records; but those who did not share their enthusiasm— i.e., the bulk of labor—were compelled to acquiesce.

---

[55] *Komsomol'skaya Pravda*, April 29, 1930.
[56] *Ibid.*

Occasionally the full rites of "trade union democracy" were outwardly observed. That their observance was a mere formality was admitted even by the central organ of the unions, in a rare moment of introspection. Early in 1930 the paper reported from Leningrad:[57]

> "The employees of the 'Rabochi' ['The Worker'] plant, observing all rules of union democracy, resolved to work overtime to fulfill the industry and finance plan. The men work two shifts, sometimes 16 hours in succession. There even are instances of work continuing beyond 16 hours. In similarly 'democratic' style resolutions are adopted wherein the workers waive their days off.
>
> "What these rules of 'union democracy' look like in practice may be seen from the example of the 'Rabotnitsa' ['Woman worker'] factory. Here the motion to work out time lost on days off is being put to a vote in the following manner: 'Those in favor of the industry and finance plan? Those opposed to the plan?'
>
> "Some wiseacres among the executives of the Voikov Metal Works suggested no more and no less than scrapping the eight-hour day and introducing the ten-hour day at regular wages [without overtime pay]. The 'Volcano' and 'Red Nailsmith' factories took the same road, waiving all days off."

This disapproval was hardly a matter of principle. The trade union newspaper lacked the courage of its convictions as much as the Young Communist daily. A news item in the very same issue of *Trud* reported that Kozlovskaya, the woman chairman of the Textile Workers Joint Board in Leningrad, had spoken up against the 'bacchanal of longer hours.' Did the union paper back her? It did not. Instead, it accused the textile workers official of "rightist deviationism"—a charge that no one in the Soviet Union carelessly invites.

So much for Leningrad. In the provinces conditions were even less gratifying. But were they any better in Moscow? In September 1930, the AUCTUC in collaboration with the central boards of various unions organized a tour of Moscow plants, a so-called "one-day campaign" to get a first-hand view of labor conditions in the capital. The outcome: "Cases are very frequent in which the unions, to overcome production difficulties, promote longer hours and waivers of days off."[58]

---

[57] *Trud*, February 25, 1930.
[58] *Trud*, September 18, 1930.

Under the impact of the results of this study tour the People's Commissariat for Labor and the AUCTUC issued a joint circular directing local labor authorities and union officials "to disallow" such violations of the Labor Code.[59] This gesture was not taken seriously either; the CPSU's *Pravda* and the Supreme Economic Council's *Za Industrializatsiyu* did not even mention it. A week later, the latter's editors called a conference of managers of the large industrial construction projects; there it was proudly stated:[60] "On industrial construction projects we work not less [*sic!*] than 10 to 12 hours a day." There was not the slightest objection either at the conference or in the press.

The overtime fever spread to official science, and a fundamental revision of the physiology of work was initiated in 1931. Professor S. Kaplun, head of the Institute for the Protection of Labor, published an article in *Pravda* under the significant title, "For a Marxist-Leninist Attitude in the Physiology of Work!"[61] in which the "fatigue theory" or "protective fatigue theory," for years the prevailing doctrine in the physiology of work, was to be refuted and pilloried as "anti-Soviet."[62]

This accepted doctrine regards the feeling of fatigue as a warning signal indicating that further exertion may have consequences harmful to the human organism. A few years earlier, Kaplun himself had shared and zealously publicized this view. Now he assailed not only the theory—suddenly recognized as dangerous—but above all its leading Russian exponents, the physiologists Levitsky and Keklcheyev:

> ". . . Levitsky proclaims: 'When the protective reaction of the sympathetic nervous system is overcome by will power—that is to say, when work is done after sensations of fatigue have set in—the inevitable result is a disorganization of the sensory reaction.' This means that the shock worker must immediately drop his work at the first feeling of fatigue. Thus the protective

59 *Trud*, September 23, 1930.
60 *Za Industrializatsiyu*, October 1, 1930.
61 *Pravda*, May 21, 1931.
62 In the same year S. Kaplun published two articles in the periodical *Gigiyena, Bezopasnost' i Patologiya Truda* ("For the Unmasking of Specific Errors through Self-Critique" in the October-November issue, and "The Reorganization of the Institute for Protection of Labor, as a Consequence of the Discussion on the Labor-Hygienic and Labor-Physiological Front" in the December issue). They apparently dealt with the same subject, but were not available to me.

fatigue theory naturally arrives at the conclusion: 'In production the workers themselves conserve their strength by reducing performance when they are overtired' (Kekcheyev)."

That the "shock worker must immediately drop his work at
the first feeling of fatigue" was a deliberate misrepresentation of
the physiological idea, unequivocally designed to discredit the
"fatigue theory." According to Kaplun, the theory dangerously
overrated "the subjective fatigue feeling" and made it an objective obstacle to "innocuous continuation of work." A worker's
weariness was a mere "subjective factor" which he could surmount
by will power and keep working without impairing his health.
Consequently those who defended and scientifically justified the
"pretense" of fatigue were to be exposed and denounced as "class
enemies":[63]

> "The activation of hostile elements among part of the scien-
> tists reflects the class enemy's bitter resistance to the socialist of-
> fensive of the proletariat. Decisively beaten all along the economic
> front, the class enemy thinks he can hold the last trench line on
> a few sectors of the ideological front. There need be no doubt
> that he will also be smashed in this, his last position."

Ideologically, the breakdown of regulations limiting hours
was further prepared in another way: by promoting the idea that
the establishment of performance records was the most progressive, the genuinely socialist approach to work. In a series of dispatches and articles carried by Moscow papers on November 7,
1931—to celebrate the October Revolution—the new creed was
presented both in theory and in model examples: "Bolshevism
must enter into scientific and technological calculations as a new
category overturning all previous views of the bases of such calculations," the newspaper of Soviet industry said in an enthusiastic report on assembly operations in the Moscow Automobile
Works. Details followed:[64]

> "The installation of the power-switch platform, the 'captain's
> bridge' of the casting department, with its fifteen band conveyors
> and forty-eight powerful motors, the mounting of sensitive con-
> trol apparatus, the installation of transformers, and the wiring

---

[63] See n. 61, *supra.*
[64] *Za Industrializatsiyu*, November 7, 1931.

were completed in a modern French plant in a month's time. After German technicians had seen what we can do, they decided to cut this period in half and do the job in two weeks. Plant manager Likhachev glanced at these calculations and said, 'Bolsheviks always do everything twice as fast,' and reduced the time to seven days. Then the chief mechanic, Barsukov, high-pressured all minor jobs and saved another two days. But Young Communists who installed the power-switch platform drew up a counter-plan and completed the entire installation in three and a half days."

In the same plant an intricate electric furnace was to be set up. According to German calculations, the newspaper said, this took three-and-a-half months. But a team of Young Communists, "pursuant to a resolution of the local bureau of the Young Communist League," completed the installation in sixteen days, for the opening of the International Youth Congress.[65]

The effects which this kind of record-hunting had on the workers themselves can easily be imagined. The newspapers proudly related that all regulations governing hours went overboard when a new record was to be set. They praised the workers of the Moscow Automobile Works who had done two consecutive daily shifts "throughout the assault period."[66] They glorified the Young Communists of the Moscow Ball-Bearing Works for staying on the job for twenty-four hours while machinery was installed.[67] They eulogized the workers of Magnitogorsk, where one team refused to go home for twenty-nine hours, another for three shifts, and a third for three days. In describing this overtime fanaticism, the correspondent of the trade union newspaper waxed quite lyrical:[68]

> "Scores and even hundreds have set examples of unforgettable revolutionary self-sacrifice. Nights were turned into days. Days grew and doubled: two days' work was done in one. Two days' work? In Magnitorsk, in scope and speed of performance, three, if not five days of work were squeezed into a single day."

The picture was the same on most industrial construction projects. Practically everywhere youth was leading in the race for

[65] *Ibid.*
[66] *Ibid.*
[67] *Trud,* November 7, 1931.
[68] *Ibid.*

records. One more instance worth mentioning is the giant construction project at Kuznetsk, where 17-year old boys worked "fourteen and sixteen hours a day, like all other workers," and Young Communists employed on installations resolved to go without any days off. "Competition between the several shift crews assumed a singular form. As soon as the first shift is through and the second has gone on duty, the crew of the first sets out to help the second. Overwhelmed by fatigue, boys of the first shift lie down right on the brick piles and after two or three hours of sleep get up and go on working."[69]

The record fever was bound to run into some opposition in the ranks of industrial executives. In the long run they could not quite overlook the inevitably fatal economic consequences of this kind of record performances. Gradual efforts were made to fence in the worst excesses, but violations of the labor laws continued widespread. It is impossible even approximately to exhaust the vast material on this theme that appeared in the Soviet press in scattered fragments, never published comprehensively. We can only try to summarize at least a part of these data so as to elucidate the overall trend.

So far we have been dealing with 1931, the peak year of the First Five-Year Plan period. Let us skip a few years to 1934, with the Second Five-Year Plan in full swing. Plant management swamps the labor inspectors with requests for the approval of overtime, "threatening non-fulfillment of Plan otherwise."[70] Many plants don't wait for approval; without even asking, they arbitrarily order the men to work overtime. Such instances are reported from the Kharkov Locomotive Works,[71] the Gorki Automobile Works,[72] the Moscow Ilyich Works,[73] etc.

At the iron foundry in Cherepovets, Moscow province, "a group of casters worked an averange of 15 hours for three months; things got to the point where overtired workers simply walked off the job without waiting for the end of the casting process."[74] In a survey conducted by the Metal Workers Union in the establishments of the "Safety-Technique Trust" [sic!] in the Ukraine, men

[69] Izvestiya, November 7, 1931.
[70] Trud, March 14, 1934.
[71] Trud, March 5, 1934.
[72] Trud, March 14 and April 21, 1934.
[73] Trud, March 21, 1934.
[74] Ibid.

were found "frequently working from fourteen to sixteen hours and more"; there were reports of workers staying on the job for "twenty, even twenty-three hours" running, without overtime pay.[75] In the Chuvyrin Mine, Donets Basin, where regulations limited work underground to six hours a day, the six-hour day was "knocked out, just so as to deliver coal," and miners were kept underground even at night, for nine or ten hours.[76]

Workers who dared object would incur open or disguised reprisals. In the Chusovaya Metal Works, Ural province, overtime was constantly scheduled on the pretext of emergency operations.[77] "Routine cleaning of furnaces in the rolling mill is called an emergency operation." Anyone venturing to doubt the emergency character of such a job was "promptly taken off the roll of shock workers and threatened with dismissal." And, from another department of the same plant: "Whoever dares to protest against work on days off and overtime is branded as loafer" and liable to punishment "under the appropriate provisions on truancy." As a result, overtime work grew apace:[78]

> "As a rule, every worker does ten overtime shifts a month. Lydia Pankratova, a woman employed in the open-hearth department, worked 49 shifts in February and 34 shifts in March; another woman, Makhnikina, did 47 shifts in February and 34 in March. Nor are these isolated cases."

These were not local phenomena peculiar to Ural province. In the Rykov Works, Donets Basin, a work gang was disbanded and "assigned to lower-paid work" because the members objected to the introduction of the twelve-hour day.[79] Several mines under the jurisdiction of the Khrustal'nyi Mine Administration, Donets Basin, branded "miners failing to report for work on their days off as refractory truants."[80] The report points out that local union and Party authorities actively sponsored such practices.

"Experiences in a number of cases show managers and plant committees cooperating on a basis of joint violation of the labor laws," said an editorial in the trade union daily.[81] This labor-

75 *Trud*, May 11, 1934.
76 *Trud*, March 29, 1934.
77 *Trud*, May 8, 1934.
78 *Ibid.*
79 *Trud*, April 12, 1934.
80 *Za Industrializatsiyu*, March 9, 1934.
81 *Trud*, April 4, 1934.

management cooperation sometimes assumed odd forms. For purposes of disguise as well as to give an appearance of legality to the unlawful non-payment of overtime rates, overtime work was occasionally presented as "socialist competition":[82]

> "Socialist competition and shock work . . . are considered easy ways of filling all gaps and veiling every 'little sin' in the organization of work. Ah, well, the shock workers, they'll get the job done! After all, it's to their own interest to fulfill the production plan, as non-fulfillment would disgrace the whole plant. So they're going to work—and it won't be overtime, either. Oh no, this will just be plain socialst competition."

To protect themselves, managers sometimes arranged for employee resolutions, real or fictitious. There was a report from the construction project of the Coke and Chemical Works in Zaporozhye on the Dnieper:[83] "On the eve of every day off a manager's order was posted enjoining the workers to work on their days off, citing resolutions passed at meetings of the workers and the technical staff, which no one had known were ever held."

Sometimes such reports were couched in terms suggesting disapproval. But even then, and even if coming from union sources, the criticism of "excesses" was based on economic, not on social considerations; the overtime epidemic was said to "increase production costs,"[84] to "drive payrolls out of bounds,"[85] to "devour huge funds," [86] etc. If a limitation of overtime work seems efficient from a purely economic point of view, the abuses are indeed checked now and then. But they soon reappear. Where the authority of the labor law dwindles, where unions have nothing to say, where no means of raising output is spurned, purely economic considerations cannot stem the breakdown of the institutionalized protection of labor.[87]

[82] *Trud*, March 8, 1934.
[83] *Za Industrializatsiyu*, April 1, 1934.
[84] *Trud*, April 4, 1934.
[85] *Trud*, March 20, 1934.
[86] *Trud*, May 10, 1934.
[87] As an illustration of this collision between social and economic considerations a characteristic case may be quoted. In 1935 the official organs of the trade unions and the economic administration engaged in unusual polemics. Sensational conditions in the "Red Profintern" railroad-car and locomotive plant in Bezhitsa stirred *Trud* to vigorous protests. But although there was no denying its facts, the union was forced to capitulate, to accept the views of the industrial paper which had attacked criticism of excessive overtime and faulty safety techniques

Let us skip a few more years, to 1937. The Second Five-Year Plan was drawing to a close. The press exulted in the country's vast industrial upsurge. A plenary session of the AUCTUC met in April, after a two-year interval, and heard from its first secretary, Shvernik:[88] "Abuse of overtime and work on days off is one of the fields in which the labor laws are most frequently broken." And President Striyevski of the Heavy Machine-building Workers Union added: [89]

> "In the Ishevsk Works [near Leningrad]—I just returned from there a few days ago—the technical director orders the men to work overtime. And when they say they are tired, he replies: 'Just take a cold shower, and go back to work!' Neither the shop committee nor the Party organization has curbed this imbecility."

Not only trade union papers but the industrial press furnished ample material to illustrate Shvernik's report. It was the story of 1934 all over again, but something new had been added: complaints of illegal overtime work for pregnant women. The following report came from the Molotov Machine Tool Works in Kharkov:[90]

> "Last year, to fulfill the production program, a great deal of overtime work was done in the plant. Now overtime is prohibited [on grounds of 'finance discipline']. Yet a few days ago, on March 11, we were in a position to observe the following in the shop which manufactures larger parts. Some comrades had worked 24 hours without leaving the plant. Comrades Poido, Chernov, and Kasyanov were kept in the plant for fourteen hours after the end of their shift. And the stockroom worker Antipova, who is to take her pregnancy leave within a few days [in 1937, such leave was granted eight weeks before delivery], was also kept in and only after much pleading allowed to go home after working a mere seven hours overtime."

Such cases affected not only the general limitation of hours but the special field of female labor protection which will be dealt with below. As for hours, the conditions described did not sub-

---

as an encroachment on the prerogatives of management, and to slap its own face for having said things "politically wrong and harmful." The story is condensed in the appendix to this chapter.

[88] *Trud*, May 16, 1937.
[89] *Trud*, May 6, 1937.
[90] *Za Industrializatsiyu*, March 17, 1937.

stantially change in subsequent years; rather, they became commonplace. Not in the sense of 10 or 12 or 15 hours of work becoming customary; seven- or eight-hour days remained the rule. But in fact the seven- and eight-hour day was no longer protected, and managers knew that the law on the seven- or eight-hour day, on overtime and days off could be ignored by them at will. In innumerable cases, they did just that.

(b) *Deterioration in Protection of Female Labor*

The breakdown of the limitation of hours was the most characteristic feature of the change in working conditions during the 1930's, but other safeguards too were on the downgrade. One flagrant instance of ignoring fundamental restriction on female labor has just been cited; such cases were in line with the trend.

As early as 1930 the trade union daily, in an article "On the Revision of the Labor Code,"[91] suggested repealing the ban on night work by women and juveniles. Soon after, *Pravda* came out against forbidding female labor underground (Sec. 129, Labor Code), and science was given the thankless task of explaning why sub-surface work would not injure a woman's health.

A survey which the Moscow Institute for Occupational Diseases—the so-called Obukh Institute—conducted in the mines of the Moscow coal region produced the thesis that the ban was unjustifiable. The North Caucasian Institute for the Economics, Organization, and Hygiene of Labor followed through in the Artem Mines, North Caucasus, with a study covering 148 women employed above ground and 444 working underground. "The results completely confirmed the findings of the Obukh Institute." Similar conclusions were reached by the Ural Institute for Labor Economics, Organization, and Hygiene, whereupon the National Conference of Research Institutes on Female Labor came out in January, 1933, against the ban on underground work by women.[92]

This closed the issue. Formally, sub-surface work remained prohibited for women until October, 1940, but these prohibitions were generally disregarded and soon forgotten. Earlier violations of the prohibition of night work for women were mentioned above in discussing the seven-hour day and the continuous week.

---

91 *Trud*, December 10, 1930.
92 G. Serebrennikov, *Female Labor in the USSR*, Moscow, 1934, pp. 204 ff.

In time, encroachments on the protection of working women grew more serious. Pregnancy restrictions were ignored: the law permits pregnant women to be employed only on jobs that do not overtax their strength, but in the 1930's this principle too was frequently disregarded. We have already quoted a story to the effect that a woman worker had to work two consecutive shifts in the seventh or eighth month of pregnancy; an even more symptomatic case was told in the trade union paper about the same time, in a letter from a woman miner, Tatyana Kreshtopova. She complained about conditions in her mine:[93]

"... I am in the seventh month of pregnancy. In the mine they refuse me the privileges of which I am entitled. It is hard for me to work underground, but I am neither transferred to work above ground nor assigned to easier work. I complained to the division chief, Samsonov, that if the winch doesn't work I have to load stones by hand. 'Never mind, you can stand it,' Samsonov said. On January 26, I was transferred: now I run a handcar in the mine gallery, again with Samsonov as chief. Working conditions are even worse. The gallery is very steep; it's tough for me to climb down there, and I suffer from the cold.

"I asked Samsonov to let me run a handcar above ground, and he threatened me: 'If you don't want to work in the gallery, I'll fire you as a truant.' I complained to the chairman of the mine committee, Comrade Zarypov; he wrote a note but that didn't help any. My co-workers, the miners Kurmayev and others, reported to Samsonov that it was too hard for me to work underground, particularly on the night shift. Samsonov replied: 'Never mind, she won't have to wait long for her maternity leave.' Another woman in my situation, Astakhova, also ran a handcar underground until the day of her maternity leave."

Before printing the letter, the editors of the trade union daily sent a reporter to check the facts. He found them worse than expected: "It turned out that twelve of the twenty pregnant women employed in the mine were refused their legal privileges." All this was known to the Public Prosecutor's office, where complaints of women workers had been on file for months, but nothing was being done.[94]

The argument that these conditions were not general cannot

---

[93] *Trud*, February 23, 1937.
[94] *Ibid.*

minimize their tragic significance. They were certainly not the rule; in many plants, such abuses were unknown. But neither were they accidental. They were the natural consequences of changes which the whole Soviet labor protection system underwent in the 1930's, and to this extent they were representative of the general trend.

(c) *Decline of Safety Standards*

There were similar developments in all fields of labor protection—of which only the most important can be taken up here. Signs of a deterioration of safety standards were visible from the early 1930's on. The initial stages may be omitted, for brevity's sake, but what happened later was clearly the result of the speed-up, which had become the gospel of economic leaders.

Let us look at conditions in tractor manufacturing, a highly regarded industry of recent origin, with new, well-equipped modern plants. President V. Sivachev of the Tractor Workers Union wrote in an article on working conditions in the Stalingrad and Kharkov tractor plants:[95]

> "The plants were designed to turn out 72 tractors per shift. With output more than doubled, they cannot meet safety requirements in their present neglected condition. The factories have been converted to Stakhanov methods, but the ventilation systems are unchanged, and as a result large quantities of gas accumulate on the premises. Checkups in the Kharkov Tractor Works showed, for example, that the air at the upper end of the conveyor belt contained ten times the permissible maximum of gas."

After listing a number of further safety hazards in tractor plants, the author concluded, "Very little attention to safety is paid by plant committees, by middle-level officials, and by the central boards of the unions." In recent times, he added, this had become particularly noticeable.[96]

Complaints of this kind grew most vocal in the years of the Great Purge, 1936-1938. Neglect of social requirements, an evil deeply rooted in the whole Soviet industrial system, was now laid to the pilloried "wreckers" and "enemies of the people." An ex-

95 *Trud*, December 8, 1935.
96 *Ibid.*

ample may illustrate the technique. Of the huge "Donsoda" chemical plant the Moscow industry paper wrote:[97] "Fascist wreckers have made labor protection and safety their favorite field of activities." The situation in the plant was intolerable:

> ". . . Damaged pipes caused steam to flow into the lime shop, and the workers had to grope their way from installation to installation, as in a fog. . . Poor visibility increased the accident rate.
>
> "Wreckers have ruined the ventilation system in all departments. In the lime shop the fans are not running at all, despite accumulated fumes. We find the same picture in the soda shop, etc. High-frequency wires lie without insulation. . . As a result, accident figures have gone up in 1936."

To blame, of course, were the "wrekers" and nobody else. And what did the plant committee do? The Party organization?

> "Stakhanovite workers Burmin, Fedorov, and others advised the organizations in the plant [the plant committee and the secretariat of the Party organization] and the management of these abuses and acts of sabotage. The outcome was that the workers who had brought the villainies of the wreckers to light were denounced as opportunists and accused of dodging work."

Was the central board of the union unaware of these conditions? Far from it. The central board knew everything, but "did nothing about it."

Did conditions improve as the "wreckers" were unmasked and eliminated? Not in the least: "Impassable filth piles up in the plant, as before . . . The pipes are damaged, leaking liquids and gas."

Another typical case was the "Sickle-and-Hammer" metal plant in Moscow. After the famous Pyatakov-Radek trial in January, 1937, when the fight against industrial "wreckers" and "enemies of the people" was at its peak, *Pravda* published an appeal in which the "Sickle-and-Hammer" plant workers called upon "all workers of the Soviet Union" for "vigilance, vigilance above all":[98]

> "We know that plant installations do not become unusable by themselves, that machine-tools do not wreck themselves, that

[97] *Za Industrializatsiyu*, April 8, 1937.
[98] *Pravda*, January 31, 1937.

boilers do no explode on their own. Somebody's hands are behind every one of these deeds. Are they not the hands of the enemy?"

Only a few weeks after publication of this appeal, the following picture of safety conditions in the cold-rolling mill of this "vigilant" plant was published:[99]

> "Acid-poisoning cases are frequent. The department with its new machine tools used to be the pride of the plant; today it is in abominable condition . . . The ventilation system is not sufficient to cleanse the air of acid fumes. The workers carry vats of acid up and down the stairs, in constant danger of burns."

Anyone who dares to criticize this state of affairs is promptly muzzled by department chief Zagaidak: "I don't want criticism. I want blind obedience. Don't forget that, if you want to work with me." This strange executive was no exceptional case:

> "The atmosphere of muzzling any self-criticism is no special characteristic of the rolling mill. In the pressing mill the picture is about the same. . . Working conditions have deteriorated. The mill is full of gas. Accidents are frequent."

Neglect of safety measures had become normal. The head of the safety department of the Moscow Dynamo Works wrote early in 1937:[100]

> "The law obliges machine-building plants to put safety devices on the machines they turn out. Yet there has not been a single case [?!] of the plant being asked to comply strictly with this provision."

The customers were glad to have their orders filled at all and to get their machines, with or without safety devices.

Indicative of the progressive disintegration of safety measures was the fact that they were soon virtually limited to ventilation systems. The bulk of the funds allocated for safety purposes was destined for ventilation. The state of the industrial ventilation systems was the subject of a comprehensive report published early in 1937 by the trade union daily. There was danger ahead, said the paper, particularly in many of the biggest plants:[101]

---

99 *Za Industrializatsiyu*, March 15, 1937.
100*Za Industrializatsiyu*, March 9, 1937.
101 *Trud*, March 11, 1937.

"Take, for instance, the copper foundry in Krasnouralsk. The foundry is so polluted by gas that workers in the main shop wear gas masks on the job, to keep from being poisoned by sulphur and other fumes.

"The hand of the class enemy has been at work in the tractor plant in Chelyabinsk. The concentration of gases in several shops is often many times the permissible maximum. Here, too, there were cases of gas poisoning.

"Examples of this kind are numerous. . . In several plants ventilation systems were found to have been put into operation without any devices for purifying the polluted air. As a result, the air around the plants and the workers' quarters is poisoned. At present, the problem of purifying air withdrawn by ventilation systems is particularly acute, for not only all foliage and grass vanishes in the neighborhood of plants causing complaints in this respect, but it becomes impossible to supply the workshops with pure air."

Conditions grew worse, especially in heavy industry. In May, 1937, at the Leningrad Provincial Conference of the CPSU, the public prosecutor for the province spoke out emphatically against "grave infractions of the labor laws, mounting accident figures, and the indifferent and at times criminal attitude of some Party, industry, and union leaders with respect to the workers' life and health."[102]

For Soviet conditions, this public airing of these vital issues was rather unusual. It was connected with the plans, drawn up at that time, to reorganize and revive the trade unions. However, as the union reform did not materialize, public discussion of safety problems and working conditions also ceased in short order.

The most striking abuses uncovered by the discussion had to be corrected—but here again the controlling point of view was the economic interest of the plants. The adverse economic effects of the race for maximum output, of record-hunting, and speed-up fanaticism were beginning to be realized in the first years of the Third Five-Year Plan. Toward the end of the decade this led to certain improvements in the internal organization of the plants. There is a good deal of available evidence to illustrate this development. And though we have hardly any data on safety improvement they are supposed to go hand in hand with the improvement

---

[102] *Pravda*, March 26, 1937.

of the internal plant organization. Thus, it is likely that better management more or less automatically resulted in relative improvement of techniques designed to protect workers' safety and health.

(d) *Ineffectual Labor Inspection*

From a cursory examination of the Labor Code and other formally still valid laws and ordinances one can conclude that the Soviet labor inspectorate is in many ways a model institution. Labor inspectors are elected by the unions; since 1933, when the functions of the labor administration were transferred to the unions, they have been government and union officials at the same time. Their number is very large, and their powers are considerable. Besides the general labor inspection, there are two special inspectorates—for safety techniques and industrial hygiene. Here also, officials are simultaneously union employees. Furthermore, the workers of every plant elect so-called "social inspectors" to serve without pay as assistants of the labor inspectorate. Their powers, though less important than those of the career inspectors, are extensive, and their position is assured by the fact that they may not be fired from their jobs without the consent of the plant committee and the labor inspector.

So much for the letter of the law. But the legal provisions have undergone in practice substantial changes. Under the Five-Year Plan policy the labor inspectors had lost almost all authority. The following report of the central trade union newspaper refers to Donets coal mining where the work of the inspectors, and perhaps even more of their unpaid assistants in the mines, should carry special weight: [103]

> "Many unions in the Donets Basin (to quote from the resolution passed by the Fifth Plenary Session of the Donets Basin Trade Union Council) 'consider the labor inspectorate a foreign body in the union organism, fail to assist it, and do not fight for the enforcement of its orders.' If even the unions regard the inspectorate as a foreign body, many economic agencies ignore it altogether. Let us cite a few facts:
> "Director Zimin of the Central Mining Group tore up an

---

[103] *Trud*, March 23, 1934.

order issued by Labor Inspector Samusov and threw him out of his office. At the mine No. 17/17 bis (in Rutchenkovo) Chief Engineer Kuznetsov threw Inspector Dubrovin out of the technical conference. The director of the Korsun' Mining Group (Artem Coal Trust) expelled Labor Inspector Vodolazkin from the mine for insisting on the elimination of safety rule violations. In the Fomino Mine District, horses provided for Inspectors Sumarokov and Vadzinski were taken away, and the inspectors now had to walk fifteen to sixteen kilometers. At Chistyakov-Ugol', a woman inspector, Sergeyeva, was ordered out of the apartment she had been assigned, on the ground that she was not employed in production, etc., etc.

"All these facts are well known to the mine committee, to the Trade Union Council for the Donets Basin, and to the All-Ukrainian Board of the Coal Miners Union. Yet they literally have not done a thing to remedy the situation."

These were unmistakable signs of decay. In line with the growing tendency to hand over the execution of social policy to the economic administration and to plant management, it was even suggested that the labor inspection too be withdrawn from the union's jurisdiction and transferred to the economic agencies. This idea was vigorously championed by one of the secretaries of the AUCTUC, V. Polonsky, in a lecture in December, 1935, and again in an article published in the industry newspaper early in 1936.[104]

No such liquidation took place, and labor inspection remained within the sphere of union activities. In practice, however, it was sharply curtailed. In 1936 the special Labor Inspection Department of the AUCTUC, the center of labor inspection, was disbanded and merged with the Production and Wages Department in a new Department of Planning and Control. Thereupon labor inspectors were "released" from the duty of making so-called "preventive checks" in newly opened plants, in direct contradiction to Sec. 138 of the Labor Code, which prescribed that "No plant shall be opened, put into operation, or transferred to new premises without the approval of the labor inspectorate and the organs of safety and industrial hygiene inspection."

Some unions went farther on the road of "cold liquidation." In May, 1936, the Central Board of the Railroad Workers Union

[104] *Za Industrializatsiyu,* January 3 and 8, 1936.

for Central Russia transferred the safety and industrial hygiene inspection to the People's Commissariat for Transportation. This example was soon followed by the Central Board of the Coal Miners Union for the Southern Region. In July, 1936, safety inspectors in the Donets Basin lost the right to order work stoppage in the mines, even in cases where "continued operations would endanger the workers' lives." Henceforth, safety and labor inspectors could only ask their superiors for remedial action in such cases.[105]

Some of these measures were repealed after a while, but labor inspection as a whole remained a stepchild of government labor policy. Lack of authority inevitably had its repercussions on personnel standards. Trained social workers were scarcely inclined to take the thankless jobs of labor inspectors. The chairman of the Central Board of the Eastern Metal Workers Union mentioned this fact at the Sixth Plenary Session of the AUCTUC in the spring of 1937:[106]

"Who will work for us as an inspector? We just have five or six people qualified for their office. Most of those who work as inspectors are strangers to the field. With hygiene inspectors, it is even worse. We have but two real hygiene inspectors, one in the Magnitorsk plant and another at central headquarters. Everywhere else, male nurses work as hygiene inspectors in the Eastern metal plants. It goes without saying that they are at a loss about problems of industrial hygiene."

Of twenty-one safety inspectors then employed by this union, only eight were graduate engineers; of the twenty-seven labor inspectors "not a single one had the required training." "Things are even worse in the plants of the Eastern lumber and wood industry. Three quarters of all inspectors there are actually semi-illiterate."[107] In the Western regions, it may not have been so bad, but things were basically similar there, too.

The press carried many reports illustrating the decline of labor inspection. Inspectors who laid well-founded complaints before management often seem to have been sharply rebuffed: "What you are doing is bureaucratism and not helpful to our

105 For more details, see my article "The Crisis of Protection of Labor," Sotsialisticheskii Vestnik, Paris, 1937, No. 12–13.
106 Trud, May 6, 1937.
107 Trud, April 9, 1937.

work." Or: "Leave my office and stop bothering me."[108] There were also instances of managers refusing to see inspectors and forbidding their staffs to accept their written complaints of violations of the labor law. "The central boards of the unions look on helplessly to all this and do not know what to do."[109]

Such reports were rather frequent during the first half of 1937 in connection with the projected revival of union activities. As nothing came of this plan, the expected improvement in the field of labor inspection did not materialize, either.

More than a year later, the question was again brought up for discussion on the eve of the Seventh Plenary Session of the AUCTUC in September, 1938. Then it was learned that the presidium of the AUCTUC "has not once taken up the questions of labor protection and safety techniques since the end of 1936,"[110] that new regulations on the reporting of industrial accidents, designed to supersede the old rules repealed in 1935, were still in the drafting stage,[111] that the temporarily revived "preventive checks" were again jeopardized. On this subject, the trade union newspaper said:[112]

> "Comrade Kurkina, head of the labor protection department of the AUCTUC [restored to its functions after the Sixth Plenary Session], recently directed the central boards of the unions not to accept for consideration any plans for new industrial construction projects that may be submitted to them by economic agencies for approval of safety techniques and industrial hygiene. The department also hastened to disband consultation bureaus set up by the Institutes for Labor Protection."

At its Sixth Plenary Session, the AUCTUC had promised improvements in labor protection and inspection. In particular, the labor inspectors were to take vigorous steps to assure a more efficient utilization of the funds appropriated for safety. Indeed, they often tried to take such steps, but rarely with success.

In the manufacture of electrical equipment, less than 20 per cent of the safety funds allocated for the year 1938 were spent on safety during the first half of the year. In Donets coal mining,

---

108 *Trud*, February 12, 1937.
109 *Trud*, April 4, 1937.
110 *Trud*, September 1, 1938.
111 *Ibid.*
112 *Trud*, August 10, 1938.

actual expenditures were only 17 per cent. "The use of safety funds is no more satisfactory in printing, shipbuilding, iron and steel, metal processing, manufacture of transportation machinery." [113] At the Seventh Plenary Session of the AUCTUC, N. M. Shvernik mentioned that in the manufacture of medium machinery only 10.5 per cent of the annual allotment for safety devices had been spent during the first half of 1938. [114] The president of the Linen Workers Union quoted an even lower figure—7.5 per cent—for the linen industry. [115]

These figures indicated average disbursements in whole industries. The picture in individual plants was often worse. A dispatch on the situation at the New Metal Works in Tula said: [116]

> "Last year a ventilating system and showers were promised to the casting department. They are still non-existent. Signaling devices for the cranes would have cost only 1,000 rubles, but they are still missing. Nor have any of the other measures laid down in the 1938 agreement materialized. The appropriation of 100,000 rubles was not spent. Labor Inspector Kuznetsov helplessly says: 'I can't do a thing. Manager Natarov wont pay attention to my orders.' "

This was not an extreme case. It was fairly typical. Nor have there been signs of a turn for the better in later years.

Curtailment Measures of 1940

In the preceding pages the story of labor protection is brought up to the end of the 1930's. Formally, the most important safeguards remained intact; actually, the law became more and more of a dead letter. The turning point was in 1940, when the trend began to extend to the letter of the law.

The first half of 1940 was marked by a perceptible economic recession. In addition, feverish war preparations started in the summer of 1940. In the field of labor legislation the consequences were drastic measures to assure work discipline and weakened protective safeguards.

[113] *Trud*, September 3, 1938.
[114] *Trud*, September 5, 1938.
[115] *Trud*, September 4, 1938.
[116] *Trud*, September 3, 1938.

The decree of the Presidium of the Supreme Soviet of the USSR of June 26, 1940,[117] which tied wage and salary earners to their places of employment (see Chapter Three), also ordered the immediate substitution of the eight-hour day for both the seven-hour day and the six-hour day, which had become traditional for a major part of salaried employees as well as for juveniles of sixteen and seventeen year of age. The "six-day week" (five work days and one day off) was abolished at the same time and replaced with the regular seven-day week. Shorter hours on the eve of Sundays and holidays—legally guaranteed and generally prevailing under the seven-day week—were tacitly abandoned.

This rearrangement of working hours may have been due to unfavorable conditions and the threat of war. But there was another conspicuous feature of the reversal of labor policy. On the same day as the decree of the Supreme Soviet, another was issued by the CPC of the USSR, dealing with the possible repercussions of the new regulation of hours on the development of wages.[118] This read as follows:

"(1) The daily wage rates and monthly salaries now in force shall continue unchanged.

"(2) Corresponding to the longer hours of work, performance quotas shall be raised and piece rates lowered."

No rise in actual earnings was to result from longer hours. Coming at a time of soaring prices (see Chapter Four), the measure dealt labor a heavy blow.

Other protective provisions remained in force for the time being, with one exception. By decree of the CPC of the USSR of October 25, 1940.[119] underground work by women in mines was officially permitted (except for some particularly strenuous jobs). The imminence of war was clearly felt in this decree.

Wartime and Postwar Development

Soviet laws for the protection of labor had begun to go on a war footing in 1940. The war brought further relaxation and curtailment of labor safeguards. The first steps immediately followed the Nazi invasion. On June 26, 1941, exactly a year after

[117] *Izvestiya*, June 27, 1940.
[118] *Ibid.*
[119] *Laws and Ordinances*, 1940:730.

the reintroduction of the eight-hour day and 48-hour week, the
Presidium of the Supreme Soviet of the USSR issued a decree
"on the wartime regulation of hours for wage and salary earners," [120] providing for mandatory overtime up to three hours a
day.

This decree abolished the last vestiges of the authority originally conferred upon trade unions and labor inspectors in
scheduling overtime. Management received discretionary powers
to order it—but, as the decree put it, "with the consent of the CPC
of the USSR." Of course, the supreme government agency could
not bother with overtime schedules in the scores of thousands of
plants and plant departments. The limitation had not the slightest practical meaning and was simply ignored in the plants. Apparently, its only purpose was to counteract the impression that
management could now regulate hours at will. The 10- or 11-hour
day and the 60- or 66-hour week were soon the rule.

The decree of June 26, 1941, also suspended the ban on
overtime work for juveniles under 18, which had remained on
the books. Most teen-age wage and salary earners were put on the
time schedules for adult workers; only children under 16 were
prohibited from doing more than two hours overtime a day.

The formal ban on overtime by pregnant women and nursing mothers stood up somewhat better. Under the decree of June
26, pregnant women were exempted from overtime work from
the sixth month of pregnancy; nursing mothers for six months
after delivery. A decree of July 8, 1944,[121] forbade overtime work
for pregnant women from the fifth month of pregnancy.

Unlike the decree of the previous year, which kept actual
earnings from rising as a result of longer hours, the decree of
June 26, 1941, provided for general payment of time and a half
for overtime. Thus the double time rates which the Labor Code
set for all overtime work exceeding two hours a day were abolished; but a considerable increase in actual daily and weekly
earnings had at least become possible and legally permissible.

Vacations also felt the impact of the trend. The decree of
June, 26, 1941, canceled all regular vacations for the duration,
substituting cash bonuses as a compensation. But in April, 1942,

---

[120] *Izvestiya*, June 27, 1941.
[121] Decree of the Presidium of the Supreme Soviet of the USSR of July 8,
1944, *Izvestiya*, July 9, 1944.

payment of these bonuses was also stopped, as inflationary; employers were directed to deposit corresponding amounts into blocked savings accounts of the workers and employees bearing 3 per cent interest.[122]

These orders were reissued for 1943 and 1944[123] and remained in force until July 1, 1945, when the prewar vacation rules were reestablished.[124]

Restoration of the prewar rules on hours was more complicated. The ten- and eleven-hour day had yielded only short-lived economic results, with the workers ill-fed and living conditions generally deteriorating. By the end of the third war year even plant management began to lose interest in ten- or eleven-hour schedules. From mid-1944 on, the reintroduction of eight-hour schedules started in individual plants. Legislation, however, failed to follow suit.

The provisions of June 26, 1941, were not rescinded; but the press on several occasions mentioned plants which had returned to the eight-hour day. Important war plants took the lead; President P. Borisov of the Automobile Workers Union said in an article on the plenary session of the union's central board in September, 1944:[125]

"Right now the most advanced plants pursue a policy of reducing overtime by improved organization of work and further increases in productivity, and of getting fewer men to produce more within the framework of the eight-hour day. The initiative was taken by the Stalin Automobile Works in Moscow. In their foundry departments, the experiment of strictly limiting overtime while simultaneously improving the organization of work has been fully justified. . .

"The plenary session of the union's central board enjoined all union organizations to do their utmost . . . to cut down overtime. In the future, in evaluating the results of nation-wide socialist competition, not only output, costs, and quality of production will be taken into account but also the observance of days off and the extent of overtime."

---

[122] Decree of the Presidium of the Supreme Soviet of the USSR of April 9, 1942, *Vedomosti Verkhovnogo Soveta*, April 24, 1942.

[123] Decree of the Presidium of the Supreme Soviet of the USSR of January 9 and December 22, 1943, *Vedomosti Verkhovnogo Soveta*, January 16 and December 31, 1943.

[124] Decree of the Presidium of the Supreme Soviet of the USSR of June 30, 1945, *Vedomosti Verkhovnogo Soveta*, July 7, 1945.

[125] *Trud*, September 6, 1944.

Soon *Trud* reported another sucessful experiment in converting a war plant to the eight-hour day; [126] similar news items
followed in rapid succession.[127] For the duration of the war these
were exceptions, however. It was only after the end of the war—
in the second half of 1945—that the eight-hour day spread rapidly.
Overtime work remained frequent, but it was no longer the
"normal" overtime of the war years which had made the ten- and
eleven-hour day the rule. As far as can be ascertained, the decree
of June 26, 1941, has never been formally repealed (save for the
vacation clauses), but in practice it was soon tacitly held invalid.[128]

There was a return to the legislation of 1940, i.e., to the
eight-hour day and the 48-hour week. After the war, overtime no
longer seemed to find the wide prevalence that had characterized
the 1930's. Longer normal hours, and the weakened physical condition of the workers after wartime privation and post-war distress, made the widespread overtime work that had marked the
First and Second Five-Year Plan periods in particular seem
scarcely possible. Still, there were a few striking instances, one
of which deserves to be cited:

On April 24, 1946, the Minister of Transportation ordered
extensive overtime work and work on days off, to provide for a
total of 2,415,000 additional work days. The Minister's order
was followed by scores of directives form his subordinates. Three
Sundays in one month—from June 15 to July 15—became work
days on the Northern Railroad. Railroad workers of the Velikiye-
Luki district did not get a single day off in June or July. In July,
railroad workers of the Volga region were ordered to work on
their days off with their families [*sic!*] for at least two days, for
track repairs.

During the war, such things were taken in stride. Now that
the war was over they caused considerable grumbling which even
found a muffled echo in the press. The Minister of Transportation at last rescinded his order on August 15.[129]

In all other fields of labor protection the general decline—

---

[126] *Trud*, October 4, 1944.
[127] *Trud*, October 26, November 25, December 7 and 10, 1944.
[128] This attitude was clearly expressed by AUCTUC Chairman Vasili V. Kuznetsov at the Fourteenth Plenary Session of the AUCTUC in December, 1945,
and left its imprint on the resolution passed by the session upon hearing his report. Cf. *Trud*, December 7, 1945, and January 24, 1946.
[129] *Trud*, July 31 and August 21, 1946.

which, along with the waning influence of the labor inspection, had been characteristic of the prewar trend—continued during the war. After the war, a certain leveling-off in this field seemed to be in the making.

APPENDIX

Conflict Between Union and Economic Authorities
Over Protection of Labor, 1935

The decline of labor protection in the 1930's left a singular memorial in a polemic between two official publications: *Trud,* the official newspaper of the trade unions, and *Za Industrializatsiyu,* the official organ of industry. The clash occurred in April and May, 1935, and concerned conditions in the "Red Profintern," a large plant manufacturing railway cars and locomotives in Bezhitsa (later Ordzhonikidzegrad) near Bryansk.

As early as December, 1934, the AUCTUC had sent an inspecting team to Bezhitsa to study conditions on the spot. The findings were released in *Trud* on December 14, 1934:

"... Systematic violation of the labor laws has become the rule in the 'Red Profintern' plant. Speed-up, unlawful overtime, work on days off—these are the means by which management time and again seeks to make up for mistakes in planning.

"For some categories of workers the work day is methodically lengthened to ten or twelve hours. Unlawful overtime is a mass phenomenon. Days off are continuously made work days, without giving the workers a chance to rest on other days. Overtime, as a rule, is not paid at all [i.e., not at overtime rates]. Scores of workers do not get a day off for months ...

"Anyone failing to report for overtime work is threatened with dismissal [apparently, punitive dismissal for infraction of work discipline]."

Unsatisfactory safety conditions were particularly stressed:

"The Labor Code and the provisions of safety protection are binding upon everyone, but not on the management of this giant plant. Negligence in technical supervision; congestion on the factory premises; movable parts unprotected by safety devices; failure to instruct the workers in accident prevention—all this resulted in a 21 per cent increase in the accident rate in the 'Red

Profintern' plant in one year. The accident rate goes up from quarter to quarter."

Did the plant lack funds for the prevention of accidents? According to the report, it had a safety fund of 140,000 rubles at its disposal in 1934. But from January through September only 32,289 rubles, less than one-quarter of the annual budget, actually was spent on safety devices. "The root of the evil," said *Trud*, "is not lack of funds but arbitrary negligence on the part of management in regard to the protection of labor."

The report concluded:

> "When the trade union agencies in the plant sought to discuss these abuses, they were accused by management of hampering fulfillment of the production program. That cooled them off."

After these public disclosures, the Bezhitsa City Committee of the CPSU directed the plant management to take remedial action. Weeks passed, but nothing changed. Four months later the AUCTUC sent another investigating committee to Bezhitsa. "A plant where disregard of labor laws is a daily occurrence," was the headline under which *Trud* printed the second committee report on April 11, 1935. Since December, the committee reported, conditions in the plant had deteriorated; a real orgy of overtime had set in:

> "To clean the factory yards, three days off were turned into work days in March, with the consent of the plant committee. During the same month, the crew of the machine shop and of the heavy freight-car department had no days off at all. In the latter department, two work gangs worked two shifts daily from February 1 to March 20, without a single day off in the whole period."

The committee found the reasons for these abuses "in the disrespect for 'the living man,' in the failure to understand the relationship between working conditions and the productivity of labor." The committee went on to say: "The plant management and the trade union organizations in the plant . . . preferred to fulfill the plan by taking the roundabout way of violating labor law."

The AUCTUC decided to act. One of its secretaries, V. Polonsky, and several leading officials of the labor inspectorate were sent to Bezhitsa. It was suggested that the Central Board of the Union of Workers in the Manufacture of Transpotration Machinery go to Bezhitsa to take the necessary steps on the spot. *Trud* announced twice that the secretary of the AUCTUC would be accompanied to

Bezhitsa by "the First Deputy of the Public Prosecutor of the Republic, Comrade Degot'." For many years, no labor dispute had received so much attention.

For a while the press of the economic administration did not enter the discussion at all. It was not until April 20, 1935, that *Za Industrializatsiyu* spoke up and launched the counter-offensive in an article entitled "The Disorganizers." It explicitly hit at those who insisted on compliance with labor legislation and thus, as the paper put it, "hampered one-man management." AUCTUC investigators who had alerted public opinion were undisguisedly denounced as saboteurs of production:

> "In March, for the first time in years, the plant over-fulfilled its production program. Morale went up. Workers, foreman, department heads had become firmly convinced that it was perfectly possible to carry out the program. And just at this time there appeared the 'helpers' from the ranks of the trade union movement . . . ."

In the Soviet Union, the charge of sabotage is an unanswerable argument. The accused quickly lose courage. Besides, *Za Industrializatsiyu* spoke in a vein that left no doubt that its accusations would be backed from higher up. On the very next day the industry newspaper could report with visible gratification: "The Deputy Public Prosecutor of the Republic, Comrade Degot', will not go to Bezhitsa, there being no reason why he should."

Trud, however, was not yet sufficiently intimidated. Its disclosures continued. Still more abuses of the "Red Profintern" management came to light. The trade union newspaper was able to report that the general manager had reprimanded several top executives for failure to observe the labor laws, and that the labor inspectorate had instituted disciplinary action against a number of plant officials. At a special session of the Central Board of the Union of Workers in the Manufacture of Transportation Machinery, held in Bezhitsa, AUCTUC Secretary Polonsky stated:

> "The unions have every reason to go to court against a number of plant officials. Yet Comrades Fushman and Stein [respectively, the head of the Main Board for Railway-Car Manufacture and the general manager of the 'Red Profintern'] assured us that all infractions of labor legislation will be eliminated with the utmost energy, and promised to take the severest action against anyone failing to observe the labor laws."

This alone, said Polonsky, had made the unions refrain from taking the plant executives into court.

Za Industrializatsiyu pursued its offensive against the trade union paper without paying attention to these facts. It continued to denounce the "disorganizers."

The effect was not long in coming. In early May, the *Trud* articles began to waver, then they were discontinued. For two weeks the trade union newspaper remained mute, and when it regained the power of speech on May 23 it was only to renounce all its heroic perseverance. An editorial announced under a sensational title: "Order Must Be Made in the 'Red Profintern' Plant!" The *Trud* editors took up the reasoning of *Za Industrializatsiyu,* which they had repeatedly and convincingly refuted; they even outdid the industry paper. They said in so many words that the unions had not "remembered" safety conditions in the plant until management had begun a serious drive for fulfillment of the production program. They denounced the unions for waging war on men "who had enabled the plant to recover."

Now *Trud* said that the *Trud* reports from Bezhitsa had "confused public opinion in the plant"; objections to overtime had been nothing but an "unprincipled scuffle over questions of detail in labor protection"; those who had taken up the fight "had become mouthpieces of the most backward elements in the plant, and in reality had headed the resistance against its reorganization"; *Trud*'s own editorials had been "politically wrong and harmful"; the union's labor inspectorate had pursued "aims hostile to the state," etc., etc.

What had happened to make the trade union paper reverse its position? A number of "Red Profintern" executives had been punished for the very labor-law violations exposed in *Trud,* whose exposure was now called a crime against the government. All charges against these executives had been discussed at hearings before the City Bureau of the CPSU, as well as at a public session of the Central Board of the Union of Workers in the Manufacture of Transportation Machinery, held in Bezhitsa in the presence of the head of the Main Board for Railway-Car Manufacture, the general manager of the plant, and the leaders of the Provincial Committee of the CPSU. In all these proceedings the charges originally made by *Trud* were corroborated in all important points. Why then the capitulation? What was it that made the trade union newspaper desert a cause which it had so brilliantly espoused? What made the valiant editors disown the truth, recant heresies, impugn their own motives, and don sackcloth and ashes in public?

The enigma was solved the following day. *Za Industrializatsiyu* printed a dispatch from Bezhitsa which said that a local paper, *Bezhitski Rabochi (Bezhitsa Worker),* on May 23rd had carried a resolution passed by the CC of the CPSU—not released in Moscow papers—

"severely censuring the union organizations in the plant and the labor inspectorate of the Union of Workers in the Manufacture of Transportation Machinery, for having taken an opportunistic attitude instead of combatting the supporters of tendencies hostile to the state." The dispatch said the CC resolution blamed *Trud* for having printed "a series of non-Bolshevik articles" on conditions in the "Red Profintern" plant. That was enough.

That was the last time a discussion of this kind find its way into Soviet publications. The fate of safeguards for labor was sealed.

Chapter Seven

SOCIAL INSURANCE

*Productivity, not Security, Becomes the Goal.—Health Insurance.
— Maternity Insurance. — Disability Insurance. — Survivors'
Insurance. — Old-Age Insurance. — Financing of Social Insur-
ance. — Organization of Social Insurance.*

Productivity, not Security, Becomes the Goal

From the early years of the Soviet regime social insurance was
the mainstay of the government's social policy. In the 1920's, all
the different forms of social insurance were brought together into
one uniform system of social security. At that time, social insurance had one indisputable aim: to give security to wage and salary
earners by insuring them against all the hazards threatening their
ability to earn a living.

One particular branch, health and maternity insurance, was
so widely developed in the Soviet Union that in some respects it
outdid what was provided in this way by the best social insurance
systems of other countries. Other insurance branches—unemployment, permanent disability, and old-age—lagged behind. But it
remained the government's goal to develop, expand and improve
them to the extent permitted by general economic conditions, in
order to assure a maximum of security to all working people.

This basic principle was abandoned when the Five-Year
Plans were inaugurated. The notion that social insurance had in
the first place to promote the security of the insured was rejected
as "opportunistic." Here, too, maximum production became the
prevailing consideration. This paralleled the revision of the legislation protecting labor (cf. Chapter Six above) and the revision
of trade union policies—a change of policy aimed in both instances at bringing about an incrase in productivity.

The revision of the principles of social insurance was first formulated—in a somewhat equivocal fashion—in a resolution of the CC of the CPSU dated September 28, 1929. The CC said that the main task of social insurance now was "to promote, by all possible means, further increases in the productivity of labor on the basis of the general plan for the industrialization of the country." But along with this new principle, the idea was that "improved security provisions for the groups forming the main cadres of the proletariat" were imperatively needed.[1]

At first, the resolution of the CC was kept secret. But the ideas which it incorporated soon found expression in the press.[2] It was emphasized time and again that social insurance must be made into an efficient instrument of industrialization. In November 1930 the Seventh All-Union Conference of Labor Agencies adopted a lengthy document dealing with "the present state and current tasks of social insurance," [3] wherein the fundamental principle which was henceforth to guide social insurance was presented as follows:

> . . . .Social insurance agencies must so readjust themselves, so reorganize their work, as by their practical operation to advance in the highest degree the successful accomplishment of socialist construction and the improvement of work discipline.

Official writers zealously developed the idea. "During the recovery period,[4] social insurance was an institution for securing the welfare of the working class. Today, in this socialist period, more is required of social insurance than 'security'; social insurance must now serve the purpose of the socialist offensive." To be able to do this, "social insurance must free itself of the vestiges of the old epoch . . . must slough off opportunistic theories," etc.[5]

---

[1] The resolution of the CC of the CPSU of September 28, 1929 was not made public until two years later, in M. Savel'yev and A. Poskrebyshev, *Directives of the CPSU in Economic Questions,* Moscow-Leningrad, 1931, pp. 589-593.

[2] Cf. especially articles by V. Kotov (Director of the Central Office for Social Insurance), "The Class Line in Social Insurance Policy," *Izvestiya,* October 19, 1929, and "Socialist Construction Requires Clarity in the Field of Social Insurance," *Voprosy Strakhovaniya,* 1929, no. 44, p. 1 ff.

[3] *Voprosy Truda,* October-November 1930, pp. 148 ff.

[4] The "recovery period" was the period of the restoration of the productive forces destroyed in the course of war and civil war; as distinguished from the "reconstruction period," the era when the national economy, having been restored to prewar level, was to be transformed by the Plans.

[5] B. T., "Social Insurance During the Period of Reconstruction," *Voprosy Truda,* January 1931, pp. 16 f.

"The task of social insurance lies in the many-sided, unre-
mitting daily struggle for increasing the yield of labor . . . This
must be the chief content of social insurance work. This is a point
of honor for social insurance agencies, for all social insurance
officers. This is their foremost duty, and by its execution their
performance will have to be judged . . ." [6]

How this attitude influenced the development of social insurance can best be seen from the analysis of developments in the
individual insurance fields.[7]

Health Insurance

Under the Labor Code of 1922 all wage and salary earners
were entitled, in the event they fell ill, to insurance benefits equal
to the amount of wages or salaries they would have earned had
they been able to work. In principle, then, sick benefit were com-
putable as full wages. Actual practice limited the benefits enjoyed
by different categories of workers, particularly wage earners only
temporarily employed (who could not only be "partly insured"). [8]
Still, at the end of the 1920's the overwhelming majority of wage
and salary earners were entitled to sick benefits equivalent to their
full wages (up to a fixed maximum).

The right to receive sick benefits equivalent to full wages
underwent various changes over the years. In the first place,
there was a general limitation which permitted payments of benefits based on wage income up to a fixed limit. This upper limit
was fixed at 120 to 180 rubles monthly (according to different
regional wage zones) in 1927, and raised to 150-180 rubles in
1929.[9] Until 1929 this limitation was of minor importance.[10] It

---

[6] A. Ya., "Social Insurance in the Last Year of the Five-Year Plan Period,"
Voprosy Truda, May-June 1931, pp. 104 ff.

[7] Unemployment insurance will not be dealt here as it was definitively abandoned in October 1930. For earlier developments, see Chapter Two above.

[8] The total number of wage and salary earners in 1928 was 11,522,000. Excluding those non-insurable (for the most part, agricultural and lumber workers),
the total number of persons insured was 9,865,000 of whom 9,234,000, or 93.6 per
cent, were fully insured. The remaining 631,000 (6.4 per cent) were only partly
insured, and enjoyed varying benefits according to their classification. (*National
Economy of the USSR. Statistical Year-book*, issued by the Central Statistical
Office, Moscow-Leningrad, 1932, pp. 411, 419).

[9] Decisions of the Social Insurance Council of the USSR of May 9, 1927 and
October 19, 1929, in *Izvestiya Narkomtruda*, 1927, p. 343; 1929, p. 744.

[10] According to I. F. Engel, *Social Insurance in the USSR*, Moscow, 1929, p.
20, average monthly *per capita* earnings for all groups of wage and salary earners

became more important when wages went up owing to inflation. In 1931, the fixed maximum was scrapped.

Other devices to limit sick benefits were more effective. Insured workers who claimed sick benefits over an extended period of time often were reclassified after a while (generally at the expiration of a two-month period) as "temporarily incapacitated," whereupon they were paid benefits at substantially lower rates.[11] The People's Commissariat for Labor repeatedly sought to check such practices; [12] apparently they were widespread.

Another means of reducing sick benefits was provided by a legislative act of December 28, 1927.[13] The Social Insurance Council of the USSR was granted the power, "in case of insufficient available social insurance funds, to reduce benefit rates by no more than one-third, for the entire territory of the Soviet Union, or for individual regions, or for individual categories of wage and salary earners." It does not appear that the Social Insurance Council made much use of this provision.

Soon all these rather minor limitations lost most of their significance. In 1931 the entire health insurance system was reorganized, and the principle of granting benefits equal to the full amount of wages lost through illness was restricted in a different fashion.

The aforementioned secret resolution of the CC of the CPSU of September 28, 1929 had only guardedly hinted at the desirability of imposing restrictions upon health insurance. It demanded the exercise by physicians and fellow workers of "more rigid control" over the granting of sick leave, and recommended "preferential treatment to production workers with respect to admission to resorts, sanatoriums and rest homes." In November

---

in the year 1927/28 came to 63.84 rubles, as compared with an average monthly sick benefit of 63.50 rubles. In practice, the limitation of benefit payments to a fixed maximum was rendered even less important by the fact that in some collective bargaining agreements (though probably not in many) it was stipulated that the plants would compensate the insured for any difference received. Cf. V. M. Dogadov, *Social Insurance, Foundations of Soviet Legislation Governing Social Insurance*, Moscow, 1928, p. 30.

[11] N. A. Vigdorchik, *Social Insurance, A Popular Exposition*, Moscow, 1927, p. 182.

[12] The last instance I know of such an attempt is the directives of October 8, 1929 (cf. *Izvestiya Narkomtruda*, 1929, p. 723).

[13] Decree of the CEC and the CPC of the USSR "concerning benefits to be paid by social insurance agencies," in *Laws and Ordinances*, 1928:33. Less specifically formulated, the idea of differentiating benefit rates had already been included in the Labor Code of 1922 (Sec. 182).

1930 the Conference of Labor Agencies made more specific recommendations. Pointing to the "enormous amounts" spent on
sick benefits, it spoke of the "great harm" this did to the nation's
economy; this, the conference said, as well as the necessity to "increase the workers' output," called for improvements in hygiene
and prevention of illness, and for rigid checks on patients' claims.
That all this was supported by purely economic arguments was
indicative of further changes to come. The projected reorganization of health insurance had begun.

On October 19, 1929 the Social Insurance Council of the
USSR decided that full compensation was to be granted only in
cases of sickness incapacitating the beneficiary for more than fifteen days.[14] In cases of shorter incapacitation, full benefits were allowed only for production workers in industry and transportation
workers (rail and waterways), and this again only on condition that
the beneficiary had been employed over a period of no less than
three years; all other insured were paid 75 per cent of wages lost
during the first five days of disability, and full compensation from
the sixth day on.

The practical importance of this provision was not great.
What mattered was the revision of insurance principles. For the
first time, benefits were made dependent on length of employment (though length of service in the last job was as yet not a
factor).

The ground was thus prepared for further changes. The
AUCTUC, at its plenary session in January 1931, formulated a
concrete program for making productivity the chief consideration
and goal of social insurance.[15] It laid down a rule requiring benefit rates to be determined not only according to total length of the
applicant's employment as a wage or salary earner, but also according to his length of service at his last place of employment.
Full compensation from the first day of illness would be paid
only to union members who could prove that they had been employed for more than three years, and that they had been working
at their present job for more than two years. Union members who

---

[14] Decision concerning "changes in and amendments to regulations governing
benefit payments in cases of temporary disability," *Izvestiya Narkomtruda*, 1929,
p. 744.

[15] *Pravda*, February 6, 1931. It was later asserted that Stalin himself had
fathered this AUCTUC resolution (cf. *Material on the Report Submitted by the
AUCTUC to the Ninth Trade Union Convention*, Moscow, 1932, p. 85).

did not meet these requirements were entitled during the first twenty days of disability to benefits amounting to 66.7 to 75.0 per cent of their total wages; those employed at their present jobs less than one year, to 66.7 per cent of their wages for the entire period of their disability.[16] Non-Union members were worse off. They were entitled to benefits, during the first month of disability, equal to only half their pay; only after the first month could they get benefits equal to 66.7 per cent of their wages.

Special provisions regulating benefits paid to shock workers were far more liberal.

Length of employment was also made a criterion for admission to health resorts, sanatoriums and convalescent homes.

At its session of January 1931 the trade union leadership also projected a new system of organization. Special insurance funds were to be created "for the main divisions of heavy industry (coal mining; mining of iron ore; metallurgy; machine-building; chemicals) and railroad transportation." These special insurance agencies were to exist apart from the regionally organized insurance system. The intention was to assure privileged financing to insurance agencies caring for wage and salary earners in industries considered the most important under the national economic plan; this was to be done at the expense of the general insurance organization.

Seven special funds (including a special seventh fund for persons employed by the waterways) were established in 1931. Their disbursements, as provided for in the 1932 budget for social insurance, compares as follows with the disbursements of the regional funds of the general insurance system:[17]

---

[16] Less stringent eligibility requirements applied to juvenile workers; to insured who had taken new jobs at the direction of the authorities; and to those employed in plants only recently placed in operation.

[17] Data from *Voprosy Truda*, May-June 1932, p. 109, where many more details can be found. Statistics on the amount of sick benefits paid out per person were not published.

	Medical	Disbursement per Person Insured (Rubles) Day Nurseries, Kindergartens, Special Diet for the Sick	Number of Referral Slips Issued for Admission to Resorts, Sanatoriums and Convalescent Homes, per 1,000 Insured
Special Funds for:			
Coal industry	53.05	39.06	224.9
Iron ore mining	44.08	44.35	170.8
Metallurgy	49.92	36.10	197.4
Machine building	44.56	29.94	146.8
Chemicals	50.28	33.73	175.8
Railroads	38.41	28.97	90.8
Waterways	47.42	37.83	90.8
Regional funds, average	24.28	10.96	46.4

The plan of reorganization drafted by the AUCTUC became law on June 23, 1931.[18] The new regulations made the limitation of benefit payments to a fixed maximum virtually meaningless. On July 20, 1931, this limitation on benefit payments was abolished for manual workers and technical employees in the socialized sector of the national economy; and the fixed maximum for benefits paid to all other insured (the bulk of non-manual employees) was raised to 300 rubles monthly.[19]

This system of organization, however, was again altered when the People's Commissariat for Labor was dissolved in 1933. The Commissariat's function were transferred to the trade unions, and individual insurance funds were so organized as to conform to the economic and industrial divisions in the trade union organizations.

The plenary session of the AUCTUC which deliberated on the reorganization of health insurance in June 1933, emphasized that social insurance had to provide for "shock workers and union members who have been employed for a considerable length of time, in the first place and to a higher degree" than it had to

[18] Decree of the CEC and the CPC of the USSR "on social insurance" in *Laws and Ordinances*, 1931:283.
[19] Decision of the Social Insurance Council, *Izvestiya Narkomtruda*, 1931, p. 507.

provide for all other wage and salary earners. This again applied
not only to benefits paid out, but also to admission to health resorts, sanatoriums and convalescent homes, and to the admission
of children of the insured to day nurseries, kindergartens, etc.[20]

In submitting the new plan, Shvernik, first secretary of the
AUCTUC, went so far as to suggest that admission to such institutions should be confined "exclusively" to wage and salary earners
who were members of trade unions and employed at their present
jobs for at least two years; and among those mainly to shock
workers.[21] The periodical of the Social Insurance Council commented as follows: [22] "Social insurance legislation must become a
powerful stimulus for increasing the yield of labor, for developing socialist competition and shock work on the largest possible scale, for reconstructing everyday life according to socialist
principles; legislation must make social insurance concentrate
all its attention on socialist production."

These developments reached their climax in the act issued
conjointly by the CPC of the USSR, the CC of the CPSU and the
AUCTUC on December 28, 1938.[23] It dealt with "measures to
increase work discipline, improve social insurance operations, and
combat abuses in this field." This act, with some changes, is still
in force today.

It aimed in the first place at establishing stricter discipline in
the plants and reducing labor turnover. Provisions governing
eligibility for sick benefits were revised accordingly, length of consecutive employment in the last job being henceforth the paramount criterion. Hereafter benefit payments equal to full wages
were allowed only to workers employed on the last job not less
than six years. Employment from three to six years in the same
job entitled the insured to receive benefits equal to 80 per cent of
his wages; employment from two to three years, 60 per cent; employment less than two years, 50 per cent. These were the rates
for union members. Non-union members received benefits at half
the rates of union members in the same categories, i.e. 50, 40, 30,
or 25 per cent, respectively.

Another restriction of farreaching importance was added:

20 *Voprosy Strakhovaniya*, July-August 1933, p. 19.
21 *Op. cti.*, p. 16.
22 *Op. cit.*, p. 6.
23 *Laws and Ordinances*, 1939:1.

"Wage and salary earners dismissed for violations of work discipline or criminal acts, as well as those voluntarily quitting their employment, shall not be entitled to claim benefit payments in case of temporary disability before having worked for at least six months in their new place of employment." Workers guilty of infraction of work discipline and those whose only offense was having lawfully[24] quit their jobs were punished alike. A worker found "guilty" on these counts may not fall sick on the new job for half a year. If he does, his penalty is loss of wages without any claim to sick benefit.

These regulations remained unchanged for almost a decade. And then on August 9, 1948 a decree[25] of the Council of Ministers of the USSR placed still more rigorous limitations on the payment of sick benefits. Instead of the insured individual's having to have been employed for at least 6 years in his present job in order to claim benefits equal to the full amount of his wages, he now had to be employed for a minimum of 8 years. To receive 80 per cent of his wages, he had to have been employed from 5 to 8 years at his present job (instead of from 3 to 6 years, as required by the law of 1938); 60 per cent, 3 to 5 years (instead of 2 to 3 years); employment of less than 3 years' duration (previously it had been less than 2 years) meant receiving only 50 per cent of one's wages. Again, these rates applied to members of trade unions only; non-members received sick benefits at half these rates.

At the same time a fixed maximum for sick benefits was reintroduced—160 rubles per day—although it was of little practical significance.[26]

In addition to sick benefits, insured wage and salary earners are entitled, when they fell sick, to free medical treatment for themselves and their dependents. In 1917-19 the health insurance agencies had developed a network of health institutions which they owned and administered. But this was soon abandoned, medical care for the insured being merged with the general public health services supervised by the People's Commissariat for Health. Until 1937, funds allotted for public health services out

24 Voluntary quitting of employment, as penalized under this provision, was perfectly lawful until the enactment of the decree of June 26, 1940. Then only was it made a criminal act (see Chapter Three).
25 State Social Insurance. Collection of Laws, Ordinances, etc., published by the Central Council of Trade Unions, 1949, pp. 52-53.
26 Soviet Labor Law, 1949 (see Chapter Three, n. 121), p. 349.

of the general budget were supplemented by contributions from health insurance funds to the People's Commissariat for Health.[27]

The majority of sanatoriums and convalescent homes remained under the jurisdiction of social insurance agencies. From the early 1930's on, however, not public health and medical prevention but "socialist construction" was the principal goal of the administration of these institutions. The idea expounded by Shvernik in 1933, that sanatoriums and convalescent homes should primarily serve those who distinguished themselves in production became generally accepted and even left its mark on legislation.[28] Moreover, from the mid-thirties on, it became customary for plant executives and high administration officials to spend their vacations at sanatoriums and convalescent homes; as a result, many of these places (especially the best ones) often can no longer be considered as medical institutions; they are rather resorts for the high placed. An American newspaperman who stayed in such a sanatorium in 1941, just before Soviet Russia's entry into the war, wrote:[29] "A sanatorium here did not mean a place for sick people. It was for the well, to keep them well."

Generally speaking, health insurance covers the risk of "temporary disability." Sickness is the most common, yet not the only instance of such disability. Anyone prevented from working by some other causes may under certain circumstances claim benefits. When an insured person cannot report for work because of a contagious disease in his immediate surroundings certified by the public health authority, he is entitled to benefits. Or when somebody is sick in the family of the insured and needs his personal care, hospitalization not being possible and no one else in the family being available, the insured is also entitled to benefits.

Maternity Insurance

Insurance against temporary disability also applies to pregnancy and confinement. Under the Labor Code, women engaged in manual work might not perform any work during the last eight weeks of pregnancy, nor for eight weeks after delivery.

[27] On the financial setup of health insurance, see below.
[28] First in the decree of the CPC of the USSR of April 10, 1934 which established the social insurance budget for 1934, cf. *Laws and Ordinances*, 1934:152.
[29] Henry C. Cassidy, *Moscow Dateline 1941-43*, Boston, 1942, p. 35.

Throughout this sixteen-week period they were entitled to benefit payments equal to the full amount of wages lost. Women doing clerical or other non-manual work were entitled to these benefits for a period of six weeks before and six weeks after delivery.

In addition to these maternity benefits proper, the Labor Code provided for an "additional" payment for the layette amounting to one month's income according to average local wage rates; it also provided for "additional" payments to nursing mothers over a period of nine months at the rate of 25 per cent of the average local monthly wage. In both cases this meant that benefits were not computed on the basis of the actual income of the person insured, but on a uniform basis. Whereas to receive maternity benefits proper, one had to be insured oneself, "additional" benefits were also to be paid to non-insured women whose husbands were covered by the insurance.

Originally, eligibility for maternity, layette and nursing benefits was not dependent on the duration of employment of the insured wife or husband. This was changed in 1927. Thereafter, "additional" benefits were to be paid only to women who had been employed for a total of six months during the year preceding maternity leave. In the case of a non-insured woman, the law required the insured husband to have been employed for six months during the year preceding childbirth.[30] Another restriction was soon introduced making layette and nursing benefits payable only when the income of the insured did not exceed the fixed maximum for sick benefit payments[31] (in 1927, a monthly income of 120 to 180 rubles). Thus, better-paid wage and salary earners were made ineligible. When the fixed maximum for sick benefit payments was abrogated in 1931, eligibility for "additional" benefits was extended to all insured whose income did not exceed 300 rubles monthly.[32]

Eligibility for maternity benefits was also restricted by the CEC and the CPC of the USSR on December 28, 1927.[33] It was now made dependent on employment for a period of six months

---

[30] Decision of the Social Insurance Council dated January 13, 1927 in *Izvestiya Narkomtruda*, 1927, pp. 68 ff.

[31] Decision of the Social Insurance Council dated May 19, 1927, *Izvestiya Narkomtruda*, 1927, pp. 346 f.

[32] Decision of the Social Insurance Council dated August 11, 1931, *Izvestiya Narkomtruda*, 1931, p. 508.

[33] *Laws and Ordinances*, 1928:33.

during the year preceding maternity leave. When maternity insurance was restricted in 1931 in a different way in connection with the reorganization of social insurance, this eligibility requirement was scrapped.[34]

Maternity benefit rates for many years were actually in accordance with the terms of the Labor Code, compensation being provided for the full amount of wages lost. On the other hand, layette and nursing benefits were never paid in the amounts prescribed by law. In the 1920's they amounted to half the official rates—layette benefits to 50 per cent of the average local monthly wage; nursing benefits, for a period of nine months, to 12.5 per cent of the monthly wage.[35] From the early 1930's on these benefits were no longer computed on the basis of average local wage rates, but were fixed uniformly throughout the country at 32 rubles for the layette, and a total of 45 rubles as nursing benefits, i.e. 5 rubles monthly.[36] In 1936 layette benefits were raised to 45 rubles, and nursing benefits to a total of 90 rubles (10 rubles monthly).[37]

The reorganization of health insurance in 1931 made eligibility for maternity insurance, as in the case of sick benefits, conditional on length of employment. Only union members employed for a total of at least three years, including two years at the last job, were entitled to maternity benefits equal to the full amount of their wages. Payment of layette and nursing benefits was made dependent upon consecutive employment over a specified period immediately preceding maternity leave (or childbirth, in the case of the non-insured wife of an insured husband). The required minimum was four months for women shock workers, engineers, and technicians; eight months for other union members, and twelve months for non-union members.[38]

The act of December 28, 1938 cut the period covered by maternity benefits almost in half. In earlier years, it will be recalled, benefits were payable for eight or six weeks before and

---

[34] Decision of the AUCTUC dated November 5, 1933, quoted by R. Kats and N. Sorokin, *Social Insurance. Collection of Laws and Directives*, Moscow, 1935. pp. 99f.

[35] Vidgorchik, as quoted *supra* n. 11, p. 183.

[36] Decision of the Social Insurance Council dated April 17, 1932, in *Izvestiya Narkomtruda*, 1932, pp. 265ff.

[37] Decree of the CEC and CPC of the USSR dated June 27, 1936, "on the prohibition of abortion, the increase in benefits granted at childbirth, extension of the network of maternity hospitals, nurseries and kindergartens, the incrase in penalties for non-payment of alimony, and various changes in the divorce laws," in *Laws and Ordinances*, 1936:309.

eight or six weeks after delivery depending on the beneficiary's occupation. In 1936 this provision was liberalized and payments for eight weeks before and eight weeks after delivery were granted to all.[39] But the act of 1938 restricted payments to a period of five weeks before and four weeks after delivery.[40]

At the same time, eligibility requirements were made more rigid. Henceforth, only persons having been employed for seven consecutive months immediately preceding pregnancy leave qualified for maternity benefits. Other restrictions imposed by the act of December 28, 1938 on sick benefit payments did not, however, apply to maternity insurance, which continued to be ruled chiefly by the provisions enacted in 1931. Thus the two branches of insurance against temporary disability—health and maternity insurance—from this time on followed basically different courses so far as benefit rates were concerned.

The curtailing of maternity insurance by the law of December 28, 1938 was sharply felt when the war caused the number of working women to rise steeply. In addition, the question of the birth rate involved political considerations which from the middle of the 1930's attracted great interest and made it seem advisable to give greater protection to mothers. In the summer of 1944, therefore, a decree was issued by the Presidium of the Supreme Soviet of the USSR announcing a number of measures for promoting the natural increase of population, and also an improvement in maternity insurance.[41] Although benefits paid during pregnancy were still limited to five weeks, the benefit period after delivery was extended from four to six weeks; where delivery was "abnormal" and in cases of twins, this was prolonged to eight weeks. The same decree raised nursing benefits from 45 to 120 rubles; soon after, layette benefits were raised from 90 to 180 rubles. These regulations are in force today.

Shortly after the announcement of the law of July 1944, the

---

[38] See n. 36 above.

[39] See n. 37 above.

[40] See n. 23 above.

[41] Decree of July 8, 1944 "concerning an increase in the assistance furnished by the state to pregnant women, mothers of large families, and self-supporting mothers; extension of the protection afforded mothers and infants; introduction of the honorary title, 'Heroine-Mother,' and creation of the order 'Mother's Glory,' and of the honorary medal, 'Medal of Motherhood,'" *Izvestiya*, July 9, 1944. Cf. the author's article, "Concerning Divorce and Other Things (Decree of July 8, 1944)," in *Socialisticheskii Vestnik*, August 1944.

regulations governing eligibility for layette and nursing benefits were also liberalized. The minimum required period of employment immediately before going on pregnancy leave was reduced to three months (for the insured husbands of non-insured wives, the period of required employment immediately preceding childbirth was likewise reduced to three months). The maximum monthly income allowed those claiming "additional" benefits was raised to 400 rubles, and in February 1947 to 500 rubles.[42] These regulations, too, are in force today.

Disability Insurance

Under the Labor Code of 1922 all wage and salary earners permanently incapacitated through "accident, sickness or old age" were entitled to pensions (Sec. 187). This also applied to surviving members of the families of deceased workers who are unable to work (Sec. 189). Disability benefits were not conditional upon length of employment (or, of course, on payment of insurance premiums, as no premiums are paid by employees under the Soviet system of social insurance). Only in the case of old-age insurance ("insurance for disability resulting from old age," in the words of the Labor Code) was the CPC "to determine the length of employment consti uting the basis for a benefit claim."

Economic conditions were extremely unfavorable and these provisions remained on paper. They constituted a vaguely outlined program that was later realized in part but never in its entirety. A system of disability and survivors' insurance was set up in the course of the 1920's that was little influenced by these provisions of the Labor Code; it was supplemented at the end of the decade by a complicated system of old-age insurance.

Disability insurance covers individuals incapacitated by work accidents and occupational diseases and also those otherwise incapacitated. Eligibility requirements and benefit rates differ; those disabled by work accidents and occupational diseases enjoy preferential treatment. For clarity's sake the first category will be referred to as "accident disability" (including disability caused by occupational diseases, but excluding disability caused by accidents

---

42 *Soviet Labor Law*, 1946 (cf. Chapter Three, n. 120), p. 379; *Labor Legislation*, 1947 (cf. Chapter Three, n. 68), p. 275.

not connected with the work of the insured), and the second as "general disability."

Basic regulations issued by the Social Insurance Council on July 4, 1928[43] divided the two categories into six groups each, according to the "degree of incapacitation":

Group 1. Persons completely incapacitated and in need of special daily care.

Group 2. Persons completely incapacitated but not needing special care.

Group 3. Persons unable to work regularly, but able to do occasional or easy work providing an income of not more than 50 per cent of their regular previous earnings.

Group 4, 5, and 6. Persons whose disabilities involve a loss of income of 30 to 50 per cent (Group 4); 15 to 30 per cent (Group 5); or less than 15 per cent (Group 6).

Permanent allowances were granted to all six groups where incapacitation was the result of an accident at work or occupational disease; in cases of general disability, only to Groups 1, 2, and 3. No specified length of employment was required as a condition of eligibility in cases of accident disability, while in cases of general disability only those who could prove that they had been employed for a period of one to eight years (according to age at time of application) were entitled to benefits.

Benefit rates were computed as fractions of previous earnings, according to the following schedule:

Degree of Incapacitation	Disability Pensions as Fractions of Last Income	
	Accident Disability	General Disability
Group 1	1/1	2/3
Group 2	3/4	4/9
Group 3	1/2	1/3
Group 4	1/3	None
Group 5	1/6	None
Group 6	1/10	None

[43] *Izvestiya Narkomtruda*, 1928, pp. 421-439. All provisions governing accident disability were equally applicable to disability caused by occupational diseases. Diseases to be regarded as "occupational" were specifically listed, as for instance in the regulations of July 4, 1928. These were changed by a decision of the Social Insurance Council of January 4, 1929 (*Izvestiya Narkomtruda*, 1929, pp 165ff.) and a more flexible list of occupational diseases was issued, with the proviso that it should not be considered exhaustive. Local insurance agencies were directed to

In cases of general disability, a fixed maximum was set for income considered in determining pension rates—180 to 225 rubles monthly (according to regional wage zones). In cases of accident disability, no such maximum existed until March 21, 1929, when it was fixed uniformly at 225 rubles.[44]

As nominal wages increased rapidly, the ratio of disability allowances to wage earnings was less favorable than shown in the table above. The annual plan for 1928/29 envisaged an average monthly (general) disability allowance of 22.65 rubles, whereas the average monthly income of insured wage and salary earners was estimated at 67.87 rubles.[45] That is, disability allowances equalled one-third of the average earnings from wages and salaries; actually, then, the average pension corresponded to the rate provided for Group 3. Yet of all those then entitled to general disability allowances, only 40 per cent were in Group 3, whereas 53 per cent were in Group 2, and 7 per cent in Group 1.[46]

In the early 1930's this discrepancy between nominal pension rates and allowances actually paid increased rapidly with the inflationary rise in nominal wages. To a certain extent the situation was remedied, in the case of manual workers, by a provision setting a minimum amount for allowance payments. On February 29, 1932 the Social Insurance Council fixed the minimum monthly allowance for disabled manual workers in Group 1 at 30 to 40 rubles (depending on length of employment and kind of industry), and at 20 to 30 rubles in Group 2.[47]

The reorganization of social insurance carried out in 1931 with increased productivity as its goal had far reaching effects on disability insurance. But in contrast to health and maternity insurance, which had reached a high level in the 1920's and was now scaled down considerably, disability insurance was expanded. The CEC and the CPC of the USSR decreed on June 23, 1931:[48]

In order to improve disability, old-age and survivors' insur-

---

refer to central headquarters all cases in which a committee of medical experts had established that disability was caused by an occupational disease not included in the official list; in such cases central insurance agencies were empowered to grant pensions at the regular rates for accident disability.

[44] *Izvestiya Narkomtruda,* 1929, p. 266.
[45] I. F. Engel, "Problems of Disability Insurance and Financial Prospects of Social Insurance," *Voprosy Truda,* 1928, pp. 41 f.
[46] *Ibid.,* p. 46.
[47] *Izvestiya Narkomtruda,* 1932, p. 117.
[48] See n. 18 above.

ance, especially for workers employed in the most important industries (coal, metals, chemicals, etc.), the Social Insurance Council is directed to revise, within a month's time, the rules for disability, old-age and survivors' insurance and to provide for:

    (a) higher allowances and reduced length-of-employment requirements for workers employed at hard and hazardous work;

    (b) increased allowances according to length of employment in one particular industry;

    (c) preferential treatment for beneficiaries continuing to do salaried work.

The new rules were not issued by the Social Insurance Council within a month's time; it took the Council all of seven months to get them out. When they finally appeared on February 29, 1932,[49] they regulated disability insurance for years to come. Though subsequently altered in some respects, they still govern this field of social insurance.

The main feature of the new system was a modified classification of disability. For both general and accident disability only three groups were retained. Groups 1 and 2 of the new system were the same as 1 and 2 of the old; but Group 3 now embraced all persons "unable to work continuously at their former occupation under the conditions prevailing, yet able to make use of their residual work capacity either in occasional employment, or for a shorter work period, or in a different occupation requiring considerably fewer qualifications."

This complicated clause could have been interpreted to extend the limits of the new Group 3 to include (at least in part), in addition to the old Group 3, old Groups 4, 5, and 6. But apparently this was not intended, for interpretation of the clause in practice was restrictive. The new Group 3 embraced merely the old Group 3 and some of the beneficiaries of the old Group 4; this was made clear by an ordinance of the Social Insurance Council also issued on February 29, 1932 dealing with "the revision of pension claims of beneficiaries in Groups 4, 5, and 6."[50] All claims of beneficiaries in Group 4 were to be reviewed by the insurance authorities with a view to assigning them to the new

---

[49] *Izvestiya Narkomtruda,* 1932, pp. 117 ff.
[50] *Izvestiya Narkomtruda,* 1932, p. 217.

Group 3. But claims of beneficiaries in Groups 5 and 6 were to be reviewed only upon their making application for reclassification. The statistical results of the regrouping of disability claims were, as far as could be ascertained, never published.

Eligibility for pensions in cases of general disability was again, as in 1928, made contingent upon length of employment. Underground workers and those employed in other hazardous occupations qualified after having been employed for one to six years (according to age groups). All other manual workers had to prove employment of two to eight years, and non-manual workers two to twelve years (all according to age groups).[51]

Not only the establishment of the claim itself now hinged on length of employment; allowance rates did as well. In computing monthly pensions, beneficiaries were classed in four different categories. Category I included underground workers and workers employed in other hazardous occupations; II, workers in a number of specified important occupations; III, all other manual workers, and non-manual workers employed in production; IV, all other non-manual workers. Differentiation of allowance rates according to these categories increased in proportion to length of employment.

For beneficiaries unable to show a long period of employment, differences in rates set for individual categories were insignificant; pensions in Group 1 ranged from 67 to 69 per cent of previous regular income; in Group 2, from 47 to 49 per cent; in Group 3, from 33 to 35 per cent.

But if the disabled person had been employed as a wage or salary earner for a longer period of time, pension rates varied substantially, as additional allowances for longer employment differed considerably in the individual categories. In Category I, the maximum rate was granted to beneficiaries with an employment record of at least eighteen years; in Category II, the requirement was twenty-three years; in Category III, thirty-one years; in Category IV, thirty-four years. Likewise, different categories were

---

[51] In the case of salary earners, length of employment (1 to 12 years, depending on the applicant's age) had been made an eligibility requirement by the CEC and the CPC of the USSR as early as February 13, 1930 (*Laws and Ordinances*, 1930:132). The length of employment required in other categories, even more prohibitive than those required by the decision of 1932 discussed in the text, were set by the Social Insurance Council on February 11, 1930 (cf. *Voprosy Strakhovaniya*, 1930, no. 8, pp. 42 ff.).

assigned different maximum rates. For beneficiaries in Group 1, the highest rate in Category I was 100 per cent of the insured person's income; in Category II, 90 percent; in Category III, 80 per cent; in Category IV, 75 per cent. The highest rates in Group 2 were, according to category, 80, 70, 60, or 55 per cent, respectively; in Group 3, 66, 56, 46, or 41 per cent, respectively.

These rates applied to cases of general disability. In cases of accident disability, pension rates in all four categories were 100 per cent of income in Group 1, 75 per cent in Group 2, and 50 per cent in Group 3. In cases where long employment would have qualified the beneficiary of accident-disability insurance to a higher rate under the general-disability classification, he was granted the higher rate.

The new pension scale based rate differentials chiefly on total cumulative employment. But length of employment at one job was also taken into consideration: only if the beneficiary could prove that he had been employed in his last job for a period of no less than two years was long employment to count in the computation of the higher pension rate.

In cases of general and accident disability alike, a maximum of 300 rubles monthly was fixed for the amount of the claimant's income to be considered in computing his pension.

Finally, as in previous regulations, preferential treatment was accorded shock workers.

The provisions of 1932 were, in accordance with the general trend of Soviet labor legislation, unfavorable to non-manual workers, most of whom were automatically classified in Category IV. This was changed by a decision of the CPC of the USSR of July 31, 1937.[52] Henceforth salary earners were to be classified in the same categories as wage earners employed in the same industries; accordingly, Category IV was abolished. Eligibility requirements were also made identical for manual and non-manual workers.

A more sweeping change was introduced with the reorganization of social insurance on December 28, 1938.[53] Now particular stress was laid on consecutive employment at one job as a criterion for computing rate differentials for disability pensions, although total cumulative employment continued to determine the estab-

---

52 *Laws and Ordinances*, 1937:203.
53 See n. 23 above.

lishment of pension claims. Under the 1938 regulations, the disability claims of workers employed underground and in other hazardous occupations were contingent on cumulative employment of two to fourteen years (instead of one to six years, as was the case under the 1932 rules); in all other occupations, cumulative employment of three to twenty years for men, and two to fifteen years for women (instead of two to eight years for both sexes under the 1932 rules. Differing requirements for men and women represented a new phenomenon). At the same time all rate differentials based on total employment were abrogated and replaced by differentials based on length of service at the last job. The highest pension was assured beneficiaries in Category I after employment of more than ten years at their last job (25 per cent above the regular rate for this category); in Category II, after more than twelve years at their last job (20 per cent above the regular rate); in Category III, after more than fifteen years at their last job (also 20 per cent above the regular rate).

The regulation of December 28, 1938 also provided that monthly allowances for beneficiaries (both of disability and old-age insurance) in Group 1 were not to fall below 50 rubles; and in Group 2 not below 40 rubles. No minimum amount was set for Group 3 (nor had one been set in 1932). For beneficiaries with one dependent, minimum rates were set at 60 or 50 rubles; for beneficiaries with two or more dependents, at 75 or 60 rubles, respectively.

These regulations have remained unaltered in all essentials since 1938. In particular, the maximum of 300 rubles monthly allowed as the basis for computing pensions has been retained, despite the steep decline in the value of the ruble and rise in the level of nominal wages. To be sure, many exceptions are allowed to these rules: the maximum monthly income considered in computing pensions goes as high as 600 rubles for many privileged groups *plus* 20 per cent of their income above 600 rubles but not above 1,500 rubles monthly.[54]

Only a few of the new measures deserve mention. We have

---

[54] *Soviet Labor Law*, 1949 (cf. Chapter Three, n. 121), p. 340. If, for example, the income of an insured person is 1,200 rubles monthly, the entire amount of the first 600 rubles is considered in reckoning his pension, as well as an additional 120 rubles (20 per cent of the remainder of his monthly income). Thus this person, if he belongs to Category I and is entitled to the highest rate (100%), receives a pension of 720 rubles monthly.

already spoken of one (in Chapter III), which during the war required all disabled persons in Group 3 to return to work. After the war this regulation was abolished.

Another was the rise of disability pensions in connection with the sharp rise—almost a trebling—of regulated prices on September 16, 1946. If, as was shown in Chapter V, this last regulation worked a hardship on the lower and middle ranks of workers and employees, it worked much more of a hardship on pensioners. This rise in prices was partly cancelled out for pensioners residing in cities by their being allowed a general monthly increase of 60 rubles in their allotments.[55]

Finally, we should mention the very strict regulation concerning the reviewing of disability classifications, which keeps pensioners in a constant state of nervous tension. The disability classification of all male pensioners under 60 and all female pensioners under 55 is regularly reviewed—yearly, in the case of individuals belonging to Group 1; semiannually, in the case of individuals belonging to Groups 2 and 3.[56]

Survivors' Insurance

Survivors' insurance in the Soviet Union is an auxiliary department of disability insurance. It is based on the principle that not all survivors of the insured are to be treated as beneficiaries, but only those among them who are unable to work and who were dependent for their support on the insured. Under the Labor Code of 1922, children and brothers and sisters of the deceased under 16 years of age, as well as parents and the surviving husband or wife, were entitled to claim benefits; a surviving disabled husband's claim being equal to that of a surviving disabled wife.

According to regulations issued on March 14, 1928,[57] benefit claims of parents and husbands (wives) were not conditional upon evidence of the beneficiary's inability to work, provided that he (she) had reached the age of 60 (55). Additional regulations of October 31, 1928,[58] provided that brothers and sisters and children

[55] *Pravda*, September 16, 1946.
[56] *Soviet Labor Law*, 1949, pp. 342-343.
[57] Decree of the CEC and the CPC of the USSR, *Laws and Ordinances*, 1928:146.
[58] *Laws and Ordinances*, 1928:596.

of the deceased were entitled to benefits up to the age of 18 if attending an educational institution.

General provisions for survivors' insurance are similar to those for disability insurance. Survivors are entitled to benefits if the deceased provider was entitled to general or accident disability claims or would have acquired such title through the accident or disease which caused his death.

According to the regulations of February 29, 1932,[59] benefit rates were to be computed as percentages of the rates which the deceased, if he had lived, would have been entitled to in Group 2 of disability insurance. The accident-disability rate in Group 2 was at least 75 per cent of the beneficiary's last earnings, while general disability rates were 47 to 49 per cent, increasing to a maximum of 55 to 80 per cent. Survivors' pensions were to be computed as follows:

Number of Survivors Entitled to Claims	Pension Rates as Percentages of Disability Rates
4	125%
3	100
2	75
1	50

The reorganization of December 28, 1938 affected survivor insurance only to the extent that rate schedules for disability insurance were revised; all other provisions remained unchanged.

Old-Age Insurance

Not until 1928 were the first steps taken toward introducing old-age insurance. At that time there was still considerable unemployment; insuring wage and salary earners against the contingencies of old age aimed at the elimination of the elderly from the labor force. Accordingly, old-age insurance was introduced first for workers employed in industries where there was abundant supply of labor. The first to receive old-age benefits were manual

[59] See n. 49 above.

workers in the textile industry.[60] Later, a decree of May 15, 1929 [61] extended old-age insurance to manual workers in the mining and metallurgical industries, and on the railroads and waterways. The limitations of old-age insurance to these sections of the economy was considered to be temporary, and the Social Insurance Council was authorized to extend old-age insurance to all other categories of manual workers, and to non-manual workers, "in accordance with the Five-Year Plan for the development of the national economy of the USSR."

The authors of the First Five-Year Plan contemplated a gradual extension of old-age insurance to cover all wage and salary earners in industry, transportation and commerce, and all employees of the administration, including those in the educational and health services, by September 30, 1933.[62] This was done, step by step, though more slowly than had been contemplated, until a decree of the Council of People's Commissars of the USSR dated July 31, 1937 extended old-age insurance to cover all workers and employees without exception.[63]

At first, men were entitled to old-age benefits only upon reaching the age of 60; women, at 55. But an act of May 15, 1929 empowered the Social Insurance Council to lower the age limit in dangerous occupations; by the regulations of May 23, 1929,[64] miners employed underground were allowed to claim old-age benefits at the age of 50. Regulations of February 29, 1932 [65] set 50 years as the general age of retirement for all those working underground and in other hazardous occupations.[66] These regulations are still in force.

To attain a certain age was not enough, however, to qualify for old-age benefits. The first regulations on old-age insurance (which concerned textile workers only) made benefits conditional upon an employment record of 25 years for men and 20 years for

60 Decision of the Social Insurance Council of January 5, 1928, in *Izvestiya Narkomtruda*, 1928, pp. 40 f.

61 Decree of the CEC and the CPC of the USSR of May 15, 1929, in *Laws and Ordinances*, 1929:289.

62 *Five-Year Plan of Economic Construction of the USSR*, Moscow, 1929, vol. II, 2, pp. 195 f.

63 See n. 52 above.

64 Decision of the Social Insurance Council dated May 23, 1929 in *Izvestiya Narkomtruda*, 1929, pp. 405-409.

65 See n. 49 above.

66 This corresponds to Category I of the occupational classification introduced in 1932 (cf. n. 49 above) for disability insurance.

women, regardless of the industry in which they had been employed. Under the regulations of May 23, 1929, another requirement was introduced in addition to this. An applicant had to
prove continuous employment, for at least one year immediately
preceding the date of his retirement, in one or more plants of
industries covered by the insurance plan. The miners' privilege
of retiring at the age of 50 was made conditional upon total employment of 20 years and below-surface employment of no less
than 10 years.

These regulations were retained in subsequent years. Only
the requirement of one year's employment in industries covered
by the insurance plan was abandoned—when old-age insurance was
extended to cover all but a few categories of wage and salary
earners on February 29, 1932.

Originally, old-age benefits were granted only to applicants
who had actually retired. The rules laid down for textile workers
on January 5, 1928,[67] required an application to be considered
only if the worker was no longer employed in a textile plant. This
was still the basis of the act of May 15, 1929. Interpreting its provisions, N. Bykhovsky, presumably its author, wrote:[68] "The
specific purpose of the law is to eliminate old people from production... The new law has great importance for our unemployed
youth, who will have an opportunity to take the jobs vacated by
old people."

But when labor shortages developed late in 1929, this attitude
changed. Old people now were wanted on the jobs they held.
Under regulations issued on February 11, 1930,[69] old-age benefits
were approved when the applicant had either retired or—and this
was new—had been "transferred to a lower-paid job, even in the
same place of employment." Since skilled workers were scarce, it
was the government's intention to keep veterans in the plants; if
aging or disabled workers were given light work and allowed to
draw wages without having to relinquish old-age benefits, there
was a chance that they would stay on.

Subsequent regulations sought to introduce more effective
provisions to achieve the desired result. On November 26, 1930
the People's Commissariat for Labor of the USSR issued instruc-

---

[67] See n. 60 above.
[68] N. Bykhovsky, "Old-Age Insurance," in *Voprosy Truda*, March-April 1929,
pp. 118, 120.
[69] *Voprosy Stakhovaniya*, 1930, no. 8, pp. 47 f.

tions [70] directing all plant managers to "revise work schedules in such a way as to permit the assigning of lighter jobs to disabled workers." Attached was a long list of jobs in which disabled workers were to be employed "preferentially." The People's Commissariat for Labor wrote: "The rapid pace of socialist construction and the complete elimination of unemployment in our country require the employment of additional skilled labor in all divisions of the national economy." Employment of incapacitated workers, it added, was of particular importance for the "training and retraining of the labor force."

Two months later the Social Insurance Council decreed that "old-age benefits shall be granted regardless of whether the insured has given up the job in which he was employed prior to applying for the allowance." [71] But pension and wages together were not to exceed a specified limit; this restriction, however, was abandoned when all social insurance was reorganized. The law of December 28, 1938 stated:[72] "Insured who continue to work after having been granted old-age pensions shall receive said pension regardless of their earnings from salaried employment." It was explicitly stated that this was to apply to old-age pensions only and not to disability benefits.

The regulations of May 15, 1929 set the old-age pension at 50 per cent of the former earnings of the insured, with the same limitations in the computation of the allowance as in disability insurance proper. When the regulations of February 29, 1932, provided for pension differentials according to occupational categories, old-age pensions were set as follows: in Category I, 60 per cent of previous income; in Category II, 55 per cent; in Category III, 50 per cent. (The insured in Category IV, which category has since been abolished, were not entitled to pensions.)

Financing of Social Insurance

Immediately following the October Revolution, social insurance was broadened and improved. Later, at the end of 1918, social insurance was supplanted by a new system of "social secu-

[70] *Izvestiya Narkomtruda*, 1930, pp. 714 f.
[71] Decision of the Social Insurance Council of January 20, 1931 "concerning persons eligible for old-age pensions but continuing to work," *Izvestiya Narkomtruda*, 1931, p. 157.
[72] See n. 23 above.

rity" to be financed out of the national budget. But as early as November 1921 this was abandoned and social insurance reintroduced. The organizational structure was completed in 1922.

The provisions of the Labor Code of 1922 explicitly stated that care of the sick, disabled and unemployed wage and salary earners was to be guaranteed by social insurance; these provisions were never abrogated. Likewise, the provision is still in force which requires social insurance contributions to be computed "according to the hazards and dangers" of the work performed by the insured (Sec. 177). And Sec. 178 of the Labor Code states: "Insurance contributions shall be made by plants, institutions, establishments and persons employing wage labor, but these shall not have the right to charge such contributions to the account of the insured nor to deduct insurance contributions from the latter's wages."

This, then, is the essential feature of Soviet social insurance. Contrary to most social insurance systems in other countries, where contributions are made by employers and employees in a specified proportion, the insured wage and salary earners in the Soviet Union make no contributions to social insurance. Under a system which rigidly controls wages, this amounts to dividing wages into two parts—one part is paid to the employee, and the other to agencies of social insurance. And, in fact, the insurance contributions of the employer are considered a component of "socialized wages" (see Chapter Five above).

Another peculiarity of Soviet social insurance is the grading of contributions in all insurance divisions (with the sole exception of unemployment insurance) according to the "hazards and dangers" of the work performed, a criterion which in other countries applies to disability insurance or "workmen's compensation" only. Here the insurance principle has been carried farther in the Soviet Union than elsewhere.

The amount of contributions required from employers was repeatedly reduced. Originally, contribution rates were very high. There were four separate "funds": Fund A, covering health and maternity insurance; Fund B, disability and survivors' insurance; Fund C, unemployment insurance; Fund D, medical care. Contribution rates for all funds except C were divided into four grades depending on the hazards of work; these rates were from 6 to 9 per cent of wages in Fund A; from 7 to 10 per cent of wages in Fund B; and from 5 to 7 per cent of wages in Fund D. For Fund C, the rate was uniformly set at 2.5 per cent of wages.[73] Thus, the sum total of contributions for the four funds was 20.5 to 28.5 per cent of the pay roll.

In actual practice, however, contributions were never made in these amounts. Industrial establishments especially were slow in paying their insurance contributions, for they were just beginning to recover from the effects of the civil war when this system was introduced. They actually paid in to the social insurance funds about one-third of the amounts due.[74]

As arrears accumulated, contributions were reduced—for the first time, in the spring of 1923. On April 12, 1923 the CEC of the RSFSR promulgated a new "scale of contributions to social insurance"[75] that amounted to some 16 to 22 per cent of the payroll (varying in accordance with occupational hazards). In fact, however, the reduction was even more substantial. In addition to the four grades of contributions previously provided for, two new grades were established "temporarily" with "reduced" rates; all contributions added up to between 12 and 16 per cent of the payroll. Many government establishments and government-owned industrial plants contributed according to these reduced rates.

A further reduction was ordered by the CEC of the USSR on February 26, 1925.[76] Previous regular rates were maintained, but new "reduced" rates were to apply—temporarily again—to most government institutions and government-owned industrial plants. In industry and administration these reduced rates came to 10 per cent of the payroll, in transportation to 12 per cent.

Contribution rates, reduced and regular, averaged some 14 per cent of the aggregate payroll; for a while, actual contributions were maintained at this level. But average payments dropped every year, partly because the industries which were allowed reduced rates expanded more rapidly than others, and partly because more and more enterprises were allowed to contribute at the reduced rates. In October 1926, "temporarily reduced rates"

---

[73] These contributions were fixed by a series of decrees of the CPC of the RSFSR; for Funds A and B, on January 2; for Fund C, on January 12; for Fund D, on February 6, 1922 (cf. *Laws and Ordinances of the RSFSR*, 1922:34, 65, 176).

[74] L. V. Zabelin and Ya. R. Emdin, *Industry and Social Insurance*, Moscow, 1928, p. 53.

[75] *Laws and Ordinances of the RSFSR*, 1923:342.

[76] *Laws and Ordinances*, 1925:107.

applied to 62.5 per cent of all contributors to the funds; in October, 1927, to 63.7 per cent; in October 1928, to 65.7 per cent. Total insurance contributions (in percentages of aggregate payrolls) were as follows:[77]

	Per Cent Payroll
1924/25	14.4
1925/26	13.4
1926/27	13.1
1927/28	12.7

The decline in contributions was even greater, for the figures for 1926/27 and 1927/28 include additional contributions for housing construction that were not levied in previous years.

The provisions of February 26, 1925, reducing insurance rates introduced an organizational innovation—Funds A, B and C were merged. Soon a new fund was established. On December 31, 1926,[78] a levy to be used to finance housing construction for workers was decreed; it was to be paid by the employers along with their insurance contributions. The levy took 1.2 to 1.6 per cent of the payroll at regular rates; at reduced rates, .75 to 1.0 per cent. Another provision, introduced on August 17, 1927,[79] required social insurance agencies to contribute from their own funds to the fund for housing construction; this contribution was to amount to .5 per cent of the aggregate wages of the insured; .2 from the general health insurance fund (A, B and C) and .3 from the fund for medical treatment (D). These contributions for housing construction went to the economic administration and to the management of individual plants, to be used for whatever housing projects were under way.

In the following years this system of financing remained practically unchanged, although the decrease in the actual rate of contributions from employers continued. But in 1937 the entire system of financing social insurance was recast. On March 23, 1937 the CPC of the USSR enacted a decree concerning the

---

[77] Engel, as quoted *supra* n. 10, pp. 59 ff.
[78] Decree of the CEC and the CPC of the USSR, *Laws and Ordinances*, 1927:19.
[79] Decree of the CEC and the CPC of the USSR, *Laws and Ordinances*, 1927:489.

"elimination of various items of expenditure from the social insurance budget, and changes in the scale of contributions to social insurance." [80] This decree relieved social insurance agencies of the burden of financing medical treatment, housing construction and pensions to non-employed beneficiaries of disability, old-age and survivor insurance. Henceforth, the cost of these services was to be charged to government funds. Contribution rates were correspondingly reduced, ranging from 3.7 to 10.7 per cent of wages, according to jurisdiction of different unions.[81] Average total contributions amounted to some 7 per cent of the aggregate payroll, perhaps a little more: in 1938, actually 7.4 per cent; in 1940, 6.9 per cent.[82] Mention was no longer made of the "temporarily reduced rates" of 1925; contributions apparently were graded according to the insurance risk for the different categories of insured, although certain concessions were made to "leading" branches of industry.

In postwar years, repeated efforts were made to increase the amount of insurance contributions without having recourse to a general increase in rates. (This did not exclude a partial raising of rates as the result of various reclassifications within the limits of the current scale of rates.) Since 1947 the authorities have at various times issued decrees and ordinances pressing employers to remit their insurance contributions promptly and in full, and, in particular, to pay up their arrears.[83] Receipts of insurance contributions have in fact appreciably risen since 1946. Estimated receipts for 1946 were set at a figure of 11,655,000,000 rubles; in 1947, at 14,875,000,000 rubles; in 1948, at 15,650,000,000 rubles; and in 1949, at 17,491,000,000 rubles.[84] If, as was assumed above, average wages came to 5,000-5,200 rubles in 1947, and 5,200-5,400 rubles in 1948 and 1949, then planned receipts of insurance contributions in 1947 amounted to 9.1-9.5 per cent of wages; in

[80] *Laws and Ordinances*, 1937:88.

[81] In 1933 the administration of social insurance was transferred to the trade unions.

[82] In 1936 total contributions to social insurance amounted to 7,167,000,000 rubles; in 1940, to 8,518,000,000 rubles (cf. *USSR's Finances in the Thirty Years*, Moscow 1947, p. 178).

[83] A series of such decrees can be found in the collection entitled *State Social Insurance*, published by the Central Council of Trade Unions in Moscow, 1948, pp. 228-232.

[84] See the reports of Finance Minister Zverev to the Supreme Soviet of the USSR, *Pravda*, October 16, 1946; February 21, 1947; February 1, 1948; and March 11, 1949.

1948, to 8.7-9.0 per cent; and in 1949, to 9.2-9.5 per cent.[85] Our sources do not permit of a more detailed analysis of these figures.

Of the other changes affecting financing that resulted from the reorganization of social insurance on December 28, 1938, we need mention here only the one requiring social insurance agencies to resume the burden of the cost of caring for non-working disabled pensioners; they were not, however, granted an increase in receipts corresponding to this increase in their obligations.

To illustrate the kind and extent of disbursements of insurance funds, we give below, in a simplified form, the budget of expenditures for 1950:[86]

Type of Expenditure		Million Rubles
Benefits:		7,027
a. Sickness	5,050	
b. Maternity	1,535	
c. Layette	181	
d. Nursing	187	
e. Burial	74	
Pensions:		8,205
a. Non-working disabled	5,334	
b. Working disabled	1,971	
c. Working disabled veterans of the Fatherland War, Group 3 of the disability insurance	900	
Convalescent homes and sanatoriums		1,942
Children's camps and sanatoriums		886
Out-of-school child care		50
Sports and travel		135
Allowances for special diets		40
Special-purpose contributions to the state budget		569
Administrative costs, training of personnel, etc.		172
TOTAL:		19,026

---

[85] These figures are relatively high and are cited by those who take a more optimistic view of recent developments in wages in Russia (cf. Appendix 2 to Chapter V) as an additional argument in favor of their opinion. But if average wages in 1948 did in fact reach 7,400 rubles, as the "optimists" assume, then planned insurance contributions for the year amounted to only about 6.4 per cent of wages—a most unlikely figure.

[86] Taken from a more detailed table in A. Krasnopolsky, "The Nature of Soviet State Social Insurance," in *Sovyetskoye Gosudarstvo i Pravo*, June 1951, p. 65.

Organization of Social Insurance

Before the revolution of 1917 Russia had known only a modest system of health and accident insurance which had been established in 1912. Though limited in scope, the health insurance organization played a unique role.

At the time, the Russian labor movement had been driven underground. Nation-wide trade unions did not exist at all. The few local unions that there were had a total membership of scarcely more than 20,000-30,000 throughout the country. The establishment of a system of health insurance allowing for some measure (however limited) of self-administration by the insured, gave the labor movement an outlet for some of its energies. Thus there arose a new type of labor movement, the so-called workers' insurance movement, which aimed at improving and extending self-administration by the insured. In a few years large numbers of talented organizers and labor leaders made their appearance.

This period of struggle for the workers' right to organize was not without far-reaching effects on the workers' attitude to the problems of social insurance. Precise ideas as to what social insurance should be, and how it should be organized and administered, became generally accepted in labor circles. These ideas outlasted Tsarism. After the revolution organized workers fought for an integrated system of social insurance encompassing health and maternity, disability and accident, old-age and unemployment insurance, and based on democratic self-administration by the insured.

The Bolsheviks themselves had fought for these ideas before the revolution; they had to accept them when they came to power. In 1917 and 1918, social insurance was extended and improved, however poor may have been its actual achievements (save in the field of health and maternity insurance) in a time of economic disintegration. Great energy was displayed by the workers in setting up a democratic organization of social insurance.

Yet this democratic development soon clashed with the dictatorial system of government. Though the social insurance organization neither pursued political aims beyond its own sphere nor directly challenged the Bolshevik dictatorship, it stood for the free and independent organization of the working class and trained members in the use of freedom and self-government. The Communist Party's effort to "conquer" social insurance from within having failed completely, the Soviet Government in the fall of 1918 decided to put an end to autonomy in social insurance. Social services were taken away from the self-governing insurance agencies and entrusted to government agencies operating with government funds and endowed with the authority of the Soviet state.[87]

But the state welfare services did not operate satisfactorily and had to be abandoned. As mentioned before, social insurance was revived early in 1922. The Soviet Government sought to substitute the trade unions for the disbanded democratic organization of the social insurance system, trade unions were to build the new insurance structure. This, however, merely disguised Communist control of insurance, for the party had already established its control over the trade unions.

Social insurance, as then organized, was a complicated system, with the jurisdiction of insurance agencies conflicting with that of supervisory bodies of the administration of labor. Demarcation lines were drawn and redrawn, but no clear separation of functions was ever achieved; the administrative structure lacked stability for many years. Not until trade unions were definitively integrated with the government machine in 1933 did social insurance acquire a stable structure; thereafter, no major changes took place.

Since 1933, social insurance has been administrated by the trade unions. The AUCTUC is the central body in the system of social insurance, and also the highest authority in the administration of labor. In particular, it has the job of drawing up the annual insurance budget, which, however, has to be approved by the CPC of the USSR. At the national level, individual unions are insurance carriers for their respective industries. At the local level, shop stewards (shop committees) serve as agents of social insurance. To assist them in performing their functions insurance councils have been created in many plants; members of these councils are elected by local social insurance officers (insurance delegates of individual plant departments, insurance physicians, etc.), but may not hold office without the approval of the shop committee. This rigidly controlled system seems to work with tolerable smoothness.

---

[87] The author has traced this development in greater detail in a monograph (as yet unpublished) prepared for the Hoover Library entitled *Social Insurance in Russia, 1917-1919.*

INDICES

GENERAL INDEX

(growth of female labor); 153-163 (planned and actual development of nominal and real wages); 252-254 (planned and actual housing construction).

Five-Year Plan, Third—22-23 (growth of the working class); 33 (workers and employees in various branches of economic activities); 72 (female labor); 167-171 (planned and actual development of nominal and real wages); 252 (planned housing construction).

Five-Year Plan, Fourth—27-29 (growth of the working class); 81-82 (labor reserves); 207-208 (wage policies); 209-214 (planned and actual development of nominal wages); 219 (de-rationing promised); 231-233 (development of real wages); 250 (planned wage fund, 1950).

Fluctuation of labor—86-89, 124-127.

FUBR—247.

Gainfully employed per worker's family—144-145.

Health insurance—310-317 (basic regulation in Labor Code: 310; limits for benefits: 310-312, "reform" of 1931, length of service decisive factor: 312-313; "leading" industries privileged: 313-314 strengthening of productivity principle: 314-315; "reform" of 1938: 315-316; more rigorosity, 1948: 316; health services: 316-317); 337 (expenditures).

Hours of work—277-288 (regulation of over-time work: 278; wide practice of over-time work in 1930: 278-281; physiology of work revised: 281-281; November celebration and race for records: 282-284; 1934 practice: 284-286; 1937 practice: 287-288); 299 ("reform" of 1940); 299-300 (war-time regulation); 301-302 (return to normalcy); 302 (over-time work on the railways in 1946). *See* also Continuous work week, Seven-hour day.

Housing—241-247 (housing construction under the first three five-year plans: 242-244; rent in workers' budget: 245-247).

Inspection of labor (Labor inspection)—294 (legal position); 294-297 (loss of influence); 296 (low quality of personnel); 303-309 (powerless in conflict with economic authorities).

International wage comparison—131-132 (1928); 175-178 (1938); 234-238 (1950/51).

Invalidity insurance—*see* Disability insurance.

Juvenile labor—76-83. *See* also "Armor", Vocational training.

Labor Code—39 (Sec. 7: compulsory hiring through employment offices); 94 (Sec. 46: termination of employment contract by the

CHRONOLOGICAL INDEX

of laws, decrees, ordinances, a.a., and of authoritative decisions of the Communist Party and the trade unions.

[Abbreviation: *AUCTUC* — AU-Union Central Trade Union Council; *CC of CPSU* — Central Committee of the Communist Party of the USSR; *CEC* — Central Eexecutive Committee; *CM* — Council of Ministers; *CPC* — Council of People's Commissars; *PC* — People's Commissariat; *PC f. L* — People's Commissariat for Labor; *SEC* — Supreme Economic Council; *SIC* — Social Insurance Council.

Some basic laws, as the Labor Code, the Constitution of the USSR, the Criminal Code, the Five-Year Plans, are mentioned in the general index and are omitted here.]

1930, December 17: PC f. L of USSR "on list of penalties for enterprises and institutions of the socialized sector"—*99*.

1930, December 23: PC f. L of USSR "on registration and utilization of job seekers"—*83*.

1930, December 28: PC f. L of USSR on the tasks of labor organs—*47*.

1931, January: 5th plenary session of AUCTUC on the tasks of the trade unions—*312-313*.

1931, January 10: CEC of USSR "on measures for training skilled labor for the national economy"—*68*.

1931, January 16: PC f. L of RSFSR on lists of occupations reserved exclusively or predominantly for women—*67*.

1931, January 16: PC f. L of the USSR "on returning to work on rail ways of people who worked formerly on rail-ways"—*117*.

1931, January 18: PC f. L of USSR "on determining the persons to be considered refractory desorganizers of production"—*95, 96*.

1931, January 20: SIC "about persons eligible for old-age pensions but continuing to work"—*332*.

1931, January 23: PC f. L of RSFSR "on fact-finding relative to man-power surpluses and the proper utilization of such surpluses"—*117*.

1931, February 8: PC f. L of USSR about the implementation of the decree of January 10, 1931—*68*.

1931, April 30: SEC of USSR on reconverting the Stalingrad Tractor Works to the "interrupted" six-day week—*275*.

1931, May 19: PC f. L of USSR "on lists of professions and posts in which the employment of women had to be considerably widened"—*67, 68*.

1931, June 23: CEC and CPC of USSR "on social insurance"—*314, 323-324*.

1931, June 30: CEC and CPC of USSR: "on *otkhod*"—*56*.

1931, July 20: SIC "on abrogation for workers and technicians of maximum limit for temporary disability benefits and on fixing for all other employees of an uniform maximum of 300 rubles"—*314*.

1931, August 11: SIC on broadening the eligibility for additional social insurance benefits—*318*.

1931, August 28: Presidium of the Central Control Commission of CPSU and PC f. Workers a. Peasant Inspection of the USSR

of CEC and CPC of the USSR of November 15, 1932, on discharging for absence from work without valid reason—*99*.

1932, December 27: CEC and CPC of the USSR "on the introduction of an uniform passport system and on mandatory registration of passports"—*97-98*.

1933, January 2: Presidium of AUCTUC "on changes in the operational activities of the RKK"—*184-185*.

1933, January 14: CPC of USSR "on issuing passports"—*98*.

1933, May 21: CPC of the USSR and CC of CPSU "on wages of workers and technicians in the coal industry of the Donbas" —*151-152*.

1933, June 27: CEC and CPC of the USSR "on supplementing Sec. 2 of the decree of CEC and CPC of the USSR of November, 15, 1932, on discharging for absence from work without valid reason"—*99*.

1933, July 8: CPC of the USSR "on rebuilding the system of wages and technical norms in railway transportation"—*151-152*.

1933, August: Public Prosecutor of the USSR about measures against *kolkhoz* members breaking their contracts with industrial plants—*60*.

1934, April 10: CPC of USSR "on social insurance budget for 1934" —*317*.

1934, May 27: CPC of the USSR and CC of CPSU "on raising the wages of low-paid workers and employees in connection with the raising of prices on rationed bread"—*156*.

1934, November 26: Plenary session of CC of CPSU "on de-rationing of bread and some other commodities"—*154*.

1934, December 7: CPC of USSR "on de-rationing of bread, flour and grits"—*154, 157*.

1935, February 17: CPC of USSR and CC of CPSU "on model statute for the agricultural *artel*"—*64*.

1935, September 25: CPC of USSR and CC of CPSU "on lowering bread-prices and de-rationing of meat, fish, sugar, fats, and potatoes"—*154*.

1936, April 19: CEC and CPC of USSR "on the fund of the director of the enterprise"—*230*.

1936, June 27: CEC and CPC of USSR "on the prohibition of abortion, the increase in benefits granted at childbirth, extension of

INDEX OF NAMES